The Sociology of Norbert Elias

Norbert Elias has been described as a great sociologist and over recent years there has been a steady upsurge of interest in his work. Yet despite the fact that he was active for nearly sixty years from the 1920s to the 1960s it was only in the 1980s that English translations of his works became widely available and the importance of his contribution to the sociological endeavour was fully recognized in the English-speaking world. This book provides a comprehensive and accessible introduction to the key aspects of Elias's work and then applies an Eliasian approach to key topics in contemporary sociology such as race, class, gender, religion, epistemology and nationalism. The editors have brought together a distinguished group of international sociologists and this book will not only change the course of Elias studies but be a valuable resource for both students and scholars alike.

Steven Loyal is a lecturer in sociology at University College, Dublin. In addition to his interest in Elias he has research interests in theory and ethnic studies. His most recent book is *The Sociology of Anthony Giddens* (Pluto Press 2003).

Stephen Quilley is a lecturer in sociology at University College, Dublin and has taught in Manchester and Moscow. He has published on Elias, urban studies and the sociology of nature. His most recent book *Exploring the Tomato: Transformations in Nature, Society and Economy* (Edward Elgar 2002) was co-authored with Mark Harvey and Huw Benyon.

The Sociology of Norbert Elias

Edited by

Steven Loyal and Stephen Quilley

CAMBRIDGE
UNIVERSITY PRESS

PUBLISHED BY THE PRESS SYNDICATE OF THE UNIVERSITY OF CAMBRIDGE
The Pitt Building, Trumpington Street, Cambridge, United Kingdom

CAMBRIDGE UNIVERSITY PRESS
The Edinburgh Building, Cambridge, CB2 2RU, UK
40 West 20th Street, New York, NY 10011–4211, USA
477 Williamstown Road, Port Melbourne, VIC 3207, Australia
Ruiz de Alarcón 13, 28014 Madrid, Spain
Dock House, The Waterfront, Cape Town 8001, South Africa

http://www.cambridge.org

First published 2004

Printed in the United Kingdom at the University Press, Cambridge

Typeface Plantin 10/12 pt.   *System* LaTeX 2$_\varepsilon$ [TB]

A catalogue record for this book is available from the British Library

Library of Congress cataloguing-in-publication data
The sociology of Norbert Elias / edited by Steven Loyal and Stephen Quilley.
    p. cm.
Includes bibliographical references and index.
ISBN 0 521 82786 8 – ISBN 0 521 53509 3 (pb.)
1. Historical sociology.   2. Elias, Norbert.   3. Civilization, Modern.   4. Social
structure.   5. Self-consciousness.   I. Loyal, Steven.   II. Quilley, Stephen.
HM487.S63   2004
301 – dc22   2003055749

ISBN 0 521 82786 8 hardback
ISBN 0 521 53509 3 paperback

For
Nikki, Mum and Dad,

and

Harjit Singh, Lakhbir Kaur and William and John
Loyal and to the memory of my grandmother,
Kartar Kaur Rehal

Contents

Contributors

BARRY BARNES is Professor of Sociology in the University of Exeter

CHRISTIEN BRINKGREVE is Professor of Sociology at the University of Utrecht

ERIC DUNNING is Emeritus Professor of Sociology at the University of Leicester and Visiting Professor of Sociology at University College, Dublin and the University of Ulster at Jordanstown

JOHAN GOUDSBLOM is Professor Emeritus of Sociology at the University of Amsterdam

PAUL KAPTEYN is Senior Lecturer in Sociology at the University of Amsterdam

RICHARD KILMINSTER is Senior Lecturer in Sociology at the University of Leeds

STEVEN LOYAL is College Lecturer in Sociology at University College, Dublin

STEPHEN MENNELL is Professor of Sociology at University College, Dublin

JOHN PRATT is Reader in Criminology at the Institute of Criminology, Victoria University of Wellington

STEPHEN QUILLEY is College Lecturer in Sociology at University College Dublin

TOM SCHEFF is Professor Emeritus of Sociology at the University of California, Santa Barbara

BRYAN TURNER is Professor of Sociology at the University of Cambridge

LOÏC WACQUANT is Professor of Sociology, University of California, Berkeley and Researcher at the Centre de Sociologie Européenne du Collège de France

CAS WOUTERS is Senior Researcher at the Department of General Social Science at the University of Utrecht

Acknowledgements

Our growing interest in the work of Norbert Elias owes a great deal to our colleagues, Stephen Mennell and Eric Dunning, who have provided a consistently challenging and stimulating foil for the development of our own ideas. Stephen offered invaluable technical advice and much encouragement in the preparation of this volume, and Eric was both generous and exacting in providing critical comments and suggestions. We should also thank the contributors for their patience and forbearance. Finally we would like to thank: the *Irish Journal of Sociology* for permission to use a revised version of Johan Goudsblom's essay which first appeared in that journal in volume 12 (1) 2003; Editions François Bourin, for the use of Loïc Wacquant's 'Décivilisation et démonisation: la mutation du ghetto noir américain', which was first published in French in Christine Fauré and Tom Bishop (1992) (eds.), *L'Amérique des Français*, Paris, pp. 103–25 (it was translated into English for this volume by James Ingram and the author); and *Amsterdams Sociologisch Tidjschrift* for the use of 'Elias in the Dark Ghetto' which appears here as Part II of Wacquant's essay, and was published in volume 24 (3/4), December 1997, pp. 340–8.

1   Towards a 'central theory': the scope and relevance of the sociology of Norbert Elias

Stephen Quilley and Steven Loyal

Introduction

There were periods during the twentieth century when sociology was imbued with a certain social and intellectual prestige. Sometimes this was for the wrong reasons, as during the late 1960s when students entering the proliferating sociology departments conflated the scientific investigation of social processes with the politics of emancipation. A decade earlier, practitioners of the newly professionalized discipline of 'systematic sociology' (Johnson 1960) confidently proclaimed the emergence of a 'mature science' (Parsons quoted in Goudsblom 1977: 23). But the accomplishments of this emerging and overly self-confident discipline were invariably disappointing. And despite the claims for a cumulative and iterative relationship between theory and empirical observation, the links remained tenuous between the theoretical edifice associated with the towering figure of Talcott Parsons and the data-gathering of mainstream sociology. Since the 1970s, the illusion of any kind of paradigmatic consensus has been shattered. Sociology remains 'a multi-paradigmatic or multi-perspectival subject . . . conflict ridden . . . [and without any] overall consensus . . . regarding concepts, theories and methods' (Dunning and Mennell 2003: 1). And this situation has been made considerably worse by the abandonment, by possibly a majority of sociologists, of the very idea that the investigation of social processes can be *scientific*, and by implication of the idea that it should be possible to build up, over time, a stock of reality-congruent ideas about the operation of social processes.[1]

Over the last twenty years, sociology has been embroiled in self-perpetuating debates driven by the epistemological relativism associated with postmodernist social theory, Foucauldian discourse analysis and poststructuralist currents emanating from literary theory. Combined with the fact that the 'post-Enlightenment' nostrums of identity politics make it almost impossible to dissociate the investigation of the emergent dynamics of social processes as they *are* from statements about how we should *like* them to be, the rationale for sociology as an autonomous and coherent field of investigation within the family of human sciences has never seemed more fragile.

This is evident in the endless proliferation of sub-disciplines reflecting the increasing division of labour and specialization in sociology: for instance, fields such as race, family, organizations, criminology and class, which at least have some empirical rationale, are now supplemented by exotic newcomers such as 'visual sociology'. Sub-disciplinary fragmentation has accompanied intellectual and empirical specialization in all areas of (natural) science. But although, in an encompassing discipline such as biology, there are bitter disputes and apparently competing forms of explanation, even antipodean areas such as molecular genetics and ecology are not intrinsically irreconcilable perspectives, but rather sub-fields corresponding to different scales and units of analysis. Moreover, the synthesis represented by the interdisciplinary field of evolutionary ecology testifies to their location within a (cumulatively) unified scientific framework. By contrast, in the absence of such a unified framework, the proliferation of sociological journals and specialisms takes on an *ad hoc* character. The differentiation and proliferation of empirical fields unfortunately owes as much to competitive institutional dynamics as to any cumulative extension in human knowledge.[2] Given this state of affairs, it is not surprising that many sociologists have become nervous about the intellectual credibility of their discipline and have perhaps taken refuge behind impenetrable jargon and theoretical obscurantism. While the worst examples of empty scholasticism are reserved for articles in specialist journals and conference papers, more public disrobings of the Emperor, as happened in the case of the infamous Sokal affair, have periodically added to our discomfort.[3]

What then should we expect from sociology? The contention animating this volume is that there is a way out of this impasse. In the writings of Norbert Elias there are the beginnings of a paradigm that establishes

(i) a coherent rationale for the relative autonomy of sociology as one discipline within a family of human sciences, and
(ii) the proper object of sociological investigation: long-term transformations in the relations of interdependence between individuals and groups.

Upon this basis it is possible to discern the embryo of what Elias referred to as a 'central theory' and the coalescence of a figurational tradition embodying greater international, interperspectival and intergenerational continuity of theorizing and research (Dunning and Mennell 2003: 2). On this foundation rests the hope of a gradual expansion in the stock of social-scientific knowledge, synthesizing the best and most productive traditions that have periodically animated the discipline: specifically, the Marxist and Weberian historical sociology of capitalism(s); the tradition of symbolic interactionism associated with George Herbert Mead through to Herbert Blumer and Erving Goffman; and in France, the tradition that eventuated in the work of Pierre Bourdieu and his school.

Furthermore, the theory of knowledge which underpins this incipient 'central theory' creates a platform for the integration of findings from across the full range of human sciences, from the *Annales* school in history, Schumpeterian evolutionary economics, cognitive and neurosciences, psychoanalysis, though to evolutionary archaeology and biological anthropology (see, for example, Goudsblom 1992; De Vries and Goudsblom 2002). That the discipline needs such an interdisciplinary interface is evident from the difficulty that sociologists have in thinking about 'human nature' (for instance, in relation to debates about 'race' or gender relations), and reconciling social constructionism with the realities of both (species-level) biological evolution and (individual) physiological growth and development. Eliasian conceptualizations of 'second' and 'third' nature (see Wouters, in this volume) provide the most durable riposte to indiscriminate (if often accurate) accusations of 'blank slate-ism' (Pinker 2002).

Coming out of a distinguished intellectual milieu, which also included figures such as Karl Mannheim, Erich Fromm and Theodor Adorno, Elias remained largely unrecognized by mainstream European sociology until the late 1960s. It took a further twenty years for his work to attract any significant attention among English-speaking sociologists, with the first complete publication of an English edition of *The Civilizing Process* coming only in 1978–82. Elias's relative obscurity for much of the latter half of the twentieth century stands in inverse proportion to the scope and ambition of his work. One of the remarkable aspects of *The Civilizing Process* was the mutually constitutive and historical relationship that Elias established between ontogenetic processes of individual psychology and socialization ('psychogenesis') and developmental trajectories of political and economic regulation at the level of the state and society ('sociogenesis'). Arising out of this relational and processual 'way of seeing', Elias was later to elaborate an encompassing sociological perspective incorporating a distinctive sociology of knowledge ('involvement and detachment') and a theoretical point of departure which, using the grounding concepts of 'figuration' and 'habitus', bypassed the epistemological tensions between the sociologies of action and social structure.

During the 1920s and 1930s, a central question for German sociologists was the synthesis of insights from Karl Marx and Sigmund Freud. The work of Erich Fromm and others associated with the Institute for

Social Research in Frankfurt was paradigmatic in this regard. As the principal assistant to Karl Mannheim in the Department of Sociology at the University of Frankfurt during this period, Elias's formative intellectual years were spent at the confluence of some of the richest streams of European sociological thought. By synthesizing aspects of Weber and Simmel, together with an understanding of the behaviourist psychology of Watson, Cannon's physiology, Freudian psychoanalytical theory, and the 'Gestalt theory' of Köhler and Wertheimer, and undertaking an equally historical, psychological and sociological study, Elias arguably succeeded where earlier authors had failed. *The Civilizing Process* shows how the superego, in Freud's sense, developed through time and in relation to specific emerging structures of social interdependence.

Probably the earliest American sociologist to use Elias was Erving Goffman in *Asylums* (1961). There, in a discussion of monasteries, he refers to Elias's examination of the historical development of sleeping patterns. But whereas Goffman's work is largely ahistorical and almost entirely micro-sociological in emphasis, Elias can be read as a historicization of key Goffmanian concepts *avant la lettre*. By showing how what is carried on behind the scenes is variable through space and time, Elias lays the basis for an historical and comparative understanding of the relationship between 'front' and 'back stage' as well as the corresponding psychical structures, and the figurational matrices to which these relate. Although Goffman read Elias in the original German long before he was translated into English, and seems to have derived key insights from his work, he never showed any interest in a developmental theory dealing with historical transformations in the 'presentation of self'. That the sociological mainstream has (rightly) celebrated the work of Goffman whilst often (wrongly) ignoring the insights of Elias, relates in part to 'hodiecentrism' or 'today-centred thinking' (Goudsblom 1977: 7). Human beings are equipped with an intellectual apparatus attuned, at a deep level, to permanence rather than to change. It requires an enormous effort of detachment from routine everyday occurrences to begin to perceive long-term processes of change. Elias's sociology is more demanding than many because it requires a degree of detachment from the behavioural assumptions and clusters of meaning attaching to everyday concepts, which over many decades and centuries have become an 'automated' aspect of our 'second nature'. From a sociological point of view, however, the rewards for such detachment are great.

Another reason for Elias's anomalous status within the sociological community was that his work did not fit easily into any of the dominant sociological traditions. He compounded this sense of intellectual dissociation by developing his ideas in a singular manner with scant reference to the intellectual contributions of his contemporaries. Despite his broadly left-liberal outlook, Elias generally eschewed participation in politics. Such detachment in part related to his sociology of knowledge, but it also contrasts markedly with the emotive and self-conscious political affiliations which have often characterized the discipline. However, this detachment from the immediacy of political engagement, combined with this empirical and historical methodology and a direct and lucid writing style, has meant that Elias's work has dated remarkably little, still striking first-time readers with its explanatory power and originality.

What then are the defining features of the figurational approach? Following Goudsblom (1977: 6–8) Elias's legacy can be summarized in terms of a series of deceptively simple propositions.

(i) Human beings are born into relationships of interdependency. The social figurations that they form with each other engender emergent dynamics, which cannot be reduced to individual actions or motivations. Such emergent dynamics fundamentally shape individual processes of growth and development, and the trajectory of individual lives.

(ii) These figurations are in a state of constant flux and transformation, with interweaving processes of change occurring over different but interlocking time-frames.

(iii) Long-term transformations of human social figurations have been, and continue to be, largely unplanned and unforeseen.

(iv) The development of human knowledge (including sociological knowledge) takes place within such figurations and forms one aspect of their overall development: hence the inextricable link between Elias's theory of knowledge and the sociology of knowledge processes (see Kilminster and Quilley, both in this volume).

From these propositions are derived a number of characteristic injunctions to sociologists. Firstly, they should studiously avoid thinking either about single individuals, or about humanity and society, as static givens. The proper object of investigation for sociologists should always be interdependent groups of individuals and the long-term transformation of the figurations that they form with each other. Human figurations are in a constant state of flux, in tandem with shifting patterns of the personality and habitus of individuals. For Elias, the foundation for a *scientific* sociology rests upon the correction of what he called the *homo clausus* or 'closed person' view of humans (the perspective underlying all forms of methodological individualism) and replacing it with an orientation towards *homines aperti* or pluralities of 'open people'. The nature of any individual's psychology and 'way of seeing' emerges out of the figurational matrices in which s/he is a participant. Recognition of this allows Elias to problematize and historicize traditional philosophical epistemologies that involve the implicit and usually unrecognized assumption that an adult Western male could serve as the basis for a supposedly universal theory of knowledge. This point of departure, in the dynamic configurations that people form with each other, allows Elias to sidestep the fruitless individual *versus* society or structure *versus* agency debates (e.g. Giddens 1984). And since the concept of figurations applies equally to interdependencies between small groups of individuals, and larger groups associated with cities, race and caste (see Dunning, this volume), classes (Loyal, this volume), nation-states (Kapteyn, this volume), and ultimately humanity as a whole, this conceptual architecture similarly side-steps the much debated dualism between macro and micro perspectives (see Dunning and Mennell 2003).

Secondly, echoing Spinoza and anticipating recent developments in neuroscience (see Damasio 2003; 1997), the *homines aperti* formulation, together with the concept of habitus, allows Elias to avoid the mind/body duality that has dogged philosophy and filtered into much sociological theorizing. In this regard, the theoretical achievement of *The Civilizing Process* can be seen in terms of a synthesis of insights from Freudian psychoanalysis with a historical sociology of long-term processes of development. Elias recognized that sequence or 'phasing' in such processes of development must correspond to long-term transformations in patterns of individual socialization and personality formation: in effect that 'human nature' has a history. In line with the parallels already suggested between the concepts of psychogenesis and *homines aperti*, and the interactionist understanding of the self advanced by Mead and Goffman, the concept of 'second nature' points always to the formation of historically located groups of 'interdependent selves' (see Scheff, this volume).

Thirdly, *vis-à-vis* this deep-seated blindness to long-term processes of change, Elias sensitizes the sociological imagination to problems of language and particularly the dominant conceptual vocabulary that reduces processes to states (*Zustandsreduktion*). As he pointed out, such a tendency is a characteristic of Western languages, which express constant movement or change by first positing an isolated object at rest, before adding a verb to express the fact that the thing with this character is now moving or changing. Thus, for instance, we say that 'the wind is blowing', as if a wind could exist somehow without blowing (1978: 111–12).[4] By consistently using processual nouns (e.g. 'courtization', 'sportization') in his work, and eschewing formulations that imply that 'social structures' can exist outside of the 'figurational flux', Elias consistently drew attention to the reifying potential of stock sociological concepts such as class (see Loyal, in this volume).

Fourthly, in line with his struggle against the tendency for sociology to separate objects from relationships, Elias was particularly concerned to develop a relational understanding of social forms. For example, in relation to the concept of power, most analyses have tended to reify it and treat it as a 'thing' which can be 'possessed', 'held' or 'seized' in an absolute sense. The implication of such constructions is either that one has power or that one is absolutely deprived and powerless. In contrast, Elias stressed the polymorphous and many-sided character of power as

[a] . . . structural characteristic . . . of all human relationships . . . We depend upon others; others depend on us. Insofar as we are more dependent on others than they are on us, they have power over us, whether we have become dependent on them by their use of naked force or by our need to be loved, our need for money, healing, status, a career or simply for excitement. (1978: 74, 93)

For Elias, as long as one party to a relationship has a function, and therefore a value, for another, he or she is not powerless, however great the discrepancy in the power ratio between them may be.

Finally, as an aspect of the more general long-term development of knowledge, sociology should be seen in terms of the continuing attempts by people to orient themselves within the social figurations that they form together. In any historical context there are differences in power between individuals within any figuration and different levels of insight about how the figuration works. But in line with the unplanned and unforeseen nature of long-term processes of development, the overall level of power, insight and control over the operations of figurations as a whole, remain generally low. Sociologists are people and, without their involvement in social life, they would be neither motivated nor able to explain social processes. However, whilst distancing himself from the Weberian understanding of value-neutrality, Elias insisted on the need for the social sciences to engender a *relatively* greater degree of detachment in order to grasp longer-term figurational dynamics and developments (Goudsblom 1977: 8; see Kilminster this volume). Without this they are more rather than less prone to images based upon fantasy thinking rather than careful investigation. In *Involvement and Detachment* Elias shows how humanity's increasingly reliable knowledge of non-human nature and our expanding techno-economic 'zone of safety' have, paradoxically, made human beings more vulnerable in relation to social processes. Nevertheless, Elias continued to maintain a critical acceptance of certain fundamental ideas characteristic of Enlightenment thinking. Just as has been the case *vis-à-vis* knowledge of non-human nature, Elias repeatedly affirmed his belief that the expansion of the stock of reality-congruent sociological knowledge will, over time, provide individuals and groups with more effective means of orientation in relation to figurational transformations. In this sense, over the long term, sociology will eventually be able to underwrite more effective interventions at various levels including that of the state. But direct political commitments and involvements must be one step removed from the immediate process of sociological investigation. As happened in the natural sciences, sociology needs to create professional procedures and conventions and institutional checks and balances which, to a degree, insulate the knowledge process and allow researchers to develop a secondary involvement in the process of detached observation: a 'partisan' commitment to unravelling connections and searching for explanations in the webs of interdependence.

Elias's major works: an intellectual and historiographical route-map

The Civilizing Process is undoubtedly Elias's *magnum opus* and established Elias as an important if somewhat dissident figure in the sociological canon. His bifocal investigation of psychological and behavioural transformations among the upper and middle classes in Europe on the one hand, and processes of 'internal pacification' and state formation (including the build-up for wars) on the other, created a rich and complex account of long-term processes of social transformation which rivals the definitive accounts bequeathed by the Holy Trinity of Marx, Weber and Durkheim, themselves canonized by writers such as Anthony Giddens. Written during the turbulent interwar period and published on the eve of the Second World War, *The Civilizing Process* (1939) can also be seen as one of the last expressions of the earliest tradition of academic sociology established by writers such as Weber, Durkheim and Mannheim, in the wake of Auguste Comte.[5]

During this period, intellectuals were less conscious of their departmental affiliations and more instinctively interdisciplinary in approach. In particular, there was a healthy, and perhaps urgent, engagement between historical sociology and institutional economics. Written during a period when the nascent liberal-democratic version of industrial-market society was being squeezed by authoritarian and state-centred models of development in the form of both European fascism and Soviet communism, Elias's epic study of the Western civilizing process should be seen alongside the work of Joseph Schumpeter (1942) and Karl Polanyi (1944).

In the first chapter of *The Civilizing Process*, Elias investigates the developmental differences underlying the contrast between the German understanding of *Kultur* and *Zivilisation* on the one hand and the concept of Civilization in France and England. His aim was to investigate the historical-sociological specificities underlying twentieth-century pathologies in German society and these arguments were later developed at greater length in his study *The Germans* (1996).

However, despite its evident importance, *The Civilizing Process* has often been read partially and incompletely. With surprising regularity, commentators from within the discipline have dwelt upon the first volume but ignored or played down everything in the second, where the corollary processes of state formation and pacification are discussed and where, in the long and brilliant 'Synopsis' (Elias, 2000: 363–447) he reveals the interwoven elements of the whole work. This neglect was undoubtedly partly a consequence of the chequered and separate publication of Volumes I and II in English, four years apart. Yet other factors came into play in the context of its reception. The suspicion with which many sociologists view psychoanalysis and psychology, combined with the more general tendency to compartmentalize domains of investigation, has led to the designation of *The Civilizing Process* as simply a 'history of manners', effectively consigning the book to relative obscurity. It has also meant that Elias's conceptual contribution is often presented as being limited to the recognition of a relationship between the development of modern society and the lowering of thresholds of shame and embarrassment – a kind of antiquarian adjunct to Goffman. As a result, the expansive synthetic vision of the book has disappeared from view.

Elias opens *The Civilizing Process* by asking how it was that certain classes in the developing nation-states of Western Europe came to think of themselves as 'civilized'. He goes on to examine how this understanding became generalized as a badge of the West's superiority *vis-à-vis* non-Western cultures. In the investigation of this question, he was led to chart long-term transformations in regimes of manners and behavioural codes, which he saw as involving the internalization of restraints. Elias's primary sources of evidence were the books of manners or etiquette manuals that were produced all over Europe from the Middle Ages onwards, mainly for the purpose of instructing adults of the upper (and later middle) classes. In particular, his work demonstrates how, in the sociogenesis of the absolutist states, a characteristic habitus involving increasing superego restraints over affective impulses and drives (significantly, but not exclusively, in relation to violent behaviour), became a compelling aspect of 'court society'. It was this pattern of upper-class manners and affective sensibility that subsequently, as a result of processes of distinction and imitation, became generalized as a model for polite behaviour, gradually diffusing through wider strata of society. This narrative pertaining to the blind and unplanned – but nevertheless structured and directional – transformation of manners, is the primary subject of Volume I of *The Civilizing Process*. However, Elias was not concerned simply with presenting a 'history of manners'. Volume I cannot be understood without reference to Volume II, which deals with questions of state formation and involves the outline of a theory of civilizing processes. Specifically, Elias shows how the process of the internalization of restraints and the resulting transformation in behavioural codes (*psychogenesis*) was intimately connected with transformations in the division of labour, demographic shifts, processes of societal pacification, urbanization, and the growth of trade and the money economy (*sociogenesis*). Briefly stated, the argument is that growth in the urban money economy facilitated, but also critically depended upon, the power and increasing monopoly on violence of the central state authority. A key aspect of this process was the formation of a rationalized administrative apparatus in the towns. The central state, with greater access to these economic circuits, gained access to greater military resources, relative, in the first instance, to the lower levels of the landed warlord nobility, whose principle source of economic and military power remained the control over finite and depreciating provincial land assets. Over time, this shifting power ratio resulted in the transformation of a formerly independent warrior class into an increasingly dependent upper class of courtiers. In this process there was a virtuous circle through which greater pacification facilitated trade and economic growth, and which in turn underwrote the economic and military power of the central authority. In these newly pacified social and economic domains, and particularly within the social dynamics of court society, these developments systematically rewarded more restrained patterns of behaviour. Over a long period of time external restraints associated with the outward authority relations of state formation were increasingly internalized as self-constraints resulting in a characteristic shift in the habitus and personality structure.[6] In a word, the relationship between processes of psychogenesis and sociogenesis has been deep-seated and iterative.

At this point we should perhaps consider the question as to whether *The Civilizing Process* is to be understood as a universal theory, applicable to all human societies. Elias has often been accused of resurrecting a version of Victorian progress theory. On this point it should suffice to say that although there are obvious problematic normative associations with the term 'civilization', Elias is explicit in his insistence on a technical concept of 'civilizing process' which refers only to path-dependencies in the sequence or phases of social development – i.e. progression, or to use his later phrase 'sequential order', but certainly not progress. Elias is interested in the use of the term 'civilization' by various groups and strata in the West – that is, its social function in constituting the self-image of Western nations. *The Civilizing Process* is most definitely a highly focused study of particular European societies over a specific time-frame – and in this sense it should not be seen as a general theory with universal validity. This should be obvious from the sub-title to Volume I: *Changes in the Behaviour of the Secular Upper Classes in the West*. There is certainly no implication of a single, universal trajectory towards a teleological notion of civilization. Having said that, the underlying conceptual architecture does point the way to a more general understanding of social processes *qua* figurations. In this sense civilizing processes are understood as having neither beginning nor end. It is the recognition of both the mechanisms for, and the implications of, the emergent dynamics of social processes that provides the fulcrum for Elias's expansive synthesis. Essentially this centres on the link between the nature, the scale and the intensity of the interdependencies between individuals with varying degrees of power and autonomy, and the psychological formation of those same individuals. That is to say, there are processual connections between the scale, internal organization and interdependence of we-groupings (which might be variously families, clans, villages, tribes, empires, nation-states), the control and management of violence within and between such groupings, and individual processes of socialization and psychological formation. A characteristic aspect of such psychogenetic processes is the achievement of goals through the exercise of habituated foresight and 'detour behaviour' (a term Elias preferred to the commoner 'deferred gratification').[7] This matrix is intrinsic to the nature of social processes, and is at work in *all* human societies, at all stages in our development (see Dunning in Dunning and Rojek 1992). It was also at work in relation to the social processes of our hominid forebears, and had significant implications for the direction of our own biological evolution. Even the most basic human innovations such as carefully knapping an axe-head from flint, rather than using more instantly available shatter splinters, necessitate such detours. However, detour behaviour becomes possible only in the context of the achievement of more 'detached' reality-congruent knowledge about aspects of the natural world (in this case the sculptural properties of different kinds of stone and flint). Goudsblom (1992) has shown with great clarity the way in which the domestication of fire by early hominids must likewise have involved a civilizing process bringing together processes of social coordination and cooperation/hierarchy, psychological restraint (for example, not to use all the fuel at once), and detour behaviour (such as collecting and storing fuel for later use).

The achievement of *The Civilizing Process* was the combination of dense, historical narrative in relation to multiple intertwining social planes, with the elaboration of a series of sophisticated but usable concepts which are always embedded in the substantive investigation. It is difficult, but not impossible, to draw out this conceptual architecture. In fact, nearly all of the major pieces of work that Elias subsequently produced can be seen as an elaboration of substantive themes and concepts first developed in *The Civilizing Process*, although there were of course numerous concepts that he developed both before and after, and his work is by no means of one piece (Van Krieken 1998). Thus Elias's *habilitation*, completed in 1933 and later published as *The Court Society* (1983 [orig. 1969]) and *The Germans* (1996), can be seen as prequel and elaboration respectively of his comparative investigation of the dynamics of state formation and psychogenesis during the early modern period in Germany, England and France. Likewise, his contribution to the sociology of sport in *Quest for Excitement* (Elias and Dunning, 1986), applies the matrix of Western civilizing processes to the links between the 'parliamentarization' of English politics and the initial codification of modern sports.

However, frustrated by repeated misinterpretation, Elias also went on to elaborate the conceptual architecture and the theoretical innovations of *The Civilizing Process* in a series of books, which have subsequently languished in comparative obscurity. *What is Sociology?* (1978) was the closest that Elias came to writing a programmatic textbook for 'process sociology'. In this book, Elias introduces the concept of the 'triad of basic controls' as a means of determining and measuring the stage of development which a society has reached. Specifically, Elias shows that the stage of development of a society can be determined:

(i) by the extent of its control chances over extra-human nexuses of events, that is, over what we sometimes refer to rather loosely as 'natural events';
(ii) by the extent of its control chances over inter-human connections, that is, over what we usually refer to as 'social nexuses';
(iii) by the extent to which each of its individual members has learned, from childhood onwards, to exercise self-control.[8]

Scientific and technological developments correspond to the first of these basic controls; the development of social organization to the second; and the civilizing process to the third. According to Elias, the three are interdependent both in their development and in their functioning at any given stage. However, he warns against 'the mechanistic idea that the interdependence of the three types of control is to be understood in terms of parallel increases in all three' (1978: 157). More particularly, the development of the three types does not occur at the same rate, and the development of one type can contradict, impede or threaten developments regarding the others. For example, it is highly characteristic of modern societies: that the extent of their control chances over extra-human natural nexuses is greater and grows more quickly than that over interhuman social nexuses (1978: 156). This is evident in the fact that the developments in the 'natural' sciences have proceeded more quickly than development in the 'social' sciences, with the result that our ability to predict, intervene and control the natural/physical world is greater at present than our ability to control social processes. A corollary of this is the fact that the less amenable a sphere of events is to human control, the more emotional and fantasy-laden people's thinking about it tends to be. For Elias, such emotional and fantasy-laden thinking about the social world represents a significant obstacle to the development of a more reality-congruent stock of social scientific knowledge.

A further crucial set of concepts that Elias outlines in *What is Sociology?* are summarized in the 'Game Models': Elias imagines the simplest hypothetical social processes in relation to games involving two or more players. In the first model – the primal contest – Elias discusses the functional interdependence, unequal strength and uneven reciprocal imposition of constraints of two competing groups, both chasing shrinking food resources. For Elias the primal contest is important because it demonstrates that, even in the absence of any active, ongoing relationship, groups and individuals provide functions for each other by the simple fact of co-presence – necessitating reciprocal anticipation, foresight and planning. A central question which follows from this, and in many ways one of the key problems of any civilizing process, is how people are able to regulate their interdependencies and meet their animalic needs in such a way that they need not resort to violence:

If one wanted to reduce the key problem of any civilizing process to its simplest formula, then it could be said to be the problem of how people can manage to satisfy their elementary animalic needs in their life together, without reciprocally destroying, frustrating, demeaning or in other ways harming each other time and time again in their search for this satisfaction – in other words, without fulfilment of the elementary needs of one person or group of people being achieved at the cost of those of another person or group. (1996: 31)

The main purpose of these models for Elias is to demonstrate the way in which social processes generate emergent dynamics which crucially:

(i) cannot be reduced to or derived from a simple aggregation of many component individual actions or decisions; and,
(ii) constrain and mould both the habitus and behaviour of individuals.

In effect, Elias uses the game models to elaborate a rationale for the autonomy of social processes as a field of investigation, and figurational dynamics as the proper object of study for sociology as a discipline. The link between the emergent dynamics of social processes and the habitus and behaviour of individuals is effectively the most abstract statement of Elias's central insight: that there is a link between sociogenesis and psychogenesis. By increasing the number of players and their arrangement in groups ('teams'), Elias goes on to explore the shifting power ratios and the capacity for individuals, in various circumstances, to dictate the course of the game. The models allow Elias to demonstrate rather conclusively that, as the number of players increases:

(i) the ties of interdependency between individuals become greater and more binding and the power ratio between players tends to become more equal. This is the simplest theoretical expression of Elias's notion of *functional democratization*: that other things being equal, greater complexity in social and economic life leads to a narrowing (if not elimination) of power ratios;
(ii) the power of individuals to dictate the course of the game declines and the tendency for the emergent and autonomous dynamics of the game to dictate and structure the 'moves' of individual players increases correspondingly.

Whereas *What is Sociology?* (1978) may legitimately be presented as a theoretical appendix, and the first part of *The Society of Individuals* (1991) was in fact an off-cut from *The Civilizing Process* (1939), *The Established and the Outsiders* (1965) is one of the few books by Elias that operates within the foreshortened time-horizons of mainstream sociology. In some ways the book could be read as a classic 'here and now' investigation of class, hierarchy and status on a working-class estate – rather in the tradition of the post-war community studies or the earlier work of the Chicago school.[9] But once again, working again with the conceptual architecture of figurations, interdependencies and power ratios, the study in fact works to demonstrate that the theoretical precepts established during an extended investigation of long-term developments in early modern societies were equally relevant to the more parochial and contemporaneous concerns of academic sociology.

The Established and the Outsiders is an account of a small suburban community, divided into three neighbourhoods or zones in Winston Parva (a fictitious name): one middle class and two predominantly working class. For Elias and Scotson the relationship between these districts serves as an empirical exemplar for more general dynamics involving power and inequality. What makes this study of social stratification atypical is that the principal difference between the two working-class groups involved could not be measured according to standard sociological taxonomies relating to class (or religion or nationality) since they occupied a similar class position. Indeed, the only difference between the groups was temporal and related to the duration of their residence in the community. This enabled one group, the 'established', to develop greater internal social cohesion; and this in its turn, enabled them to dominate local organizations and gossip networks, to the detriment of the less-established 'outsider' community. According to Elias, the purely figurational fact of their greater cohesion provides a major key to understanding 'established–outsider figurations'. And it is the structural characteristics that bind the two groups to each other in specific ways, such that the members of one feel impelled, and have sufficient power resources, to treat those of the other as collectively inferior.

According to Elias, the established group in Zone 2 in Winston Parva 'felt exposed to a three-pronged attack – against their monopolized power resources, against their group charisma and against their group norms'. It was precisely because of this that the established group used stigmatization and exclusion as weapons to maintain their distinct identity, assert their superiority and 'keep the outsiders in their place'. And this in turn was only possible because of the cohesion, which had developed in their group over the course of some generations and the correlative lack of cohesion which characterized the newcomers.

Elias sought to demonstrate that such views of outsiders as tainted are maintained and reproduced by the established on a day-to-day basis through 'blame-gossip'. Tied to this are processes of group charisma and group disgrace which involve the established maintaining a positive 'we-image' and imposing a negative 'they-image' on the outsiders by stigmatizing them and propagating collective fantasies about them. As a result of the power differential, outsiders often come to accept that they belong to a group of lesser virtue and respectability: they internalize both their 'group disgrace' and the 'group charisma' of the established. However, over time such processes of exclusion and stigmatization are liable to change as functional democratization results in equalizing power ratios between groups. In such changed circumstances, outsider groups begin to challenge and contest their lower social position and blocked access to various power resources.

Finally, one of the most important aspects of Elias's work related to problems which philosophers and philosophically minded sociologists refer to as 'epistemology', but Elias himself preferred to refer to, more simply and straightforwardly, as a sociological theory of knowledge. Again, developing concepts and theoretical precepts that are intrinsic to the logic of his substantive historical investigations but rarely explicated, in later life Elias was repeatedly drawn back to consideration of the scientific nature of sociology and its relationship with neighbouring disciplines among the human sciences. In *Involvement and Detachment* (1987), *The Symbol Theory* (1989) and *Time: An Essay* (1992), Elias sought to combine a modified Comtean theory of knowledge with a sociology of knowledge processes.[10] His work in this area is elaborated at some length elsewhere in this volume (see the essays by Kilminster and Quilley).

In summary, it is perhaps useful to understand Elias's major works in relation to three categories (these categories are indicated against key publications in Table 1.1):

A. *Sociology within the human sciences*: Contributions to the theory of knowledge and the sociology of knowledge processes. These works establish the basis for a *scientific sociology* and the *object of sociological investigation* (the dynamics and long-term transformations of human figurations), whilst elaborating the rationale for the *relative autonomy of the subject in relation to neighbouring disciplines* (the irreducible and 'emergent' character of such dynamics). In this aspect of his work, Elias also elaborated the dynamics of sociology as a dimension of more general knowledge processes, emerging from the spiralling interplay between 'involvement' and 'detachment', and the gradual widening and enlargement of the social fund of more reality-congruent understandings.

B. *Processual concepts and theoretical precepts for a 'figurational sociology'*. Elaborating concepts such as the *figuration, established–outsider relations, functional democratization* and the relational understanding of power expressed in terms of *power ratios*, these works make explicit the underlying conceptual architecture that animates all of Elias's substantive studies in historical sociology.

C. *Substantive studies in historical sociology*. Constituting the earliest and most definitive elements of Elias's legacy, these works are certainly the best known and often the least understood. *The Court Society, The Civilizing Process* and later *The Germans*, all express and build upon both the theory of knowledge and the sociology of knowledge processes subsequently outlined in *Involvement and Detachment*. For instance, the concept of 'second nature' that is so central to *The Civilizing Process*, depends on an understanding of socialization as a neurobiological (as well as social) process, and human beings as animals biologically predisposed to learn. These studies likewise embody the figurational and processual concepts that are developed more explicitly in later, more self-consciously 'sociological' works.

Table 1.1 *Norbert Elias – life and writings*

Life events	Selected key publications[a]
1897 Born in Breslau, Germany	
1915 Soldier in Signal Corps; saw action on both the Eastern and the Western fronts	
1918–24 Studied philosophy and medicine, later dropping medicine. Anatomical studies lead Elias to question philosophical mind/body dualisms, culminating in rift with supervisor and intellectual shift away from philosophy	1924 Thesis: 'Idea and individual: a contribution to the philosophy of history', supervised by Richard Honigswald
1925 Arrives in Heidelberg to study sociology. Works with Alfred Weber and becomes Mannheim's unofficial academic assistant	1929 'On the sociology of German anti-Semitism'. Finishes Habilitationsschrift (later published as *The Court Society* (*Die Hofische Gesellschaft*) 1969) (C)
In 1929 Academic assistant for Mannheim in Frankfurt (located in the same building as the Frankfurt School, directed by Horkheimer)	
Elias flees Germany, 36 years old, a refugee in Paris, and without a university position	
1935–40 London. Spent three years researching and writing *The Civilizing Process* at the British Museum. Elias's father dies in 1940 in Breslau and his mother (almost certainly) in Auschwitz in 1942. Receives Senior Research Fellowship at the LSE	1939 *Uber den Prozess der Zivilisation* (C)
1940 War-time internment on the Isle of Man	
In 1954 receives offer of an academic post from Ilya Neustadt at University College, Leicester. Already 57	1950 'Studies in the genesis of the naval profession' (C) 1956 'Problems of involvement and detachment' (shorter essay) (A)
In 1962 went to Ghana as Professor of Sociology at the University of Ghana at Lagon	1965 *The Established and the Outsiders* with J. Scotson (B) 1969 *The Court Society* (C)
Returns to Britain. Lectures part-time at University of Leicester	1970 *What is Sociology?* (B)
From 1978 rarely in England	1982 *The Civilizing Process* translated into English in two separate volumes (C)
1977 Theodore Adorno Prize	
1979–84, Lived in a flat at University of Bielefeld	1984 *Time: An Essay* (A)
1987 90th Birthday marked by two major conferences, one attended by Pierre Bourdieu	1986 'The changing balance of power between the sexes' in *TCS* (B,C) 1986 *Quest for Excitement* with Eric Dunning (C)
1988 Presented with *Premio Europeo Amalfi* for 'The Society of Individuals'	1987 *Involvement and Detachment* (A) 1987 *Die Gesellschaft der Individuen* (trans. *Society of Individuals* 1991) (B)
1990 Elias dies at the age of 93	1989 *Studien uber die Deutschen* (trans. *The Germans* 1996) (C) 1989 *The Symbol Theory*. (A)

Elaborations: the scope and relevance of 'figurational sociology'

There have been a number of book-length commentaries on Elias's work. The most comprehensive and systematic exposition remains Stephen Mennell's *Norbert Elias: An Introduction* (1998 [orig. 1989]). Other useful contributions include Jonathan Fletcher's *Violence and Civilization* (1997) and Robert van Krieken's shorter and more accessible student text (1998). Johan Goudsblom's (1977) *Sociology in the Balance* combines a critical overview of the development of twentieth-century sociology with an embedded exposition of the Eliasian perspective. There have also been a number of monographs that do a good job of contextualizing Elias's contribution. These include Bogner (1977), Goudsblom (2000), Kilminster (1993) and Kuzmics (1991). Dunning (1977), Van Krieken (1990), Kilminster and Mennell (2000) and Kilminster (1999) also provide useful general orientations to Elias's work. Substantial scholarly critiques – both sympathetic and unsympathetic – include Gordon (1994), Goody (2002), Layder (1986), Mouzelis (1993) and Robinson (1987). For a general overview of criticisms see chapter 10 of Mennell (1998).

The enormous potential for the application of Eliasian ideas across the widest range of sociological problems is only just beginning to be realized. Eliasian scholars have, however, already made significant contributions in diverse areas, including: the sociology of race and class; informalization processes; the sociology of organizations; crime and punishment; (de)civilizing processes, war and violence; art and aesthetics; processes of state formation; sport; religion; food; medicine and psychoanalysis; drugs, alcohol and tobacco use; and animal–human relations.[11]

For this volume we have commissioned a series of essays ranging across the full range of sociological enquiry and which, taken as a whole, summarize the 'Eliasian' point of departure whilst also extending the reach of the figurational perspective. The book is divided into four sections. Section I, *Sociology as a human science: Norbert Elias and the sociology of knowledge*, concerns the status of sociology as a relatively autonomous discipline within the family of human sciences. Richard Kilminster sets the scene by detailing the emergence of Elias's distinctive framing of the problem of value neutrality in his theory of involvement and detachment. Stephen Quilley's chapter elaborates further the links between Elias's theory of knowledge and the sociology of knowledge processes, before examining the resulting interface between sociology and the range of biological sciences. Barry Barnes examines Elias's attempt to move beyond both social constructionist and realist accounts of the notion of time.

Section II, *Processes of stratification: figurations of race, class and gender*, deals with issues which have always had a central and defining impact on the sociological imagination. Essays by Eric Dunning, Steve Loyal, Loïc Wacquant and Christien Brinkgreve demonstrate the powerful and distinctive insights that are made available by the processual perspective.

One of the distinctive aspects of *The Civilizing Process* was the manner in which Elias established connections between (macro-level) processes of state formation and the extension in the scale and scope of human interdependencies on the one hand (sociogenesis), and (micro-level) processes of individual socialization, personality and habitus formation (psychogenesis), face-to-face behaviour and norm-formation on the other. Section III, *The formation of individuals and states*, further explores these issues, with essays variously from Stephen Mennell on state formation in America, Paul Kapteyn on processes of pacification and relationships between states, Cas Wouters on processes of informalization in Western societies, John Pratt on the relationship between civilizing processes and modern penal development, and finally, Thomas Scheff who explores the links between Elias, Freud and Goffman and their understandings of shame.

Finally, in Section IV, *Religion and civilizing processes: Weber and Elias compared*, Bryan Turner and Johan Goudsblom present rather different perspectives on the legacy of, on the one hand, one of the most clearly established theorists within the sociological canon, and on the other, one of the most influential outsiders. This is an appropriate note on which to end because ever since Weber's *The Protestant Ethic*, the role of religion in explaining long-term processes of social change and social order has remained highly contested. In this section Turner and Goudsblom assess the importance of religion as a factor in explaining civilizing processes. Their contributions provide a useful illustration of both the continuities and the underlying differences between Weberian and Eliasian approaches to sociology – ontologically, epistemologically and substantively.

NOTES

1. On its website, in answer to the question 'What is Sociology?' the British Sociological Association implies that sociology has backed away from claims to scientific status: 'From its original purpose as the "science of society", sociology has moved on to more reflexive attempts to understand how society works. It seeks to provide insights into the many forms of relationship, both formal and informal. . . . The task for sociologists . . . is to capture this understanding in a more systematic way and provide substantive explanations which nevertheless are understandable in terms of everyday life.' This implies that sociology can

at best aspire to provide systematic insights. Oddly enough, explanations are required to be 'understandable', rather than themselves contributing towards the understanding of social processes.

2. Elias's understanding of the relationship between 'involvement and detachment' allows for a more effective treatment of what Giddens (1984) refers to as 'the double hermeneutic': i.e. the distinctive methodological and theoretical problems posed by 'subject–object relations' in sociology as compared with the natural sciences.

3. Professor of Physics at New York University, Alan Sokal achieved both notoriety and critical acclaim when he wrote a spoof article which was accepted for publication in America's leading cultural studies journal *Social Text* (see Sokal 1996a). For his original revelation and explanation of the hoax see Sokal 1996b, and also the books *Intellectual Impostures* (Sokal 2003) and *Fashionable Nonsense* (Sokal and Bricmont 1998).

4. Exactly this same point was made to rather more acclaim some two years later by the oft-cited physicist David Bohm (1980).

5. In *Reflections on a Life* (1994), Elias bears this out when he says that he was of a generation in which few if any sociologists had themselves trained initially as sociologists. The debt to Comte is particularly evident in relation to Elias's theory of knowledge, advanced in *Involvement and Detachment* and in many other essays that have never been collected in book form. His most explicit discussion of Comte is in *What is Sociology?* ch. 1, 'Sociology: the questions posed by Comte'. See also Eric Dunning (1977).

6. For Elias circumstances which involve a steady and consistent but moderate pressure favour the transformation of external constraints into internal constraints.

7. Elias discusses this at length in *The Civilizing Process* in a section entitled 'The Spread of Pressure for Foresight and Self-Constraint' (2000: 379–82).

8. See Elias 1978: 156–7 for a discussion of this concept. Also see Mennell 1992: 169–72, 236.

9. More precisely, Elias emphasized that time was always one axis of any sociological explanation, and in his own work that is mainly associated with long-term historical perspectives; but a process explanation can have quite a short time-span – it depends on the problem you are studying.

10. Derived in part from his understanding of Mannheim and Levy-Bruhl.

11. A large selection of the most notable essays, including many of those listed above, have been brought together recently in a four-volume collection edited by Dunning and Mennell (2003).

REFERENCES

Bohm, D. 1980, *Wholeness and the Implicate Order*, London: Routledge and Kegan Paul.
De Vries, B. and Goudsblom, J. 2002, *Mappae Mundi. Humans and their Habitats in Long-Term Ecological Perspective*, Amsterdam: Amsterdam University Press.
Damasio, A. 2003, *Looking for Spinoza: Joy, Sorrow and the Feeling Brain*, London: Heinemann.

1997, *The Feeling of What Happens: Body Emotion and the Making of Consciousness*, London: Vintage.

Dunning, E. 1977, 'In defence of developmental sociology, a critique of Popper's *Poverty of Historicism* with special reference to the theory of Auguste Comte', *Amsterdams Sociologisch Tijdschrift* 4 (3): 327–49.

Dunning, E. and Mennell, S. 2003, *Norbert Elias: Sage Masters of Modern Social Thought*, 4 vols. London: Sage.

Dunning, E. and Rojek, C. 1992, *Sport and Leisure in the Civilizing Process: Critique and Counter Critique*, London: Macmillan.

Elias, N. 1978 [orig. 1970], *What Is Sociology?*, London: Hutchinson.

1983, *The Court Society*, Oxford: Blackwell.

1987a, *Involvement and Detachment*, Oxford: Blackwell.

1987b, 'The retreat of sociologists into the present', *Theory, Culture & Society* 4 (2–3): 223–49.

1989, *The Symbol Theory*, London: Sage.

1991, *The Society of Individuals*, Oxford: Blackwell.

1992, *Time, an Essay*, Oxford: Blackwell.

1996 [1989 orig. in German], *The Germans*, Cambridge: Polity.

2000 [orig. 1939], *The Civilizing Process*, rev. edn, Oxford: Blackwell.

Elias, N. and Dunning, E. 1986, *Quest for Excitement*, Oxford: Blackwell.

Elias, N. and Scotson, J. 1965, *The Established and the Outsiders*, London: Frank Cass, rev. edn, London: Sage, 1994.

Fletcher, J. 1997, *Violence and Civilisation: An Introduction to the Work of Norbert Elias*, Cambridge: Polity.

Giddens, A. 1984, *The Constitution of Society*, Cambridge: Polity.

Goffman, E. 1961, *Asylums: Essays on the Social Situation of Mental Patients and Other Inmates*, New York: Double Day.

Goody, J. 2002, 'Elias and the anthropological tradition', *Anthropological Theory* 2 (4): 401–12.

Gordon, D. 1994, 'The civilizing process revisited', in *Citizens without Sovereignty: Equality and Sociability in French Thought, 1670–1789*, Princeton, NJ: Princeton University Press, pp. 86–128.

Goudsblom, J. 1977, *Sociology in the Balance: A Critical Essay*, Oxford: Blackwell.

1992, *Fire and Civilisation*, London: Allen Lane.

2000, 'Norbert Elias and American sociology', *Sociologia Internationalis* 38 (2): 173–80.

Johnson, H. M. 1960, *Sociology: A Systematic Introduction*, New York: Harcourt Brace and Co.

Kilminster, R. 1993, 'Norbert Elias and Karl Mannheim: closeness and distance', *Theory, Culture and Society* 10: 81–114.

Kilminster, R. and Mennell, S. 2000, 'Norbert Elias', in *The Blackwell Companion to Major Social Theorists*, G. Ritzer (ed.), Oxford: Blackwell.

Van Krieken, R. 1998, *Norbert Elias*, London: Sage.

Kuzmics, H. 1991, 'Embarrassment and civilisation: on some similarities and differences in the work of Goffman and Elias', *Theory, Culture & Society* 8 (2): 1–30.

Layder, Derek 1986, 'Social reality as figuration: a critique of Elias's conception of sociological analysis', *Sociology* 20 (3): 367–86.

Mennell, S. 1998, *Norbert Elias: An Introduction*, Dublin: University College Dublin Press.

Mouzelis, Nicos 1993, 'On figurational sociology', *Theory, Culture and Society* 10: 239–53.

Pinker, S. 2002, *The Blank Slate: The Modern Denial of Human Nature*, London: Viking.

Polanyi, K. 1957 [orig. 1944], *The Great Transformation*, Boston: Beacon Press.

Robinson, R. J. 1987, 'The civilizing process: some remarks on Elias's social history', *Sociology* 21 (1): 1–17.

Schumpeter, J. 1942, *Capitalism, Socialism and Democracy*, London: Harper.

Sokal, A. 1996a, 'Transgressing the boundaries: towards a transformative hermeneutics of quantum gravity', *Social Text* 46 (4): 217–52 (spring/ summer).

Sokal, A. 1996b, 'A physicist experiments with cultural studies', *Lingua Franca* May/June: 62–4.

Sokal, A. and Bricmont, J. 1998, *Fashionable Nonsense: Postmodern Intellectuals' Abuse of Science*, New York: Picador.

Part I

Sociology as a human science: Norbert Elias
and the sociology of knowledge

2   From distance to detachment: knowledge
     and self-knowledge in Elias's theory of
     involvement and detachment

Richard Kilminster

> 'Detachment' and 'involvement' belong to the not very large group of
> specialized concepts referring to the whole human person.
>
> (Norbert Elias 1987: xxxii)

Introduction: after Weber

Max Weber famously declared that the vocation of sociology requires that
sociologists should suspend certain values in the pursuit of the ideal of
'value-freedom'. It is obvious reading Elias's first systematic statement
of his theory of involvement and detachment (Elias 1956) with Weber
in mind, that on the subject of science and values, although he departs
from Weber in significant ways he, too, must have been stimulated by
Weber's observations. In common with many other social scientists outside Marxist circles in Weimar Germany, early in his career Elias probably
acquiesced in the all-pervasive Weberian position on value-freedom (or
some version of it) as a set of working principles for social-scientific work.
Indeed, it was partly this broad orientation which set the sociology department of Mannheim and Elias in Frankfurt apart from the subsequently
more famous 'Frankfurt School' of Adorno and Horkheimer with whom
they shared a building (Shils 1970; Bogner 1987; Mennell 1998: 15). In
a Marxian manner the latter group emphatically rejected value-freedom
in any form because they saw it as part of a positivistic ideology in social science that excluded partisanship on behalf of the underprivileged
(Kilminster 1979: 195–201).

I think it is possible to breathe further life into this venerable subject
of value-freedom through understanding how Elias took the Weberian
model as a *point of departure*. As Alan Sica has astutely observed, Elias's
'independence of mind' was such that unlike many others of his contemporaries, 'Elias did not tremble in the shadow of Max Weber' (Sica 1984:
50). Through a specific integration of sociology and Freudian ideas, carried out in *The Civilizing Process*, Elias created a synthetic theoretical

framework to counteract the rationalism of Weber, from which Eliasian perspective the issues as posed in Weber on the subject of scientific values were transformed.

To counteract also Weber's individualism (as well as the solipsism of phenomenology) Elias started from the sociological assumption of interdependent people rather than congeries of individuals. Or, to use his later language: he came up with *homines aperti* formulations to counter the *homo clausus* asumptions underlying many of the methodological discussions of the time (Elias 1978: 125). From very early on he argued solely and uncompromisingly from this extra-individual viewpoint, which was greatly strengthed later by the findings of *The Civilizing Process*. It provided him with the simple but powerful means by which to show that many conventionally posed epistemological problems, such as 'How do I know what I know?', 'How do we perceive social patterns when all we experience is individual action?' or 'Is my action free or determined?', embodied individualistic, *homo clausus* assumptions. These simply did not arise if one took the *homines aperti* standpoint. It was a way of arguing indebted to the sociology of knowledge (Elias 1971; Kilminster 1993; Kilminster and Wouters 1995) and, as such, it was never going to satisfy the philosophers.

The general problem area of value-freedom in the sciences was much discussed in the 1920s in Germany (Lassman, Velody and Martins 1989). As Dunning (1986: 6–7) rightly said, Elias embarked upon his sociological career at a specific conjuncture in the twentieth-century German *Methodenstreit* (that is, the ongoing dispute over the appropriate methods for the natural and social sciences: see Frisby 1976). On the intellectual plane, this controversy stimulated debate on a number of the key problems and dualisms (such as individual/society or free will/determinism) that Elias, like many others at the time, sought to solve, resolve or otherwise to transcend. The general issue of how to achieve 'valid' knowledge of society whilst investigating it from within, which Elias was centrally addressing in his theory of involvement and detachment, was one of these problems. It was also a very prominent issue in strands of phenomenology and existentialism in the 1920s (Schutz 1932; Gadamer 1985) as well as in Weber. Other Kantian discussions about psychic distancing doubtless also played a part in stimulating Elias's reflections on this subject (more on this later).

The work of Alfred Schutz (Schutz 1932; 1940) contained amongst other things a philosophical solution to the problem of how to develop an objective science of society whilst the investigators are inextricably bound up with the subject matter. Schutz's solution was that social scientists must, whilst investigating society, 'bracket out' the 'natural attitude' (which includes values) that they possess in common with everyone else, thereby distancing themselves in a disciplined fashion from their own status and position. For Schutz, this is a shift of point of view in which the observer is no longer concerned with his or her own self, but is freed from a constant orientation to his or her own problems in favour of investigating the social world in general. The investigator does not leave the social world (impossible) but simply *switches focus*. As Berger and Kellner, following Schutz, subsequently characterized the starting point of the sociologist's inquiries: 'I now establish a greater kind of *distance* from the situation within my own mind' (1981: 31–2, emphasis in original). The abiding rationalism of this kind of approach is evident. For the social phenomenologists, distance refers to *acts of consciousness*, the maintenance of the inner emotional balance of the investigator, as well as his or her relations with others in scientific communities, being placed analytically and firmly in methodological 'brackets'.

For Elias, Weber and writers such as Schutz took for granted the self-awareness, capacity for self-regulation and all-round conscience formation of modern people, including their own, the genesis of which has been long forgotten in the Western civilizing process. From this experience those writers abstracted personality and behavioural features (rationality, reflection, distance, self-control) the possession of which seemed self-evident to them, and generalized these as representative of humans *as such*. Elias's perspective on involvement and detachment assumes, on the contrary, a view of people 'in the round' (a phrase he uses a number of times in his writings), as bodies, relatively more or less involved or detached in their activities *as whole people*, and the product of specific social transformations. As Elias explains: 'Basically the two concepts refer to different ways in which human beings regulate themselves' (Elias 1987: xxxii).

In this chapter I shall be arguing that Elias renders historically specific the generalized model of self-autarkic individuals implied in Weber's observations on science and value-freedom. Elias suggests that only under specific societal conditions do people develop the capacity to manage their emotions in such a way, *in their relations with others*, as to make scientific detachment, which is a social accomplishment, possible. Scientific detachment is not, in other words, synonymous with individual acts of consciousness or cognitive distanciation.

Weber scrutinized: Mannheim, Kris and Elias

During the interwar years, the whole value-freedom problematic established by Weber came under close scrutiny from writers of Elias's generation. The psychoanalytic perspective of Freud played a significant part in the questioning of Weber's rationalism. The first explicit pairings of the terms involvement and detachment used as technical terms defining the poles of a social-psychological continuum occur in the writings of Karl Mannheim, Ernst Kris and Elias. As far as I know there was no contact between the psychoanalyst Ernst Kris and either of the other two (even though they were all living in London during the late 1930s). However, an important part of the work of all three converged on a psychoanalytically informed treatment of the issue of psychic distancing that had been much debated by Kantians and phenomenologists. All three took for granted a psychoanalytic conception of embodied human beings possessing an inner psychic structure of emotional self-controls. This assumption is explicitly deployed in Kris (individualistically) and Elias (sociologically) as a counter-balance to the rationalistic model of people found in many philosophical models of people's capacity for psychic distancing. In contrast to Kris, for Mannheim and Elias, in different ways, the psychological and social properties of humans are interdependent.

Turning first to Mannheim, in his essay 'The Democratization of Culture' of 1933, written during his Frankfurt period immediately prior to his exile, there occurs another of the explicit pairings of the two concepts of involvement and detachment in a related, though different, sense from that of Elias. Mannheim accepts that the nominalists aim to understand the behaviour of individuals, but opposes their view that individuals can be studied as separate from their participation in overlapping groups. He continues: 'What makes a single being sociologically relevant is not his comparative detachment from society, but his multiple involvement' (Mannheim 1933: 110). For Mannheim, the capacity of people to detach themselves from groups is bound up with social distance. He saw the latter as an entirely social phenomenon, produced by people themselves in their social relations (Mannheim 1933: 207). He traced the effects of the longer-term process of social democratization, i.e. the relative levelling (though by no means the total disappearance) of social hierarchies in the modern period, on social and *psychic* distanciation (1933: 206ff.) Like Elias, Mannheim had a clear conception that social group conflicts and interdependencies will be mirrored in the internal psychic make-up of people.

Vertical distance, for Mannheim, is the principle by which hierarchically organized groups maintain their power. This principle becomes an organic part of people's thinking, something Mannheim calls a form of 'psychic distanciation' (1933: 210). It is also reinforced by standards of conduct, patterns of culture and language use, all of which function to keep the requisite social distance between the groups in place. A reduction in the vertical distance between social strata, brought about by the growing complexity of the social and economic process, brings about a 'de-distanciation' (1933: 210). As groups of 'outsiders' (1933: 215) begin to make their presence felt in political participation, this social democratization process will manifest itself in language, customs, behaviour and ways of thinking generally (echoes of Elias here). For Mannheim, the phenomenon of de-distanciation is explained largely by positing a static contrast between traditional and modern society, de-distanciation being said to result from increasing social and economic complexity in the modern world (1933: 210).

In summary: Elias was able to take Mannheim's depiction of distanciation and de-distanciation a stage further by more consistently stressing: (i) the psychological mechanism of fear of social degradation that underpins fear both of others' gestures of superiority and of lapsing into inferiority oneself (see Kuzmics 1991; Wouters 1998); and (ii) how the fantasy content of established images of outsiders as well as the latter's internalized images of themselves, rise or fall according to the relative steepness of the power gradient of the relationship between the two groups in given cases and, hence, the *stage of development* of the relationship between them (see Elias 1976; Mennell 1998: 138). Elias's dynamic principle (suggesting stages or phases) supplanted Mannheim's static traditional/modern contrast in the explanation of shifting degrees of distanciation/de-distanciation.

In the case of Kris, there seems to have been a parallel discovery or a convergence of perception about problems with Kantian rationalism in all its forms. In his essay 'Aesthetic ambiguity' (1948) Kris developed a theory of aesthetic experience partly in a dialogue with the now little read English philosopher Edward Bullough's (1912) concept of distance in the field of aesthetics. Bullough argued, following Kant, that for aesthetic appreciation to take place there must be a shift in 'psychic distance'. The aesthetic experience is at its optimum if the person experiencing the work of art avoids either of two poles: either extreme identification with characters, themes or symbols in the work, or a total distancing that transforms the experience from an aesthetic one to a pragmatic or intellectualistic one. Bullough developed a continuum between the two poles, with shifts in distance being seen as matters of degree.

Kris argued that Bullough was right about aesthetic experience but that his analysis would be more complete with the integration of Freudian ideas that show the internal mechanisms of the psyche that make those aesthetic experiences, in their various gradations, possible. Kris maintained that central to artistic creation was a form of controlled psychic regression, involving a 'relaxation . . . of ego-functions' (1948: 253). On the part of painters and other artists, this form of regression was 'purposive and controlled'. Too much regression produces unintelligible symbols and at the other extreme of control the artistic result is cold, mechanical and uninspired. This theory of psychic levels represents a Freudian critique of Kantian rationalism in the aesthetic field. Its structure parallels Elias's 'sociologized' Freudian reformulation of Weber's Kantian rationalism in the field of social science (Elias 1939: 412–15).

In the course of commenting on Bullough's continuum, Kris also paired the terms 'involvement' and 'detachment' as opposites at either end of a continuum, in Kris's case one that embraced the crucial idea of individual emotional self-regulation. He commented that 'The response is not aesthetic at all unless it also comprises a shift in *psychic distance*, that is, fluctuation in the degree of involvement in action . . . In poetry, the Kantian emphasis on detachment can be expressed by Coleridge's formula of "willing suspension of disbelief"' (Kris 1948: 256, emphasis in original).

In his late work on Mozart (Elias 1993: 56–63) Elias wrote, in a way not incompatible with Kris's analysis of the importance of controlled regression in artistic creation, about 'de-privatized fantasies' and a 'controlling element of the personality' that checks the 'libidinal fantasy-stream' of the artist. Elias also pointed out that where this stream is relatively unchecked the resulting artistic forms can appear dislocated and disconnected, as seen in the drawings of schizophrenics (1993: 60). Kris had made a similar point in his classic essay 'Comments on the spontaneous artistic creations by psychotics' (Kris 1936: 116). Kris not only argued that a relaxation of ego functions that is purposive and controlled is important in artistic creation and inspiration, but he also used the expression 'regression in the service of the ego' in a more general sense (cited by De Swaan 1990: 164). As De Swaan says, there is a parallel between the latter concept and Elias's idea of 'an enjoyable and controlled de-controlling of emotions' (in Elias and Dunning 1986: 44) achieved in public spectator sports.

Returning to Weber, we can see that Elias transposed Weber's theory of scientific values on to another level informed by the basic idea that people's purposive rational conduct and capacity to exercise conscious distance from values presupposed that the continuous and more all-round self-control of affects was highly developed, taken for granted and (*contra* Kris) continuously *socially* reproduced. More specifically, that the pursuit of science, as part of the process Weber identified as rationalization, was made possible in internally pacified state societies by a personality in which the superego was highly developed. In reformulating the Weberian (and implicitly the relevant Kantian and phenomenological) ideas as explained above, the problem of psychic *distance* was transmuted by Elias into the problem of sociological *detachment*. The two perspectives carried with them different human self-images, representing different challenges. The first yielded the problematic of '*know* thyself' through psychic distancing whilst the second, Eliasian, one corresponded to '*face* thyself' through sociological detachment (see Elias 1987: 39–40).

Involvement and detachment as a balance

The relationship between involvement and detachment in Elias is not conceived of as a 'zero-sum' relation, that is, it does not imply that as involvement increases, so detachment decreases. Nor is the relationship a dualism between two mutually exclusive opposites. Rather, it is to be seen as a dynamic tension balance embodied in social activities. For Elias, rational conduct, including exercising detachment as part of a scientific group or institution, presupposes that the individuals doing this are already adults capable of controlling their affects and steering themselves (internally and in relation to others) in a such a way as to detach themselves from urgent personal problems of the moment in favour of impersonal, systematic, scientific problems. Only small babies or insane people, Elias argues, can either abandon their feelings to the here and now or, conversely, remain completely unmoved by what goes on around them. Adult behaviour lies on a scale somewhere between these two extremes, and social life as we know it would come to an end if standards of adult behaviour went too far in either direction. The sociological problem, Elias says, is to develop criteria to determine the *continuum* that lies between the two poles.

Nor do the terms involvement and detachment refer to two separate classes of objects. Elias writes: 'In using these terms, one refers in short to changing equilibria between sets of mental activities which in human relations with other humans, with objects and with self (whatever their other functions may be) have the function to involve and to detach' (Elias 1956: 227). Elias is working here with a multilevelled model of the embodied human personality that derives its specific character from the complex self-steering activities of people. What we call reflection, Elias says, 'combines and often struggles with drives, affects and emotions in the steering of muscular actions' (Elias 1987: 115). As 'reason', it is celebrated by philosophers as an unchanging human characteristic.

The capacity for such intense reflection in people is only possible *to that degree* if they possess a particularly well-developed and all-round capacity to regulate their drives and emotions internally – and also to the extent that they live in regularized and relatively pacified societies or enclaves. Far from being an unchanging characteristic of all humans, it is only consolidated at a comparatively late stage in social development in people for whom, internally, a longer gap exists between an impulse to act and the act itself, than existed in people in the Middle Ages. From this widening gap emerges the characteristic feature of thinking-about-thinking so typical of learned and cultured people in Western societies in particular. In Eliasian terminology, it is a personality in which the balance between id, ego and superego functions has become tilted towards superego functions producing, through the strong mechanism of the authoritative conscience, a consciousness 'less permeated by drives', as Elias (1939: 410) puts it.

Elias argues that it would be misleading to describe one type of sciences, those dealing with natural processes, as 'value-free' and the others, including sociology, as value-laden. Rather, he argues, in scientific inquiries different *kinds* of evaluations are more dominant than other kinds. He distinguishes, on the one hand, *autonomous* evaluations (such as an interest in the inherent order of events or fact orientation) which have become institutionalized in the natural sciences and are protected by professional standards. On the other hand, there are *heteronomous* evaluations, which embody strongly felt human needs experienced in the immediacy of the moment. The latter evaluations prevail in the social sciences at present.

For Elias, the social sciences, and sociology, in particular, await a breakthrough towards greater detachment to help humans control their interdependent social relations that are 'experienced by many as an alien external force not unlike the forces of nature' (Elias 1987: 10). In the case of the non-human forces of nature, humans gradually, over many thousands of years, managed to break out of a '*vicious circle*' (1987: 10). That is, people had little chance of controlling their own strong feelings in relation to natural forces and to develop the greater detachment needed to understand nature conceptually, as long as they still had little control. This is because that lack of control continually generated the fears that engendered more emotional, involved ways of thinking about nature, which itself impeded the development of greater detachment which would have enabled people to control the forces. People had little chance of extending their control over their non-human surroundings 'as long as they could not gain greater mastery over their own strong feelings in relation to them and increase their control over themselves' (1987: 9). Elias speculates that in relation to non-human nature, the breakthrough probably came as the result of the '*principle of increasing facilitation*' (1987: 9), i.e. that the more control people gained over various processes of nature, the easier it was for them to extend this control.

However, greater human control of natural forces has left people with the problem of controlling social forces. As Elias comments: 'The same process which has made people less dependent on the vagaries of nature has made them more dependent on each other' (1987: 10). In such circumstances, it is difficult for vulnerable and insecure people to be more emotionally detached about *social* relations and events, to control for their own strong feelings about events that deeply affect them, when their ability to control those events is small. At the same time, it is difficult for them to extend their understanding and control social processes as long as they cannot approach them with greater detachment, which entails greater control *over themselves*. Hence this 'circular movement between inner and outer controls, a feedback mechanism of a kind' (1987: 11) works not only in relation to natural forces, but also in people's *relations with each other*, that is, in society. Here the 'objects' are also the 'subjects' (1987: 12). It is this idea of a dynamic interplay between internal and external controls, as well as the conception of vicious circles playing themselves out in different ways in relation to natural forces and social relations, that constitutes the distinctiveness of Elias's model.

Secondary involvement and the sociological vocation

In the introduction to the late work, *Involvement and Detachment* (Elias 1987: xliv–xlv), Elias introduced the concept of *secondary involvement* which was developed in relation to the effect of realism achieved by Renaissance perspective painters such as Masaccio, van Eyck and Velazquez. Through detachment those painters achieved the effect of realistic perspective on the canvas, something that came to be supplemented later by a secondary involvement, whereby viewers of the paintings become involved in the aesthetic qualities of the ensemble of details assembled in the paintings. The painters provided an illusion of three-dimensional space, a feat achieved in virtue of their detachment, at the same time appealing to the viewers' capacity for the same. The painters provided various clues in the pictures which viewers picked up, clues that were designed to arouse the feelings of the viewers whose pleasure then derived from their becoming secondarily involved in the aesthetic qualities of the way in which the elements of the picture were arranged.

By analogy, I would argue that the achievement of self-perpetuating greater detachment in the emerging discipline of sociology would entail that the kind of passion normally associated with political and religious beliefs and similar commitments is channelled into the pursuit of a kind of detached sociological knowledge that transcends the one-sidedness of involved viewpoints of society. Sociologists embracing such greater detachment in their inquiries, themselves become secondarily involved in that activity and take pleasure from the comprehensive understanding made possible by the standpoint and relish its potentialities.

It is compatible with Elias's conception of sociology (as I have argued elsewhere (Kilminster 1998: 178)) that at the present stage in the development of societies and of the discipline itself, sociologists committed to 'autonomous evaluations' (Elias) should face the challenge of conducting themselves professionally in the following way. They should apply in their practice of sociology the criteria of cognitive evaluation and the standard of detachment which *would* be widely taken for granted if the discipline, as a special science, had achieved a higher degree of self-perpetuating, institutional autonomy, and a corresponding authority, than at present. The consistent application of these criteria and the standard of detachment anticipates their future embodiment in a stronger institutionalization of the discipline and, hopefully, will help to bring it about. Although there are no guarantees as to how far such a process can go.

I would also argue that this *anticipatory motif* in Elias is robustly sociological. It has a different character from other conceptions of the regulative character of idealized states of affairs found in political theory and social criticism (for example, the ideal speech situation of Apel and Habermas, or the 'utopian moment of the object' in Adorno (Kilminster 1998: 50–4), or Bauman's (1993: ch. 3) concept of 'being-for-the-other'). Those writers, unlike Elias, rely upon philosophical transcendental arguments for the derivation of regulative principles. In Elias, however, the controlling imperative of greater detachment, as a research guide, has neither an absolute metaphysical status nor a logical necessity. He is able to specify the concrete social and psychological forces and relations which would hinder or facilitate the achievement of *greater* self-perpetuating institutionalized standards of detachment, without assuming a final state of pure detachment can be achieved. For Elias, that would be a highly 'involved', teleological assumption that assumed that sociology was being drawn towards a preconceived notion of what it could ideally be. Rather, for Elias, the sociological enterprise is in a continuous process of becoming (see the final section of this chapter).

A final point of clarification needs to be made to conclude this section. It is a common misunderstanding of the sciences that they embody a cold, calculating rationalism that is inimical to warm, close human emotions. This common misconception of science perpetuates a misleading Romantic dichotomy between reason and passion that has got into intellectual currency. I think that Elias had moved away from this assumption. It would be a misunderstanding of Elias's notion of 'secondary involvement' to equate detachment with emotionless rationality and involvement with affect and feeling. In recent years, as part of the 'postmodern' sensibility (see Kilminster 1998: 110, 164, 170–1) the assumption of cold rationalism has been uncritically projected back on to the Enlightenment, said to be the source of the pernicious and 'inhuman' coldness and indifference of rationality and science. Then, by extension, this view has shaded over into a pervasive anti-science sentiment in the present period which attributes to science many of the catastrophes of the modern world such as the Holocaust, global pollution and nuclear warfare. In the social sciences we live in a period of Enlightenment bashing. But, as Peter Gay has said of the Enlightenment, 'It was passionate in its own right, and [passion] played a part in all irreverence, every call to rebellion, every moral tirade [of the *philosophes*]' (Gay 1973: 624–5).

In contrast to the Romantics, Elias's argument is, on my interpetation, that for any science (social or natural) to become established and institutionally self-perpetuating many preconditions have to be fulfilled, one of which is the *sustained transfer of controlled affect into 'autonomous evaluations'* through a process of institutionalization. It is an interpretation consistent with Elias's theory to say that through this process the practitioners of an emerging science, in the developing institutional practices in which they participate, gradually begin to be emotionally moved by specifically scientific activities and values. They come to experience pleasure and excitement in relation to activities such as discovery in which they are habitually applying a standard of detachment and an orientation to factual research, thereby developing a very strong, emotionally reinforced, commitment to the science concerned.

Richard Brown (1987: 535) recalls that at the University of Leicester in the 1950s Elias's first-year lectures: 'included several . . . which became inspirational as the importance and potential of sociology were advocated with powerful conviction'. Anyone who knew Elias could attest to this aspect of his character. Ironically, Elias's passionate commitment to sociology may have provided a further source of misunderstanding and even suspicion of him, which may (along with other factors) have contributed to the delayed reception of his work, particularly in Britain. For many people in academic circles passionate advocacy and scientific detachment are mutually exclusive. To the liberal mind that wants to keep rationality and irrationality strictly *separated*, Elias's passion for greater detachment in sociology would have seemed contradictory, incongruous, embarrassing or even suspicious. For that reason, Elias's approach would very possibly have been regarded as unreliable and even as possibly masking hidden, and perhaps dangerous, political biases, simply because of the seemingly inappropriate fervency of his commitment to a *discipline*, a fervour that for other people is normally reserved for ideologies or religious beliefs.

Concluding remarks: detachment in a new key

The struggle-for-detachment argument, prominent in Elias's programmatic writings about the role and prospects of sociology (e.g. Elias 1987b and 1984), bears the marks of the psychic structure characteristic of an earlier, disciplining, stage of a civilizing process, or at least one prominent strand of it. However, convincing evidence is beginning to accumulate (Waldhoff 1995; Wouters 1998; Kilminster 1998: 163–5) to suggest that in the contemporary period there has been the development of what Wouters has called a 'Third Nature' (Wouters 1998) psychic structure (see his chapter in this volume). This has been brought about by an opening up of the psychic dividing lines between id, ego and superego functions. This process has developed as part of the social dividing lines opening up further in a far-reaching phase of functional democratization and informalization and attendant social integration. The balance between functions within the psyche has, evidence is beginning to suggest, consolidated into a new, higher, pattern in which ego-functions play a stronger role and the superego functions have been transformed.

The superego functions do not any longer automatically operate as they did in the disciplining phase *solely* to forbid and to repress dangerous emotions. Now superego functions are involved to a much greater extent in automatically warning people, triggering pressures to take more aspects of other people and of oneself more into account. The multilevelled balance of psychic functions has thus reached a higher level of integration. This emergent new level has enabled in the present period a higher level of *mutual identification* between people, which corresponds to a higher level of social interdependency. In the earlier, disciplining, phase the particular character of superego functions (as part of the overall balance between id, ego and superego functions) was more associated with the automatic containing and repressing of certain affects and impulses. This particular balance of psychic functions blocked those emotions from playing a more *controlled* part in the flow and balance of psychic functioning, which they now arguably do.

It is highly plausible that these social and psychic developments have given rise to a different, more flexible, more malleable, pattern of internal controlling and self-regulation that is showing itself in many areas of culture. It is a characteristic kind of behaviour that many sociologists in the present period are conceptualizing as 'reflexivity' and 'individualization' (e.g. Giddens 1991; Beck 1992) although without a sociological theory of shifting psychic functions. People generally, *including sociologists*, now arguably have a higher capacity for self-organization and self-orientation than in the formalizing/disciplining phase. They can adjust themselves in manifold ways to the increasing demands of contemporary society which arise from the extending chains of interdependency at the regional and global levels of integration. Accumulating evidence suggests that emotionally people today are increasingly able to bring to the surface, and control, strange feelings and other previously more severely suppressed emotions. But, these are precisely the emotions, strange feelings and fantasies (as expressed in ideological convictions) that were always to be rigorously *excluded* from sociology in the greater detachment model of science advocated by Elias – lest they shape sociological inquiries in deleterious ways.

The models of science that stressed the suspension of value-judgements or the controlling of involvements, associated with Weber and as adapted by Elias, presuppose a particular balance between id, ego and superego functions characteristic of earlier phases of the Western civilizing process. This was a balance in which superego functions were closely bound up with the rigorous repression of dangerous emotions. The same balance of functions could be said to have underpinned the social phenomenologists' classical procedure of rigorous methodological 'bracketing'. It is also a psychic pattern that had its expression in R. K. Merton's (1968: 175, 185) strict methodological exclusion of psychology and psychoanalysis from sociology, in favour of the functionalist study of social institutions and culture.[1] What I am drawing attention to here is not merely the 'analytical' bracketing of certain questions or the intellectual exclusion of psychology as a matter of preference, but rather the strictness and rigour with which what was bracketed or excluded had to be *erased from the consciousness* of researchers. These were highly disciplined precepts and doctrines.

The same processes of functional democratization and informalization and 'Third Nature' personality formation would appear to have *already* become reflected in the upsurge in recent years of types of action research, the advocacy of 'taking the findings back to the people', dialogic approaches, more tolerance towards literary knowledge, folk knowledge, invoking personal experience, legitimizing gay, lesbian and ethnic knowledges, concern with morality, etc. which have become widely practised or advocated in sociology (e.g. Seidman 1998: Introduction and 347–9; May 1996: chs. 10 and 11; May 2001). These attitudes and kinds of inquiries are congruent with the experience and sensibilities of younger contemporary sociologists who are themselves bound up with the same social and psychic developments. The reflexive and democratizing tenor of the new types of sociology attests to a higher degree of *mutual identification* having been attained in the contemporary period.

The younger practitioners in sociology will probably experience their relations with others, inside and outside their institutional, professional sociological relations, in ways that will make the methodological imperative of greater detachment and suspension of value-judgements, pursued rigorously and *in its pure form* alone, seem simply inflexible and even authoritarian. On the other hand, sociologists still wedded exclusively to the greater detachment, fantasy-control, ideology banishing model of scientific activity will find the contemporary kinds of sociological activities and preferences briefly mentioned above decidedly disconcerting. To them, those research trends and attitudes will seem strange, unrigorous and uncontrolled, constituting a dangerous blurring of the much-fought-for clear boundary between scientific knowledge and personal and lay experience. This boundary was always previously policed by a more predominantly repressive, prohibiting, superego, the character of which, and its relationship to other psychic functions, have now, arguably, been transformed as social dividing lines have opened up. How can these two perspectives be reconciled? Are we witnessing the death throes of detachment, as is claimed by some groups within and on the periphery of sociology? I think not.

Sociologists of the contemporary sensibility who do continue to accept the importance of the scientific detachment, ideology-extirpating model are simply likely to be doing so in a less automatic, austere and martial fashion. But this will not make the inquiries they undertake in its name any less detached in practice. The same investigators also probably possess the psychic wherewithal to live with being committed, on the one hand, to a highly detached sociology geared to investigating long-term social compulsions, and, on the other hand, to one or other of the 'interactive' or quasi-political sociologies. But, embracing a higher level of more differentiated self-control, they may be better able than earlier generations of sociologists to live with this seeming incongruity.

The traditional scientific imperative was closely associated with the classical models of scientific sociology (including that of Elias in significant respects) that grew out of a disciplining phase of the Western civilizing process. But it was an ideal that, as subsequent social and psychic developments are clearly demonstrating, did not *by itself* signify the end state or *final* destination of sociology. Its transformation in the contemporary period by no means constitutes its demise, however, but simply its continuation on a higher level. To paraphrase Elias's judgement about the process of civilization which he made at the end of volume II of *The Civilizing Process*, one might say that the process of the development of sociology is not yet completed.

NOTE

1. R. K. Merton was an important figure in the promoting of a kind of sociology which methodologically excluded (i.e. suppressed) psychological realities
from sociological inquiry. In doing so, he was able to stake out a claim to the
independent subject matter of sociology as a human science, something which
had obvious professional benefits. His model had a considerable impact in the
1950s and 1960s as a professional ideology and continues to do so. This is
despite the fact that the level of behavioural formality, formal self-regulation
and social distance associated with that social phase and which made the
model plausible in the self-experience of sociologists, have long since been
superseded by more flexible patterns in society as a whole, as explained in
the text. When the Merton/Parsons research programmes were at their height,
Benjamin Nelson (1962: 151) made a prescient observation:

> In Merton's case there was operative from the outset an effort to provide as precise as
> possible a purely sociological mode of analysis which was not entangled with psychology
> and above all with psychoanalysis. In his early paper, *Social Structure and Anomie* [he] . . .
> carefully bracketed psychodynamic perspectives. The achievement of Professor Merton
> and those who have followed his lead since that day have been undeniable. Yet one day
> the dividends and costs of his decisions will have to be calculated together.

On these issues see Devereux 1967 and Hunt 1989.

REFERENCES

Bauman, Zygmunt 1993, *Postmodern Ethics*, Oxford: Basil Blackwell.
Beck, Ulrich 1992, *The Risk Society: Towards a New Modernity*, London: Sage
Publications.
Berger, Peter and Kellner, Hansfried 1981, *Sociology Reinterpreted: An Essay on
Method and Vocation*, Harmondsworth: Penguin Books.
Bogner, Artur 1987, 'Elias and the Frankfurt School', *Theory, Culture & Society*
4 (2–3): 249–85.
Brown, Richard 1987, 'Norbert Elias in Leicester: some recollections', *Theory,
Culture & Society* 4 (2–3): 533–9.
Bullough, Edward 1912–13, 'Psychical distance as a factor in art and an aesthetic
principle', *British Journal of Psychology* 5: 1912–13.
De Swaan, Abram 1990, *The Management of Normality: Critical Essays in Health
and Welfare*, London: Routledge.
Devereux, George 1967, *From Anxiety to Method in the Behavioral Sciences*, The
Hague: Mouton.
Dunning, Eric 1986, 'Preface', to Norbert Elias and Eric Dunning, *Quest for
Excitement: Sport and Leisure in the Civilizing Process*, Oxford: Basil Blackwell.
Elias, Norbert 2000 [1939], *The Civilizing Process: Sociogenetic and Psychogenetic
Investigations*, trans. Edmund Jephcott, rev. edn, eds. Eric Dunning, Johan
Goudsblom and Stephen Mennell, Oxford: Blackwell Publishers.
  1956, 'Problems of involvement and detachment', *British Journal of Sociology*
7 (3): 226–52 (also in *Involvement and Detachment* 1987).

1971, 'The sociology of knowledge: new perspectives', *Sociology* 5, 2 (3): 149–68, 355–70.

1976, 'Introduction: a theoretical essay on established and outsider relations', in Norbert Elias and John L. Scotson 1994, *The Established and the Outsiders*, 2nd edn, London: Sage.

1978, *What is Sociology?*, London: Hutchinson.

1984, 'Knowledge and power: an interview by Peter Ludes', in Nico Stehr and Volker Meja, eds., *Society and Knowledge: Contemporary Perspectives on the Sociology of Knowledge*, New Brunswick/London: Transaction Books.

1987a, *Involvement and Detachment*, Oxford: Basil Blackwell.

1987b, 'The retreat of the sociologists into the present', *Theory, Culture & Society* 4 (2–3): 223–47.

1993, *Mozart: Portrait of a Genius*, ed. Michael Schröter, trans. Edmund Jephcott, Cambridge: Polity Press.

(with Dunning, Eric) 1986, *Quest for Excitement: Sport and Leisure in the Civilizing Process*, Oxford: Basil Blackwell.

Frisby, David 1976, 'Introduction to the English translation', in Theodor Adorno, Hans Albert, *et al.*, *The Positivist Dispute in German Sociology*, trans. Glyn Adey and David Frisby, London: Heinemann.

Gadamer, Hans-Georg 1985, *Philosophical Apprenticeships*, trans. Robert R. Sullivan, Cambridge, MA: MIT Press.

Gay, Peter 1973, *The Enlightenment: An Interpretation: Volume Two, The Science of Freedom*, London: Wildwood House.

Giddens, Anthony 1991, *Modernity and Self-Identity: Self and Society in the Late Modern Age*, Cambridge: Polity Press.

Hunt, Jennifer C. 1989, *Psychoanalytic Aspects of Fieldwork*, London: Sage.

Kilminster, Richard 1979, *Praxis and Method: A Sociological Dialogue with Lukács, Gramsci and the Early Frankfurt School*, London: Routledge & Kegan Paul.

1993, 'Norbert Elias and Karl Mannheim: closeness and distance', *Theory, Culture & Society* 10 (3): 81–114.

1998, *The Sociological Revolution: From the Enlightenment to the Global Age*, London: Routledge (paperback 2002).

Kilminster, Richard and Wouters, Cas 1995, 'From philosophy to sociology: Elias and the neo-Kantians: a response to Benjo Maso', *Theory, Culture & Society* 12 (3): 81–120.

Kris, Ernst 1936, 'Comments on spontaneous artistic creations by psychotics', in Kris 1964, *Psychoanalytic Explorations in Art*, New York: Schocken Books (fourth printing 1974).

1948, 'Aesthetic ambiguity', in Kris 1964, *Psychoanalytic Explorations in Art*, New York: Schocken Books (fourth printing 1974).

Kuzmics, Helmut 2001, 'On the relationship between literature and sociology in the work of Norbert Elias', in Thomas Salumets (ed.), *Norbert Elias and Human Interdependencies*, Montreal & Kingston: McGill-Queen's University Press.

Lassman, Peter, Velody, Irving and Martins, Herminio (eds.) 1989, *Max Weber's 'Science as a Vocation'*, London: Unwin Hyman.

Mannheim, Karl 1933, 'The democratization of culture', in Mannheim 1956, *Essays on the Sociology of Culture*, London: Routledge & Kegan Paul.

May, Tim 1996, *Situating Social Theory*, Buckingham: Open University Press.

2001, *Social Research: Issues, Methods and Process*, Cambridge: Polity Press.

Mennell, Stephen 1998, *Norbert Elias: An Introduction*, Dublin: University College Dublin Press.

Merton, Robert K. 1968, *Social Theory and Social Structure*, London: Collier Macmillan.

Nelson, Benjamin 1962, 'Sociology and psychoanalysis on trial: an epilogue', *Psychoanalysis and Psychoanalytic Review* 49 (2): 144–60.

Schutz, Alfred 1932, *The Phenomenology of the Social World*, trans. George Walsh and Frederick Lehnert, London: Heinemann, 1972.

1940, 'Phenomenology and the social sciences', in Farber, Marvin (ed.), *Philosophical Essays in Memory of Edmund Husserl*, London: Greenwood Press, reprinted 1968.

Seidman, Steven 1998, *Contested Knowledge: Social Theory in the Postmodern Era*, 2nd edn, Oxford: Blackwell Publishers.

Shils, Edward A. 1970, 'Tradition, ecology and institution in the history of sociology', *Daedalus* 99(ii) (also in his *The Constitution of Society*, Chicago & London: University of Chicago Press, 1982).

Sica, Alan 1984, 'Sociogenesis versus psychogenesis: the unique sociology of Norbert Elias', *Mid-American Review of Sociology* 9 (1): 49–78.

Waldhoff, Hans-Peter 1994, 'On secondary involvement and the perception of strangers', Paper presented to the *Ad hoc* Sessions on Figurational Sociology, XIII ISA World Congress of Sociology, Bielefeld, 18–23 July.

1995, *Fremde und Zivilisierung. Wissensoziologische Studien über der Verarbeiten von Gefühlen der Fremdheit. Probleme der modernen Peripheri-Zentrums-Migration am türkisch-deutschen Beispiel*, Frankfurt am Main: Suhrkamp.

Wouters, Cas 1977, 'Informalization and the civilizing process', in Peter Gleichmann, Johan Goudsblom and Hermann Korte, *Human Figurations: Essays for Norbert Elias*, Amsterdam: Sociologisch Tijdschrift.

1986, 'Formalization and informalization: changing tension balances in civilizing processes', *Theory, Culture & Society* 3 (2): 1–19.

1987, 'Developments in the behavioural codes between the sexes: the formalization of informalization in The Netherlands, 1930–85', *Theory, Culture and Society* 4 (2–3): 405–27.

1998, 'How strange our feelings of superiority and inferiority to ourselves?', *Theory, Culture & Society* 15 (1), February.

3 Ecology, 'human nature' and civilizing processes: biology and sociology in the work of Norbert Elias

Stephen Quilley

Introduction

One of the great strengths of Norbert Elias's work is that he sought to develop sociology as a rigorous science of society.[1] He argued that the scientific investigation of social processes, although at an early stage of development, could be potentially as rigorous and as open to generalization as any of the natural sciences. 'The structure of a given system of rules, as a figuration of interdependent people, can be determined with almost the same rigour as that of a specific molecule by a scientist' (1983: 119). This was also one of the reasons for the slow appreciation of his work in the anglophone world. Since the 1970s wider awareness of substantive studies such as *The Civilizing Process* and *The Court Society* has not led to a revival of interest in the more programmatic and epistemological works such as *Involvement and Detachment*. One reason for this was the intellectual ascendance, in recent decades, of epistemological relativism in a variety of forms (poststructuralism, postmodernism, the 'linguistic turn', discourse analysis etc.) and a pronounced retreat from any scientific ambitions for sociology. This has also been combined with a deep scepticism of any theories of long-term development, which became associated with unfashionable Marxist teleology and Eurocentric progress theory. Another consequence of this new sociological 'common sense' was the rigid codification of what Pinker cruelly, if in part accurately, caricatures as commitment to the 'blank slate – the modern denial of human nature' (Pinker 2002). Social constructivism in sociology owes a great deal to the early twentieth-century anthropological programme of Franz Boas and Margaret Mead, which sought to chart the diversity of human cultures, whilst self-consciously eschewing consideration of long-term historical development (see Freeman 1983). Their legacy was an ingrained insistence upon developmental autonomy and difference. In recent decades this has left both sociology and cultural anthropology ill-equipped to integrate the rapid advances across an enormous range of (broadly biological) neighbouring disciplines in the human sciences – evolutionary ecology, neuroscience, evolutionary archaeology, developmental biology, genetics – to name a few. A feature of these developments is a growing interdisciplinarity, from which mainstream sociology in particular is excluded. A good illustration of this is that it has been left to a biologist (a trained ornithologist no less!) to develop one of the grandest works of synthesis of the last fifty years; Jared Diamond's *Guns, Germs and Steel* (1998), sets out to bring together insights from evolutionary ecology, environmental history and epidemiology to answer questions that should be of central interest to sociologists interested in development, racism, stratification and colonialism, namely, why it was Europeans who invaded Papua New Guinea and not the other way around. How did colonized Africa remain full of Africans whilst in the Americas, Europeans replaced indigenous populations on a massive scale?

Elsewhere the field has been left to the more gene-centred and reductionist forms of biology to explain – or in many cases 'explain away' – the intricacies of human social processes as the outcome of our evolutionary history. However, in the defensive vilification of the original programme of sociobiology advanced by E. O. Wilson (1975), and more recent incarnations in the guise of evolutionary psychology (Barkow, Cosmides and Tooby 1992), sociology has squandered an opportunity to engage with biology. In such an engagement there was, and still is, an opportunity to develop a common programme with areas of biological investigation that are more sensitive to multiple scales, and processes working at different levels of complexity, engendering 'emergent' dynamics that cannot be reduced or 'explained' by lower-level processes. This is true of developmental biology in general, where in explicit rejection of the selfish-gene imagery associated with neo-Darwinians such as Richard Dawkins, there is more emphasis on complex, two-way, iterative interactions between genes and environments (see Rose 1997). Across the field of evolutionary biology there is also a growing recognition that the neo-Darwinian paradigm has to be opened up to incorporate a growing body of evidence as to the evolutionary significance of cooperation, association and symbiosis (Margulis 1998; Sapp 1994), group and multilevel selection (the 'trading up' of evolutionary fitness – see Michod 1999), and – the ultimate Lamarckian heresy – the (albeit limited) possibility of the inheritance of acquired characteristics. It is also true of developments in theoretical biology associated with the complexity theory of Stuart Kaufman and colleagues at the Sante Fe Institute (Kaufman 2000; see also Goodwin 1994), whose articulation of a 'general biology' focusing on the concept of emergence and the modelling of the interdependent interactions or autonomous agents, is potentially reconcilable with Elias's vision of sociology as an aspect of 'the great evolution': i.e. the investigation of the emergent dynamics of the complex social processes which occur when a biological species acquires language ('symbol emancipation') and both its own social and ecological pattern of life, and that of the species around it, are subject to the development of culture (the growing anthroposphere within the biosphere – see below).

In this chapter, my aim is to present the integrated epistemology and sociology of knowledge that is central to Elias's substantive works in the area of historical sociology, and to demonstrate that in this theory of knowledge there is also a systematic vision of the relationship between sociology and the biological sciences. This is integral to the distinctions that Elias makes between history, long-term processes of development and (phylogenetic) evolution. It is central to his recognition that processes of psychogenesis and personality formation coincide with biological (and neurological) growth and development. But, most importantly, this integrated theory of knowledge provides a rationale for sociology as a *scientific* discipline taking its place among an array of human sciences, but also for its *autonomy* as a discipline, which derives ultimately from the irreducibility of the emergent dynamics of human social processes. Sociology is autonomous and unique because, in relation to our own biosphere, human language is unique. Elias would, however, have been happy to locate sociology within the overarching rubric of a general biology in Kaufman's sense, precisely because he would have recognized that there are almost certainly other biospheres in the universe, and quite probably other 'symbolically emancipated' species (Elias 1989) engaged in social processes with their own distinctive dynamics. Finally, Elias's sociology of knowledge also sheds light on the sequence of scientific developments and, at least to some extent, explains why the emergence of a more detached understanding of social processes has lagged behind the development of natural sciences. As with the latter, the development of a scientific sociology depends not upon the eradication of passion or a deep sense of 'involvement' on the part of social scientists, rather it requires the emergence of forms of 'secondary involvement' in the process of sociological investigation itself (as opposed to immediate politico-ethical attachments), and a 'passion for detachment'. At the very least such a development will require sociologists to develop a rationale for their own discipline which is sufficiently robust to allow incursions from neighbouring biological disciplines to be welcomed as challenges rather than dismissed defensively, and out of hand.

Sociology as science: contributions to epistemology and the sociology of knowledge

In the introduction to this volume it was argued that in his post-war career, in relation to both his substantive contributions to historical sociology and the limited attempt to formulate an abstract theoretical rationale for process sociology, as well as his most apparently orthodox sociological study of a working-class community near Leicester, Elias was in fact elaborating themes and concepts that were already woven into the dense narrative and innovative conceptual architecture of *The Civilizing Process* (1939). This is even more clearly the case with respect to three books which arguably constitute his most important contribution to sociology: *The Symbol Theory* (1989), *Time: An Essay* (1992) and *Involvement and Detachment* (1987). It is these works, and particularly the last, which elaborate both a distinctive Eliasian epistemology and an illuminating sociology of knowledge (although see also Elias 1971; 1984). Characteristically, Elias seeks to replace philosophical questions as to the possibilities for cognitive individuals to acquire 'truthful' knowledge about the world, with sociological questions about the relationship between social development and the expansion of the social stock of reality-congruent knowledge about the world. For this reason, his theory of knowledge is inextricably intertwined with a sociology of the knowledge process. The resulting matrix combines a theoretical rationale for the scientific investigation of social processes as an autonomous plane of integration and complexity, with an historical interpretation of the growth of human knowledge and, more specifically, the sequential emergence of successive scientific disciplines – including sociology. On this basis, Elias provides the most rigorous account, from within the discipline, of the relationship between the biological and social sciences. In what follows, I will summarize Elias's contributions to epistemology and the sociology of knowledge, before going on to elaborate the implications for our understanding of both 'human nature' and 'non-human nature'. It will be argued that Elias provides the basis for a more engaging sociology of 'life on earth' which is more competent to act as the societal interlocutor of the life sciences revolution currently accelerating the anthropogenic transformation of the biosphere, and threatening to launch a paradigmatic process of reflexive evolution – the semi-conscious human steering of human nature.

In *Involvement and Detachment* (*I&D*) Elias elaborates a theory of knowledge that seeks to establish the relationship across the full spectrum of scientific disciplines within the arc of a 'comprehensive process model'. As a contribution to epistemology, *I&D* provides a convincing rationale for a spectrum of methodological priorities across a hierarchy of scientific disciplines, and relating principally to the complexity and order of integration of the phenomenal subject matter in each case. The relevance of this model to the social sciences is that it establishes a strong rationale for the autonomy of sociology, whilst establishing more precisely the nature of the continuities and overlaps with neighbouring disciplines in the natural sciences.

Following a schema originally outlined by Auguste Comte (1907)[2] Elias argues that different scientific disciplines can be arranged along a continuum according to the nature of the data they seek to understand (1987: 121–33). These fields of investigation exhibit different degrees of differentiation, interdependency and functional integration. At one end of this spectrum lie the physical sciences whose basic units of observation – sub-atomic particles, atoms, molecules etc. – form composite units that exhibit low levels of complexity, little functional differentiation and low levels of integration. In consequence, component part units of any such composite structure are only minimally influenced by the emergent dynamics of the whole. Such fields of investigation are well suited to the characteristic analytical and reductive procedures of the physical sciences: dissection, isolation, experimentation and reduction to component parts, and law-like generalizations. However, moving across the spectrum, through organic chemistry, the natural sciences and eventually to anthropology and sociology, the fields of investigation become more complex. Composite structures form systems. Systems within systems entail multiple levels of integration. At each successive level, part units exhibit greater functional differentiation and are involved in overlapping planes or modalities of integration. Moving in this direction, such atomistic reductive methods become less appropriate. An important reason for this is that in such fields of investigation the qualities and characteristics of component part units are increasingly determined by the nature of their connections and relationships within such higher-level systems. In this context Elias observes that in moving away from physics there is a subtle but consistent devaluation in the cognitive status of scientific laws and a corresponding increase in the importance of non-law-like theoretical formulations, modelling temporal and spatial processes and structures (1987: 125). A prime example in the field of evolutionary biology would be Darwin's essentially 'historical' theory of evolution.

For Elias, this spectrum of disciplines and their corresponding fields of investigation is also a hierarchy. The reason for this is that each more complex, more functionally differentiated field of investigation refers to composite units and systems that 'contain' (but cannot be reduced to) all lower levels of integration. For instance, atoms and molecules are clearly components of all biological processes. However, biological systems involve structures whose part units one level lower are linked by a complex division of functions (e.g. the different organs in relation to the overall metabolism of the body). The behaviour and characteristics of such part units are irreversibly adjusted to the functioning of a composite unit of a higher order. 'Life' is a concept that simply refers to this irreversible order of integration. The shift from the physical to the biological sciences can be seen as a move upwards through 'a hierarchic order within which, over a number of stages, part units together form composite units of a higher order and so lead, through a growing number of planes of differentiation and integration, to more and more complex formations' (1987: 129). Within this schema, social processes consequent upon language and culture represent the highest order of integration. A single cell is estimated to have between ten and twelve interlocking planes of integration. At the level of human beings, culture escalates this complexity to an almost unquantifiable degree. Units representing higher stages of integration possess stage-specific behavioural and functional properties that are derivable only in relation to their mode of integration – i.e. the manner in which they are organized functionally and interdependently. It follows that the behaviour of human beings has stage-specific dimensions that emerge from the pattern of interdependent interaction and participation in social processes. But this pattern is a function of the social configuration and not of particular persons. This provides a convincing rationale for the relative autonomy of social processes as a field of investigation, whilst specifying fairly precisely the relationship to natural scientific disciplines.

A final feature of Elias's conception of this 'model of models' is that the continuum of scientific disciplines and fields of investigation also represents a temporal sequence in 'the grand evolution'. 'The different sciences can then be understood as each contributing to solving the problems which different stages of an evolutionary process pose, their respective theoretical models as symbolizing different stages' (1987: 146). Anticipating the current biological thinking in relation to complexity theory (Kaufman 2000), Elias argues that there is an unambiguous direction to the grand evolution towards increasing complexity. By creating matter, 'the big bang' set in train the physical processes that constitute the first dimension in the ongoing transformation and evolution of the universe. This process of physical expansion provides the field of investigation for cosmology. Successive dimensions form a temporal sequence, with evolutionary-biological processes, and the plane of integration that we call 'life', emerging (on our planet) only 3.5 billion years ago. With human 'symbol emancipation', biological evolution eventually engenders the plane of integration we understand as culture: the anthroposphere within the biosphere.

In summary, Elias presents a *hierarchy of scientific disciplines* that relates to a *spectrum of fields of investigation* arranged according to their degrees of complexity and levels of integration. This spectrum is also understood as a *temporal sequence in the 'great evolution'*. However this 'model of models' is combined with an *historical sociology of the 'knowledge process'*. For Elias the historical emergence of successive scientific disciplines is but the most recent movement in the spiralling iteration between very long-term processes of social development on the one hand, and the expanding stock of reality-congruent knowledge about the world. His principal point of departure in the analysis of this knowledge process, is the interdependence of the safety/danger balance on the one hand, and the involvement/detachment balance on the other. The relationship between knowledge and social development hinges, Elias argues, on the complex feedback loops – both 'virtuous' and 'vicious' – between these two balances. Early in human development, what Elias calls animistic, magico-mythical knowledge about the world was characterized by higher degrees of fantasy (than later become the case), consequent upon greater degrees of involvement. Putative connections between events and phenomena were, to a much greater degree, posited in relation to the direct meaning they had for the self. The paradigmatic questions would not concern 'how' a phenomenon occurred, but 'why it happened to me' or 'what it means for us/me'. Elias shows how high levels of danger induce greater degrees of involvement – making more detached observation and induction of possible connections between events and phenomena more difficult – and hence creating obstacles to the expansion of the social stock of reality-congruent knowledge about the world. As a result of this 'double bind' the early stages of the knowledge process are relatively slow and tortuous. An early example would include the time, foresight, affective restraint (deferral of gratification) and the relatively detached understanding of the qualities of the raw material[3] required to collect the correct stone and create stone tools for use in a subsequent hunting expedition. However, to the extent that the knowledge process does move forward, each extension of detachment consistently enhances the capacity of human beings to control non-human nature.[4] Over many millennia, in consequence of hundreds of small technological innovations, and in tandem with a steadily increasing stock of concepts and terms expressing more reality-congruent understandings about the connections between processes and events in the natural world, the balance between danger and safety shifts steadily in favour of the latter (at least *vis-à-vis* non-human nature). Thus for Elias, there is a consistent and reciprocal relationship between (a) the level of detachment represented by public standards of thinking about natural events, and (b) the level and manner of control of non-human nature represented by conventional procedures for manipulating them (1987: 8). This gradual shift from a vicious loop or double-bind in the relationship between the involvement/detachment and safety/danger ratios, to a virtuous loop, proceeds according to 'the principle of facilitation'. As the size of this relatively insulated sphere of safety increases (the anthroposphere within the biosphere), the achievement of more detached understandings becomes progressively easier to achieve. It is for this reason that the knowledge process and concomitant technological innovation exhibit a glacial inertia in the earliest phases of hominid development before accelerating rapidly, almost exponentially, in later phases.

Central to the theory of civilizing processes is the idea of 'social constraint towards self-constraint' – that is to say, the internalization of progressively more restrained codes of conduct, greater and more or less automatic patterns of self-control, the increasing mediation of affective drives and short-term impulses, by processes of calculation and foresight – and in short, the formation of a more complex 'superego' agency in the psychical structure. Crucially Elias points out that 'civilization' is a process and is absolutely not a characteristic of 'mind' or 'nature' – and certainly not an essential attribute of European societies. Rather, civilization as the internalization of restraints is the unplanned outcome of blind social processes, over many generations. 'Civilisation is not "reasonable"; not "rational", any more than it is "irrational". It is set in motion blindly, and kept in motion by the autonomous dynamics of a web of relationships, by specific changes in the way people are bound and live together' (2000 [1939]: 366). And in so far as the kind of social figurations – the interdependencies, processes of socio-economic differentiation and pacification – are extending across the planet (not least in the wake of globalization), the theory would predict a corollary extension of 'social restraint towards self-restraint'.

What is interesting about this formulation is that it suggests a historical-sociological way of reconciling the observable malleability of human nature with its essential universality as a function of the human genome. In phylogenetic terms human nature is an attribute of the species. In this sense only, it can be equated with the range and frequency of occurrence of all the versions (alleles) of all of the genes that are present in the human gene pool. Our genomic nature is an evolved genetic profile whose contours can be related to our unique history of adaptation to a changing ecological environment over many millennia. At the level of genes, evolution refers to allelic mutations, and the changing frequency of the resulting genes in the population. For any species there is not only a gap between the actual combination of alleles present in a particular organism (genotype) and the pattern of their expression in somatic growth and development (phenotype), but there is also an enormous degree of phenotypic plasticity consequent on the fact that processes of individual growth and development involve complex, iterative and open-ended interactions between the organisms and their environment. Biologists refer to this problem in terms of 'reaction norms' (see Pigliucci 2001 for an comprehensive review of these debates). What this means is that for any species there is a gap between a phylogenetically defined 'nature' and actually observed characteristics and patterns of behaviour. Wild chimpanzees have not been observed using complex symbolic communication. Chimps raised in human society can learn to make considerable use of such symbols, and develop fairly extensive vocabularies. These two situations point to two rather different phenotypic 'chimp-natures', both of which unfold within limits of a phylogenetic species-nature.

Symbol emancipation and culture have progressively expanded the range and variability of human reaction norms to an extent that makes the concept of human nature far more difficult to pin down. For hundreds of thousands of years human evolution has involved an expanding circuit of material culture, most notably in respect of the progressive domestication of fire and a learned capacity to construct wooden and stone tools. Both Goudsblom (1992) and Elias (1987: xxxiv) highlight the interlocking of biological and social processes as a pervasive feature of these earliest stages of human evolution. This canalizing and steering of our evolutionary trajectory by social processes amounted to the sociological modification of (biological) norms of reaction. For around 50,000 years the possibilities for intergenerational transmission and retention of knowledge has multiplied almost exponentially as a result of the evolution of fully fledged language. 'Symbol emancipation' (Elias 1989) was the defining point in the acceleration of human cultural development because it had the effect of dramatically stretching the phenotypic plasticity of human nature. How was this so? Although we are predisposed to consider single, individual organisms and persons as the base-line unit of analysis in both the social and the biological sciences, this becomes even more problematic in the case of sociology. Humans are born into language, which is an emergent property of groups of individuals interacting in the context of regular, structured but largely unplanned social processes. The concepts and ideas that we acquire through language provide axial modes of orientation in relation to both the social world and non-human nature. By allowing much more complex processes of communication and coordination, language precipitated the extension and elaboration of social interdependencies between individuals and groups. The codes of conduct and standards of behaviour regulating such interactions could become increasingly complex. Cultural patterns, which allow for the storage and gradual modification of such formal and informal codes and standards, are an emergent property of social processes – the unplanned outcome of the interweaving plans, actions, emotional and rational impulses of individual people. 'From this interdependence of people arises an order *sui generis*, an order more compelling and stronger than the will and reason of the individual people composing it' (Elias 1939: 366).

Analysing civilizing processes in Western Europe, Elias's argument is basically that social differentiation and the extension of the division of labour engendered a progressive ordering of social relations that compelled more and more people to attune their conduct to that of others. Over time, external controls to this effect were increasingly complemented by internalized patterns of self-restraint, discernible as a particular psychological trait. Only in the context of the social and economic stability effected by centralized monopolies over wealth transfers and physical violence, combined with consistency in patterns of childhood socialization, 'does this kind of self-restraint require a higher degree of automaticity, does it become, as it were, a "second nature"' (1939: 369). It is this 'automaticity', consequent upon the ontogenic 'wiring up' of such a psychical habitus during the process of childhood socialization, that makes it second *nature*.

In summary, the emergence of social processes consequent upon language had a significant impact on our own evolution. Symbol emancipation was an autocatalytic evolutionary event in so far as it resulted in a positive feedback loop, accelerating the expansion of the higher plane of integration and complexity engendered by culture and social processes. However, culture also intervenes in relation to developmental biology (the ontogenic processes of individual growth, development and socialization). Long-term processes of social development, and the enormous range of societal formations, entail a corresponding variety in the expression of human nature and 'wiring up' of particular human beings. Elias's concept of 'second nature' and his recognition of 'symbol emancipation' as an evolutionary process, provide the basis for an accommodation of sociological perspectives with both evolutionary biology and developmental biology.

Reflexive evolution of humanity

One important factor that emerges from Elias's theory of knowledge relates to 'the great evolution' and the successive emergence of higher levels of complexity and planes of integration. In this schema, Elias notes the tendency for higher orders of integration to channel and steer lower orders. For instance, with the evolution of organic life and the emergence of the biosphere 3.5 billion years ago, emergent biological processes begin to steer development on lower chemical and physical planes of integration. The most important instance of this steering of the lithosphere by the biosphere was the oxygenation of a previously anaerobic atmosphere by primitive photosynthetic bacteria – among the first life forms to emerge on the earth. Other examples include the geological transformations

associated with the creation of limestone consequent upon the fossiliza-
tion of aquatic micro-organisms, and similarly the emergence of the
'carbon sink' from petrified organic matter in the form of oil and coal
deposits. Such steering and channelling effects occur at all levels of biological complexity, from the organization and evolution of single-celled organisms, through to the climatic ecology of the biosphere. Symbol emancipation and the emergence of culture are the most recent and graphic
examples of this process. Such evolutionary steering is evident in relation
to the anthropogenic transformation of the biosphere and global evolutionary ecology (see below). However, it is also becoming a probable
trajectory in relation to the reflexive evolution of our own species. Since
Watson and Crick received the Nobel prize for deciphering the genetic
structure of DNA in 1953, the life sciences revolution has been threatening to transform just about every sphere of economic and social life. With
the completion of the human genome project genetic science is progress-
ing so rapidly that ethical and regulatory debates are barely able to keep
up. What seems certain is that starting over the next hundred years a combination of screening, gene therapy and genetic engineering will engender
escalating opportunities for the radical genetic reconstruction of human
beings (Dyson 1997: 157). This amounts to the semi-conscious, reflexive
steering of human evolution. It has always been a misconception among
social scientists that with the onset of cultural evolution, the biological
evolution of our species effectively ceased. In fact, there has been an ongoing two-way interaction between social development and genomic evolution. Examples of this include the textbook relationship between sickle
cell anaemia and resistance to malaria in some African populations, and
the recent evolution of adult lactose tolerance in response to the development of a culture of milk drinking, among pastoralists and farmers (Wills
1999). The problem from a conceptual point of view has always been to
keep simultaneously in view multiple time-frames, relating to biological
evolution, long-term processes of social development, history and individual growth and development. However, reflexive evolution, at least in
relation to our own phylogenetic trajectory as a species, by rapidly accelerating the pace of human evolution, is likely to bring the time-frames of
evolutionary biology and social development into phase with each other.
As Dyson points out, however, the time-frames for such processes may
still operate over thousands rather than tens or hundreds of years.

The biosphere within the anthroposphere

Goudsblom (2002) uses the term anthroposphere to refer to the expanding range and ecological impacts of human culture. In ecological terms,

humanity is often seen as a rampant, plague species – a consummate ecological opportunist moving from niche to niche and creating havoc in its wake. Certainly anthropogenic ecological change is a major cause for concern. However, it is important to remember that such ecological crises, including catastrophic declines in biodiversity as a result of an accelerated rate of extinction, are not unprecedented. One such event occurred over 3 billion years ago when certain forms of photosynthetic bacteria ('blue-green algae') 'poisoned' the atmosphere by releasing oxygen – deadly to the great majority of species then constituting the biosphere, and resulting in 'the greatest environmental crisis ever' (Westbroek 1991: 202 – quoted in Goudsblom 2002: 22). Whilst human culture is transforming planetary ecology, our propensity for language, culture and technology is a natural product of evolution. Anthropogenic transformation of the earth began with the gradual domestication of fire – thousands of years before symbol emancipation and the dawn of modern human culture in the upper Palaeolithic, some 30,000–50,000 years ago (Klein 2002). Anthropogenic extinctions of large mammals on all continents at various times during the Palaeolithic bear witness to the ecological implications of the Promethean trajectory of human culture. More recently, processes of agrarianization and industrialization have further transformed the human ecological regime with escalating impacts on the biosphere. In short, the expansion of the anthroposphere within the biosphere is an intrinsic and unavoidable aspect of human ecology. As a symbolizing species humanity developed the capacity for the unbroken (as a whole, at least) transmission of an expanding stock of reality-congruent knowledge about non-human nature across successive generations (see Kilminster in this volume). This social stock of knowledge provides the basis of material culture that continually enhances the human capacity to transform and manipulate non-human nature.

Over the last two centuries, processes of industrialization, global integration and the faltering extension of nation-territorial forms of pacification, have lead to a paradigm shift in the relationship between the anthroposphere and the biosphere. For the first time, the former can be said to contain the latter. Ecological and evolutionary biological processes increasingly take place within the constraints established by human development and social processes. Nash (1969) describes the manner in which European settlers conceived of themselves as carving out an American civilization within a vast sea of wilderness. Within three centuries, with the closure of the frontier, Theodor Roosevelt's federal reserves sought to protect the final vestiges of wilderness from the rapid encroachment of civilization. At the start of the twenty-first century, the greater part of the earth's surface is fenced off, criss-crossed by roads, railways, fences and communications wires. The air is teeming with aircraft, and the upper atmosphere with satellites. Developers and oil tycoons are lining up to exploit the remaining wilderness areas in the Antarctic, the Amazon and Alaska. And even the world's oceans, having served as hunting grounds, transport corridors and industrial waste sinks, are now being actively farmed. This last point is perhaps the most telling in evolutionary terms. By the end of the present century, between 60–70 per cent of the terrestrial biomass of the planet will be accounted for by human controlled agriculture – and most probably by genetically modified organisms (GMOs). Animals and plants which are not directly part of our agrarian regime, must nevertheless adapt to a life at its margins. Images of large predators such as wolves or lions as the apex of evolutionary adaptedness abound in popular natural history. But in fact such species are evolutionary hangovers, maladapted to the post-Neolithic environment, and will survive only at the discretion of human beings – a discretion motivated by the kind of aesthetic impulses referred to above. It is domestic dogs and cats that are truly adapted to a world in which the biosphere has become subordinate to the anthroposphere. However, this is not to say that this humanization of nature is not natural. It is in fact the outcome of the evolutionary strategies of not only human beings, but a large number of allied species which have tied their colours to the mast of human culture (Budiansky 1994; Eisenberg 1998). It is in this context that Coppinger and Smith (1983) argue that biologists should begin to recognize a new evolutionary paradigm based on a human-centred web of symbiosis – the 'age of interdependent forms'.

This concept dovetails well with Elias's theory of knowledge in which human social processes are seen as an aspect of 'the great evolution' and constituting the most recently evolved field of investigation. The 'domestication of evolution' refers to the fact that the expanding anthroposphere is now channelling and steering biological evolutionary processes at lower levels of integration. However, this is not to say that human beings should be complacent about the pace of ecological change. Evolutionary ecology is full of examples of species that become too successful or too specialized for their own good. Extinction is the regular and normal fate for most species and there is no particular reason why human beings should be any different. However, whilst symbol emancipation launched our species on a Promethean trajectory of ecological expansion and domination, the capacity for culture and social development also involves a capacity for politics and self-regulation. It is possible that the species with the greatest capacity for destabilizing impacts on non-human nature, may yet prove to be the only species capable of exercising evolutionary self-restraint – the semi-political and semi-conscious internalization of restraints in relation to nature and environment. However, such an outcome will depend to a great extent on a progressive shift in the involvement–detachment balance in relation to our understanding of social processes. Greater detachment and more reality-congruent knowledge of figurational dynamics might create the basis for the kind of interventions and remodelling of human social and economic systems implied by the notion of sustainable development. Concepts such as 'anthroposphere', 'biosphere' and 'sustainability' suggest that such a shift may already be under way.

For Elias, the massive reduction in levels of daily violence within nation-states and the continuing emergence of a less violent and more affectively restrained personality structure, are a function of pacifying state processes and intensive and extended patterns of socialization consequent upon economic productivity and extended and binding figurations of interdependency between individuals and communities. It is likely that the combination of regulation of anthropogenic impacts on the biosphere and the internalization of restraints in the context of a 'biophilic' personality structure are only conceivable in the context of more extensive global interdependencies combined with supranational state processes and forms of governance (Quilley 2003; see also Aarts *et al.* 1995). In relation to this, biophilic civilizing processes are unlikely to have much impact over the long term without the further extension of classical Eliasian civilizing processes at a supranational level – i.e. in relation to pacification and the internationalization of psychological restraints against violence. However, even the abortive Kyoto summit suggested that the ecological sword of Damocles that is becoming increasingly evident in relation to problems such as global warming, may play an important role in the extension of such supranational forms of governance. There may be a principle of facilitation in the relationship between biophilic civilizing processes and supranational state processes.

Conclusion

Elias's simultaneous focus on multiple time-frames and processes working along different planes of integration is integral to the conceptual architecture of *The Civilizing Process*. The insistence on process allows him to reconcile the iterative and dynamic connections between state processes, social differentiation and the expansion of the division of labour, and the psychogenesis of individuals. But by the same token, Elias goes further than any sociologist in reconciling the reality of human beings as biological organisms. This is true in relation to individual persons endowed with a species 'human nature'. It is also true in relation to the evolutionary ecology of humanity as the dominant species in a global eco-system – a dominance that is a function of symbol emancipation and the biological capacity for language and culture. All of the main elements of Elias's epistemology and sociology of knowledge were either developed or alluded to in *The Civilizing Process*. The recognition of symbol emancipation and social development as an evolutionary (biological) departure is combined with an appreciation of psychogenesis as an aspect of individual ontogeny (biological growth and development). And finally, in *TCP* there is a clear appreciation of the link between the expansion of reality-congruent knowledge of non-human nature and an ecological dominance mediated by culture and technology.

However, the fact that *TCP* in a sense 'contains' at least the germs of just about everything that Elias wrote subsequently, does not make it the most logical point of departure for an analysis of his contribution. The very density and imbricated quality of this work makes it easy to overlook important insights. In fact, it makes more sense to see *Involvement and Detachment* (1987) as the meta-theoretical key to the rest of Elias's *oeuvre*. Although characteristically embedded in historical themes (as with the opening discussion of perspective in Renaissance painting, or Poe's allegory of the fishermen in the maelstrom), the combined epistemology and sociology of knowledge set up a framework which both establishes the rationale and the meaning of sociology as a *scientific* discipline, alongside, without being subsumed by, neighbouring biological disciplines (as has been implied by advocates of evolutionary psychology and socio-biology). His theory of knowledge establishes both the difference and the relationships between evolutionary and social-developmental processes. *What Is Sociology?* can be seen to provide a similar cognitive mapping of the conceptual tools required in the sociological investigation of the latter. *The Civilizing Process* (1939) and books such as *The Germans* (1996), *The Court Society* (1983) and *The Established and the Outsiders* (1965), are thus to be seen as concrete sociological investigations, embodying these principles and conceptual tools, whilst periodically, if elusively, reflecting also the relationship that Elias established between sociology and other scientific disciplines.

NOTES

1. There is an argument that Elias himself should be seen as the true exponent of a 'positive science of society' in Comte's original sense i.e. as a subject based upon comparative historical methods and in which mathematics and especially statistics were eschewed (see Dunning 1977). However positivism in the social sciences has become identified with the narrow perspectives associated with statistical analysis, and the identification and quasi-experimental manipulation of variables in a search for law-like associations.

2. This is the edition cited by Elias in *What is Sociology?*, p. 176*n*.
3. A piece of flint 'as such' – rather than an animistic conception of the living stone as an active agent, with intentions and motivations and possibly concerning 'me' directly.
4. Elias also points out that the expansion of the overall knowledge stock has often involved the *loss* of knowledge. An example would be the knowledge, detailed natural history and understanding of the ecology of particular places associated with hunter-gathering – knowledge diminished and often lost completely in the process of agrarianization, even if the latter represents, on balance a higher level of synthesis, a greater degree of detachment, a greater social stock of knowledge and an enhanced capacity to manipulate non-human nature.

REFERENCES

Aarts, W., Goudsblom, J., Schmidt, K. and F. Spier 1995, *Towards a Morality of Moderation: Report for the Dutch National Research Programme on Global Air Pollution and Climate Change*, Amsterdam: Amsterdam School for Social Science Research.
Barkow, J. H., Cosmides, L. and Tooby, J. 1992, *The Adapted Mind: Evolutionary Psychology and the Generation of Culture*, New York: Oxford University Press.
Botkin, D. 1990, *Discordant Harmonies: A New Ecology for the Twenty-First Century*, Oxford: Oxford University Press.
Budiansky, S. 1994, *The Covenant of the Wild*, London: Weidenfeld & Nicholson.
    1995, *Nature's Keepers, The New Science of Nature Management*, London: Weidenfeld and Nicholson.
Comte, Auguste 1907 [1830 orig.], *Cours de philosophie positive*, 1830–42, 5th edn, Paris: Schleicher frères.
Coppinger, R. P. and Smith, C. K. 1983, 'The domestication of evolution', *Environmental Conservation* 10, 4, Winter 1983, 283–92.
De Vries, B. and Goudsblom, J. 2002, *Mappae Mundi. Humans and their Habitats in Long-Term Ecological Perspective*, Amsterdam: Amsterdam University Press.
Diamond, J. 1998, *Guns, Germs and Steel: A Short History of Everybody for the Last 13,000 Years*, London: Vintage.
Dunning, E. 1977, 'In defence of developmental sociology, a critique of Popper's *Poverty of Historicism* with special reference to the theory of Auguste Comte', *Amsterdams Sociologisch Tijdschrift* 4 (3): 327–49.
Dyson, F. 1997, *Imagined Worlds*, Cambridge, MA: Harvard University Press.
Eisenberg, E. 1998, *The Ecology of Eden*, London: Picador.
Elias, N. 1939 [orig. 2000], *The Civilizing Process*, rev. edn, Oxford: Blackwell.
    1971, 'The sociology of knowledge: new perspectives', *Sociology* 5, 2, 3: 149–68, 355–70.
    1984, 'Knowledge and power: an interview by Peter Ludes', in Nico Stehr and Volker Meja, eds., *Society and Knowledge: Contemporary Perspectives on the Sociology of Knowledge*, New Brunswick and London: Transaction Books.
    1989, *The Symbol Theory*, London: Sage.
    1987, *Involvement and Detachment*, Oxford: Blackwell.
    1992, *Time, An Essay*, Oxford: Blackwell.

1983, *The Court Society*, Oxford: Blackwell.

1996 [1989 orig. in German], *The Germans*, Cambridge: Polity.

1987, 'The retreat of sociologists into the present', *Theory Culture & Society* 4 (2–3): 223–49.

Elias, N. and E. Dunning 1986, *Quest for Excitement*, Oxford: Blackwell.

Elias, N. and Scotson, J. L. 1965, *The Established and the Outsiders*, London: Frank Cass, rev. edn, London: Sage, 1994.

Freeman, D. 1983, *Margaret Mead and Samoa: The Making and Unmaking of an Anthropological Myth*, Cambridge, MA: Harvard University Press.

Goodwin, B. 1994, *How the Leopard Changed its Spots: The Evolution of Complexity*, New York: Charles Scribner's Sons.

Goudsblom, J. 2002, 'Introductory overview: The expanding anthroposphere', in J. Goudsblom and B. De Vries, eds., 2002, *Mappae Mundi: Humans and their Habitats in a Long Term Socio-Ecological Perspective. Myths, Maps, and Models*, Amsterdam: Amsterdam University Press.

Kaufman, S. 2000, *Investigations*, Oxford: Oxford University Press.

Klein, R. G. with Blake, Edgar 2002, *The Dawn of Human Culture. A Bold New Theory on What Sparked the 'Big Bang' of Human Consciousness*, London: John Wiley & Sons.

Margulis, L. 1998, *The Symbiotic Planet*, London: Weidenfeld & Nicholson.

Michod, R. E. 1999, *Darwinian Dynamics. Evolutionary Transitions in Fitness and Individuality*, Princeton: Princeton University Press.

Nash, R. 1969, *Wilderness and the American Mind*, New Haven: Yale University Press.

Goudsblom, J. 1992, *Fire and Civilisation*, London: Allen Lane.

Goudsblom, J., Jones, E. and Mennell, S. 1996, *The Course of Human History, Economic Growth, Social Process, and Civilization*, New York: M.E. Sharpe.

Pigliucci, M. 2001, *Phenotypic Plasticity. Beyond Nature and Nurture*, London: Johns Hopkins University Press.

Pinker, S. 2002, *The Blank Slate: The Modern Denial of Human Nature*, London, Penguin.

Quilley, S. 2003, 'Biophilia as a civilizing process', Paper presented to the University College, Dublin Sociology Department Seminar Series, January.

Rose, S. 1997, *Lifelines: Biology, Freedom, Determinism*, London: Penguin.

Sapp, J. 1994, *Evolution by Association: A History of Symbiosis*, Oxford: Oxford University Press.

Westbroek, P. 1991, *Life as a Geological Force: Dynamics of the Earth*, New York: W. W. Norton & Co.

Wills, C. 1999, *Children of Prometheus, The Accelerating Pace of Human Evolution*, London: Penguin.

Wilson, E. O. 1995 [orig. 1975], *On Human Nature*, Cambridge, MA: Harvard University Press.

4   Between the real and the reified:
Elias on time

Barry Barnes

Introduction

A burgeoning interest in knowledge has been one of the most striking and significant developments in the social sciences over the last quarter of a century. Nor has this shift in attention resulted merely in the relocation of the debates and controversies characteristic of these fields. Something close to an agreed conception of knowledge has emerged, even if how precisely knowledge should be analysed and understood remains hotly disputed. Knowledge is now routinely perceived as something akin both to language and to practical skills, in being a part of the cultural tradition of society, something passed on down the generations as the shared possession of its members. And, indeed, this conception can seem so obviously correct to social scientists today that it is important to remember that the grip of individualistic, ahistorical conceptions of knowledge was until quite recently a strong one, and that for some at least the transition to the current perspective was not altogether easy. Only as we saw how to treat the natural sciences, including mathematics, as parts of our inherited culture, and began to grasp the full implications of the claim that 'scientific knowledge, like language, is intrinsically the common property of a group or else nothing at all' (Kuhn 1970: 210), did the transition at last occur. Only then was the current conception acknowledged as applicable to all knowledge, and hence to knowledge *qua* knowledge as it were, rather than *qua* mere belief.

Even so, the transition did occur, and what it is tempting to call a properly sociological conception of knowledge has now established itself. Above all, this involves an understanding of knowledge as intrinsically a collective phenomenon and not something residing in an independent individual mind; but there are other aspects of the sociological conception that are scarcely less important. As a collective phenomenon, knowledge has a history and must be understood in part by reference to that history: along with the rest of the cultural tradition, it evolves and develops over the generations and builds upon itself. Again, as a part of the cultural tradition, knowledge is bound up with practice and activity, and grows and develops along with practice; so intimately bound up with practice is it, indeed, that it is impossible fully to describe the characteristics of the one without making reference to the other, if one and other they are. And all this, of course, has implications for how members evaluate their knowledge. At the collective level, the constant adaptation and development of practice, so that it more efficaciously serves human needs and objectives, entails the adaptation and development of knowledge: knowledge will be evaluated and re-evaluated in specific contexts, along with practice, in terms of its efficacy in those contexts. At the individual level, knowledge is acquired, in the first instance, from the ancestors, as part of a larger social process of cultural transmission, and however active the individual may be in relation to what the collective knows, her evaluation of that knowledge is simply not intelligible in terms of the use of an independent power of reason. It can only be authority – the authority of tradition, or rather of those licensed to dispense it – that permits an individual to identify knowledge. The authority of the collective must underpin anything that is to count as knowledge, whether directly, or else by guaranteeing the standing of some practice or procedure that may be applied to the putative knowledge as a test of its validity.

Here then is a rudimentary outline of a conception of knowledge now very widely diffused throughout the social sciences, and close to being taken for granted therein by those for whom knowledge is the primary focus of research. In this latter group, at least, the conception is frequently said to derive from Emile Durkheim, whose seminal texts on knowledge and classification have long been influential in sociology and anthropology and continue to inspire sociologists of knowledge today. And indeed perhaps the simplest way of paying tribute to Norbert Elias as a sociologist of knowledge is to recognize his work as of a comparable stature to that of his predecessor. What I have described as the current sociological conception of knowledge may be drawn from Elias as readily as from Durkheim, and, whilst he is of course the later writer, his work has its own distinctive merit. It is largely free of the solecisms that can easily distract the reader of *Primitive Classification* (1902) or *The Elementary Forms of Religious Life* (1915), and offers insight into the processes wherein knowledge develops that is largely absent from those sources.

There are many close parallels between Elias and Durkheim. Both were genuine sociological theorists, concerned to understand and explain social life at every level. No mere purveyors of words as substitutes for understanding, they wrote at length in an effort to do justice to the historical and empirical materials with which they worked. And they were in close agreement on many, perhaps most, of the major theoretical issues that have confronted the mainstream of sociology. Both were hostile to individualism, and inclined to express their alternative understandings of the human condition through critical reflection on those philosophers most inclined to the celebration of individual reason, notably Descartes and (especially) Kant. Both favoured developmental accounts of social life and social institutions. Both convincingly transcended the micro/macro dualism that so many other theoretical perspectives have been unable to overcome. And so it is scarcely surprising that both were also in close agreement on the nature of knowledge. In Elias, as in Durkheim, the stock of knowledge exists prior to the individual and to individual reason: 'in acquiring knowledge, no human being is a beginning' (1971: 165). Knowledge is the product of a long historical development wherein it is transmitted from generation to generation and in the course of which it systematically changes and evolves. It is at once a part of and affected by parallel, long-term developmental processes – differentiation and division of labour in Durkheim, the civilizing process in Elias. Yet both are clear that at any given time the same knowledge is being received, applied, modified and passed on, in and as the actions and interactions of human beings, engaged in the routine business of living their lives, in a specific setting, over a particular time-span.

Of course, positions so closely analogous will share weaknesses as well as merits, and face much the same range of problems and challenges. Thus, precisely because they focus so intensely on the carriers of knowledge, Durkheim and Elias are both ambiguous, to say the least, about the relationship of knowledge to its referents, and/or whatever other externalities condition its development and use. It is not that they deny that knowledge is in some sense about something, and conditioned by human awareness of what it is about; on the contrary, both speak of the 'object-adequacy' of knowledge and of its tendency to increase over time. The problem is rather that the relationship of 'adequacy' between knowledge and 'objects' is acknowledged by both as relevant to an understanding of the developmental processes in which they are interested, and yet neither provides even a rudimentary account of what that relationship consists in. There is a special piquancy about this problem in Elias's work, because of his particular interest in the very highly elusive entity, time. And indeed his monograph, *Time: An Essay* (1992), is at once testimony to the extent of its author's achievement, and an exemplification of some of the major problems and difficulties that his sociology of knowledge failed to resolve, and that remain unresolved in the sociology of knowledge today.

Elias on time

Elias's essay on time appeared very late in his long career and does not stand amongst his finest works. It is poorly organized, repetitive and marred by puzzling digressions. Even so, it conveys his general perspective very effectively, as it applies to conceptions of time. These conceptions are indeed collective possessions, according to Elias. They have been developed and elaborated over the course of many generations, in processes that reveal systematic, patterned features when subjected to sociological study. They are bound up with the procedures and activities of human beings and cannot be identified and described without reference to them. And they are evaluated in use in relation to human needs and purposes.

For Elias, conceptions of time are collective possessions inseparable from 'the social institution of time' (1992: 11). Individuals learn those conceptions, and assimilate those institutionalized practices associated with them, specific to the societies wherein they are born and to which they belong. Elias constantly returns to these points, although it is not their intrinsic interest and the need to address them in greater detail that draws his attention back to them. It is his anxiety to rebut all individualistic perspectives in this context that is responsible, an anxiety born of the conviction that any form of individualism implies semantic fixity and an ahistorical view of time. If time is an enduring feature of nature that an independent individual may address and examine, then concepts of time will be fixed into correspondence with time itself, as it were. If the individual apprehends time *a priori*, in Kantian fashion, then her conceptualization of it will likewise be fixed. Elias wants to deny the fixity of our conceptions of time, in the face of what he believes to be our tendency as individuals to experience time precisely as fixed and compelling. And in support of this he invokes the familiar theme that what is institutionalized, and hence liable to vary over the generations, is experienced by individuals as fixed and compelling, and indeed often as something internally compelling. 'The conversion of external compulsion coming from the social institution of time into a pattern of self-constraint . . . is a graphic example of how a civilizing process contributes to forming the social habitus which is an integral part of each individual personality structure' (1992: 11).

By characterizing time as a social institution, Elias identifies it as something with a history and thereby prepares the ground for what is to follow; for much of the subsequent essay is indeed concerned with how conceptions of time have changed, over time as it were, and with how that change represents not mere variation but systematic, patterned development. Thus, what individuals experience as fixed, unchanging and external, historical sociology may reveal as part of a secular macro process. In particular:

> The idea that people have always experienced . . . sequences of events . . . as an even, uniform and continuous flow . . . runs counter to evidence we have from past ages as well as from our own . . . In fact, it is the development of time-reckoning in social life and of a relatively well-integrated grid of time-regulators such as continuous clocks, continuous yearly calendars and era time-scales girding the centuries . . . which is an indispensable condition of the experience of time as an even uniform flow. (1992: 33, 41)

These are indeed interesting passages. In them Elias invited us to understand the incidence of the modern scientific conception of time, that has been accepted and employed in both the physical and biological sciences, not by reference to 'what time really is' but rather through an understanding of historical developments extending back beyond what is generally reckoned to be the period of the emergence of science itself.

Considered as a historical study there are many intriguing suggestions to be found in Elias's essay, although most of them merit discussion in general appreciations of his thought and especially of his account of civilizing processes, rather than in the narrower context of this chapter. One of them is, however, of immediate interest: Elias consistently treats conceptions of time as inseparable from practice and activity, indeed as close to being reducible to practice and activity. He lays heavy emphasis on this connection, to the extent that he describes his own concerns as being not so much with time as with timing activities. He congratulates the English language for possessing not just the noun, 'time', but the verb, 'to time', as well, as many languages do not. And he repeatedly deplores the tendency, ubiquitously encountered, but all the more likely to be encountered in settings where the language is lacking in verbal forms, to reify activities into objects and to treat processes as things.

> with the concept of time . . . Western linguistic tradition has transformed an activity into a kind of object . . . The verbal form 'to time' makes it more immediately understandable that the reifying character of the substantial form, 'time', disguises the instrumental character of the activity of timing . . . speaking and thinking in terms of reifying substantives can gravely obstruct one's comprehension of the nexus of events. (1992: 42, 43)

There remains, finally, the question of how conceptualizations of time are evaluated, or as we may now say, of how timing activities and the associated conceptualizations are evaluated. Again, Elias's answer to the question is of just the kind foreshadowed earlier: 'Like many other social skills, timing has grown into its present condition slowly . . . in reciprocal conjunction with the growth of specific social requirements. Foremost among them is the need for people to coordinate, to synchronize – their own activities with each other and with the succession of non-human natural events. Such a need does not exist in all human societies' (1992: 121–2). Thus, Elias suggests that people develop and sustain timing activities that suit their needs, and on this basis purports to account for the systematic elaboration and development of these activities as societies have evolved from simple systems wherein 'the need for actively timing or dating events is minimal' (1992: 122), to today's vast state societies. In these, the need for timing is inescapable, and individuals must internalize a social habitus replete with finely structured time grids, and sustain an ever-present awareness of 'what time it is'.

The plausibility of Elias's general vision of the historical development of timing activities need not concern us here, which is perhaps fortunate. It is open to criticism for its apparent claim that the relevant practices came into existence just as the need arose, as if there were no inherent impediments to the development of the associated instruments and technical artefacts. And, more generally, it is bound to be treated with reserve in the present theoretical climate simply because it involves a form of macro-functional sociological explanation. On the other hand, what Elias has to say about the sort of needs served by timing activities is both more relevant here and more plausible. In particular, the suggestion that timing activities are evaluated as coordinating and synchronizing devices is one that he discusses further and elaborates upon in interesting ways. Since we have now completed the task of identifying the four major components of a sociological conception in Elias's account, let us move on and shift our attention to this further discussion, wherein he sought to describe just how timing activities can serve to coordinate and synchronize what we do. What he proposed here is perhaps just a little surprising.

Amongst the concepts and practices that make up our shared inheritance of knowledge, those pertaining to time may seem, on the face of it, atypical. Most of our shared concepts and practices function only in so far as we employ them appropriately to describe and/or manipulate externalities. But those pertaining to time seem to function simply by virtue of being shared. With agreed conceptions of time and agreed timing activities the collective simply is coordinated. There is nothing more that needs to be done. And in this respect conceptions of time can seem different from conceptions of, say, elephants, where a further problem of correct reference appears to exist. Those who believe that 'time', like 'elephant', refers to something 'out there' are forced to speak of some mysterious, invisible, intangible referent, which tends to confirm the thought that there is indeed no referent there at all. And since the upshot of all this is that agreement seems the be-all and end-all where the institution of time is concerned, it must surely have been tempting, particularly for someone like Elias, who opposed a realist view of time, to describe it as wholly conventional in character, entirely a matter of human agreement, nothing to do with how the world actually is – the ideal exemplar, it would be said today, of a radical constructivist view of knowledge. Elias himself however suggested nothing remotely like this.

'Time' does not refer to any material thing or object. To believe that it does so refer is to reify, to fall victim to the malign consequences of the widespread use of reifying substantives, as the *Essay* puts it. Even so, the concept does refer to something: '"Time" refers to certain aspects of the continuous flow of events in the midst of which people live and of which they themselves form part' (1992: 70). But how is it possible to refer to, and time, this continuous flow, given that referring activities, including timing activities, must themselves be a part of it? Elias accepts that in a 'single-strand universe', wherein there was awareness of but one flow of events, it would indeed not be possible to speak of time. There needs to be awareness of different flows or continua, different 'strands of continuous changes' (1922: 72), so that one may be identified as a timing standard and employed to measure and mark out temporal durations upon the others. Thus, when timing and drawing conclusions about time and duration, we make reference not to objects but to relationships, the relationships between one continuum of events and others.

There is much that is valuable in this account. It does seem to put into words successfully much of our intuitive understanding of timing activities and what they have in common. And it does identify plausibly how these activities may be at once conventional and variable, and also externally constrained. It is surely true that we are sensitive to the match of one entity or interval with another, as we time, and that in this sense what we do is constrained by the externalities we are involved with. And clearly our sensitivity to matching must be shared, experienced by different timers independently, if timing is indeed to function as a social institution that permits coordination and synchronization. Yet the account also indicates why the institution of time may vary from one context to another, and, in a given context, from one time to another. Which of the available sequences or continua of events will count as a measure of time is a matter for timers themselves. One sequence among others will be designated as the measure, and the intervals between the events along it will be defined as (equal) time intervals, whereupon the intervals between events along other continua will be identified as of such and such a duration as a matter of contingent fact, ascertained by measurement and validated through agreement in measurement. Clearly, the continuum chosen as measure may vary, but so too may the extent to which it is divided up, the accuracy with which it is divided, and the status of the divisions – as, for example, indicators of sequence or interval measures of magnitude. It is perfectly possible, for example, when using sunrises as the definitive sequence for timing, either to assume, or to refrain from assuming, that each day thus defined is an equal unit of time.

For all its merits, however, there are problems with this account of timing activities. Filled with what seems to have been genuine intellectual curiosity about them, Elias calls attention to features of them that shake the framework of his normal, sociological mode of thought. Thus, his major concern is to display time as an evolving social institution. But he repeatedly makes it clear that the culturally specific, learned elements of the institution build upon, and depend for their existence upon, universal human intuitions that permit us to orient ourselves to, and bring what we have learned to bear upon, externalities in the world about us. Moreover, these include an intuitive ability to apprehend sequence, a sense of before/after relations, and a preconceptual awareness of succession, duration and speed. It is tempting to say, although Elias does not, that these are all intuitions of time, or temporality, standing prior to and as an essential support for institutional representations of these things.

The important point here is not that Elias is wrong to identify primitive intuitions of sequence, succession and so forth. It is perfectly plausible to do so, and indeed any reader of Elias's text (or, for that matter, of this chapter) will find themselves constantly having to draw on very general temporal intuitions in order to make sense of what is being said about time. What does amount to a significant criticism is that Elias's theoretical account of time would seem to be intelligible only to someone who knows what time is already – somebody, that is, who has the intuitions, properly describable as primitive temporal intuitions, referred to in his theory. In brief, the criticism is that the theoretical account is circular. And many critics would probably want to add that the place on the circle upon which to focus, if one would truly understand time, is that occupied by primitive intuitions, and that this is just where Kant and other individualistic philosophers focused their attention.

It might be said in defence of Elias that his concern is solely with historical changes in the institution of time, that is, in shared concepts of time and methods of timing. But this is not what Elias himself says. Recall his assertion that 'human beings did not always experience connections of events in the manner now symbolically represented by the concept "time"' (1992: 38). This is by no means the only passage wherein he refers to changes, not simply in concepts, but in the 'experience' (of time) they 'represent'. Similarly, he never contrasts changing concepts of time with an unchanging referent of the concepts: the most he is willing to do is to contrast a changing experience of time with an unchanging intuition of sequence – where sequence is treated as distinct from time. And, of course, efforts to separate conceptions of time and timing activities from 'time itself' are repeatedly criticized, in the *Essay*, as misconceived reifications. Elias simply did not want to be read merely as the chronicler of changes to the institutionalized ways of conceptualizing, identifying and measuring an independent, persisting, possibly unchanging, externality, not even if that externality was a mode of relation or connection. But he noticed nonetheless that externalities did bear upon timing activities and their outcomes, and he felt an obligation to make mention of them.

Thus, we find Elias inclined to identify that which does not change as a primitive intuition of sequence and succession, and that which does change as a learned conception of time. Similarly, he contrasts what now is the inherited view that time passes in an even, uniform and continuous flow, with the simple awareness that events are connected in sequences, one after another. The latter is genuine awareness of something that is there, but is not awareness of time. The former is awareness of time but not of something really there. And indeed it is remarkable to what extremes Elias will go in asserting what time is not: 'clocks . . . can certainly be used to measure something. This something is not really invisible, intangible time but something very tangible, such as the length of a working day . . .' (1992: 1). There is a sense that forced distinctions are being made here, in an effort not so much to dismantle a reifying metaphysic of time as to engage with one metaphysic on behalf of another.

'Time' and time

Although it is little more than a decade since Elias ceased to contribute to sociology, the tendency in the sociology of knowledge is to honour him as a major historical figure rather than to look to him as an inspiration for research. In this sub-field, his thought is experienced as that of an earlier generation, dominated by concerns and frames of reference now far less salient than once they were. In the *Essay*, for example, the most obvious thematic obsession, returned to again and again, is the overcoming of Kant and his individualistic vision of the timelessness of time; but even at the time of its first publication the issues were being formulated rather differently, and realist and constructivist views of knowledge were being utilized as the frames and sets of resources with which to structure debates. Given this, and given also that Elias's writing can easily appear confused and inconsistent when read from either of these perspectives, the case for continuing to read him as a sociologist of knowledge is not everywhere accepted. The case can be made, however, and one way of making it is precisely to turn our attention onto current realist and constructivist positions.

On a realist view, our talk of time is talk about something. 'Time' is used (in an effort) to talk about time; that is, the concept of time is used to refer to time as it exists, as something incarnate in external reality. As Elias says, time is not visible or tangible. But we are aware of temporality, and we have clues as to its true nature and constitution. In efforts to learn more about time, we produce models wherein it appears. And we use and evaluate the models, not just in efforts to coordinate, but also in efforts to predict events, something not emphasized sufficiently by Elias. Timing permits us to coordinate not just with a clock but using separate clocks, acting entirely independently of each other, predicting that we shall meet again, at a set time as it were, because the clocks are 'the same' on our model of time. And the extent of the success of such a model, along with the associated activities and conceptualizations, will be a basis on which to evaluate it, and possibly change it to increase its predictive utility. We may redesignate what are definitive time measures and what cheap and cheerful stand-ins. We may amend how we read the measures. We may adjust the internal relations of the model, the relations wherein 'time' is incarnate. And if the model performs better afterwards we may be tempted to say that we have come to understand time better 'as it really is'.

Unfortunately, however, this way of relating 'time' (the concept) and time (its supposed referent) has changed, under the influence of the intellectual division of labour. We all use 'time'; but the duty and privilege of creating and modifying models of time, and authoritatively identifying the model truly revelatory of the nature of time, have been delegated to specialists, namely a sub-set of natural scientists. As a result, the way we contrast 'time' and time has subtly shifted, so that the distinction now tends no longer to be between concept and referent, but rather between concept and the authoritative model of its referent. The scientists' model has become a stand-in, as it were, for reality itself. Now, when we talk about time, we may find ourselves being told that we are 'really speaking about' a dimension of the universe, or a constituent of a four-dimensional space/time continuum, and we may even come dimly to accept or believe that this is indeed what we are doing. This, I suspect, is what prompts so much hostility to the realist view amongst sociologists today. It is not the thought that what we may know is constrained by reality that is intolerable to them, as much as the thought that what we may know is constrained by professional scientists and the powers with which they are associated, something that the realist view appears to imply if we cease to mark a distinction between scientists' models of reality and reality itself.

It is perfectly possible that this confusion of scientists' models and reality itself is also what helped to turn Norbert Elias away from a realist view of time. Elias not only criticized the view that time is a real entity, he fearlessly criticized natural scientists for reifying it. And it was the experience of time produced by scientifically authoritative models and conceptions, above all, that he sought to make visible as 'the result of humanity's long learning process' (1992: 5). Even so, Elias's purpose here was not to criticize science and scientific models, for which he had an obvious respect, but only to caution against a reified view of them. And indeed no sociologist is in a position to criticize our current science by asserting that reality is other than as natural scientists currently describe it, and Elias, much impressed with the 'object adequacy' of current scientific conceptions of time, had no inclination to do so. Nowhere did he seek to demonstrate, for example, that time is not a constituent of a four-dimensional space/time manifold intrinsic to the physical universe. All that his analysis implied in this case was that the scientific model of our universe as such a manifold, simply by virtue of being a model, is *ipso facto* not identical with what it is a model of. This is no criticism of science *qua* science. Indeed it permits us to continue in the view that for scientists, whose interest is in understanding the nature of the external world, it may be appropriate to relate models solely and simply to physical externalities, and even perhaps functional to regard models as revelations of reality. It is only where an understanding is sought, not of the externalities that scientists seek to understand, but of scientists and their science, that it is necessary to relate models to their history and to the situated actions of their creators. Only then, in relation to that purpose, is it crucial to avoid any confusion between models and 'reality itself'.

Elias helps us to avoid the dangers inherent in confusing time with scientists' 'time', a confusion particularly encouraged by realism in the forms in which it is presently most commonly encountered. Even so, in the present context of debate, he will not be read as an exemplary anti-realist. Nor is it merely that talk of progressive developmental change and the increased 'object adequacy' of knowledge is alien to that view in its currently dominant form. Elias's entire style of thought could be said to be coloured by realism, and his very project of chronicling the history of the institution of time may itself be described as a form of reification.

What are the grounds for asserting any connection at all between the putative 'components' of the institution of time as delineated by Elias? His own work could be used to call the existence of any such connection into question, and to support a radical constructivist account of these 'components' as so many separate speech acts, or items of discourse, to be addressed not in terms of a general historicist framework but as the one-off productions of particular human beings. Certainly, Elias gives us no reason to assume that when members of other cultures speak of time (on our interpretation of their language), what they are talking about is either the 'time' or the time of scientists, or for that matter of any connected set of things or relations at all. Indeed he gives no account of how it is possible validly to identify the utterances of other cultures as expressing conceptions of time in the first place. He relies on a strong shared intuition in his audience that the different 'components' of his history are 'the same', in that they are instances of, or references to instances of, timing.

However strong and shared it may be, this intuition is difficult to rationalise. The tokens used to stand for concepts will not establish same-concept relations, since they obviously vary between cultures and subcultures. But if the concepts themselves vary as well, and the associated practices and activities, and the externalities constraining the use of, or constituting the referents of, the activities, then what is a historical sociology of time a historical sociology of? How is 'humankind's experience of what is now called "time"' (1992: 38) to be picked out in different periods and contexts? Not by the direct identity of that experience with what we now experience as time; for the whole thrust of Elias's argument is that 'experience' of time *varies* with period and context. But how else is a sense of sameness between different conceptualizations and activities to be generated, of a kind that will permit cross-cultural references to time and timing of the kind that Elias assumes he is entitled to make? And what will be the standing of any such references in relation to members' own conceptions, with which through the very manner of their creation they are bound to clash? It is striking that this unresolved and extremely difficult problem, especially awkward to deal with in the frame of a realist epistemology, and long debated by anthropologists and sociologists in various forms and guises, as in Gellner (1962), is not highlighted by Elias himself.

Elias, we might say, if he was an anti-realist at all, was not an anti-realist in the way that modern radical social constructivists are. His concern was with the historical sociology of institutions, not with their deconstruction and dissolution. He did not share the characteristic constructivist obsession with words and talk. Irritated though he was by 'reifying substantives', it was no part of his project to convert the lot back into verbs; even in the *Essay* he never goes so far as to speak of 'doing time'. Indeed, a doctrine that denies, as radical constructivism does, the power of our speech to refer, save in that one special case where the referent is speech itself, would surely have struck him as restrictive and arbitrary. Elias, it is tempting to say, would never have made a passable constructivist because of his inability to keep his mind from digressing onto externalities. He could not relax, and switch off his curiosity, in the face of regularities that appeared to be captured in discourse but not created by discourse, or when confronted by the difficulties evidently experienced by members in applying their concepts and practices. He was fascinated, for example, by the recalcitrant problem of matching the intervals of the diurnal calendar to those of the solar 'equivalent': the difficulties seemed to have to do with the nature of the earth's motion (1992: 55).

In summary then, whether read from a realist, or an anti-realist, radical-constructivist, perspective, Elias is liable to appear as at once vague, confused and inconsistent, and as too close to the alternative position. From a realist perspective, he creates problems of intelligibility by his use of vague notions like 'object-adequacy', and by failing systematically to distinguish between concept and referent, between 'time' and time, for example. And he is an anti-realist in so far as he treats time as a reification of instrumentally efficacious timing activities. But from a radical-constructivist perspective the concept about which he is most vague is the time that is the subject of his essay, even if his failure to enclose it in inverted commas is entirely laudable. And despite his selective attention to 'reifying substantives', his undisciplined interest in externalities is just the most striking of a number of features of his work that seem to mark him out as a kind of realist.

Much could be said about these criticisms, but their immediate relevance here is that quite apart from any judgement of the extent of their validity they actually indicate why Elias's *Essay* remains of interest. No account of a general theoretical perspective in the social sciences is ever going to be wholly internally consistent, and devoid of vagueness and apparent confusion. And if some accounts seem more satisfactory than others in those respects it is often because they recapitulate settled wisdom, or well-established models and frames, in routine ways. Conversely, accounts that clash with settled wisdom, or seek to modify it or extend it, will often upset the semantic order it represents, with the result that they appear, or indeed are, confused. Confusion of this sort may be the price paid by, or even a desideratum of, work that helps research forward, and some at least of the confusion that it is now possible to identify in Elias's *Essay* is arguably of this sort. In pursuit of its own agenda, it transgresses the boundaries of both realism and constructivism as presently constituted in this sphere, and is not afraid to engage with some of the most challenging and awkward problems currently facing the sociology of knowledge in the contested ground between them. Problems of this sort have an especial importance in the context of ongoing research, and it is far from obvious that those at issue here will be satisfactorily dealt with wholly within either a realist or a (radical-)constructivist frame. Indeed current research, particularly research on scientific knowledge, increasingly recognizes the inadequacy of both of these frames. Simply put: 'Experimental scientists do not read the book of nature, they do not depict reality. But they do not construct reality either' (Rheinberger 1997: 225).

REFERENCES

Durkheim, E. [1915] 1976, *The Elementary Forms of Religious Life*, 2nd edn, London: Unwin.
Durkheim, E. and Mauss, M. [1902] 1963, *Primitive Classification*, London: Cohen & West.
Elias, N. [1987] 1992, *Time: An Essay*, Oxford: Blackwell.
1971, 'Sociology of knowledge: new perspectives', *Sociology* 5 (2): 149–68.
Gellner, E. [1962] 1970, 'Concepts and society', reprinted in B. Wilson (ed.), *Rationality*, Oxford: Blackwell.
Kuhn, T. S. [1961] 1970, *The Structure of Scientific Revolutions*, Chicago: Chicago University Press.
Rheinberger, H. J. 1997, *Towards a History of Epistemic Things*, Stanford: Stanford University Press.

Part II

Processes of stratification: figurations of race, class and gender

5   Aspects of the figurational dynamics of racial stratification: a conceptual discussion and developmental analysis of black–white relations in the United States

Eric Dunning

Introduction

The sociological problem considered in this chapter is ostensibly simple.[1] It is, why, after some four centuries of oppression by whites, should blacks in the United States have begun to fight back openly and on a large scale only in the 1950s and 1960s? This is not to imply that American blacks failed totally to fight back before that period but rather to suggest that the civil rights movement and the urban riots of that era marked a watershed regarding the openness, scale and organization of their struggle against white domination. The fact that the slogan 'black is beautiful' was coined at the same time, suggests that this period also formed a turning point regarding the group consciousness of blacks, namely that they began in the 1950s and 1960s to have a more positive 'we-image' than hitherto. The point is to explain why this constellation of interrelated changes occurred and why the 1950s and 1960s represented a critical juncture in this process.

In approaching questions of this sort, it became conventional in sociology in the 1960s and 1970s to use variants of class and stratification theory (Kahl 1961; Marx 1969; Blauner 1972). I do not wish to deny the utility of this convention. It certainly helped to push the understanding of 'race' relations beyond the level possible within the largely psychological framework of 'prejudice' and 'discrimination' theories which had hitherto prevailed (Allport 1954). Nevertheless, there are, I think, distinct limits to what stratification theory can achieve without being radically revised. Perhaps that is why it fell into comparative disuse? Accordingly, what I propose to do in this chapter is to review aspects of the 1960s/70s work on racial stratification and to discuss aspects of the 'figurational' theory of Norbert Elias in order to explore whether they can help to get us out of the theoretical-empirical impasse within which the sociological analysis of 'race' relations arguably became trapped. What I shall do is examine:

(i) Elias's theory of 'established-outsider' figurations (Elias and Scotson 1994 [1965]); (ii) his concept of power (Elias 1978); and (iii) his theory of 'functional democratization' (Elias 1978). I shall then apply this body of theory empirically in an attempt to illuminate: (i) how the development of American society in the eighteenth and nineteenth centuries was conducive to the emergence of a social figuration characterized by virtually total dominance of whites over blacks, together with an internalization by the latter of their 'group disgrace' and, as a corollary, of the white man's 'group charisma'; and (ii) how the development of American society in the twentieth century contributed to a slight but nonetheless detectable shift in the balance of power between these 'racial' groups. It was arguably such a figurationally generated change in the balance of racial power that led American blacks to begin to reject their stigmatization by whites and to fight more openly and systematically against white dominance, contributing in the process to the racial violence that flared up in the 1950s and 1960s.

Before I embark on such an analysis, I shall critically review some of the older sociological approaches to 'race' relations, aspects of which I regard as worth reviving. The approaches that I have chosen to examine are those of Lockwood (1970), Warner (1949), Davis and the Gardners (1941), and finally, that of black sociologist, E. Franklin Frazier (1962). I do not pretend that these constitute an exhaustive list; nor is it representative or up-to-date. I have chosen to focus on the work of these authors because it will enable me to bring some neglected aspects of 'race' relations into the discussion.

Because it is the most sophisticated theoretically, I shall start with Lockwood's contribution. He shares my view concerning the inapplicability of class and stratification theory at least to aspects of this problem area. However, whereas Lockwood focused solely on the possibility that this may stem from the uniqueness of 'race' relations as an area of social facts, what I want to suggest is that the specificity of 'race' relations is in some ways more apparent than real. More particularly, it appears to be more an artefact of the inadequacy of class and stratification theories in their current forms than of the total uniqueness of racial inequality as a form of social stratification. In the context of this discussion, I shall refer to aspects of Durkheim's (1964) theory of the division of labour, more specifically to his concept of 'mechanical solidarity', and I shall use it, in part, as a means of reintroducing the concept of 'caste' into the analysis of 'race' relations. Only then will I examine the aspects of Elias's theory referred to above.

'Race' relations and class

In the late 1960s, largely following the widely acknowledged failure of earlier approaches to foresee the 'racial explosion' of that decade, an

attempt was made to delineate precisely what the nature of 'race' relations is as an area of sociological problems. The discussion focused
centrally on the degree to which 'race' relations can be considered to be
a type of social stratification. Most American sociologists, whether of a
functionalist or Marxist persuasion, more or less explicitly accepted the
view that 'race' relations are a form of class and status relations. However, Lockwood (1970) raised doubts about the definitional consensus
between these 'strange bedfellows', suggesting that there are limits to the
analysis of 'race' relations in class and stratification terms. That, he said,
is partly because class inequalities stem from the division of labour but
racial inequalities do not; partly because racism leads to forms of intra-
class tension and the alignment, within groups that are socially defined
as races, of protest movements that involve patterns of identification and
unification across class lines. The first of Lockwood's arguments appears
to stem from a failure to appreciate aspects of Durkheim's analysis of
the division of labour, more specifically, its developmental focus. Thus,
whilst Durkheim held that division of labour is conducive to the emergence of 'organic solidarity' based on 'bonds of interdependence', he also
maintained that such a process takes place only gradually, leading, in the
first instance, to types of solidarity in which 'mechanical' and 'organic'
forms are mixed. In addition, he argued, there has been a historical tendency for advancing division of labour to be correlated with the decline
of 'caste'. I do not think that Durkheim said so explicitly, but one form of
social organization in which mechanical and organic solidarity are mixed
occurs where a society is divided into racial castes. That is because racial
alignments are based on specific 'bonds of similitude', e.g. similitudes of
colour, rather than on bonds of interdependency established through the
division of labour. Hence, they are mechanical in Durkheim's sense. If this
argument has any substance, the degree to which racial alignments exist
in an urban-industrial society is an index of the fact that such a society
remains 'mechanically' integrated in part. It would also appear to follow
that, to the degree that the social experiences of some groups lead them
to be bonded in forms that approximate to an ideal type of mechanical
solidarity, such groups are liable to extreme forms of racist identification.
Poor whites in racially mixed rural communities and the poorest sections
of the urban-industrial working class in 'multiethnic' areas are examples.
This suggests that it may not be, as is commonly supposed, only the
status ambiguity of such groups (i.e. their low-class, high-caste status)
that leads them to be prone to racism, but their segmental solidarity as
well (i.e. their bonding by means of similitudes). Such an analysis does
not find it difficult to cope with the propensity of such groups towards
conflict with racially different members of the same class. It follows as a
corollary of the degree to which they are segmentally bonded. Nor does it

WHITES

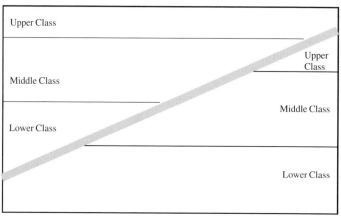

NEGROES

Figure 5.1   Class and Race Lines
Taken from Joseph A. Kahl's (1961) adaptation from *Deep South: A Social-Anthropological Study of Caste and Class*, by Allison Davis, Burleigh B. Gardner and Mary R. Gardner, Chicago 1941: University of Chicago Press

find it difficult to cope with racial identifications across class lines. Such identifications follow from the degree to which the members of different classes are constrained into identifying mechanically or segmentally with other members of the same racial group.

The concept of caste

Use of the concept of caste to describe a racially divided society is a sociological tradition that goes back at least as far as Weber who argued that 'caste is . . . the normal form in which ethnic communities . . . live side by side in a "societalized" manner' (Weber 1946). This tradition was criticized by Leach (1960) and others but, as Berreman (1960) showed, on arguably spurious grounds. I do not wish to reopen the controversy over the cross-cultural applicability of the concept of caste but reference to usage of the concept in the work of Warner (1949) and his associates, Davis and the Gardners (1941), will be illuminating. In their book, *Deep South*, Davis and the Gardners depicted the structure of caste relations in what they regarded as a typical Southern US town in the form of a diagram (see Figure 5.1).

The fact that the 'caste' or 'colour' line depicted in the diagram does not follow the horizontal axis but is skewed towards the vertical, represents a structural fact of some importance. According to Warner, it must have been closer to the horizontal at the end of the Civil War, i.e. at the time of the emancipation of the slaves. Since that time, it has skewed towards the vertical largely on account of the internal stratification of the 'Negro caste', that is, because of the emergence of black upper, middle and lower classes. The significance of this process, more particularly of the emergence of what Frazier (1962) called the 'black bourgeoisie', lies primarily in the fact that it involved the creation of socially marginal upper and middle classes, that is, class groupings of high 'class' but low 'caste' status. That, of course, has been commonly observed. Nevertheless, its significance has tended to go unnoticed, especially the fact that it involved the emergence of potentially radical upper and middle classes, more specifically of upper and middle classes which, although the majority of their members may not be radical in terms of their political ideologies and allegiances, are radical in terms of the implications of their existence for the dynamics of racial stratification. Thus, whilst not all members of the black bourgeoisie in the United States are affiliated to racial protest organizations, a majority of such organizations were founded by members of the black bourgeoisie (and some whites). Similarly, many members of black protest organizations are black bourgeois, especially younger members, and it is from this source that much of the leadership, funds and organizational expertise of such organizations derives. As I shall argue later, the formation of the black bourgeoisie has been one of the principal sources of the changing balance of power between blacks and whites in the United States. More specifically, it has been a principal source for allowing what Elias called 'functional democratization' to occur in American 'race' relations.

There are at least two reasons why the significance of this structural transformation may have been overlooked. It could derive from the adherence of American sociologists predominantly to nominalist paradigms and from the correlative fact that, whilst they have been sensitized to the consequences of this emergent status-inconsistency for intercaste *behaviour*, for example to the anomalies that arise when low-caste, high-class blacks interact with high-caste, low-class whites, they have been simultaneously blinded to its consequences for the *dynamics* of racial stratification, that is, as a source for the genesis of structural change. Alternatively, it could derive from the general tendency for sociologists to expect the upper and middle classes to be politically conservative and for the lower classes to be politically radical, an expectation which tends to be confounded where caste and class systems are intermixed for, in such cases, there is a tendency towards the generation of distinct types of upper- and middle-class radicalism and lower-class conservatism. In his book, *Black Bourgeoisie*, Frazier (1962) rightly stressed the tendency for the black upper and middle classes to engage in status-conscious attempts to imitate their white counterparts. The fact that the class hierarchy of blacks in the United States is itself, in part, a colour-caste hierarchy, i.e. that there is an inverse correlation among American blacks between class position and lightness of skin pigmentation, provides further testimony to the degree to which they have internalized the values of the dominant whites (Frazier 1962). Yet, whilst Frazier was correct to emphasize these facts, it is nevertheless reasonable to suppose that his 'insider' perspective may have led him to underestimate the simultaneously radical propensities that are generated by the marginal status of the black bourgeoisie. Status consciousness and the internalization of white values may seem *logically* inconsistent with radical potential but they are not necessarily *structurally* incompatible with it. Frazier admitted that black bourgeois organizations like the National Association for the Advancement of Coloured People are characterized by 'racial radicalism', i.e. by a belief in the equality of blacks and whites. But, at the same time, he was blinded by their ostensible class conservatism, and particularly by their anti-communist stance in the 1950s and the commitment to dominant values that this implied, into underestimating the consequences of such organizations for the long-term dynamics of 'race' relations. In short, he seems to have fallen into the not uncommon trap of believing that a radical ideology and posture are necessary prerequisites for the contribution by a group or organization to the genesis of structural change.

Established–outsider relations

It is precisely in relation to the weaknesses of these approaches that Elias's theory scores. Elias's *The Established and the Outsiders* (1994) is a study of a dominance–subordination figuration formed by two working-class groups in 'Winston Parva', a suburb of the East Midlands English city of Leicester. According to Elias, these groups were identical in terms of all conceivable indices of social stratification. They differed only in the fact that the 'established' group had lived in the community for several generations, whilst the 'outsiders' were relative newcomers. Yet the whole constellation of social symptoms normally associated with class and racial oppression was detectable in the relations between them.

This depended, according to Elias, principally on the fact that their 'oldness' of association enabled the established to develop greater cohesion relative to the outsiders and this, in turn, enabled them to monopolize official positions in local associations. Such greater cohesion of established relative to outsider groups is, Elias suggested, a common, 'purely figurational' aspect of all dominance–subordination relations. The implied criticism of Marxian and other conflict approaches was later taken up by Elias explicitly. He recognized the sociological value of what he called Marx's 'great discovery' but was critical of what he regarded as the tendency in some circles 'to see in it the end of the road of discovery about human societies. One might', he added, 'rather regard it as one manifestation of a beginning' (Elias 1994: xxxiii).

Elias would not have denied that Marx's theory of class-formation (for example, his theory of the emergence of 'classes for themselves' out of 'classes in themselves') deals with aspects of the figurational generation of social cohesion and, hence, with a crucial power resource. What he would have denied was that such processes are to be understood solely in relation to a society's mode of production. These 'economic' forms are socially structured and structuring but, Elias contended, they are not alone in that respect: other aspects of social figurations such as state formation, interdependency chains and the relative cohesion of and balance of power between groups, are equally structured and determining and no less 'real'. Under specific circumstances, these other aspects also enjoy autonomy in relation to and even dominance over the mode and means of production as determinants; that is, in this, as in other aspects of his work, Elias rejected the notion of universal 'law-like' relationships between social 'parts' or 'factors' (Elias 1974). And, consistently with this, he suggested that the degree to which economic conflicts are paramount in a society is partly a function of the balance of power between groups. Here is how he put it:

the supremacy of the economic aspects of established-outsider conflicts is most pronounced where the balance of power between the contenders is most uneven – is tilted most strongly in favour of the established group. The less that is the case, the more clearly recognisable become other, non-economic aspects of the tensions and conflicts. Where outsider groups have to live at a subsistence level, the size of their earnings outweighs all their other requirements in importance. The higher they rise above the subsistence level, the more does even their income – their economic resources – serve as a means of satisfying other human requirements than that of stilling their most elementary animalic or 'material' needs; the more keenly are groups in that situation liable to feel the social inferiority – the inferiority of power and status from which they suffer. And it is in that situation that the struggle between established and outsiders gradually ceases to be, on the part of the latter, simply a struggle for stilling their hunger, for the means of physical survival, and becomes a struggle for the satisfaction of other human requirements as well. (Elias 1994: xxxii)

As I shall show, this analysis is particularly apt regarding the status struggles of the American black bourgeoisie. Let me examine those aspects of Elias's theory that are more directly relevant to 'race' relations.

'Race'-relations as a dominance–subordination figuration

What Elias shows in respect of 'race' relations, in my view more clearly than anyone else to date, is that 'race' relations are not unique as a type of social stratification. Four features that he singles out as shared by intraclass established–outsider relationships of the kind investigated in his study and interclass, interethnic and international dominance–subordination relationships as well, are: (i) a tendency for the established group to perceive the outsiders as 'law-breakers' and 'standard-violators', that is, in Elias's modification of Durkheim's term, as 'anomic'; (ii) a tendency for the former to judge the latter in terms of the 'minority of the worst', that is in terms of the minority of outsiders who actually do break the law and violate standards; (iii) a tendency for the outsiders to accept the established group's stigmatization of them, that is, to internalize the 'group charisma' of the dominant group and their own 'group disgrace'; and (iv) a tendency for the established to perceive the outsiders as in some way 'unclean'. It is the fourth of these common features that I shall focus on here.

Elias shows that members of the established group in Winston Parva believed that the houses of the outsiders, especially their kitchens, were 'unclean'. That is similar, he suggests, to the tradition that gained currency in Britain from about 1830 of referring to the 'lower orders' as 'the great unwashed'. It is similar also to the notions of 'uncleanliness' and 'pollution' in the Indian caste system; to the fact that the Burakumin in Japan are stigmatized by the label 'Eta' which literally means 'full of filth'; and to the fact that comparable notions are generally associated with established–outsider relations that are based on 'real' rather than 'supposed' racial differences. The distinction between 'real' and 'supposed' racial differences can be illustrated by a discussion of Elias's analysis of the Burakumin or Eta of Japan.

Elias maintains that a common property of established–outsider figurations is the generation of 'collective fantasies' by the dominant group about its subordinates. Although there are no detectable genetic differences between them, one of the collective fantasies of the dominant Japanese about the Burakumin is the idea that the latter have a bluish birth-mark under each arm. In that way, the social stigma attached by the established to the outsider group is reified, transformed in their imagination into a material stigma. 'It appears', says Elias, 'as "objective" – as implanted upon the outsiders by nature or the gods. In that way, the stigmatizing group is exculpated from any blame. It is not *we*, that is what such a fantasy implies, who have put a stigma on these people, but the powers that made the world.' And he concludes:

terms like 'racial' or 'ethnic' widely used in this context both in sociology and in society at large are symptomatic of an ideological avoidance action. By using them, one singles out . . . what is peripheral to these relationships (e.g. differences of skin colour) and turns the eye away from what is central (e.g. differences in power ratio and the exclusion of a power inferior group from positions with a higher power potential) . . . [T]he salient aspect of their relationship is that they are bonded together in a manner which endows one of them with very much greater power resources than the other and enables that group to exclude members of the other group from access to the centre of these resources and from closer contact with its own members, thus relegating them to the position of outsiders. Therefore, even where differences in physical appearance and other biological aspects to which we refer as 'racial' exist in these cases . . . the socio-dynamics of the relationship between groups bonded to each other as established and outsiders are determined by the manner of their bonding, not by any of the characteristics possessed by the groups conceived independently of it. (Elias 1994: xxx–xxxi)

Later, I shall use these insights to explore the manner in which the figurational dynamics of American social development led to the emergence of virtually total dominance of whites over blacks. I also want to use Elias's theory of 'functional democratization', together with the ideas about 'caste-formation' that I introduced earlier, to shed light on the manner in which twentieth-century American social developments led to the emergence of a social figuration in which a slight but nonetheless detectable redress in the balance of racial power occurred. Accordingly, it is necessary to discuss Elias's theory of 'functional democratization'.

According to Elias, the social transformation usually referred to by terms relating to particular aspects such as 'industrialization' and 'economic growth' is, in fact, a transformation of the total social structure. And, he contended, one of the sociologically most significant aspects of this total social transformation has consisted of the emergence of longer and more differentiated chains of interdependence. Concomitantly with this, according to Elias, there has occurred a change in the direction of decreasing power differentials within and among groups, more specifically a change in the balance of power between rulers and ruled, the social classes, men and women, the generations, parents and children. Such a process occurs, Elias maintained, because the incumbents of specialized roles are interdependent and able to exert reciprocal control. The power chances of specialized groups are further enhanced if they organize since, then, they become able to disrupt the wider chains of interdependence by collective action. It is in ways such as these, according to Elias, that increasing division of labour and the emergence of longer chains of interdependence lead to greater reciprocal dependency and, hence, to patterns of 'multipolar control' within and among groups. Let me apply this body of theory to aspects of American 'race' relations.

From slavery to the urban ghetto: a figurational–developmental analysis of 'race' relations in the United States

A figurational–developmental analysis of the genesis and subsequent modification of the 'established–outsider' relations between whites and blacks in the United States has to accomplish at least two things: it has to show, firstly, how the relations between American blacks and whites concentrated power chances in the hands of the latter, leading the former to be readily exploitable, to accept in large numbers their stigmatization as inferior, and to be unable to offer effective resistance to white rule; secondly, it has to show how the long-term development of that country, more specifically, the emergence of an urban-industrial nation-state figuration, led, especially *via* a process of functional democratization, to a shift in the balance of racial power, enabling blacks to begin to slough off their negative group image and to be able to fight more effectively against white dominance. Such an analysis also has to be, in Elias's sense, 'post-Marxian'; that is, it has to incorporate the analytical gains made by Marxism, but it has to avoid the 'economism' of the latter, its tendency to see all forms of power as ultimately economically determined and to reduce social figurations and processes to determination by a single, 'economic' factor or 'prime mover'. Instead, it has to show how the fluctuating balance of power between racial groups, their variable capacity to impose or resist dominance and exploitation, was generated, not by abstract and reified 'economic' forces, but dynamically and polymorphously by the figurations within which such groups were, and remain, interdependent. Let me be clear about what this means. It is not meant totally to deny the value of the Marxian and other, similarly 'economistic' explanations but rather to suggest that it is necessary to go beyond them in at least two senses: (i) by seeking to incorporate the misleadingly labelled 'economic' sources of power in a wider, figurational, explanation, i.e. an explanation which locates them in their figurational context and sees them as one source of social power among others; and (ii) by seeking to avoid law-like, prime-mover explanations in terms of economic 'forces' which abstract and reify a particular aspect of social figurations and which, correspondingly, deflect attention away from such complex patterns of interdependence *per se*, and which simultaneously mask the polymorphous manner in which specific figurations generate specific inter- and intragroup power ratios. In what follows, I shall attempt to incorporate but simultaneously to go beyond the partly fruitful, partly limiting Marxian and other similarly economistic analyses of 'race' relations.

Black–white relations in America have passed through three broad, overlapping stages: a stage of plantation slavery; a stage of colour castes; and a stage of urban ghettoes.[2] During the second stage, the pattern of extreme white dominance and widespread black acceptance of their stigmatization by whites, first developed on the slave plantations, continued to exist though in a modified figurational setting that witnessed the embryonic formation of the black bourgeoisie. The formation of this caste-class fraction constituted a slight shift in the power ratios of blacks and whites, but it was in the stage of urban ghettoes that the more significant long-term change in the balance of racial power which led to the riots of the 1960s was set in motion. The expansion of the black bourgeoisie and the occurrence of functional democratization were centrally implicated in this process.

Plantation slavery

One source of the relative powerlessness of blacks in the first stage of white dominance in the United States was the fact that they had been forcibly transported there as slaves. Both on the slave ships and the plantations, their power chances were reduced by the stratagem of keeping the members of tribal and language groups apart, thus making difficult that degree of communication which is one of the figurational preconditions for effective group resistance. The power chances of the slaves were further reduced by their transplantation to an unfamiliar cultural context and by the systematic use of physical violence. Frequent whippings, use of the stocks and, on the larger plantations, imprisonment in the plantation jail were not uncommon. Runaways were sometimes hunted with dogs – this variant of the English 'hue and cry' seems to have been a favourite leisure activity in the South – and, when caught, clapped in irons, branded and sometimes castrated. Ill-treatment was limited to some extent by the fact that slaves were valuable property in which considerable money capital had been invested and because they had to be fit enough to work on the plantation or in the master's house. Furthermore, physical damage could reduce their re-sale price and, in the case of house slaves, their value for purposes of display. Against this, recalcitrant slaves were expendable, especially on the larger plantations where punishment in public could serve as an effective means of control.

From the slaves' standpoint, the plantation figuration approximated closely to what Goffman (1959) would have called a 'total institution'; i.e. they were 'closed systems' in the sense that slaves were not allowed legitimately to leave their confines except in the company of their masters or, in the case of slaves who were considered trustworthy, with a 'pass' that showed they were not runaways but transacting their master's business. Sometime slaves were allowed to tend their own gardens and livestock but, for the most part, they worked solely for their masters, not themselves. Moreover, they were kept to a large extent outside direct involvement in the money economy in at least three senses: (i) most of the necessities of life were usually purchased by their masters; (ii) they were not paid a money wage; and (iii) the produce of their labour was marketed by their masters and the revenue obtained belonged solely to him.

However, the powerlessness of the slaves was relative in the sense that aspects of the plantation figuration gave them a degree of autonomy. For example, the larger plantations could not be effectively policed at night and the slaves were thus afforded the chance for some relatively independent activities; e.g. religious gatherings in the slave quarters or elsewhere on the plantation. In addition, slaves who developed a degree of expertise in specific fields could make their masters dependent on them, in that way reducing somewhat the degree of asymmetry otherwise inherent in the pattern of master–slave interdependence. In general, however, such figurationally generated autonomy of slaves was slight.

In some parts of the South, the numerical predominance of blacks led whites to fear slave insurrections, a fear reinforced by occasional bloody uprisings, but the overall social figuration made the dominance of whites, especially of plantation owners, secure. State formation in colonial and early postcolonial America was in its early stages and the planter aristocracy, the owners of the largest plantations and the bulk of the slaves, controlled each Southern state. Poor whites formed a numerical majority among the whites but most of them were small farmers and landless agricultural labourers. They were also ecologically scattered and unorganized. As a result, the planter aristocracy were not subject to effective pressure from above or below and this meant they were able to control the plantations and exploit the human capital on which they depended in their own interests, virtually untrammelled by external constraints.

It is hardly surprising, given such a figuration, that blacks came to develop forms of extreme dependency on their masters and to internalize the 'group charisma' of the latter and their own 'group disgrace'. Elkins (1959) wrote of the 'infantilization' of the majority of slaves. Such a term is reminiscent of a collective fantasy of the dominant whites but there may be something in what he said. The plantations were similar in some ways to Nazi concentration camps and may well have produced similar effects on their victims: for example, extreme dependency patterns, identification with their oppressors and a degree of 'infantilization' in the sense that, like children, they had only limited chances for initiating independent action. But, unlike children, their dependency was total, permanent and maintained by sanctions which, in industrial societies, tend to be the prerogative of the state, e.g. the right to imprison, fine or physically punish. Under such circumstances, violence and the fear of it played a key part in the emergence and persistence of a form of legitimacy which stemmed from identification with the oppressors.

Colour castes

The emancipation of the slaves came about, not because of a figurationally generated change in the balance of power between whites and blacks, but in conjunction with the Civil War, i.e. a struggle of a type common in post-colonial figurations where the fissiparous tendencies inherent in the local social structure had hitherto been masked by common opposition to the colonial power. Viewed retrospectively, the American Civil War was a war connected with the formation of the United States as an urban-industrial nation-state and the correlative rise of the bourgeoisie to national dominance. It was, that is, a war connected with struggles among the dominant whites in which blacks were not centrally involved. It is, accordingly, not surprising that emancipation did not lead, in the short run, to significant changes in their social position. Although a few managed to gain seats in Southern legislatures during the so-called 'Reconstruction era', blacks as a whole were not sufficiently powerful in the period following emancipation to force whites to take their interests into account. They were scattered, either in small rural settlements or in the 'coloured quarters' of what were essentially market towns tied to the 'cotton monoculture'. Such 'ecological scatter' was not conducive to communication among them, nor to recognition of their common interests in opposition to the dominant whites. By keeping them out of direct involvement in the money economy, moreover, slavery had not permitted the occurrence even of the forms of capital accumulation that are usual among peasants, e.g. hardly any equivalent of a 'kulak' class was able to form. The majority of blacks were poor and had to devote most of their energies simply to keeping alive. As a result, their powerlessness meant that slavery was replaced by a dominance system in which blacks, though nominally free, continued to be subject to multiple forms of exploitation.

Yet, while emancipation did not significantly alter the material position of blacks, apart from freeing them to a degree from the paternalism of their former owners and making them more directly subject to the vicissitudes of the markets for land and labour, it did alter the overall social figuration of the South in at least one respect: it brought blacks into *direct* competition with poor whites, leading the latter to develop exaggerated fears about 'black domination'. Loss of their human 'property' led such fears and fantasies to be common in the white middle and upper classes, too. That is, partly because of the segmental solidarity of such groups – i.e. the fact that they bonded principally around the similitude of colour – the dominant response of whites was violent and racist, taking, for example, the form of the establishment of racist organizations like the Ku Klux Klan. Such organizations operated clandestinely during Reconstruction but came into the open once the federal troops started to leave the South. A central consequence of the movement of groups like the Ku Klux Klan into the open was that the lynching rate grew annually from about 1870 to about 1890. It started to decline around the turn of the century because that period marked the legal consolidation of the caste-like figuration that had begun to emerge as soon as slavery was abolished.

This process began in 1890 with the passage of an act in Louisiana that legalized the segregation of railway carriages. That act was declared constitutional by the US Supreme Court in 1896 in the case of Plessy *vs.* Ferguson, a crucial decision since, under the masking ideology that 'separate' could mean 'equal', it gave federal backing to the constitutions that were framed in all Southern states during this period, whereby not only transport, but also schools, residential areas and public facilities generally were increasingly segregated by law. Such legally buttressed segregation, and the caste-like system of white dominance that underlay it, secured important gains for whites of all classes. For the upper and middle classes, it secured a permanent supply of cheap, easily exploitable labour and removed the threat of a racially united working class; for poor whites, it limited black competition in the field of employment in two main ways: firstly, through the creation of 'job ceilings' that prevented blacks from rising above the ranks of unskilled and semi-skilled labour; and secondly, by the permanent restriction of blacks to pariah occupations. At the same time, it provided poor whites with an important psychological gain by ensuring that, even though they might have been at the bottom of the *white* social hierarchy, they did not stand at the bottom of the *overall* Southern social order. In order to secure the implementation of this gain, all interracial contact was forced to take a ritual form in which deference to all whites was demanded from all blacks. Breaches of the rules of interracial etiquette were severely punished, nowhere more than in the case of violations of the sexual aspects of the code, e.g. if a black man so much as glanced at a white woman. This is indicative of a further gain for white males, namely of the fact that they had available two classes of women, black as well as white. Blacks as a group were insufficiently powerful to resist such encroachments into their lives by the dominant whites.

It would be wrong to imply that the replacement of slavery by a colour-caste figuration had no long-term effects on the relations between blacks and whites. One crucial long-term consequence was the formation of an embryonic black bourgeoisie, a process that was implicit in the formation of colour-castes since this implied that a number of crucial services, e.g. hairdressing, teaching, legal, medical and funeral services, had, given the existence of an inflexible pattern of segregation, to be performed independently by blacks, hence giving rise to the internal stratification of blacks as a caste. This process was intensified by the ghettoization of blacks that occurred when they migrated in large numbers from the South.

Urban ghettoes

The seeds of the downfall of the colour-caste figuration were present even as its consolidation began. America's position in the system of international interdependencies had been crucial to the initial consolidation of white dominance. The power of the colonizing British had made it possible for them to dominate the slave trade, and Britain's industrialization, more specifically, the emergence of the cotton industry, had facilitated the emergence of the cotton monoculture in the postcolonial South. International contingencies were similarly implicated in the downfall of that system and in the transformation of the wider social figuration with which it was intertwined. The emergence of countries such as Egypt and China as producers of cotton for the world market, and the manufacture of artificial fibres, let to a decline in the competitiveness of the American South and subsequently to a decline of the cotton monoculture and the related colour-caste figuration. As a result, blacks and poor whites were forced in large numbers to leave the South. They were simultaneously attracted to the North and West by the employment opportunities opened up by industrial expansion, a process intensified during the two world wars. The strict immigration legislation enacted in the face of mounting prejudice against immigrants from Southern and Eastern Europe, led to a drastic decline in the capacity of American industry to import cheap labour. It was forced to rely increasingly on domestic sources, and blacks and poor whites from the South came to form the chief means of filling the gap.

The effects of this migration on the social situation of American blacks were dramatic. In 1900, 90 per cent of the black population of the United States lived in the South. By 1960, only just about one half remained there. The migration was not simply a move out of the South but from rural to urban areas as well. A comparable rural–urban migration also occurred in the South itself as, latterly, industrialization and urbanization began to take root there, too. Thus, again by 1960, blacks had come to constitute between 14 per cent and 54 per cent of the populations of most major US cities. This representation of blacks in urban America did not reflect their proportional membership of the US population – about one-tenth – but the fact that their movement to the cities coincided with and was, in part, the stimulus for an exodus of whites to the suburbs. In that way, the urbanization of blacks was a process of 'ghettoization'.

At first, this process simply involved a reconstitution in an urban context of the colour-caste figuration that had developed in the preindustrial South. The emergent system of urban racial castes was more impersonal but the fact that it was based on physical marks of difference meant that it was relatively easy to re-establish in an urban context. The deep-rooted anti-black feelings of a majority of Northerners – 'Jim Crow' legislation was enacted in some Northern states even before the Civil War, i.e. long before similar legislation was enacted in South – provided the motive. In the longer term, however, ghettoization had important consequences for the balance of power between blacks and whites, leading gradually to a slight increase in the power of the former relative to the latter, to a more positive group image on their part and, simultaneously, to the adoption by many of them of a more militant and aggressive political stance. This long-term process was complex. Although they interacted, I shall conclude this chapter by singling out what seem to me to have been its most important components. They were:

(i) The fact that the ghettoization of blacks and their incorporation into a caste-like urban figuration facilitated more effective communication, organization and perception of the common interests that they shared in opposition to whites than had been possible given the ecological scatter of their situation in the rural South. In short, this process was conducive to the incipient formation of blacks as what Marx might have called a 'caste', racial or ethnic group 'for themselves'.

(ii) The fact that urban concentration facilitated rioting. Whites became fearful of the black ghettoes, and the race riots that occurred in America in the 1960s are a measure of the power increment gained by blacks under urban conditions. Even though they were directed typically at small, white-owned (often Jewish) businesses in the ghettoes, they tended, nevertheless, to be perceived by whites as posing a more general threat, e.g. to their own residential areas and to capital concentrations such as factories, machines, power plants, office blocks, political, judicial and administrative buildings. It would be wrong to see the threat posed in this connection as simply economic. Such capital concentrations are one index of the complex interdependency networks characteristic of urban–industrial societies. It is the operation of these networks that is threatened by riots just as much as the capital equipment.

(iii) The integration of blacks into the urban-industrial occupational structure, albeit principally at lower levels in the overall stratification hierarchy, also began to increase their power chances, especially where they formed trades unions or managed to enter white ones. Such an effect is a principal source of functional democratization. It follows generally as a result of occupational differentiation, since specialist groups, when their members become conscious of common interests and begin to organize, can, by withdrawing their labour or threatening to do so, effect a breakdown in the wider system of social interdependencies and thus put pressure on others.

(iv) The integration of increasing numbers of blacks into the money economy as wage-earners as opposed to subsistence farmers and 'debt peons' – itself an index of their growing integration into the nationwide network of interdependency chains – had among its consequences the fact that the organized withdrawal of their purchasing power enabled them to hurt firms which refused to employ black labour or practised other forms of discrimination. Simultaneously, the increase of black purchasing power increased the dependency of business generally on the so-called 'negro', 'black' or 'African-American' market.

(v) The internal stratification of the urban 'black caste', with the gradual emergence of a comparatively affluent, comparatively well-educated 'black bourgeoisie', began to provide leadership, funds and organizational expertise for rational, non-violent protest organizations such as the NAACP (National Association for the Advancement of Coloured People) and the SCLC (Southern Christian Leadership Conference). Through the long-term strategies they pursued, though there were conflicts between them that simultaneously lessened their impact, these organizations played a significant part in preparing the way for the protests of the 1960s, helping to create a situation in which more militant 'black power' groups such as the Black Panthers could emerge. A crucial moment came in 1954 when the Supreme Court overruled the 'separate but equal' doctrine that it had legitimated in 1896. That reversal was achieved primarily as a result of a long-term legal campaign organized and financed by the NAACP. It was the signal for the overt civil rights struggle of the 1950s and 1960s to begin.

At the root of the motivation of members of the black bourgeoisie in supporting organizations like the NAACP lay status-frustration at the ambiguities inherent in their position as the dominant group in a subordinate 'caste'. Their comparative affluence meant that questions of status could take precedence in their lives over bread-and-butter issues, whilst their rejection by whites of comparable social standing forced them into ambivalent identifications with poorer members of their own 'caste'. Once the dynamics of the protest movement thus set in motion had got under way, the stage was set for the emergence of more militant and radical protest groups. Even here, however, large numbers came from the black bourgeoisie, though, in this case, principally from its younger age-groups, especially blacks at university. But that only serves to underline the dependency of the US civil rights movement on the process of internal stratification of the black 'caste' that occurred contingently upon the absorption of blacks into the urban-industrial figuration of American society as a whole.

Despite the many conflicts between them, the black protest organizations began to succeed in the 1960s in obtaining better employment opportunities for blacks, in securing voting rights in the South, and in forcing the desegregation of public facilities. By and large, however, such changes were of immediate benefit principally to the black bourgeoisie. The reasons why were inherent in the deep structure of the overall social process. Since it was initially a product of ghetto life, in particular of the fact that segregation forced blacks to perform virtually all service and professional functions for themselves, the power and influence of the black bourgeoisie were, at first, restricted almost solely to the ghetto context. As a result, the pressures of functional democratization in the United States tended to be caste-specific, i.e. they operated mainly among whites, to a lesser extent among blacks and hardly at all in the relations between blacks and whites. Now, however, blacks began to be elected as mayors and more than ever before began to work in racially integrated contexts, for example, for the Federal Government, and that meant in contexts where the pressures of functional democratization could operate *between*, rather than as had previously been the case, mainly *within* castes. And that meant, in turn, that, for such groups, the gains of the civil rights movement could be preserved.

However, for the vast mass of poorer blacks, this process and, more specifically, the rhetoric of the civil rights movement, served merely to kindle aspirations which, especially in a period of declining employment opportunities for unskilled workers, could not be satisfied in the short run and which contributed, correspondingly, to the ghetto riots of the mid-1960s. The effects of these riots on the dynamics of racial stratification and protest were complex. In part, they led younger black activists to become disillusioned with moderate leaders, to press for 'black power' and to reject non-violent tactics. This served to split the moderate leadership, pushing some into a more radical stance. It also served to increase the 'white backlash' that had been in evidence ever since the changing balance of power between whites and blacks began to be translated into organized protest and to meet with a measure of success. It was partly for this reason that the civil rights movement only managed to make a comparatively small dent in the power of the dominant whites and that its principal long-term effect so far, apart from leading the black bourgeoisie to grow larger, has been to exacerbate the class division of blacks that began to be intensified correlatively with their ghettoization.

NOTES

1. This chapter is based on a paper that I gave to the Sociology Department at the Ruhr University Bochum, Germany, in 1979. The paper derived from two principal sources: the first was my marriage to the daughter of a black American newspaper publisher in the early/mid-1960s and the insights I obtained in that connection into the black bourgeoisie. The second was the course on race relations that I taught at the University of Leicester in the 1960s and 1970s. I believe the chapter retains its value as an illustration of the light that can be shed on race relations and related issues by an 'Eliasian' approach. It has to be acknowledged nevertheless that the paper is outdated in two respects. The first is the fact that the literature on which I was dependent came mainly from the 1950s, 1960s and 1970s. I freely admit that there has probably been conceptual, theoretical and empirical work on race relations carried out since those decades to which I could have fruitfully referred. The second respect in which the paper is outdated relates to changes that have taken place in American race relations since the 1960s and 1970s, especially those connected with immigration into the United States of people of Hispanic and Asian descent. These have added to the complexity of the structure and dynamics of American race relations in numerous ways and suggest that it would probably be fruitful to think in this connection of the overlap and interpenetration of multiple established–outsider figurations with groups that are established in some contexts having become outsiders in others. That said, it remains arguably the case that a figurational/process sociological perspective can be of help in unravelling and explaining complexities of these kinds.
2. The analysis offered here is based on reading a wide range of secondary sources. Principal among them are Blassingame (1972); Blauner (1972); Davis and the Gardners (1941); Fitzhugh (1854); Franklin and Moss (1994); Frazier (1962); Genovese (1974); Marx (1969).

REFERENCES

Allport, G.W. 1954, *The Nature of Prejudice*, New York: Doubleday.
Berreman, G.I. 1960, 'Caste in India and the United States', *American Journal of Sociology* 66: 120–7.
Blassingame, J.W. 1972, *The Slave Community*, New York: Oxford University Press.
Blauner, R. 1972, *Racial Oppression in America*, London: Harper and Row.

Davis, A., Gardner, B.B. and Gardner, M.R. 1941, *Deep South*, Chicago: University of Chicago Press.
Durkheim, E. 1964, *The Division of Labour in Society*, New York: Free Press.
Elias, N. 1974, 'The sciences: towards a theory', in R. Whitely (ed.), *Social Processes and Scientific Development*, London: Routledge & Kegan Paul, pp. 21–42.
1978, *What is Sociology?* London: Hutchinson.
Elias, N. and Scotson, J. 1994, *The Established and the Outsiders*, London: Sage (first published in 1965 by Frank Cass: London).
Elkins, S. 1959, *Slavery: a Problem in American Institutional Life*, New York: Grosset and Dunlop.
Fitzhugh, G. 1854, *Sociology for the South*, Richmond, VA.
Franklin, J.H. and Moss, A.A. Jr. 1994, *From Slavery to Freedom*, New York: McGraw-Hill.
Frazier, E.F. 1962, *Black Bourgeoisie*, New York: Collier.
Genovese, E. 1969, *The World the Slaveholders Made*, London: Allen Lane.
Goffman, E. 1959, *Asylums*, New York: Doubleday Anchor.
Kahl, J.A. 1961, *The American Class Structure*, New York: Holt, Rinehart and Winston.
Leach, E.R. 1960, ed., *Aspects of Caste in South India, Ceylon and North-east Pakistan*, Cambridge: Cambridge University Press.
Lockwood, D. 1970, 'Race, conflict and plural society', in S. Zubaida (ed.), *Race and Racialism*, London: Tavistock.
Marx, G. 1969, *Power and Prejudice*, New York: Harper Torch Books.
Parsons, T. 1953, 'Revised analytical approach to the theory of social stratification', in R. Bendix and S.M. Lipset (eds.), *Class, Status and Power*, Glencoe: Free Press.
Warner, W.L. 1949, *Social Class in America*, Chicago: Science Research Associates.
Weber, M. 1946, 'Class, status and party', in H.H. Gerth and C.W. Mills (eds.), *From Max Weber: Essays in Sociology*, New York: Oxford University Press.

6 Decivilizing and demonizing: the remaking of the black America ghetto

Loïc Wacquant

This chapter is divided into two parts.[1] In Part I, I analyse the post-sixties transformation of America's black ghetto in material reality and public discourse as the product of two interconnected processes. At the *social-relational level*, the ghetto has undergone a process of 'de-civilizing' in Elias's sense of the term, caused not by economic 'mismatches', the excessive generosity of welfare, or the 'culture of poverty' and 'anti-social' impulses of its residents, but by the withdrawal of the state and the ensuing disintegration of public space and social relations in the urban core. This process is echoed, at the *symbolic level*, by the demonization of the black sub-proletariat via the trope of the 'underclass', a scholarly myth anchored by the loathsome imagery of the fearsome 'gang banger' and the dissolute 'welfare mother'. Decivilizing and demonization form a structural-cum-discursive couplet in which each element reinforces the other and both serve in tandem to legitimize the state policy of urban abandonment and punitive containment responsible for the parlous state of the contemporary ghetto.

In Part II this processual approach to the formation of class, caste and urban space is further elaborated using the theoretical tools of Norbert Elias's figurational sociology. Adopting a relational perspective and bringing fear, violence and the state to the analytical forefront makes it possible to specify the transition from the mid-century 'communal ghetto' to the contemporary 'hyperghetto', in terms of the dynamic interaction of three master processes: the *depacification of everyday life, social dedifferentiation leading to organizational desertification* and *informalization of the economy*. I argue that each of these processes is set off and abetted by the collapse of public institutions and by the ongoing replacement of the 'social safety net' of welfare by the 'dragnet' of police, courts, and prisons. Elias thus helps us spotlight the distinctively political roots of the urban patterning of racial and class exclusion of which today's hyperghetto is the concrete materialization.

I THE SOCIAL AND SYMBOLIC REMAKING OF THE BLACK GHETTO

To approach the controversial reality of what has become of the black American ghetto a quarter-century after the wave of race riots chronicled in the famous Kerner Commission Report of 1968 (see NACCD 1968), I would like to highlight two interconnected processes, the one material and relational, the other symbolic or discursive, whereby has operated an urban and racial mutation specific to *fin-de-siècle* America.

The first process is what I will call, after Norbert Elias, the *de-civilizing* of the segregated core of large US cities, these veritable domestic Bantustans that are the ghettos of the old industrial centres of the Rustbelt states, such as New York, Chicago, Detroit, Philadelphia, Pittsburgh, Baltimore and Cleveland, owing to the retreat of the state in its various components and the ensuing disintegration of public space.

The second process, tightly linked to the first by a complex functional relation, is the *demonizing* of the black urban sub-proletariat in public debate, that is, the extraordinary proliferation of discourses on what has been called the 'underclass' for a little over a decade now on the Western shores of the Atlantic – a term that is better left untranslated in so far as it points to an alleged location in American social space and carries with it a specifically American semantic halo. We will see that the semi-journalistic, semi-scholarly trope that has given 'birth' to this fictitious group by refurbishing century-old prejudices concerning the supposed cultural peculiarities of the black community for contemporary tastes tends to effect a veritable 'symbolic enslavement' of the residents of the ghetto (see Dubin 1987).[2] This symbolic confinement in turn serves to justify the policy of abandonment of this segment of society by public authorities, a policy to which the theory of the 'underclass' owes its considerable social plausibility.

Because my analysis focuses on an aspect of US society that is not well known, including by indigenous social science, owing especially to the notions of the national common sense, ordinary and scholarly, which tend to screen it from view, it is liable to be mistaken for a polemic against the United States stamped in the coin of anti-Americanism. To indicate that it is no such thing, it will suffice to suggest that an analysis of the same type could be made, *mutatis mutandis*, of the situation of the declining working-class estates that ring France's large cities and of the recent explosion of apocalyptic discourses on the '*cités-ghettos*' in the media and the political field, a thematic which constitutes in many regards a sort of French structural equivalent of the American debate on the 'underclass' (see Wacquant 1992).

The de-civilizing of the ghetto

In his masterwork *Über den Prozess der Zivilisation*, Norbert Elias (1994) describes what he labels the 'civilizing process'. By this term the German sociologist designates not some Victorian idea of moral or cultural progress of which the West would be bearer and beacon, but the long-term transformation of interpersonal relations, tastes, modes of behaviour, and knowledge that accompanies the formation of a unified state capable of monopolizing physical violence over the whole of its territory and thus of progressively pacifying society.

For the sake of clarity, this process can be analytically decomposed into four levels. The first is a structural modification of social relations, of the form and density of social 'figurations', that manifests itself in the growth of the division of labour and the lengthening and multiplication of networks of interdependence and interaction among individuals and groups. In the second place, the civilizing process is distinguished, according to Elias, by a series of associated changes in modes and styles of life: the repression and privatization of bodily functions, the institutionalization and diffusion of forms of courtesy, and the increase in mutual identification bringing about a decline of interpersonal violence. A third family of transformations touches the structure of the habitus, i.e., the socially constituted schemata that generate individual behaviour: on this level one notes an increase in the pressure towards the rationalization of conduct (particularly by the elevation of the thresholds of shame and embarrassment) as well as the sociocultural distance between parents and children; with the domestication of aggression, self-control becomes more automatic, uniform and continuous, and governed by internal censorship more than by external constraints. The fourth and final transformation impacts modes of knowledge, whose fantasmatic contents regress as the principles of cognitive neutrality and congruence with reality are affirmed. The originality of Elias's analysis lies not only in linking these diverse changes to one another but, above all, in showing that they are closely connected to the increasing hold of the state upon society.

The evolution of the black American ghetto since the 1960s can, following this schema, be interpreted in part as the product of a *reversal* of these trends, that is, as a process of *de*-civilizing[3] whose principal cause is to be found neither in the sudden upsurge of deviant values run amok (as the advocates of the 'culture of poverty' thesis, an old theoretical carcass periodically exhumed from the graveyard of stillborn concepts, would have it), nor in the excessive generosity of what one analyst has rightly termed the 'American semi-welfare state' (as maintained by conservative ideologues Charles Murray 1984; and Lawrence Mead 1985), nor in the mere mechanical transition from a compact industrial economy to a decentralized service economy (as claimed by partisans of the so-called 'mismatch' hypothesis, such as William Julius Wilson (1987); and John Kasarda (1988)), but in the multifaceted retrenchment, on all levels (federal, state and municipal) of the American state and the correlative crumbling of the public sector institutions that make up the organizational infrastructure of any advanced urban society. This is to say that, far from arising from some economic necessity or obeying a cultural logic specific to the black American lower class, I demonstrate that the current predicament of the ghetto and its unending deterioration pertain essentially to the political order of state institutions and actions – or the lack thereof.

I propose to treat briefly *in seriatim* three trends that materialize this decivilizing of the ghetto: the depacification of society and the erosion of public space; the organizational desertification and the policy of concerted abandonment of public services in the urban territories where poor blacks are concentrated; and, finally, the movement of social de-differentiation and the rising informalization of the economy that can be observed in the racialized core of the American metropolis. Along the way, I will provide a compressed statistical and ethnographic sketch of this concentration-camp-like space into which the black American ghetto has turned, relying mainly on the example of that of Chicago, which I know well for having worked on and in it for several years.

The depacification of everyday life and the erosion of public space

The most striking aspect of daily life in the black American ghetto today is no doubt its extreme dangerousness and the unprecedented rates of violent crime that afflict its inhabitants. Thus, in the course of 1990, 849 murders were recorded in Chicago, 602 of which were shootings, the typical victim being a black man under 30 living in a segregated and deprived neighbourhood on the South Side or West Side (the city's two historic 'Black Belts'). A murder is committed in Al Capone's old fief every 10 hours; there are 45 robberies per day, 36 of them involving guns. In 1984 there were already 400 arrests for violent crimes per 100,000 residents; this figure had increased fourfold by 1992. A disproportionate share of these crimes are committed, but also suffered, by the residents of the ghetto.

Indeed, a recent epidemiological study conducted by the Center for Disease Control in Atlanta shows that homicide has become the leading cause of male mortality among the black urban population. Of the rising tide of macabre statistics published on this subject in recent years, one can recall that young black men in Harlem run a greater risk of violent death today simply by virtue of residing in that neighbourhood than they would have walking to the front lines at the height of the Vietnam War. In the Wentworth district, at the heart of Chicago's South Side, the homicide rate reached 96 murders per 100,000 inhabitants. A police officer assigned to this neighbourhood laments: 'We have murders every day that don't even make the news. Nobody knows or cares.' And he complains that young criminals commonly have access to high-powered weapons, automatic handguns and Uzi submachine guns: 'Before, the kids tended to use clubs and knives. Now they have better firearms than we do.' In the course of the single year 1990, the city police seized more than 19,000 handguns during routine operations (*Chicago Tribune* 1991a). A number of big cities have instituted 'gun exchange' programmes, offering a fixed sum of money for firearms turned in in the hope of reducing the number of pistols and rifles circulating in poor neighbourhoods.

It is true that in some public housing concentrations in the ghetto, gunfire is so frequent that children learn when they are little to throw themselves to the ground to avoid bullets as soon as they hear shooting; as for little girls, they are also taught to guard against the 'rape men'. Thousands of high-school students abandon their studies every year on account of the insecurity that prevails inside Chicago's public schools. Indeed, it is not unusual for families to send their offspring off to board with parents in the suburbs or in the Southern states so that they can follow a normal academic cursus without risking their lives. A recent study of residents of a large low-income housing complex on the South Side compares the area around the projects to 'a war zone where the non-combatants flee the frontlines'. The dangers to which the children of these neighbourhoods are exposed are, in decreasing order, shootings, extortion by gangs, and obscurity, propitious to violence of all kinds – in contrast a random sample of suburban mothers cite fear of kidnapping, car accidents and drugs as the main threats looming over their offspring. One South Side mother describes a typical scene as follows: 'Sometimes you see boys running from two directions; they start calling names; then they start shooting' (Dubrow and Garbarino 1989: 8). Another adds: 'People start shooting and the next thing you know you have a war on your hands.' In the projects of the West Side, families surviving on welfare payments allocate a share of their meagre resources to pay for funeral insurance for their adolescent children.

In this environment of pandemic violence, the mere fact of surviving, of reaching the age of majority and *a fortiori* old age, is perceived as an achievement worthy of public recognition. In the neighbourhood of North Kenwood, one of the South Side's poorest, murders became

so frequent in the late 1980s that the young people there 'seriously discussed whether it was possible to get past your thirties'. Some analysts
of urban problems go so far as to speak openly of young black men as an
'endangered species' (see Duncan 1987; Gibbs 1988). Dying a violent
death and going to prison have become eminently banal events, with the
result that incarceration is often perceived as a simple continuation of life
in the ghetto:

To a lotta *poor blacks America is a prison* . . . Jail, jail jus' an' extension of America,
for black people anyway. Even in jail, the whites got the better job, I'm serious!
They give the whites the *high-payin' jobs*, they give the blacks the *wors' jobs in
d'jail*: cleanin' the basement, all kindsa har' an' crazy stuff.

So I was told by one of my informants, a former leader of Black Gangster
Disciples, the gang which ruled the South Side at the turn of the 1980s,
at the end of seven years spent in the penitentiary. In fact, today there
are more black men between 19 and 25 under correctional supervision
(jailed in preventive custody, serving prison sentences, and on probation
or parole) than are enrolled in four-year colleges (Duster 1988).

The first reaction of ghetto residents who are victims of violence is
to flee, when they can, or to barricade themselves into their homes and
to withdraw into the family circle, when it is not to avenge themselves.
The reflex of resorting to law enforcement agencies quickly fades when,
on the one hand, one is equally afraid of police violence, itself endemic
(as was recently revealed during the trial following the brutal beating
of black motorist Rodney King by the Los Angeles police, caught on
videotape by an amateur cameraman), but also and above all when state
services, overextended and direly short of means, are unable to respond
to demand and incapable of guaranteeing the victims minimal protection
against possible reprisals by the criminals. Alex Kotlowitz recounts the
fruitless efforts of a South Side family to get the police or social services
of the city to intervene to get back their 11-year-old son, who had been
in effect kidnapped by a dealer who used him to distribute drugs to his
resale network (Kotlowitz 1991: 84ff.). A paradox that speaks volumes:
it is in the most dangerous neighbourhoods of the ghetto that the calls to
911 are the least frequent.

The organizational desertification of the ghetto

At once cause and effect of this erosion of public space, the decline of local
institutions (businesses, churches, neighbourhood associations and public services) has reached such a degree that it verges on an organizational
desert. The origin of the spectacular degradation of the institutional and

associative fabric of the ghetto is, here again, to be found in the sudden retreat of the welfare state, which has undermined the infrastructure enabling public and private organizations to develop or subsist in these stigmatized and marginalized neighbourhoods.

It is well established that, on the heels of Richard Nixon's re-election, the United States made a U-turn in urban policy. In the course of the seventies, the scaffold of government programmes put in place at the time of Johnson's Great Society was gradually dismantled and then abandoned, depriving the big cities of the means to meet the needs of their most disadvantaged residents. The policy of disengagement from the metropolis accelerated to reach its acme under the successive presidencies of Ronald Reagan: between 1980 and 1988, the funds allocated for urban development were cut by 68 per cent and those destined for federal public housing by 70 per cent. It was the same with social assistance: in the state of Illinois, for example, the real-dollar value of the basic package (the allowance for a single mother with offspring under Aid to Families with Dependent Children, plus food stamps) decreased by one half between 1977 and 1988. The maximum amount a family of three can claim is now barely equal to the average rent of a *one-room* apartment in Chicago. And only 55 per cent of those entitled to it receive public aid.

At the municipal level, deep cuts have been made selectively in the budget for public services, on which blacks living in poor neighbourhoods are the most reliant, whether it be public transport, subsidized housing, social and medical services, schools, or city services such as trash collection and housing inspection. Thus today there is not a single public hospital left on the South Side of Chicago, nor a single functioning drug rehabilitation programme that accepts patients who do not have the means to pay. And a chain of fire station closings allows the city to claim the highest rate of death by fire in the country. Indigenous institutions, which flourished up to the mid-sixties, are in their death throes. Even the two traditional pillars of the black community, hinges and mouthpieces of the ghetto in its classical form (as described by St Clair Drake and Horace Cayton in their masterful book *Black Metropolis*, 1962[1945]), the press and the pulpit, have all but lost their ability to shape life in the inner city as the exodus of the black (petty) bourgeois and stable working-class families, who leave to find refuge in the adjoining neighbourhoods left vacant by whites fleeing the city, deprived them of their main clientele and source of support.

But it is the accelerated degradation of the schools that best reveals this process of institutional abandonment. Public schooling has become, according to the testimony of a former superintendent of the Chicago Board of Education, 'a reservation of the poor': 84 per cent of its clientele is black and Latino and 70 per cent comes from families living below the official poverty line. Of 100 children entering the sixth grade in 1982, only 16 reached the twelfth grade six years later, even though no examination is required to move on at any level of the curriculum. In the eighteen poorest schools of the district, all of them located inside the ghetto, this percentage drops to a paltry 3.5. Three-quarters of the city's secondary establishments do not offer courses leading to college admission; most are cruelly lacking in rooms, books, basic equipment such as typewriters, desks or blackboards, and, even more so, teachers – a quarter of the city's teaching body is made up of permanent substitute teachers. No local elected official to the municipal council sends his or her children to a public school and the teachers who risk theirs there are far and few. And for good reason: Chicago spends, on average, only $5,000 per student per year, as against $9,000 annually for the pupils of the rich towns of the Northern suburbs (Kozol 1991).

The pauperization of the public sector has debased schools to the level of mere *custodial institutions* incapable of fulfilling their pedagogic functions. At Fiske Elementary School, on 62nd Street, no more than a couple of hundred yards from the overaffluent University of Chicago Business School, the two daily priorities are, first, to ensure the physical safety of the children and staff by means of a parents' militia that patrols the school grounds all day long armed with baseball bats; and, second, to feed the children, a large number of whom come to school with empty stomachs and fall asleep from exhaustion during class. In May 1991, when the Chicago Board of Education announced the imminent closing of thirty-odd ghetto schools due to an unforeseen budget deficit, some 300 parents went on a protest march which culminated in a stormy meeting with the academic authorities: 'When you start closing these schools and transferring these kids, tell us if you're going to ensure that our kids will be able to stay alive when they walk out of one territory to enter another gang's territory? Do you want to have the blood of our children on your hands? (*Chicago Tribune*, 1991b). The lapidary response of the mayor on the evening news: 'We can't put a policeman behind every student.'

Social dedifferentiation and economic informalization

In keeping with the predictions of Elias's model, one can observe inside the black American ghetto a trend toward *social dedifferentiation*, that is, a functional and structural decrease in the division of labour, at the level of populations as well as institutions. This retreat of differentiation can be seen first in the growing occupational uniformity of the residents of the segregated urban core, due principally to the vertiginous rise of unemployment: in 1950, half of ghetto dwellers over 16 years of age had a job; in 1980, three adults in four were without work and over half of all households subsisted mainly on public aid. At the institutional level, a parallel tendency towards forced multifunctionality asserts itself, such that an organization finds itself compelled to take on functions that ordinarily redound to other (especially public) organizations owing to the latter's crisis or outright disappearance. Thus the churches strive, as best as they can, to make up for the deficiencies of the schools, the labour market, and a social, medical and judicial system in an advanced state of decay, by running soup kitchens and food pantries, setting up drug rehabilitation programmes and literacy campaigns run by volunteers, and by maintaining 'job banks'. But they are themselves confronted with such a fall in their financial and human resources that they often have to devote most of their energies to their own survival. The same is true of the city's 'political machine', which, unable to maintain the networks of clientelism responsible for channelling the voters of poor neighbourhoods, now exists only on paper. At the close of the 1988 presidential campaign, the local Democratic Party was reduced to offering a free meal in a desperate attempt to attract potential voters to its meetings in Woodlawn in support of its candidate Michael Dukakis.

The dedifferentiation of the social structure is directly tied to the decline of the formal economy and the collapse of the job market in the ghetto. In the post-war decades, the segregated neighbourhoods of the big cities served as a convenient pool of cheap manual labour for a booming industrial economy. The restructuring of American capitalism during the period from 1965 to 1982 put an end to this role of reservoir of workforce, bringing about a rapid withering away of the productive fabric. The fate of the community of Woodlawn, on Chicago's South Side, provides a vivid illustration of this process of economic marginalization of the ghetto. Woodlawn counted over 700 commercial and industrial firms in 1950; today it holds little more than 100, the great majority of which employ no more than two or three people. The most common businesses in the neighbourhood are liquor stores, hair and cosmetics salons and storefront churches, small independent religious establishments the majority of which have closed down and are rotting away.

To this collapse of the official economy corresponds the vertiginous growth of the informal economy, and especially the drug trade. The commerce in narcotics is, in many sectors of the ghetto, the only expanding economic sector and the main employer of jobless youths – nay, the only type of business that the latter know firsthand and for which they can begin working as early as age six or eight. It is true that it is also the only sector in which racial discrimination is not a barrier to entry (see Williams 1989, and also Bourgois 1992). As a West Side informant explained to me as we drove past a row of abandoned buildings near his home: 'That's the thing, to be *a gang-banger*, to be a drug-dealer. An' that's what they doin', hangin' there, on the street corner, sellin' drugs, an' rippin' off people – that's *they art*. See they don' have anything else, so that's they art.'

Aside from the drug economy and informal work – whose development is visible in other sectors of the American economy, including the most advanced[4] – the heart of the ghetto has witnessed a proliferation of small sub-proletarian 'trades' typical of Third World cities: itinerant hawkers, resellers of newspapers, cigarettes or soft drinks by the unit, porters, parking lot attendants, day-labourers, etc. There is no South Side neighbourhood without its 'gypsy cabs', its 'jackleg mechanics', its 'after-hours' clubs and its teenagers who offer to carry your grocery bags at the exit of the local food mart or to fill up your car at the gas station for a bit of change. Everything can be bought and sold on the street, from counterfeit Louis Vuitton handbags (for $25 dollars each) to refinished stolen cars to handguns ($300 for a 'clean' revolver at the current rate, half that sum for a 'dirty' one), defective clothes, homemade Southern-style cooking and dollar-store jewelry. The gambling economy – the 'numbers game', lottery, lotto and illegal card and dice games – knows no recession.

The development of this parallel irregular economy is closely tied to the disintegration of public space and the depacification of the local society. According to anthropologist Philippe Bourgois, the ghetto streets have become the crucible of a 'culture of terror' that grows functionally with the drug trade:

Regular displays of violence are necessary for success in the underground economy – especially the street-level, drug-dealing world. Violence is essential for maintaining credibility and for preventing ripoff by colleagues, customers, and holdup artists. Indeed . . . behaviour that appears irrationally violent and self-destructive to the middle-class (or the working-class) outside observer can be reinterpreted according to the logic of the underground economy, as a judicious case of public relations, advertising, and rapport-building. (Bourgois 1989: 631–2)

To complete this summary portrait of the decivilizing process in the ghetto, one would need to evoke the shortening of networks of interdependency (as in the case of one resident of the South Side who no longer visits her cousins on the West Side due to the intense insecurity prevailing there, or the children of public housing projects who resign themselves to not having friends out of fear of finding themselves entangled in dangerous situations – Kotlowitz 1991: 154); the production of structurally unstable habitus due to the internalization of socioeconomic structures that are increasingly precarious and contradictory; the rise of political-religious fantasies of a millenarist kind, of which the growing popularity of Nation of Islam leader Louis Farrakan is one indicator among others, etc. In short, all the practices of an 'infra-civil' society that has developed to fill the organizational vacuum created by the retrenchment of the state and the collapse of public space as well as of the social regulations of which the state is the bearer.

The invention of the 'underclass', or the demonizing of the black ghetto sub-proletariat

The symbolic flank of this decivilizing process is the invention of the *underclass* as a novel, yet pivotal, category of political and scholarly common sense in the debate about the ghetto after the Civil Rights revolution.[5] If we are to believe the media, policy research experts, but also a good number of sociologists, a new 'group' has made its appearance at the heart of the country's urban 'Black Belts' in the course of the past three decades: the 'underclass'. One would be tempted to translate this term as *quart-monde* [Fourth World], the excluded, or sub-proletariat if it did not precisely designate an indigenous 'reality' without true counterpart outside of the United States (much like, for example, the notion of '*cadre*' in French society – Boltanski 1987), which justifies our retaining the American word, even as, unbeknownst to most of its users, it derives from the Swedish *onderklasse*. This 'group' can be recognized by a collection of supposedly closely interconnected characteristics – pell mell: an out-of-control sexuality, female-headed families, massive absenteeism and failure rates in school, drug consumption and trafficking and a propensity for violent crime, an abiding 'dependency' on public aid, endemic unemployment (due, according to some versions, to a refusal to work and to fit into the conventional structures of society), isolation in neighbourhoods with a high density of 'problem' families, etc.

Definitional criteria vary, as do the estimates of the size of the group, which range from a modest 0.5 million to a gigantic 8 million. Some analysts depict the 'underclass' as a category that includes vast numbers and is growing at a frightening pace; others argue, to the contrary, that its volume is quite restricted and that it is stagnating, even shrinking. But nearly all agree on one key point: the 'underclass' is a new entity, distinct from the traditional 'lower class' and separate from the rest of society, which bears a specific culture or nexus of relations that determines it to engage in pathological behaviours of destruction and self-destruction.

Genesis of a scholarly myth

Whence comes the 'underclass'? The name strictly speaking emerged in that murky zone situated at the intersection of the political field and the field of the social sciences, from where it was first propagated in the media before making a forceful return within sociology. Borrowed by journalists from the Swedish economist Gunnar Myrdal (1962), who used it to designate something else altogether – those fractions of the proletariat marginalized on the labour market due to an ethnic stigma and technological upheavals in the production system – the term has become virtually synonymous not simply with the 'undeserving poor' (Katz 1989), but with the undeserving *black* poor. For, curiously, there seems to be no white 'underclass', or if there is, it is so insignificant as to be hardly worthy of mention.

One can sketch an abbreviated genealogy of the emergence of the swirling discourse on the 'underclass' by retracing its course through the media, since it is they who gave the term its remarkable power of attraction. Its first national appearance dates from the summer of 1977, when, following the looting that broke out during the great blackout in New York City, *Time Magazine* (29 August: 14–15) devoted its cover to 'The American Underclass', which it presented in these terms, buttressed by the picture of a young black man sporting a fearsome grimace: 'Behind its crumbling walls lives a large group of people who are more intractable, more socially alien and more hostile than almost anyone had imagined. They are the unreachables: the American underclass.' And it defined the 'underclass' by the deviant norms and the pathological practices of its members: 'Their bleak environment nurtures values that are often at radical odds with those of the majority – even the majority of the poor.'

In 1982, journalist Ken Auletta published a book soberly entitled *The Underclass*, which caused a sensation and gave the term broad currency in public debate. According to this author, 'millions of social dropouts' who 'prey on our communities', would be the chief culprits for the 'street crime, long-term welfare dependency, chronic unemployment and anti-social behaviour in America today'. Auletta identified the four components of the underclass as 'the passive poor', 'the hostile street criminals', 'the hustlers' and 'the traumatized alcoholics, drifters, homeless shopping-bag ladies and released mental patients'. And he lamented the fact that 'traditional anti-poverty programmes and the criminal justice system have both failed to socialize these most virulent and increasingly disorganized members of our society'.

Very quickly, the trickle of more or less sensationalist stories swelled into a veritable torrent. The image of a new group endowed with a culture

at once passive, hostile and destructive was consolidated, and the implicit association between blackness and the 'underclass' was cemented.
In 1986, *US News and World Report* could authoritatively present the
'underclass' as a 'nation apart, a culture of have-nots that is drifting
further and further from the fundamental values of the haves', and whose
'growth constitutes the main problem of [the] country's urban centers'
(17 March 1986). An article in *Fortune Magazine* appeared the next year,
under the worried title, 'America's Underclass: What To Do?' and described 'underclass communities' (for the term was by then also used as
an adjective) as 'urban knots that threaten to become enclaves of permanent poverty and vice' (Magnet 1987). And always these pictures of poor
blacks, alternatively threatening and pitiable, irrefutable visual proof of
the emergence and spread of a untamable new social animal. By 1989,
the Joint Economic Committee of the US Congress found it urgent to
organize a hearing to officially alert the nation to 'the tragedy of the underclass' and shine a light on 'underclass neighbourhoods' in which 'poverty
is being passed from generation to generation'. Remarkably for a panel
ostensibly concerned with economic issues, two of the three experts asked
to testify were African American. Economist Ronald Mincy supplied bold
statistical measurements of the size, evolution and demographic makeup
of the alleged group; political scientist Lawrence Mead adduced as the
cause of its emergence a 'complex of social isolation, permissive welfare
and attitudes contrary to work'; and sociologist Elijah Anderson insisted
that 'a lot of the problem of the underclass is drug related now'. Worrying
that 'the threat' of the 'underclass' was 'beginning to spread', Chairman
Lee Hamilton, representative of Indiana, closed the discussion by musing:
'It is still going to take a lot more work to understand the phenomenon:
is that right?' (Joint Economic Committee 1989: 1, 19, 24, 47, 64–5).

Indeed it was. Today, one can barely keep track of all the books, articles
and reports devoted to the 'underclass'. Conferences are regularly organized where the most eminent specialists of the country grimly debate
the distinctive characteristics of the 'group', its extent and location, the
causes of its formation and the ways of integrating (that is, of domes-
ticating) it into the 'mainstream' of American society. Most of the big
private and public foundations – Ford, Rockefeller, the Social Science
Research Council and even the National Science Foundation – presently
finance gigantic research programmes on the 'underclass', underwrite
dissertations, diffuse publications and put forth policy recommendations
about it. Impeccably scholarly books, such as *The Truly Disadvantaged* by
William Julius Wilson (1987), *The Urban Underclass* edited by Jencks and
Peterson (1991), and *Streetwise* by ethnographer Elijah Anderson (1990),
have taken up and developed this concept – (retroactively) granting it

titles of academic nobility. Even though these authors deny, with good reason for some, sharing the openly culturalist theses propagated by the advocates of continued state retrenchment,[6] it remains that they lend credibility to the idea that a new group has 'crystallized' in the ghetto which is, in whole or part, responsible for the crisis of the cities. And one can find even in the writings of the most progressive among them, with greater or lesser degrees of euphemization, a number of moral and moralizing elements that explain the enthusiastic welcome their work has received from the politicians and bureaucratic intellectuals charged with articulating the public policy of urban abandonment, the first victims of which are the supposed members of the 'underclass'.

'Gang-bangers' and 'welfare mothers': a fantasmatic social threat

The iconography of the 'underclass' rapidly became polarized around two paradigmatic figures: on one side, the 'gangs' of young, arrogant, violent black men, who refuse to occupy the scarce, unskilled, low-paying jobs for which they could apply, and thereby take up their appointed function at the bottom of the social ladder; on the other side, the 'teenage mothers' who subsist 'on the backs' of the taxpayer via receipt of social assistance in large public housing estates, who typically get photographed complacently sitting doing nothing, infants sprawled across their knees, in front of their lit television sets. These emblematic figures are in fact but the two visages of the same fantasy, that of the threat that 'uncivilized' blacks – those who have no place in the new caste and class order – pose for the integrity of American values and the nation itself: the 'gang-bangers' represent moral dissolution and social disintegration on the public side, in the streets; the 'welfare mothers' are the bearers of the same dangers on the private side, inside the domestic sphere. Conceived according to a punitive logic, the state management of these two categories 'by excess' translates, on the one hand, in the astronomical rise in incarceration rates, and, on the other, in the overcrowding of the welfare offices of the ghetto. For it is not so much their poverty and desperation that is a problem as their *social cost*, which must be reduced by all means necessary.[7]

One finds a hyperbolic expression of this loathsome fantasy in an article by Charles Murray, published in England in the *Sunday Times* (for a princely fee), and for this reason less subject to the censorship of the national academic field, where the famed author of *Losing Ground*, the Bible of Reaganite social policy, could for a moment disregard the rules of socioracial decorum that normally govern American public policy discourse, and say plainly what most analysts of the 'underclass' must ordinarily content themselves with writing between the lines. In two call-outs taken from the text of this paper, entitled in huge letters, 'UNDERCLASS: THE ALIENATED POOR ARE DEVASTATING AMERICA'S INNER CITY – IS THE SAME HAPPENING HERE? (Murray 1989: 26, 39, 43), one reads: 'Young [black] males are essentially barbarians for whom marriage is a civilizing force'; 'Single young women get pregnant because sex is fun and babies are endearing.' Murray's analysis (if one may call it that), which presents the ghetto residents as a tribe of savages bent on cannibalizing their own community, is not so much a *reductio ad absurdum* as a return of the repressed. Is not this the same vision that is unapologetically projected by the (Italian and Jewish) lower-class whites in the neighbourhoods adjoining New York's black 'inner cities', for whom 'the ghetto is a jungle infested with dark-skinned "animals" whose wild sexuality and broken families defy all ideas of civilized conduct'? (Rieder 1985: 25–6, 58–67).

From the late nineteenth-century 'theorists' of the race question to Charles Murray by way of Edward Banfield, there exists a long tradition of pseudo-scientific analyses aiming to buttress the stereotypical representation of ghetto blacks as lazy, deviant, amoral and unstable beings who bathe in a pathogenic culture that is radically discontinuous with the dominant American culture. What is new is that the terminology of the 'underclass' claims to be *race-blind*: it has this great virtue that it allows one to speak of African Americans in a superficially 'de-racialized' language. The theory of the 'underclass' presents this other significant advantage of being tautological, since the two defining elements of the 'group' – a deviant and devious 'culture of poverty', a gamut of pathological and destructive practices – reciprocally warrant one another in a process of circular reasoning: the members of the 'underclass' conduct themselves in 'aberrant' manner (another term that recurs to describe them) because their values are abnormal; the proof that they participate in an abnormal culture resides in their errant behaviour.

CODA: WHAT USE IS THE UNDERCLASS?

It should be clear by now that the notion of an 'underclass' is nothing other than what Pierre Bourdieu (1980) calls a 'scholarly myth', that is, a discursive formation which, under a scientific wrapping, reformulates in a way that is apparently neutral and based on reason social fantasies or common prenotions pertaining to differences between the so-called races. Historian Lawrence Levine (1982) has shown that the masters of Southern plantations had much to gain by emphasizing the cultural distance that separated them from their slaves by use of qualifiers such as 'barbaric', 'primitive' and 'childlike' so as better to justify reducing them to chattel. Similarly, there exists an 'unconscious interest' in exaggerating the cultural differentiation of the urban black sub-proletariat to the point of radical alterity. Its demonization allows it to be symbolically isolated and cast off, and it thereby justifies a state policy combining punitive measures, such as programmes of forced labour or workfare, the 'War on Drugs' (which is above all a guerrilla war on drug addicts and dealers in ghetto neighbourhoods) and penal policies that have led to the doubling of the prison population in a decade, and confinement in crumbling inner-city neighbourhoods left fallow.

A fuzzy and malleable term with changing and ill-defined contours, the notion of 'underclass' owes its success to its *semantic indeterminacy* which allows for all manner of symbolic manipulations aiming to contract or enlarge the frontiers of the 'group' according to the ideological interests at hand. But what then is the principle of unity of this concept of variable geometry? It does seem that, as in the case of the marginals of Paris in the high Middle Ages according to Bronislaw Geremek (1976: 361), it is mainly the 'feeling of animosity, of mistrust and contempt' that ghetto blacks inspire in the rest of American society that serves to cement this category.

The ultimate reasons for the success of the concept of 'underclass', then, are to be sought not in its scientific fallout, which is nil in the best of cases,[8] but in its social effects, which are threefold. The first effect is the *dehistoricization* (or naturalization) of the dereliction of the ghetto: the illusion of the radical novelty of this group makes one forget that a sub-proletariat – black and white – has always existed in the United States and that the 'hyperghetto' of the 1980s is nothing but the sociospatial exacerbation of a double logic of racial and class exclusion tendentially at work since the very origins of the dark ghetto a century ago. The second effect is the *essentialization* of the racial/urban question: the slide from substantive to substance makes it possible to attribute to the individuals whose mere statistical aggregation constitutes this fictive group properties that pertain in reality either to the mental structures of the analysts or to national urban structures, and thus to falsely circumscribe within the ghetto itself a problem that finds its roots in the racial division of US politics, city and state. Thirdly, and relatedly, the thematic of the 'underclass' tends to *depoliticize* the dilemma posed by the accelerating decline of the dispossessed black neighbourhoods of the American metropolis: for, if the 'underclass' is indeed a collection of failing individuals carrying within themselves the germ of their predicament and of the bane they inflict upon others, then collective responsibility cannot be invoked either at the level of causes or when it comes to remedies.

The discourse on the 'underclass' is an instrument of discipline in Foucault's sense of the term, not so much for the poor themselves as for all those who struggle not to fall into the urban purgatory that the name symbolizes (that is, the working class in its various components, especially black and Latino), and the best warrant for the policy of *de facto* abandonment of the ghetto by the country's dominant class. Far from illumining the new nexus that links together race, class, and state in the American metropolis, the tale of the 'underclass' contributes to masking the preeminent cause of the decivilizing of the ghetto in Elias's sense: the political will to let it rot away.

II ELIAS IN THE DARK GHETTO

Norbert Elias's theory of the 'civilizing process' and his notations on its obverse, spurts of 'decivilizing', offer a potent tool for diagnosing the mutation of the black American ghetto since the sixties. An adaptation of his framework can help us overcome some of the perennial limitations of conventional analyses of the conundrum of race and class in the US metropolis (on these see Wacquant 1997a).

The ghetto in light of figurational sociology

First, Elias warns us against *Zustandreduktion*, the 'reduction of process to state' built into the idiom of poverty research, which typically fastens on descriptive properties of disadvantaged individuals and populations, as induced by the positivist philosophy of science that animates it. Instead of thinking of the ghetto in static and morphological terms, he suggests that we conceive of it as a system of dynamic forces interweaving agents situated both inside and outside its perimeter. Forms, not rates (of segregation, destitution, unemployment, etc.), connections, not conditions, must be our primary empirical focus.

Secondly, Elias's notion of *figuration* as an extended web of interdependent persons and institutions bonded simultaneously along several dimensions invites us to skirt the analytic parcelling favoured by variable-oriented social analysis. 'It is a scientific superstition that in order to investigate them scientifically one must necessarily dissect processes of interweaving into their component parts' (Elias 1978: 98). Race or space, class or race, state or economy: these artificial oppositions that splinter the normal science of urban poverty in America are unfit to capture the complex causal ensembles and processes involved in making and remaking the ghetto as social system and lived experience.

Thirdly, Elias offers a model of social transformation that spans and *ties together levels of analysis* ranging from large-scale organizations of political and economic power to institutionalized social relations to patterns of interaction to personality types. This model exhorts us to hold together conceptually the most 'macro' of all macro-structures and the most 'micro' of all micro-formations – all the way down to the 'bio-psychosocial' constitution of the individual, to speak like Marcel Mauss (1968). For sociogenesis and psychogenesis are two sides of the same coin of human existence and changes in the one cannot but reverberate upon the other.

Fourth, and most importantly for our purpose, Elias places *violence and fear* at the epicentre of the experience of modernity: together, they form the Gordian knot tying the outermost workings of the state to the innermost makeup of the person. The expurgation of violence from social life via its relocation under the aegis of the state opens the way for the regularization of social exchange, the ritualization of everyday life, and the psychologization of impulse and emotion, leading in turn to 'courtly' and thence courteous human commerce. As for fear, it supplies the central mechanism for the introjection of social controls and the self-administered 'regulation of the whole instinctual and affective life' (Elias 1994: 443).

Now, fear, violence and the state are integral to the formation and transformation of America's dark ghetto. Fear of contamination and degradation via association with inferior beings – African slaves – is at the root of the pervasive prejudice and institutionalization of the rigid caste division which, combined with urbanization, gave birth to the ghetto at the turn of the century (Jordan 1974; Meier and Rudwick 1976). Violence, from below, in the form of interpersonal aggression and terror, as well as from above, in the guise of state-sponsored discrimination and segregation, has been the preeminent instrument for drawing and imposing the 'colour line'. And it plays a critical role also in redrawing the social and symbolic boundaries of which the contemporary ghetto is the material expression.

Depacification, desertification and informalization rearticulated

Elsewhere I have characterized social change on the South Side of Chicago, the city's main historic 'Black Belt', as a shift from the 'communal ghetto' of the mid-century to the *fin-de-siècle* 'hyperghetto' (Wacquant 1994), a novel sociospatial formation conjugating racial and class exclusion under the press of market retrenchment and state abandonment leading to the 'deurbanification' of large chunks of inner-city space.

The communal ghetto of the immediate post-war years was the product of an all-encompassing caste division that compelled blacks to develop their own social world in the shadow – or between the cracks – of hostile white institutions. A compact, sharply bounded, sociospatial formation, it comprised a full complement of black classes bound together by a unified racial consciousness, an extensive social division of labour and broad-based communitarian agencies of mobilization and voice. It formed, as it were, a 'city within the city', standing in a linked oppositional relation with the broader white society whose basic institutional infrastructure it strove to duplicate.

This 'Black metropolis', to borrow the eloquent title of the classic study of Chicago's 'Bronzeville' by St Clair Drake and Horace Cayton (1945), has been replaced by a different urban form. The hyperghetto of the 1980s and 1990s both expresses an *exacerbation of historic racial exclusion sifted through a class prism* and exhibits a novel spatial and organizational configuration. Because it weds colour segregation with class bifurcation, it no longer contains an extended division of labour and a complete set of classes. Its physical boundaries are more fuzzy and its dominant institutions are not community-wide organizations (such as churches, lodges and the black press) but state bureaucracies (welfare, public education, the courts and police) targeted on marginalized 'problem populations'. For the hyperghetto serves not as a reservoir of disposable industrial labour but as a mere dumping ground for supernumerary categories for which the surrounding society has no economic or political use. And it is suffused with systemic economic, social and physical insecurity due to the mutually reinforcing erosion of the wage-labour market and state support. Thus, whereas the ghetto in its classical form acted partly as a protective shield against brutal racial exclusion, the hyperghetto has lost its positive role of collective buffer, making it a deadly machinery for naked social relegation.

The shift from communal ghetto to hyperghetto may be pictured dynamically in terms of the structured interaction of three master processes. The first is the *depacification of everyday life*, that is, the seeping of violence through the fabric of the local social system. Mounting physical decay and danger in America's racialized urban core, detectible in the dereliction of neighbourhood infrastructure and in astronomical rates of crime against persons (homicide, rape, assault and battery), have forced a thorough revamping of daily routines and created a suffocating atmosphere of distrust and dread (Freidenberg 1995).

A second process entails *social dedifferentiation* leading to the withering away of the organizational fabric of ghetto neighbourhoods. The gradual disappearance of stable working- and middle-class Afro-American households, the stacking of degraded public housing in black slum areas and the deproletarianization of the remaining residents have undercut local commercial, civic and religious institutions. Persistent joblessness and acute material deprivation have set off a shrinking of social networks while the political expendability of the black poor allowed for the drastic deterioration of public institutions. From schools, housing and health care to the police, the courts, the prison and welfare, the latter operate in ways that further stigmatize and isolate ghetto dwellers (Wacquant 1997b).

A third process is *economic informalization*: the combined insufficiencies of labour demand, organizational desertification of neighbourhoods and failings of welfare support have fostered the growth of an unregulated economy led by the mass retail sales of drugs and assorted illegal activities. Nowadays most inhabitants of Chicago's South Side find the mainstay of their sustenance in street trades and the social assistance sector: wage work is too scarce and too unreliable for it to be the main anchor of their life strategies (Wilson 1996).

State retrenchment and hyperghettoization

The causal nexus driving the hyperghettoization of the urban core comprises a complex and dynamic constellation of economic and political factors unfolding over the whole post-war era – and further back since many of them can be traced to the era of initial consolidation of the ghetto in the wake of the 'Great Migration' of 1916–30 – that belies the short-term plot of the 'underclass' narrative as a product of the 1970s. Against monocausal theories, I argue that hyperghettoization has *not one but two fundamental roots*, the one in revamping of the urban economy and the other in the structures and policies of the American federal and local state. And that rigid spatial segregation perpetuated by political inaction and administrative fragmentation (Massey and Denton 1993; Weiher 1991) provides the lynchpin that links these two sets of forces into a self-perpetuating constellation highly resistant to conventional social mobilization and social policy approaches.

All told, the *collapse of public institutions* resulting from the state policy of social abandonment and punitive containment of the minority poor emerges as the most potent and distinctive root of entrenched marginality in the American metropolis. Shorn of specifics, the theoretical model of the role of the state in hyperghettoization that Elias helps us specify may be sketched as follows. The erosion of the presence, reach and efficacy of public institutions and programmes entrusted with delivering essential social goods in the racialized urban core sends a series of shock waves that destabilize the already weakened organizational matrix of the ghetto. These shock waves are independent of, though closely correlated with and further amplified by, those emanating from the postfordist restructuring of the economy and ensuing dualization of the city (Sassen 1990, Mollenkopf and Castells 1991).

The massive *social disinvestment* spelled by the curtailment of state provision (i) accelerates the decomposition of the indigenous institutional infrastructure of the ghetto; (ii) facilitates the spread of pandemic violence and fuels the enveloping climate of fear; and (iii) supplies the room and impetus for the blossoming of an informal economy dominated by the drug trade. These three processes in turn feed upon each other and become locked into an apparently self-sustaining constellation that presents every outward sign of being *internally* driven (or 'ghetto-specific'), when in reality it is (over)determined and sustained *from the outside* by the brutal and uneven movement of withdrawal of the semi-welfare state.

The fact that the involutive trajectory of the ghetto appears to be driven by self-contained, endogenous processes is pivotal to the political-ideological redefinition of the question of race and poverty in the 1980s. For it gives free rein to blaming its victims, as in the stigmatizing discourse of the 'behavioural underclass' (Gans 1995), which justifies further state retrenchment. The latter then 'verifies' the view that the ghetto is now beyond policy remediation as conditions within it continue to deteriorate.

Thus the thinning of the ghetto's organizational ecology weakens its collective capacity for formal and informal control of interpersonal violence, which, in the context of widespread material deprivation, leads to increased crime and violence (Bursick and Grasmick 1993). Above a certain threshold, the tide of violent crime makes it impossible to operate a business in the ghetto and thus contributes to the withering away of the wage-labour economy. Informalization and deproletarianization, in turn, diminish the purchasing power and life stability of ghetto residents, which undermines the viability of resident institutions – and thus the life-chances of those who depend on them. It also increases crime since violence is the primary means of regulation of transactions in the street economy, which violence feeds organizational decline that yet furthers economic informalization, as indicated in Figure 6.1.

From social safety net to penal dragnet

State retrenchment should not be taken to mean that the state withdraws *in toto* and somehow disappears from America's neighbourhoods of relegation. To stem the public 'disorders' associated with acute marginality caused by the downgrading – or termination – of its (federal) economic, housing and social welfare component, the (local)

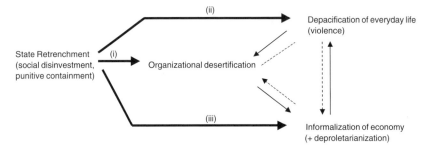

Figure 6.1   Simplified model of the relations between state retrenchment and hyperghettoization

state is compelled to increase its surveillance and repressive presence in
the ghetto.

In point of fact, the past two decades have witnessed an explosive
growth of the penal functions of the American state as prisons and related
carceral devices (parole, probation, electronic monitoring, bootcamps
and curfews) were deployed to stem the consequences of rising destitution caused by the shrinkage of welfare support. Today, the United States
is spending upwards of $200 billion annually on the crime-control en-
terprise and the 'face' of the state most familiar to young ghetto residents is that of the policeman, parole officer and prison guard (Miller
1996). For the tripling of the incarcerated population in fifteen years, from
494,000 in 1980 to over 1.5 million in 1994, has hit poor urban African
Americans with special brutality: 1 black man in 10 between the ages of
18 and 34 is presently incarcerated (as compared with 1 adult in 128 for
the nation) and fully 1 in 3 is under supervision of the criminal justice
system or admitted in detention at some point during a one-year period.

However, the substitution of disciplinary functions, carried out by
the police, criminal justice and prison system, for social provision functions has been only partial, so that the net result of this 'simultaneous
reinforcing-weakening of the State' (Poulantzas 1978: 226) is a marked
diminution of the depth and breadth of state regulation in the urban core.
This is visible even in the area of public order, notwithstanding the guerrilla war on the urban poor waged by the police and the courts under
cover of the 'War on Drugs'. Even in those parts of the ghetto where police forces are highly visible, the 'dragnet' simply cannot make up for the
unravelling of the 'social safety net'. For instance, despite the presence
of a police station *inside* the Robert Taylor Homes, the country's most
infamous concentration of public housing and social misery, the Chicago
Housing Authority found it necessary to create its own, supplementary,

private police force to patrol the project grounds. And, even then, it cannot deliver minimal levels of physical safety to its residents (in the early 1990s, the homicide rate in that section of the South Side exceeded 100 per 100,000, highest in the city), let alone effect a finer control of the so-called 'underclass behaviours' that worry political elites and policy experts.

This is because welfare state retrenchment impacts the ghetto not simply by curtailing the investment and income streams flowing into it but also, more significantly, by unknitting the entire web of 'indirect social relations' (Calhoun 1991) sustained by public institutions and by the private organizations that these in turn support. The substitution of the penal state for the semi-welfare state cannot but reinforce the very socioeconomic instability and interepersonal violence it is supposed to allay (Wacquant 1996).

Elias thus helps us to 'bring the state back in' in the analysis of the nexus of caste, class and space in the American hyperghetto. Examination of the state's role ought to include (i) all levels of the governmental apparatus (federal, state, county and municipal) as well as the strategies and practices of ghetto residents towards them; (ii) not only welfare and 'anti-poverty' policies but the whole gamut of state activities that affect the sociospatial structuring of inequality, including criminal and penal policies; (iii) both what public authority does and what it fails to do, for the state moulds urban marginality not only by commission but also – and perhaps most decisively in the case of the United States – by (socially and racially selective) omission.

Taking Elias into America's dark ghetto suggests that theoretical models of the latter's transformation (and beyond it, of the reconfiguration of the metropolitan order) that omit the state, its organizational capacities, policies and discourses, and its actual street-level modalities of intervention, do so at the cost of forbidding themselves to unearth the *distinctively political roots of the patterning of racial and class exclusion* of which today's hyperghetto is the concrete materialization. And they are at grave risk of being invoked to recommend prescriptions that can do little more than provide *ex post facto* legitimation for the policies of urban abandonment and repressive containment of the black (sub-)proletariat that are the main cause of the continued aggravation of the plight of America's urban outcasts.

NOTES

1. Part I of this chapter is based on two talks: the first was delivered at the Conference on 'Transatlantic Man/L'Amérique des Français' organized by

the University of Paris-Sorbonne and New York University in Paris on 10–12 June 1991; the second was given to the Sociology Department Colloquium Series, University of California at Berkeley, 18 February 1992. It appeared as 'Décivilisation et démonisation: la mutation du ghetto noir américain', in Christine Fauré and Tom Bishop (eds.), *L'Amérique des français*, Paris: Editions François Bourin, 1992, pp. 103–25 (it was translated into English for this volume by James Ingram and the author). Part II is based on a lecture given at the Amsterdam School for Social Science Research on 26 November 1996; it was published as 'Elias in the Dark Ghetto', *Amsterdams Sociologisch Tidjschrift* 24(3/4) (December 1997), pp. 340–8.

2. The notion of 'underclass' thus tends to fulfil a role similar to that bestowed in an earlier era upon that icon of American racial ideology that is the familiar character of Sambo (cf. Boskin 1986).

3. Stephen Mennell discusses four possible cases of de-civilizing – the onset of the 'permissive society' in the 1950s, the recent rise of violence in the United States, the Holocaust and the collapse of the great empires – but none of them accords fully with his proposed definition of the process (1990: 205–23). The trajectory of the black American ghetto, on the other hand, comes very close.

4. The informalization of the American economy is a structural and not a cyclical phenomenon, spurred by its leading sectors (Sassen 1989). However, the growth of the informal sector of the ghetto economy is also 'residual', that is, due to the withering of formal wage work and regular economic activities.

5. For a useful review of various 'theories' of the 'underclass', see Marks (1991); for a devastating critique of the policy uses of this bogus concept, see Gans (1991). Two paradigmatic expressions of the orthodox view are Ricketts and Sawhill 1988; and *Chicago Tribune* 1986. One can readily detect from them the near-complete convergence of scholarly and journalistic visions of the alleged group.

6. This is the case of William Julius Wilson, who, more than any other author, rightfully insists on the economic roots of the decline of the ghetto and has recently declared himself ready to forsake the term 'underclass' if it turned out that it restrains research more than it facilitates it (see Wilson 1991).

7. In this respect, the 'underclass' is similar to (North African) immigrants in current French sociopolitical reasoning (Adbelmalek Sayad 1986).

8. One could make a strong case that it is in fact *negative*, as the prefabricated problematic of the 'underclass' prevents organized research into the social bases and intersection of deproletarianization and racial division in the US city and its articulation (and obfuscation) in public discourses and state policy.

REFERENCES

Anderson, Elijah 1990, *Streetwise: Race, Class and Change in an Urban Community*, Chicago: University of Chicago Press.
Auletta, Ken 1982, *The Underclass*, New York: Random House.
Boltanski, Luc 1987 [orig. 1981], *The Making of a Class: Cadres in French Society*, Cambridge: Cambridge University Press.

Boskin, Joseph 1986, *Sambo: The Rise and Demise of an American Jester*, New York: Oxford University Press.

Bourdieu, Pierre 1980, 'Le Nord et le midi. Contribution a une analyse de l'effet Montesquieu', *Actes de la recherche en sciences sociales* 35 (November): 21–5.

Bourgois, Philippe 1989, 'In search of Horatio Alger: culture and ideology in the crack economy', *Contemporary Drug Problems* Winter: 631–2.

1992, 'Une nuit dans une "shooting gallery": enquête sur le commerce de la drogue à East Harlem', *Actes de la recherche en sciences sociales* 94 (Spring): 59–78 (English trans. 'Just another night in a shooting gallery,' *Theory, Culture & Society* 15, 2 (June 1998): 37–66).

Bursik, R.J. and Grasmick, H.G. 1993, 'Economic deprivation and neighbourhood crime rates, 1960–1980', *Law and Society Review* 27, 2: 263–83.

Calhoun, Craig 1991, 'Indirect relationships and imagined communities: large-scale social integration and the transformation of everyday life', in *Social Theory for a Changing Society*, ed Pierre Bourdieu and James Coleman, Boulder: Westview Press, pp. 95–121.

Chicago Tribune 1986, *The American Millstone: An Examination of the Nation's Permanent Underclass*, Chicago: Contemporary Books.

1991a, '849 Homicides Place 1990 in a Sad Record Book', 2 January.

1991b 'Protesters gather to save their schools', 22 May, sect. 2, pp. 1, 10.

Drake, St Clair and Cayton, Horace 1962 [orig. 1945], *Black Metropolis: A Study of Negro Life in a Northern City*, New York: Harper and Row, 2 vols., new expanded edition.

Dubin, Steve C. 1987, 'Symbolic slavery: black representations in popular culture', *Social Problems* 34(2): 122–40.

Dubrow Nancy F. and Garbarino, James 1989, 'Living in the war zone: mothers and young children in a public housing development', *Child Welfare* 68(1): 8.

Duncan, Arne 1987, 'Profiles in poverty: an ethnographic report on inner-city black youth', paper presented at the Urban Poverty Workshop, University of Chicago, October.

Duster, Troy 1988, 'Social implications of the "New" black underclass', *The Black Scholar* 19(3): 2–9.

Elias, Norbert [1970] 1978, *What Is Sociology?* New York: Columbia University Press.

1994, *The Civilizing Process*, trans. Edmund Jephcott, Oxford and Cambridge, MA: Blackwell.

Freidenberg, J. (ed.) 1995, *The Anthropology of Lower Income Urban Enclaves: The Case of East Harlem*, Annals of the New York Academy of Sciences, vol. 749, New York.

Gans, Herbert H. 1991, 'The dangers of the underclass: its harmfulness as a planning concept', in *People, Plans and Policies: Essays on Poverty, Racism, and Other National Urban Problems*, New York: Columbia University Press, pp. 328–43.

1995, *The War Against the Poor: The Underclass and Anti-Poverty Policy*, New York: Basic Books.

Geremek, Bronislaw 1976, *Les marginaux parisiens aux XIVe et XVe siècles*, Paris: Flammarion.

Gibbs, Jewelle Taylor (ed.) 1988, *Young, Black and Male in America: An Endangered Species*, New York: Auburn House Publishing Company.

Jencks, Christopher and Peterson, Paul (eds.) 1991, *The Urban Underclass*, Washington, DC: The Brookings Institution.

Joint Economic Committee 1989, *The Underclass, Hearing Before the Joint Economic Committee of the 101st Congress of the United States*, 25 May, Washington, DC: US Government Printing Office.

Jordan, Winthrop D. 1974, *The White Man's Burden: Historical Origins of Racism in the United States*, Oxford: Oxford University Press.

Kasarda, John D. 1988, 'Jobs, migration, and emerging urban mismatches', in M.G.H. McGeary and L.E. Lynn (eds.), *Urban Change and Poverty*, Washington, DC: National Academy Press, pp. 148–98.

Katz, Michael 1989, *The Undeserving Poor: From the War on Poverty to the War on Welfare*, New York: Pantheon.

Kotlowitz, Alex 1991, *There Are No Chidren Here*, New York: Doubleday.

Kozol, Jonathan 1991, *Savage Inequalities: Children in America's Schools*, New York: Crown Books.

Lehmann, Nicholas 1986, 'The origins of the underclass', *The Atlantic Monthly* (June): 31–55.

Levine, Lawrence W. 1982, 'African culture and U.S. slavery', in Joseph E. Harris (ed.), *Global Dimensions of the African Diaspora*, Cambridge, MA: Harvard University Press, pp. 128–9.

Magnet, Myron 1987 'America's underclass: what to do?', *Fortune*, 11 May: 130.

Marks, Carole 1991, 'The urban underclass', *Annual Review of Sociology* 17: 445–66.

Massey, Douglas and Denton, Nancy 1993, *American Apartheid: Segregation and the Making of the Underclass*, Cambridge, MA: Harvard University Press.

Mauss, Marcel 1968, *Essais de sociologie*, Paris: Editions de Minuit/Points.

Mead, Lawrence 1985, *Beyond Entitlement: The Social Obligations of Citizenship*, New York: The Free Press.

Meier, August and Rudwick, Elliott 1976, *From Plantation to Ghetto*, New York: Hill and Wang.

Mennell, Stephen 1990, 'Decivilizing processes: theoretical significance and some lines of research', *International Sociology* 5(2): 205–23.

Miller, Jerome G. 1996, *Search and Destroy: African-American Males in the Criminal Justice System*, Cambridge: Cambridge University Press.

Mollenkopf, John H. and Castells, Manuel (eds.) 1991, *Dual City: Restructuring New York*, New York: Russell Sage Foundation.

Murray, Charles 1984, *Losing Ground: American Social Policy, 1950–1980*, New York: Basic Books.

  1989, 'The alienated poor are devastating America's inner city. Is the same happening here?', *Sunday Times Magazine* (London), 26 Nov.: 26, 39, 43.

Myrdal, Gunnar 1962, *Challenge to Affluence*, New York: Pantheon.

NACCD 1989, *The Kerner Report: The 1968 Report of the National Advisory Commission on Civil Disorders*, New York: Pantheon.

Poulantzas, Nicos 1978, *L'Etat, le pouvoir et le socialisme*, Paris: Presses Universitaires de France.

Ricketts, Erol R. and Sawhill, Isabell V. 1988, 'Defining and measuring the underclass', *Journal of Policy Analysis and Management* 7 (Winter): 316–25.

Rieder, Jonathan 1985, *Canarsie: Italians and Jews of Brooklyn against Liberalism*, Cambridge, MA: Harvard University Press.

Sassen, Saskia 1989, 'New York City's informal economy', in Alejandro Portes, Manuel Castells and Lauren A. Benton (eds.), *The Informal Economy*, Baltimore: The Johns Hopkins University Press, pp. 60–77.

1990, 'Economic restructuring and the American city', *Annual Review of Sociology* 16: 465–90.

Sayad, Adbelmalek 1986, '"Coûts" et "profits" de l'immigration: les présupposés politiques d'un débat économique', *Actes de la recherche en sciences sociales* 61 (March): 79–82.

Time Magazine 1977, 'The underclass', *Time*, 29 August: 14–15.

Wacquant, Loïc 1992, 'Pour en finir avec le mythe des "cités-ghettos"', *Les Annales de la recherche urbaine* 52 (September): 20–30.

1994, 'The new urban color line: the state and fate of the ghetto in post-fordist America', in Craig Calhoun (ed.), *Social Theory and the Politics of Identity*, Oxford: Basil Blackwell, pp. 231–76.

1996, 'De l'Etat charitable à l'Etat pénal: notes sur le traitement politique de la misère en Amérique', *Regards sociologiques* 11: 30–8.

1997a, 'Three pernicious premises in the study of the American ghetto', *International Journal of Urban and Regional Research* 21, 2 (June), 'Events and Debate': 341–53.

1997b, 'Negative social capital: state breakdown and social destitution in America's urban core', *The Netherlands Journal of the Built Environment* (Special issue on 'Spatial Segregation, Concentration, and Ghetto Formation') 13(1): 25–40.

Weiher, George 1991, *The Fractured Metropolis: Political Fragmentation and Metropolitan Segregation*, Albany: State University of New York Press.

Williams, T. 1989, *The Cocaine Kids: The Inside Story of a Teenage Drug Ring*, Reading, MA: Addison-Wesley.

Wilson, William Julius 1987, *The Truly Disadvantaged: The Inner City, the Underclass and Public Policy*, Chicago: University of Chicago Press.

1991, 'Studying inner-city social dislocations: the challenge of public agenda research', *American Sociological Review* 56(1): 1–14.

1996, *When Work Disappears*, New York: Knopf.

7   Elias on class and stratification

Steven Loyal

Introduction

Unusually for a sociologist, Elias was not prone to extended reflection on the relative theoretical merits of the 'grand masters' (although see Elias 1994). Nevertheless, his work does bear the imprint of both Marx and Weber, if less obviously than that of Comte and Durkheim. Like both Marx and Weber, Elias sought answers to rather big historical questions. For all three the origins and development of the patterns of social stratification and class conflict associated with the kind of advanced, capitalist societies found in Western Europe were central theoretical and empirical concerns. Although Elias rarely systematically discussed the concept of class, it nevertheless plays a fundamental role in the analytical rubric of 'process sociology'. This is clearly the case in his books dealing specifically with processes of stratification – *The Established and Outsiders* (1994) and *The Court Society* (1983). It also applies to the more abstract elaboration of the 'game models' in *What is Sociology?* (1978). But, most importantly, in view of the genealogy of his work, class also functions as a central dynamic concept in *The Civilizing Process* (2000). In this chapter, Elias's processual understanding of class is outlined and compared with the concept of class as it appears in the Marxian and Weberian traditions.

Marx and Weber on class: some shared assumptions

Despite recent flirtations with 'post-class' formulations and the relativist and discursive currents associated with late twentieth-century identity politics, class analysis retains a pivotal role in sociological analyses. However, paradigmatic longevity has not engendered conceptual clarity, let alone consensus. Class remains, in Gallie's terms, 'an essentially contested concept' (1955). However, for the sake of argument, it is useful to distinguish three theoretical orientations. Firstly, there are interpretations in which class refers to patterns of structured inequality consequent upon the possession of economic resources (and thereby power).

122

Secondly, there is a more pragmatic tradition that takes a combination of more heterogeneous factors such as prestige, status, culture or lifestyle, as the point of departure in the analysis of social stratification and inequality. And thirdly, there is an action-centred approach in which the idea of class is invoked only in relation to actual or potential social and political actors in the context of specific, historical conflicts and struggles (Crompton 1993).

The Marxian tradition has been predominantly associated with the first and third orientations, that is, class as an index of the differential access to economic resources, and, given Marxism's status as primarily a political practice, class as manifesting itself in conflict and struggle. However, despite the centrality of class in his work, Marx never provided an explicit and systematic definition of the concept, and there is voluminous and ongoing debate about the 'conceptual slippage' in his work. The simple binary view contained in *The Communist Manifesto* (1848) is complicated by the more complex and nuanced account of class fractions in *The Eighteenth Brumaire* (1858) and diverse and sometimes inconsistent formulations in *Theories of Surplus Value* (1863) and *Capital, Volume III* (1865). This conceptual fluidity, as Sayer (1987) rightly points out, reflects both the relational and the historical character of social reality itself and the various different levels of abstraction at which Marx, like Elias, applied his categories.

Such empirical and historical complexity notwithstanding, there is a consistent kernel in Marx's interpretation of class. This emerges from his vision of an overarching trajectory in historical development, and the commitment to social relations of material production as the key analytic point of departure (see, in particular, Marx 1846). The architecture of this interpretative schema was summarized rather succinctly in the *Grundrisse* in which Marx made a fundamental distinction between the patterns of personal domination characterizing pre-capitalist social relations, and the pattern of domination through objects and private property which is the defining feature of the wage relation under capitalism (1858: 95).[1] Although class as a general category applies to all previous agrarian societies, Marx insisted on the specificity of class relations under capitalism. In pre-capitalist societies, the processes of exploitation and surplus production were based upon a multiplicity of 'extra-economic' factors (and notably included legally sanctioned violence), which characterized a situation of 'personalized dependence'. Under capitalism, processes of economic exploitation for the first time came to operate purely in relation to objective and abstract economic criteria. With the severing of property from its 'former social and political embellishments and associations' (1865: 618), the subordination of the labourer was guaranteed by the 'dull compulsion of economic relations' (1867: 737).

For Weber, in the context of a multidimensional approach to social stratification, class along with status and party are seen as major factors shaping power relationships. But although class is seen as only one factor among many, Weber does, at least provide a clear sociological definition of class in modern society. For Weber, class situation reflected the market determination of life chances. Class had an intrinsic connection to the market to the extent that it could only be understood in terms of a market situation where various assets attributed to individuals are recognized as resources. These resources are primarily private property, skills and education. And it is the ability to *utilize* such resources in a market that determined an individual's life chances. Class then referred primarily to economic criteria. Weber posited a fourfold classification of class which includes: the working class as a whole; the petty bourgeoisie; technicians, specialists and lower-level management; and classes privileged through property and education.

Weber, like Marx, made much of the contrast between class and status: '"classes" are stratified according to their relations to the production and acquisition of goods; whereas "status groups" are stratified according to the principles of their consumption of goods as represented by special "styles of life"' (1970: 193). Status is determined by a specific, positive or negative, social estimation of 'honour'. Whereas for classes, where 'class consciousness' remains generally contingent, status groups refer to collections of 'conscious' individuals, often pursuing material and sym-bolic rewards, with shared identities formed through a process of social closure.

Despite the fact that, within the sociological tradition, the Marxian and Weberian traditions are generally posited as incompatible alternatives, there are definite continuities and areas of overlap. And, ironically, it is this corpus of shared assumptions that is in fact most problematic in the approaches of both to problems of class and social stratification. In different ways, both place a very strong emphasis on economic factors in shaping class. As a result, they both tend, though Marx more so than Weber, to neglect other non-economic processes of stratification in modern societies, particularly those associated with race and gender. Likewise, they both tend to downplay the role of symbolic and cultural factors in class structuration and domination.

More recently, Erik Olin Wright and John Goldthorpe have reformu-lated the Marxist and Weberian approaches to class respectively. And, ironically, given their rhetorical opposition, these approaches increasingly resemble each other. Both recognize that class advantages derive from the ownership and possession of property, knowledge, skills and creden-tials, and labour power. They also share the assumption that occupational categories can serve as a useful proxy for class position. Classes are seen to be determined by economic factors with social, cultural and psychological factors having little explanatory role in their formation. Tied to this is a conception of class as an objective phenomenon, which exists independently of the consciousness and intentions of the individuals who constitute it.

Elias and class

While the concepts of class, stratification and functional differentiation appear as central themes in *The Court Society* (1983), *The Established and Outsiders* (1994), *The Germans* (1996) and various essays (1950, 2000b[1929]) they also play a fundamental role in Elias's magnum opus, *The Civilizing Process* (*TCP*) (2000a). The new translation of the book has rectified one major omission from the previously published English versions: Volume I is sub-titled *Changes in the Behaviour of the Secular Upper Classes in the West* in place of *The History of Manners*. The implications of this correction, *prima facie*, seem fairly trivial and unnecessarily pedantic. However, I want to argue that they are of crucial significance, underlining the central role of Elias's conception of class and highlighting the importance of class dynamics in the European civilizing process.

In *TCP*, Elias provides a delineation of class relationships and their complex and shifting transformation from the medieval to the modern period, with the development of the absolute monarchies constituting a decisive intermediary phase. According to Elias, in medieval society, land constituted the most important means of production and source of property, wealth, and power. After the ninth century, demographic pressure, population movements and declining opportunities for the acquisition of new land by conquest created a situation in which the division between those who had land and those who did not formed an increasingly significant *horizontal* line of demarcation within society, cutting across vertical class divisions. On the one hand, there stood land-monopolizing warrior families, noble houses and landowners, but also peasants, bondsmen, serfs and hospites who occupied a piece of land that supported them. On the other hand, we see individuals from both classes deprived of land. Thus both the knightly and the labouring classes became increasingly divided in their relationship to ownership of and access to land. *Vis-à-vis* the former, Elias identifies a tripartite distinction between those knights who ruled over one or more small estates, a smaller number who ruled large estates, and those without land, who placed themselves in the service of greater knights. The landless knights went on to take on a variety of different social functions including becoming *Minnesanger* or joining the Crusades. Of the lower classes, those serfs who worked on land could be distinguished from those displaced by a shortage of opportunities who joined the growing ranks of urban artisans in the rapidly growing towns. Particularly after the eleventh century the growing complexity of the urban economy saw the proliferation of exchange relationships, increasing use of money and the extension of the division of labour. The growth of the money economy carried different implications for different strata, in particular the warrior nobility, kings and princes, and the bourgeoisie. The inflation of prices which followed the increase in monetary flows had profoundly disastrous consequences for those on fixed incomes, and particularly the feudal lords who were dependent on fixed rents from their estates. Over time, the declining relative value of rental incomes saw the impoverishment of formerly powerful knights and weaker nobles who were forced variously to sell off their estates and or move into paid the employment of kings and more powerful nobles. On the other hand, those whose incomes rose from growing monetary circulation and commercial activity – principally certain sections of the bourgeoisie and the king – benefited greatly from these processes.

From about the eleventh century these dynamics saw the reversal of the processes of fragmentation and decentralization that marked the early feudal period. The growing power of the centre was tied to the monarch's greater access to the growing money economy. Monopolies on taxation underwrote and reinforced a growing monopoly on the means of violence. These 'centripetal' forces signalled processes of internal pacification and the earliest phases of state formation. And these processes in turn saw the emergence of the two major fractions of the bourgeoisie: the commercial merchants and the administrators of the *noblesse de robe*.

According to Elias, the structure of the *Ancien Régime* displayed a complex, fluid configuration of class forces with many major class groupings containing within them their own class fractions. These can again be delineated according to a division between the rural and the urban:

The secular society of the French *Ancien Régime* consisted, more markedly than that of the nineteenth century, of two sectors: a larger rural agrarian sector, and an urban-bourgeois one which was smaller, but steadily if slowly gaining in economic strength. In both there was a lower stratum, in the latter the urban poor, the mass of journeymen and workers, in the former the peasants. In both there was a lower middle stratum, in the latter the small artisans and probably the lowest officials too, in the former the poorer landed gentry in provincial corners; in both an upper middle stratum, in the latter the wealthy merchants, the high civic officials and even in the provinces the highest judicial and administrative officials, and in the former the more well-off country and provincial aristocracy. In both sectors, finally, there was a leading stratum extending into the court, in the latter the high bureaucracy, the *noblesse de robe*, and the courtly nobility, the elite of the *noblesse d'épée* in the former. In the tensions within and between these sectors, complicated by the tensions and alliances of both with a clergy structured on a similar hierarchy, the king carefully maintained equilibrium. (2000a: 361–2)

This equilibrium was maintained and reproduced through the royal mechanism: the internal balance of social forces that were leading to the concentration of power chances in the social position of the king, within the developing state. Here, it was not simply a monopoly of the means of violence (and the tax monopoly which reinforced it) that allowed the king to hold the different classes in check, but the social constellation which made these groups dependent on a coordinating and arbitrating function. However, the interests and divisions between these groups were by no means simple and clear-cut, as they had been to a greater degree during the medieval period. The increasing division of functions in society transformed the pattern of human relations: clear uncomplicated relationships of friendship or enmity gave way to a more complex situation in which contradictory feelings, interests and valuations coexisted within interdependent individuals as a 'mixture of muted affection and muted dislike' (2000a: 318). In consequence of a growing social and economic complexity people and groups became in some way dependent upon one another. They were potential friends, allies or partners and at the same time potential opponents, competitors or enemies. Denser figurational complexes also meant that every action taken against an opponent could also threaten its perpetrator by disturbing the whole mechanism of chains of interdependent checks and balances. As a result, individuals and groups were cast back and forth between their shared, split and contradictory interests. They oscillated between the desire to win major advantages over their social opponents and the fear of unbalancing the whole social apparatus, on the functioning of which their social existence depended. It was the very multipolarity of this system that underpinned the power of the absolute monarchs who were able to steer intergroup conflicts and balances to their own advantage. To preserve this stalemate the absolute monarchs were careful not to become overidentified with those of any other class or group.

Conscious of the historical relativity of the figurations to which sociological concepts refer, Elias was wary of comparing the bourgeoisie of the absolutist period with those of later periods. In addition, both the bourgeoisie and the nobility were far from homogenous groupings with numerous class fractions and divisions of interest within each stratum (1983: 270–1). This complex division of interests meant for Elias that the objective of some sections of the bourgeoisie in the sixteenth and seventeenth centuries was not, as it became in 1789, to eliminate the nobility as a class and social institution, but rather to supplement or supplant the aristocracy by obtaining an aristocratic title and its attendant privileges. This was especially the case of the leading group of the third estate, the *noblesse de robe* who carried out largely administrative functions and who wished to see themselves as a nobility equal to the 'nobility of the sword'.[2] It was this defence and pursuit of the institution of privilege that ensured that the bourgeoisie, as a 'dual fronted class', could never deliver the final blow against the nobility, for to do so would have meant seeing an end to their own privileges, and hence their social existence.

In his discussion of the royal mechanism, Elias was careful to note that the antagonisms between the various classes and strata did not, on the whole, take the form of overt conflict. Rather, dynamic figurational processes including increasing monetarization and commercialization saw the shifting of power ratios to the advantage of the emerging bourgeoisie and the central authority on the one hand, and the disadvantage of the weaker lords on the other.

In Part I of *TCP* changes in social constraints are linked to shifts in self-restraint. Elias aims to show how the personality structure is integrally tied to the social structure. That is, he demonstrates how the changes in a particular order and direction of the psychical habitus, as it is expressed in standards of behaviour and psychological makeup, has changed in European society since the Middle Ages as a result of shifts in social relationships, figurational interdependencies and social functions. The formation of court society involved a number of such changes. These included: increasing social pressure to exercise a stricter, more even self-control of the affects; the removal behind the scenes of many bodily functions and an increasing threshold of repugnance; an advance in the frontiers of modesty and shame; a change in standards of delicacy; a growth of distance in the behaviour between adults and children; and a changing balance between external and internal constraints. The significant class dimension of these shifts in the mental and emotional structure of these individuals related not only to the affective expression in outward behaviours – in bodily carriage, gestures, facial expressions, the increasing use of visual cues and dress – but also in the inner, psychical structure of individuals, in the relation between superego and the affects. That is to say, there were very marked differences in social personality structure at various levels of society according to class position.

This is brought out more fully in his discussion of medieval society. On one hand, Elias points to the marked overall social differences *between* medieval and absolutist social formations, for example in relation to the pervasiveness and intensity of violence. On the other hand, he also acknowledges the differences between social and class strata *within* these societies. In addition, within both social formations class is expressed not only in terms of the social relationships between individuals but also within individuals in their personality makeup and habitus.

The medieval psyche and structure of feeling corresponded to the specific structure of medieval society, and, in particular, the existence of extreme differences in wealth and the absence of a central power strong enough to compel individuals to exercise restraint. In such a society individuals were quicker to respond: their drives were more open, and more spontaneous than in later periods, and emotions less evenly regulated and liable to oscillate between extremes. But, at the same time, in relation to these psychic structures and the balances between the affects and superego, there were also marked differences between social groups.[3] Just as the contrast of wealth between the highest and lowest classes of this society was extremely great, so too was their behaviour. Thus, for example, the greater aggressiveness of the secular upper warrior class meant that it possessed a different scale of values and distinctive psychic economy from those of other classes such as the clergy and the peasantry. Killing and plundering were attributes of the knightly class, a part of its social function and a source of pride. This expressed a specific balance in the relationship between the superego and various drives and affects. In other respects the nature of the constraint on the upper classes differed from that on the lower classes for straightforward material reasons:

. . . by and large the lower strata, the oppressed and poorer outsider groups at a given stage of development, tend to follow their drives and affects more directly and spontaneously, that their conduct is less strictly regulated than that of the respective upper strata. The compulsions operating upon the lower strata are predominantly of a direct, physical kind, the threat of physical pain or annihilation by the sword, poverty or hunger. That type of pressure, however, does not induce a stable transformation of constraints through others, or 'external' constraints, into 'self-restraints'. (2000: 382)

As the upper warrior classes, through increasing social competition and the formation of denser figurational chains, became increasingly dependent on other classes and upon the king, they began to cultivate a conspicuously affluent mode of life involving status display. The new modes of behaviour and function of the warrior class in court society reflected both their loss of power in relation to the monarch and their attempt to maintain social distinction from the rising bourgeoisie. In due course, these behaviours engendered a transformation of their whole drive and affect economy in the direction of a more continuous, stable and even regulation of drives and affects in all areas of conduct and in all sectors of

life. The ability of the upper classes to maintain their position by effect-
ing social closure required considerable sanctioning behaviour within the
group. Elias reveals the prestige/shame mechanisms through which this
was achieved (see Scheff, this volume):

> The effort and foresight which it costs to maintain the position of the upper
> class is expressed in the internal commerce of its members with each other by
> the degree of reciprocal supervision they practise on one another, by the severe
> stigmatization and penalties they impose upon those members who breach the
> common distinguishing code . . . it is this fear of loss of prestige in the eyes of
> others, instilled as self-compulsion, whether in the form of shame or a sense of
> honour, which assures the habitual reproduction of distinctive conduct, and the
> strict drive-control underlying it, in individual people. (2000a: 385)

However, as the bourgeoisie adopted the behavioural models of the nobility these models of conduct became progressively devalued as a means
of distinguishing the upper class. This in turn led to further refinement
of upper-class behaviour. It was through this mechanism that 'the development of court customs, their dissemination downwards, their slight
social deformation, their devaluation as marks of distinction – the perpetual movement in the behaviour patterns of the upper class received its
momentum' (2000a: 86). However, the adoption of either manners or
patterns of speech by the bourgeoisie, was not a simple downward movement, but expressed a 'double movement' – a courtization of bourgeois
people and a bourgeoisification of courtly people. This 'double movement' of 'colonization' and 'repulsion' (2000a: 430) became increasingly
reciprocal from the seventeenth to the eighteenth century as the power
balance between the two groups shifted. By the end of the eighteenth
century, the French upper class had attained the standard of manners
that was to be taken for granted in the whole society. There had been a
penetration of the middle classes, the working classes and the peasantry
and a corresponding change in their economy of drives and emotions
as models spread and became fused with others and modified in accordance with the position of the groups carrying them. As we shall see later,
the specific contours of this process has considerable implications for the
development of individuals' national habitus.

For Elias, increasing figurational interdependence facilitates the diffusion of behavioural norms within and between countries. The most
influential courtly society in the eighteenth century was in France, the
richest, most powerful and centralized country of the time. And it was
French codes of conduct, manners, language and taste that spread to
other European courts. The gradual result of this diffusion of manners
and behaviour between countries was the gradual formation of a courtly

aristocracy embracing Western Europe. Differences between countries were overlain by class differences. That is those in courtly-aristocratic society generally shared a uniformity in language (Italian then French) as well as a shared literature, and a similarity in manners and taste, a similar lifestyle. Then, however, from about middle of eighteenth century, though again at different times in different countries, a reversal occurred as national integration began to displace integration based on social estate. That is to say, national differences between people became more important than class differences. The rise of the middle classes led to a shift of power away from the court-aristocracy to various national bourgeois societies. Concomitantly the ties between the court-aristocracies of different countries became considerably weakened as marked by the emergence of various national languages.

Such a spread and corresponding modification of the forms of life of the upper classes through specific models of conduct to those below them was followed by the spread of Western behavioural models to the upper strata in other nations outside of the West, and eventually to the lower classes in those nations too, through a process of colonialism. Looked at historically and globally, as a process functional democratization involves 'diminishing contrasts, increasing varieties' (2000a: 382).

As we can see, in *TCP* Elias's distinctive approach to class, inequality and power involves the examination of the emergent dynamics of pluralities of interacting and interdependent individuals (figurations). This perspective posits a strong connection between the social structure and the personality structure: webs of relationships (figurations) form the conditions of possibility for the shaping and constitution of the habitus and psyche of individuals and groups. Any discussion of figurations as structured, yet dynamic, webs of interdependent individuals presupposes a relational understanding of power ratios between individuals. All human relationships are characterized by differential balances of power. Power here is conceptualized as a polymorphous characteristic of relationships between interdependent individuals. The idea of power ratio presupposes the concepts of function and dependence: 'we depend on others; others depend on us. In so far as we are more dependent on others than they are on us, more directed by others than they are on us, they have power over us' (1978: 132).

Elias's approach to class is coloured also by two characteristic tenets of his epistemology. Firstly, aware of the inadequacy of sociological categories for capturing the social world, Elias seeks to develop concepts which attend to both the *processual* and *relational* nature of social life. Secondly, given the propensity of accounts of stratification and inequality to embody heteronomous valuations, Elias attempts to provide a less 'involved' characterization of class and inequality *vis-à-vis* 'a detour via detachment' (see Kilminster in this volume).

At one level, Elias's work on class, like Bourdieu's in *Distinction*, both draws upon and attempts to reconsider the distinction between class and *Stand* found in Marx and Weber.[4] In *Court Society* he talks of the existence of two different world-views – an estate ethos and an economic ethos:

> On the one hand we have the social ethos of the professional bourgeoisie, whose norms oblige the bourgeoisie to subordinate expenses to income, and where possible, to keep present consumption below the level of income so that the difference can be invested in savings in the hope of increased future income . . . Prestige consumption diverges. In societies in which the status consumption ethos predominates, the mere preservation of the existing social position of the family, not to speak of an increase in social prestige, depends on the ability to make the cost of maintaining one's household and one's expenditure match one's social rank, the status one possesses or aspires to. (1983: 67)

Elias's discussion has close parallels both with Marx's distinction between the personal forms of domination characterizing feudalism and the social relationships which are increasingly being mediated by things in capitalism, as well as with Weber's discussion of 'conspicuous consumption' seen not simply as a luxury, but as a necessity for the existence of status groups. But he extends these insights by moving beyond the stark opposition between feudal and capitalist/industrial social formations. Elias's processual approach is more sensitive to the distinctive transitionary stage involving absolutist forms of rule in the later stages of court society.

Although his work is clearly influenced by Marx and Weber, Elias's approach shares little with contemporary neo-Marxist and neo-Weberian standpoints.[5] These approaches are problematical on ontological, epistemological, substantive and political/normative grounds. In terms of epistemology, their conceptual apparatus is both unreflective and clumsy, simplifying what are acutely complex processes. Such conceptual problems are compounded by a tendency both to transform analytical abstractions of various spheres in society (the social, political, economic, etc.) into independent causal forces and to 'process-reduction'. Thus by utilizing static models based on linear ladder-like metaphors they impose straightforward binaries on complex, amorphous and fluid class configurations. Contemporary quantitative approaches to class often assume, for example (though they use a different conceptual idiom), that when a bourgeois group rises, other groups such as the nobility will simultaneously fall, or that when the proletariat rises, the bourgeoisie will decline. Like Wittgenstein, Elias recognizes that language often misleads us by obscuring both difference and dynamic processes. Thus not only does the content of our class concepts change historically, but also the same class designation often covers social formations of different types or, in other words, different stages of an overall social development. For instance, later members of the nobility may not necessarily have descended from earlier ones (many were in fact descendants of non-noble families); and, similarly, the rise of a new type of noble formation (a courtly nobility) can go hand-in-hand with the decline of an older type within the same class (a warrior nobility). In contrast to other approaches to stratification, Elias does not confuse social rank with social power. For instance, although the nobility constituted the highest-ranking class in the *Ancien Régime* it was by no means the most powerful. The extraordinary power of the royal family within the overall balance of social forces in eighteenth-century France made it possible for them, in order to strengthen their position or to satisfy their personal inclination, to reduce the effective power of people of high rank and to increase that of people of lower rank.

Secondly, contemporary neo-Marxist and neo-Weberian approaches are profoundly unhistorical, positing an essentially synchronic present-centred analysis of class and symptomatic of what Elias terms elsewhere, 'a retreat of sociologists into the present' (1987). Thus, fundamentally important questions such as the formation of classes as well as the historical construction of the labour market (Polyani 2001 [1944]) remain well outside their purview. By contrast, Elias's historical sociology allows for a processual model of class which recognizes the importance of long-term structural changes and transformations in class structure. It is only in this context, across the sweep of centuries, that one can see the sharp contrasts between the behaviour of different social groups steadily diminishing. Here, classes are made and remade in specific conjunctures of figurational complexes where balances of power remain tensile and fluid. This perspective brings into view the permanent interdependence of rising and sinking movements, and processes of class integration and disintegration. With shifts in the power balance between rising and declining groups, we can also begin to see established groups becoming outsiders and outsiders becoming established. Such a processual perspective allows a break with the manichean view of dominant and dominated agents.

Moreover, an acknowledgement of the reciprocal forms of dependency characterizing class relations also means that the forms of life of upper and lower strata are continually mingling, in a two-way process, albeit differentially. A good example is the diffusion of lower-class characteristics: for example, the expectation in Western society that all individuals should earn their own living and 'pay their way' is spreading to all social classes. And, at the same time, upper-class models of behaviour are likewise spreading to society at large. Again, this implies the dissolution of hard and fixed boundaries between classes. However, it is important to note that Elias is not positing a one-way progress theory. Processes whereby individuals are subject to progressively greater constraints – both internal and external – are open-ended. Although a definite dynamic associated with the lengthening and increasing density of interdependency chains is built into figurational models, processes involving class dynamics nevertheless remain, on the whole, empirical questions. Examined from a long-term and global point of view, increasing functional democratization has undoubtedly led to the amelioration of class conflict and invoked growing processes of informalization (see Wouters in this volume). Yet, progressive movements have also been punctured by decivilizing spurts precipitating increasing social distance between groups and solidifying and augmenting variegated forms of domination (see Wacquant in this volume).

For Elias, the boundaries between classes are less exact and more blurred than conventional views of class would admit. Figurations are characterized by a multipolar balance of tensions where boundaries are constantly shifting in the course of social struggles and changes in power ratios. Economic growth and the extension of the division of labour creates a long-term shift towards lengthening and intensifying interdependencies and 'denser' figurational complexes. As individuals come to experience more overlapping and possible contradictory sets of interests and allegiances, their actions become correspondingly constrained. That is to say, the increasing likelihood of unforeseen 'boomerang' effects, constrains individuals to reflect upon, preconsider or otherwise exercise restraint in the conduct of daily life. Nevertheless, for Elias, class processes are not wholly contingent and unstructured. On the contrary, figurations have immanent dynamics, which, if understood, can reveal the emerging shapes and dynamics of social processes generally, and class struggle, specifically. The principles of these dynamic processes are elaborated in the game models.[6]

The game models together with the concept of figuration also provide a resolution to the agency/structure dichotomy. Unlike other approaches to class which are hampered either by an overemphasis on structure or agency, the subjective or the objective, the individual or the society, a figurational approach transcends the limitations of all these dualisms.

It was noted that in some ways Elias's model has many affinities with Marx's, rather than neo-Marxist approaches. In terms of later Marxist writers, it shares some conceptual symmetry with E. P. Thompson's work on class as a process: 'By class I understand a historical phenomenon, unifying a number of disparate and seemingly unconnected events . . . I emphasize that it is a historical phenomenon. I do not see class as a "structure", nor even as a "category", but as something which in fact happens' (1968: 9). Or again:

When, in discussing class, one finds oneself too frequently commencing sentences with 'it', it is time to place oneself under some historical control, or one is in danger of becoming the slave of one's own categories. Sociologists who have stopped the time machine and, with a good deal of conceptual huffing and puffing, have gone down the engine room to look, tell us that nowhere at all have they been able to locate and classify a class. They can only find a multitude of people with different occupations, incomes, status-hierarchies, and the rest. Of course they are right, since class is not this or that part of the machine, but the way the machine works once it is set in motion – not this interest and that interest, but the friction of interests – the movement itself, the heat, the thundering noise . . . When we speak of class we are thinking of a very loosely defined body of people who share the same categories of interests, social experiences, traditions and value-system, who have a disposition to behave as a class, to define themselves in their actions and in their consciousness in relation to other groups of people in class ways. But class itself is not a thing, it is an happening. (1978: 295)

Thompson's dialectical approach rejects both unsophisticated forms of conceptualization and crude impositions of a base/superstructure model operating on the basis of an ideal/material dichotomy. He is also emphatic that classes cannot be identified independently of class consciousness or experience, yet, still regards class structuration in terms of processes embedded in relations of production. Like Elias, he argues that it is the separation of the subjective and the objective or the substantive division of the social world into separate spheres that is problematic: 'in the actual course of historical or sociological (as well as political) analysis it is of great importance to remember that social and cultural phenomena do not trail after the economic at some remote remove; they are, at their source, immersed in the same nexus of relationship' (1978: 292).

Elias shares this materialist framework and similarly aims to transcend the limitations of economically reductionist views of class. Symbolic and cultural factors are regarded as equally important as economic criteria in structuring class relationships. In order to understand power differences it is not simply a question of looking at economic factors, such as which group holds a monopoly of the means of production. For Elias, one also has to look at who possesses a monopoly of the means of violence and orientation, as well as to figurational aspects of power differentials due primarily to differences in the degree of organization of human beings. This applies equally to cases where a struggle for economic resources is *prima facie* dominant, for example in the conflict between workers and factory managers. Even here other sources of dispute tend to be operative. In fact, Elias argues that the economic aspects of established–outsider conflicts are most pronounced where the balance of power between the contenders is very uneven. Consequently, as the balance of power becomes more equal through functional democratization, non-economic conflicts tend to come to the fore. Thus, the more outsider groups move away from meeting basic subsistence needs, from satisfying their basic animalic or material needs including survival and physical threats, 'the more keenly they feel social inferiority, the inferiority of power and status from which they suffer' (1994: xix). Yet, although emphasizing the importance of non-economic needs, Elias continues to recognize the fact that the meeting of primary needs still remains a major goal of vast sections of humankind.

Like Thompson, Elias connects social structure and class position to the habitus of individuals through concrete analysis. However, in this respect he goes beyond Thompson's work in which, according to Anderson (1980), the concept of experience tends to remain vague, by systematically discussing the psychic structure and experience of individuals. Finally, Thompson's attempt to write history from 'below' is matched by Elias's analysis of history and class struggle – facilitated by the concept of figurations – from both above and below, as well as from both 'we' and 'they' perspectives (1996: 44–6).

Thus we can discern a number of parallel arguments in the work of Thompson and Elias. These general facets could in fact also be extended to the work of Bourdieu.[7] However, these similarities should perhaps be understood in terms of 'family resemblances' (Wittgenstein 1969: 17) since there is a stronger focus on non-rational factors in Elias's work on the dynamics of class relationships than is found in most other writers on the issue. In his writings, Elias not only looks at the use of distinction strategies, but also at the function of collective fantasies in maintaining social boundaries. This is most evident in his discussion of outsiders in *TCP*, *The Germans* and, importantly, in *The Established and the Outsiders*. In the *Established and the Outsiders*, Elias and Scotson note how, when the established group felt exposed to an attack against their monopolosized power resources they used stigmatization and exclusion as weapons to maintain their distinct identity, assert their superiority and keep outsiders in their place. Processes of group charisma and group disgrace involved maintaining a positive 'we-image' and a negative 'they-image' through the stigmatization of outsiders and the propagation of collective fantasies. This in turn involved generalizing the worst characteristics from the anomic minority of a group to the whole group whilst simultaneously attributing the best, most respectable behaviour onto the established group. After some time the outsider group takes on the 'they' image or group disgrace and sense of inferiority:

Where the power differential is very great, groups in an outsider position measure themselves with the yardstick of their oppressors. In terms of their oppressors' norms they find themselves wanting . . . Just as established groups, as a
matter of course, regard their superior power as a sign of their higher human
value, so outsider groups, as long as their power differential is great and submis-
sion inescapable, emotionally experience their *power inferiority* as a sign of *human
inferiority*.[8] (1994: xxvi)

As was the case with the nobility in eighteenth-century France, the
established group maintained its group charisma through a 'fear of pollution'. However, such processes of exclusion and stigmatization alter
as power ratios between groups become less uneven (see Dunning this
volume). Functional democratization tends towards equalizing power
ratios. Outsider groups which had formerly accepted their inferiority and
low position in the social hierarchy, come to challenge and contest their
stigmatization and pursue a more equal access to various power resources.
Over the long term, as power differences lessen between established and
outsiders, the fantasy-laden collective 'we-images' of social superiority
characteristic of the former do begin to diminish, if very slowly.

Thus, for Elias, class is one, albeit highly significant, aspect of social
stratification.[9] It is the degree of social differentiation and the nature and
length of chains of interdependency between two (or more) groups which
provide the key to understanding established–outsider figurations. Sociologists need to examine the structural characteristics which bind groups
to each other in a specific way so that the members of one of them feel
impelled, and have sufficient power resources, to treat those of another
group collectively as inferior. These shifting social structures are intrinsically tied to psychic structures whereby modes of interaction and interdependence between individuals are modulated in class ways through
differentiated structures of feeling. The significance in class terms of the
balance between the superego and the various effects within the individual
is equally important in Elias's analysis of class.

Elias's overall approach to class is at once historical, concrete, reflexive,
relational and processual. This is achieved in part by his use of a deceptively simple figurational model to understand class processes. This allows
him to see the two-way pressures on individuals from both above and below, but also horizontally, in relation to intra-class relations and power
ratios. On this basis, intra and interclass dynamics are theorized from both
a 'we' and 'they' perspective. Here boundaries between groups are fluid
and shift as the overall nexus of interactions and interdependencies within
a figuration changes. To this we can add Elias's grounding in a sociology
of knowledge which allows him to use a reflexive approach both in terms
of concept formation and in providing the basis for a more 'detached'

reality-congruent standpoint (see Kilminster, this volume). Sensitivity to the changing emotional and substantive content of apparently enduring concepts such as class makes Elias less prone to unreflectively interpreting historical processes in terms of contemporary psychic and emotional structures, or conceptual levels of integration.

The issue of class analysis on the whole has remained largely absent in most discussions of Elias's work generally, and *TCP* in particular. This is odd given the influence of Marx, Weber and Mannheim on his intellectual development. However, given the current ontological preoccupations of sociology, contemporary readings of his work have tended to emphasize the concept of figurations *vis-à-vis* the consideration of a series of what are seen to be problematic dualisms (i.e. individual versus society, agency versus structure, and micro versus macro dichotomies). Alternatively, and partly reflecting increasing academic specialization, commentators have focused entirely upon the substantive themes relating to emotions and transformations in relation to the regulation of violence. Such one-sided interpretations have been compounded by what Wood (1986) calls the current historical/sociological 'retreat from class'. One can, however, come to understand the importance of class in *TCP*, for example, only by placing the text within the wider social, political and historical context within which it was formulated. By drawing on Bourdieu (1988) we can come to understand the unfolding logic of the intellectual field in relation to a relatively autonomous social and political field. In *TCP* Elias's discussion of the sociogenesis of the conceptual antithesis between *Kultur* and *Zivilisation* should be read, in part, as an attempt to examine and understand problems confronting German society in terms of both class conflict, rising nationalism and violence, and the exclusion of the Jews following the First World War.[10] This is developed further in *The Germans* which examines the long-term factors facilitating the rise of National Socialism, including the conflict between the court-aristocratic strata and the middle classes in eighteenth and nineteenth-century Germany. For Elias the manner in which the models of the nobility are adopted and modified by the middle and lower classes constitutes a crucial component in the formation of the national habitus. The marked power ratio, social and spatial segregation, and steep formality–informality gradient between the upper and middle classes in Germany meant that the latter adopted, almost wholesale, the lifestyle, norms and behavioural codes of the military nobility while retaining or enforcing few of their own codes and values including humanism and democratization. It is for this reason that Elias's neglected essay on the naval profession (Elias 1950), in which he acknowledges the historical primacy of the behavioural codes of the navy over the army in the seventeenth century, is so important for understanding the social habitus which emerged from Britain's long-term national development.[11]

However, on another level, protracted questions concern with both representing and capturing reality, of communication and expression, of art and science were also pervasive in Germany both prior to and after unification (Janek and Toulmin 1973). It is in relation to the context of the proliferation and innovative use of metaphors and analogies, of concepts and theories that we should also situate Elias's work, later described as figurational sociology. As Goudsblom (1986) notes in his semantic approach to class, the enduring appeal of the high–low metaphor in sociology has fostered a misleading and limited image of social stratification. The concept of figuration helps us to break out of this unilinear, static and dehistoricized picture of reality that has long held sociology captive.[12] Specifically, it stands in sharp contrast to the standard one-dimensional ladder-like image of class which hampers most other sociological approaches to class.

NOTES

1. I take this and much of the following account of both Marx and Weber from Sayer (1991).
2. For an excellent discussion about the *noblesse de robe* see Goldmann (1964).
3. As Elias notes (2000a: 180): 'however uniform, therefore, the Medieval standard of control of emotions appears in comparison to later development, it contained considerable differences corresponding to the stratification of secular society itself'.
4. Of course there are many parallels with Bourdieu's work including a shared intellectual vocabulary (see Chartier 1988) and a similar grounding in the sociology of knowledge. The remarkable similarities in the thought style and world-view of Bourdieu and Elias, should, however, not be overstated. The differences in their intellectual formation both geographic and generational as well as the political context that shaped the gestation of their sociological standpoint – the rise of Nazism, and the war in Algeria – may partly account for this.
5. The question of course here is one of balance. Elias did not simply reject quantitative approaches in sociology as is evident in his essay, 'Technization and civilization' (1995).
6. For a discussion of game models see Introduction.
7. For Bourdieu's use of class see (1984; 1987; 1996). Also R. Brubaker (1985).
8. Bourdieu (1984: 471) holds a parallel view: 'Dominated agents, who assess the value of their position and their characteristics by applying system of schemes of perception and appreciation . . . tend to attribute to themselves what the distribution attributes to them . . . adjusting their expectations to their chances, defining themselves as the established order defines them.'
9. Elias actually came to prefer the term 'established–outsider relations'. But like class, it is equally prone to reification. Moreover, although more capacious than

class and constructed partly to remedy the limits of reductive class explanations in the light of broader conflicts of power, especially rising nationalism,
it can, by its very generality, hide the specific modalities and mechanisms
of class stratification as compared to say racial forms of domination, which
have their own peculiar logic. This of course probably would have been
accepted by Elias. Moreover, it may be confusing to apply the concept in
certain contexts, while studying colonialism, for example, where of course
the established have less power than the outsiders.

10. As Elias notes (2000a: 9) 'It is clear that the function of the German concept
of *Kultur* took on new life in the year 1919, and in the preceding years, partly
because a war was waged against Germany in the name of "civilization" and
because the self-image of the Germans had to be defined anew in the situation
created by the peace treaty. But it is just as clear, and can be proved, that to
a certain extent the historical situation of Germany after the war only gave
a new impulse to an antithesis which had long found expression through
these two concepts, even as far back as the eighteenth century.' See also Elias
(1994: 56–7).

11. In 1935 an Anglo-German naval agreement was concluded under which the
British government allowed Germany to build up to 35 per cent of British
naval strength. This may provide the context for this essay.

12. 'A picture held us captive. And we could not get outside it for it lay in our
language and language seemed to repeat it to us inexorably': Wittgenstein
(1958: paragraph 115).

REFERENCES

Anderson, P. 1980, *Arguments within English Marxism*, London: New Left.
Bourdieu, P. 1984, *Distinction: A Social Critique of the Judgement of Taste*, London:
    RKP.
    1987, 'What makes a social class: on the theoretical and practical existence of
    groups', *Berkeley Journal of Sociology* 32: 1–18.
    1988, *The Political Ontology of Martin Heidegger*, Cambridge: Polity.
    1996, *The State-Nobility*, Cambridge: Polity.
Brubaker, R. 1985, 'Rethinking classical theory: the sociological vision of Pierre
    Bourdieu', *Theory and Society* 14: 745–75.
Chartier, R. 1988, *Cultural History: Between Practice and Representations*, Cam-
    bridge: Polity.
Elias, N. 1950, 'Studies in the genesis of the naval profession', *British Journal of
    Sociology* 1 (4): 291–309.
    1978, *What Is Sociology?*, London: Hutchinson.
    1983 [1969], *The Court Society*, Oxford: Basil Blackwell.
    1987, 'Retreat of sociologists into the present', *Theory, Culture and Society*
    4 (2–3): 223–47.
    1994, *Reflections on a Life*, Cambridge: Polity.
    1995, 'Technization and civilization', *Theory, Culture & Society*, 12(4): 7–42.
    1996, *The Germans*, Cambridge: Polity.
    2000a [1939], *The Civilizing Process*, Oxford: Blackwell.

2000b [1929], 'On the sociology of German anti-semitism', *Journal of Classical Sociology* 1 (2): 219–25.

1994 [1965], *The Established and Outsiders*, London: Sage.

Gallie, W. 1955, 'Essentially contested concepts', *Proceedings of the Aristotelian Society* 56.

Goldmann, L. 1964, *The Hidden God: A Study of Tragic Vision in the Pensées of Pascal and the Tragedies of Racine*, London: RKP.

Goudsblom, J. 1986, 'On high and low in society and in sociology: a semantic approach to social stratification', *Sociologisch Tijdschrift* 13(1): 3–17.

Janik, A. and Toulmin, S. 1973, *Wittgenstein's Vienna*, London: Weidenfeld and Nicolson.

Marx, K. and Engels, F. 1846, *The German Ideology*, 5, London: Lawrence and Wishart.

1848, *The Communist Manifesto*, London: Lawrence and Wishart.

1852, *The Eighteenth Brumaire of Louis Bonaparte*, 11, London: Lawrence and Wishart.

1858, *Grundrisse*, 28, London: Lawrence and Wishart.

1963, *Theories of Surplus Value*, Moscow: Progress.

1865, *Capital, vol. III*, Moscow: Progress.

1867, *Capital, vol. I*, London: Lawrence and Wishart.

Polyani, K. 2001 [1944], *The Great Transformation*, Boston, MA: Deacon Press.

Sayer, D. 1987, *The Violence of Abstraction*, Oxford: Blackwell.

1991, *Capitalism and Modernity: An Excursus on Marx and Weber*, London: Routledge.

Thompson, E. P. 1968, *The Making of The English Working Classes*, Harmondsworth: Penguin.

1978, *The Poverty of Theory and Other Essays*, London: Merlin.

Weber, M. 1970, *From Max Weber*, ed. H. Gerth & C. W. Mills, London: Routledge.

Wittgenstein, L. 1958, *The Philosophical Investigations*, Oxford: Blackwell.

1969, *The Blue and Brown Books*, Oxford: Blackwell.

Wood, E. M. 1986, *The Retreat from Class*, London: Verso.

8 Elias on gender relations: the changing balance of power between the sexes

Christien Brinkgreve

Introduction

Relations between the sexes are among the most fundamental human relations: they are necessary for the continuation of the species. In this sense men and women rely upon each other and are mutually dependent, which however does not mean that power relations between them are in a state of balance. On the contrary, in almost all known human societies men enjoy supremacy over women. Although women do possess certain power resources, men managed to acquire their superior power position early in human history and have maintained it through the ages.

Yet, in the course of time power ratios between the sexes have become less unequal. This development has not been linear but has moved in spurts and regressions, and has followed different directions in various spheres of life. It is a process which takes place in various fields of life and on various levels: in intimate relations, in the economy of feelings, in the course of state formation, in legislation and in economic developments. The part-processes which make up this process are not independent of one another, and should be rather viewed as an interrelated whole. As we shall see, Elias's concept of 'figuration' and his model of established–outsiders relations seem to throw light on the problematic of gender relations.

The riddle of male power

In most known societies, the power ratio leans towards the advantage of males. Most societies have either now or in the past displayed the same pattern of division of labour and hierarchy between the sexes. Almost everywhere it has been the women's task to take care of children, collect firewood, bring water and prepare food. In contrast, hunting for wild animals, slaughtering them, waging war, making weapons, ruling and law-making are the activities most often reserved for males. Nearly everywhere males occupy the highest positions in decision-making and politics. Why is that so? Why do men dominate over women of equal age and status? That is what Goudsblom (1997) calls 'the riddle of male power'.[1]

The answer to this question can be sought in a number of ways. Religions have looked for an answer in God's will and say that God made men supervisors over women, who deserved the right of care and protection as long as they were virtuous and obedient. Some philosophers, for their part, would claim that women are less intelligent and generally less capable than men, and as such should be subordinated to men. Quite obviously, these explanations sanctioned and effectively helped to maintain the existing inequality between the sexes. At present, other types of explanations seem to be the order of the day, namely those derived from science. Evidence from palæoanthropology and sociobiology enables us to reconstruct certain hypothetical scenarios. According to one of these, the division of labour came into being very early in human history, enabling men to participate collectively in hunting and leaving women confined within a much narrower sphere of action centring on childcare and food preparation. In the long run – that is, over many generations – this division of labour effected a differentiation in personality traits. Men became predisposed towards collective hunting, and women towards collecting crops and childcare. Accordingly, this role division would have promoted a kind of natural selection of robust male individuals and more gentle and caring female ones. Such a social and mental organization offered optimal chances of survival.

In this process men attained a superior power position traceable to these original circumstances. Through hunting together they also developed superior organizational capacities. Thanks to their greater physical strength they were able to fight better, which provided them with a form of power important in a society in which readiness and capacity for the exercise of physical violence was vital for survival, and in which warfare was a frequent affair. Their supremacy grew even stronger thanks to their acquiring a monopoly of weapons. Finally, the knowledge that men accumulated consolidated their superior position. That form of cultural supremacy resulted first of all from men's greater experience in and capacity for organization. In Western Europe, for centuries men successfully monopolized a number of fields of organization and knowledge, such as religion, science, politics, administration and jurisdiction, and access to various professions which required specialized knowledge.[2]

In the course of time men managed to preserve this advantage, sometimes even to increase it, although history has seen shifts in the balance of power between men and women. This history of mutual power relations between the sexes developed neither in a linear nor monodirectional way.

Shifts in the balance of power

Taking a long view of the balance of power between men and women in Western European history, we cannot but notice the pattern of male power superiority, enduring yet complicated by particular shifts in power relations that occurred in the course of time. In his article about the changing power balance between the sexes in ancient Rome, Elias presents an interesting point of departure for this study (Elias 1987).[3] He describes how in the earlier phases of Roman society a woman was no more than her husband's property. In fact the husband was in a position to do whatever he wanted with his wife. Women had no name of their own, so if the father's name was Claudius, the daughters were called Claudia, possibly numbered, if their number was plural. Men's violence towards women was legitimate. According to the contemporary marital law, beating, wounding or even killing a wife could go unpunished. A woman had to be virtuous and obedient towards her husband. Adultery was considered a very serious offence, and (like drinking of wine, now perceived innocent) could lead to punishment by divorce or even death. Less serious offences, such as copying house keys, concocting poison, performing abortion, attending public games without the husband's permission, were punishable by divorce (Dobash and Dobash 1979). Women had hardly any rights. But, according to Elias, in the second century before Christ gender inequality among the Roman elite diminished. Looking for reasons for this trend, Elias points to such social factors as the development of a strong state with its monopoly of physical violence, able to guarantee the safety of individuals, women included, together with their income and property, as recorded in the legislation. He also argues for the importance of alliances, pointing to the fact that women maintained close ties with their own families and had their own social networks. Another important factor is the stage of development of civilization: a specific degree of civilization in manners, capacity for mutual identification (and thus of the stronger party with the weaker one too) as well as self-control. The decline of the Roman Empire was accompanied by a corresponding erosion of married women's position.

The basic pattern of male domination and female subordination remained intact for centuries, certain shifts notwithstanding. It can also be safely assumed that some variations existed, as mutual bonds and the balance of power between the sexes differed in various social strata. Thus in medieval agrarian societies power differences between the sexes among the elite played a far more important role than among lower social states. In order to survive, peasants and manual labourers relied heavily on cooperation with their wives. In their case, within the hierarchy of sexual relations and with a manifest mutual division of roles, historians note the indispensable solidarity between the spouses. Besides, women performed other important functions, such as assisting at birth, sickness, marriage or death, as well as acting as a source of news and information (Dresen-Coenders 1978; Klapisch-Zuder 1991). Although not formalized into specific professions, these vital tasks made women enjoy a certain degree of power.

With the growth of towns, which in the Low Countries (especially in Flanders and Brabant) had by the fourteenth century gradually come to be the political and cultural centres, all these functions hitherto fulfilled by women were taken over by various institutions, such as the city surgeon, the magistracy and public education system, ousting women from the public sphere, and increasingly banishing them to the household. In the division of labour which developed in the late Middle Ages and in early modern urban societies, the man was assigned the task of earning money and the woman that of household management and administration, along with the rearing of children. Over time, that development subsequently spread and intensified among wider strata of the population.

Industrialization effected an even stricter division of tasks and fields of activity between the sexes: men became breadwinners, whereas women were assigned the major task of looking after family and children. Before the advent of industrialization, besides caring for the family, women had an important share in productive work in family businesses, whether it was a peasant farm, a craftsman's workshop or a trading company. The part that women then played in work and business is apparent, for example, from the correspondence of a married merchant couple, Magdalena and Balthasar (Ozment 1986). When Balthasar was on a trip to buy fabrics, Magdalena would run the business and from a distance advise him about possible purchases. But with industrialization the fault lines already developed earlier between women's and men's work, and women's and men's worlds, grew increasingly rigorous and impenetrable. Various functions that women had performed for a long time, in shops and workshops, in trading and accountancy, were taken over by men. It came to be perceived as a woman's task, or even her vocation, to create a quiet protected climate at home in which husband and children would thrive. These ideas about women's place – at home and living in obedience to their husbands – were supported by the Church. The Church already had a long patriarchal tradition, with God in heaven as the supreme fount of authority, delegated on earth to the clergy, and at a lower level to the man as a head of the household. In this period, the concepts of domesticity and family intimacy became the hegemonic moral and emotional ideals. Initially, that situation affected only the well to do, who could afford to exempt their women from wage-work, but in the nineteenth and twentieth centuries this pattern trickled down to the other social strata as well.

This process, which barred women from public functions and made them financially dependent on their husbands, meant for them loss of certain territory and authority, and produced a balance of power even further to the advantage of men. The women's struggle for emancipation that developed during the nineteenth century was orientated first of all towards gaining access to the public domain. It culminated in the campaign for the right to vote: women's franchise was the major goal of the first wave of feminism around the turn of the nineteenth century. Later on, the struggle included access to paid work, job markets, and thus for the economic independence which became the target of the second wave of emancipation in the 1960s and 1970s. The struggle for emancipation concerned wider areas of life, including the reform of the private sphere (marital law and legal regulation of sexuality – Sevenhuijsen 1992), access to politics, culture, and education, and redistribution of paid and unpaid work.

Emancipation struggles and ideals of equality which found their expression at that time were not a self-contained phenomenon but rather part of larger social changes. They accompanied changes in the job market (from an industrial to a service society) and the rising education level of women; they exerted influence upon the law (various restrictive regulations were abolished), and brought about changes in manners and standards of emotional control among both men and women. Now men were expected to possess more empathetic capacities: they had to reckon with the wishes, ambitions and feelings of women, whereas heavy-handed ways to enforce female obedience fell into discredit.

Towards a more equalized power ratio

The three sources of male power over women that existed for centuries – physical strength, knowledge and organization – are now more equally distributed between the sexes, or (in the case of physical strength) have lost their importance. In modern industrial society, armed violence is no longer connected with physical strength, which has eroded part of the foundation of male supremacy.[4] In the fields of knowledge and organization women have largely made up for their arrears. At the close of the nineteenth century, girls obtained access to secondary and university education. As a result, gradually – and at an accelerating speed as late as the 1970s and 1980s – men lost their supremacy in the field of knowledge, which for centuries was an important source of their superiority over women. As for the field of organization, women are now catching up with men, with a number of women's organizations, networks and alliances arising that further that process. Women have entered the labour market and now attain higher positions in it. Legal obstacles, such as the prohibition on married women's employment, have been abrogated.[5] Economic independence, an important power factor, is now within their reach. Power and territory gains achieved by women have also been greatly facilitated by a number of technological developments. Modern contraception means that women's lives are no longer determined by pregnancy and childcare. In addition, rapid advances in household technology (washing machines, tumble dryers, vacuum cleaners, microwave ovens and other devices) enable them to engage in activities and ambitions other than housekeeping and childcare. Their entry into the public domain and winning certain positions in the labour market erased the sharp demarcation line between men's and women's domains. As a consequence, women have regained the power they lost with the separation of public and private spheres and have escaped their confinement within the domestic domain.

Civilization – blindness

As mentioned above, in a high-tech society physical strength loses its importance. When we think about life and work in agrarian or early industrial societies, it becomes clear how much physical strength has lost its decisive weight as a factor in power ratios. In feudal societies notoriously plagued by warfare, physical strength was an important source of power that facilitated survival and protection of one's home and property, much more than is the case in nation-states with their regulated monopoly of violence. Yet physical strength was not only vital for the survival and protection of women and children, but was a source of power in another sense too: the very threat of violence can work as a means of power and domination. In a patriarchal culture physical violence is a means of forcing women to act as men want them to. The masculine image of power is part of the culture (*machismo*).

In the meantime, abuse of women has become illegal and is no longer socially accepted, thanks in part also to changes in moral values which have taken place. Remarkably, this norm of 'civilized' behaviour has for a long time kept men blind to the male violence against women which still persists. With male supremacy losing validity, and such forms of conduct now considered coarse and primitive, people seem to display a form of cultural blindness to the existent physical violence towards women (Römkens 1992).

Analysing conditions which promote safety from physical violence as an instrument of power, we can venture the following conclusions. Of great importance is governmental protection, or legal regulations, which protect the safety of an individual (man or woman) and his/her property; so too are bonds and alliances with one's family members or people in the outside world, which fall under the category of networks or organizations. A certain standard of civilization, meaning a capacity for emotional control and mutual identification, is a prerequisite for this. In their book about women who left their husbands, most often as a reaction to abuse, Van Stolk and Wouters present a fine description of differences between the two sexes' capacity for empathy. Often, men are shown to have had no idea about their wives' experience, being unaware of the need to give it serious thought. Women, as a subordinated party, on the contrary, felt obliged to empathize with their husbands and to consider their wishes (Kapteyn 1977; Van Stolk and Wouters 1983). Economic independence is also an important factor. Besides eliminating the long-lasting male monopoly of economic resources, the elimination of the monopoly over ideological resources deserves a note too. Thus, apart from their own right to work, to have their own income and property, it is also important for women that their voice is heard, that their own vision matters, and that they have an influence upon intellectual matters and upon decision-making processes. The functioning of religion and of other systems of thought which legitimated inequality had already been questioned, but in the 1970s feminism went on to attack the androcentrism of scientific theories. The importance of the development of women's 'own voice' should be viewed from this perspective.[6] It involves not only their access to knowledge and education and to university and the Church as former bastions of male power,[7] but also the development of knowledge and meaning-generating systems in which women should also have their place.

Stubborn inequalities

Although relations between the sexes have become less unequal, we cannot claim that relations between the sexes, either in intimate or work-related circumstances, are those of equality. The ideal of harmonious inequality (Wouters and Van Stolk 1983) has given way to an ideal of equality, of equivalent partnership. However, this equality is often precarious, sometimes controversial and certainly not free from tension. It absolutely has not penetrated all social groups as an ideal, let alone as a form of practice. The unequal balance of power between the sexes, as we have seen, came into being long ago, and has been long perpetuated, although with periodical counter-movements in which this inequality was reduced when women had more power resources at their disposal. Today, ideals of equality have gained ground and the balance of power has become relatively more equal, but the old ideals and practices of male supremacy and female subordination have not disappeared and are still experienced socially as a vital reality. This situation sometimes generates conflict, not only *among* individuals, but also *within* them – in the form of an inner conflict or mental ambivalence.

In some groups inequality is still the predominant ideal of gender relations, which goes against the ruling ideal of equality. This is especially the case with Islamic groups in which, seen from the Western perspective, women's subordination and the division between women's and men's spheres are unacceptably rigid. Instances of inequality, such as a prohibition on entering public spaces or even talking with males other than one's own husband, were virtually unknown in Western societies. That leads in Holland to friction between the Dutch and Islamic groups, and also within Islamic groups – that is between women who want to live an emancipated life, and women who cannot or do not want to do so. Religion, in this case Islam, just like Christianity before, functions to legitimate inequality and the subordination of women to men.

However, it is not only between groups and within groups but also within an individual mind that a struggle can develop between the model of dominance and subordination and the ideal of equality. In their book *Vrouwen in Tweestrijd* [Women Torn Two Ways], the Dutch sociologists Wouters and Van Stolk search for an answer to the question of why women, having left men who abused them, in many cases still returned to them. They look for an answer in the conflict between the modern ideal of equality and a longing for guidance and protection still very vivid among those women, which fits the pattern of male dominance they are accustomed to, or the 'figurational ideal of harmonious inequality' which they still cherish.

How powerful this ideal of relations remains emerges from a conversation with one of the women who had deserted her husband but returned home a few days later. According to the authors, she sounded still a bit overstressed. 'Well, yeah, he thought we still had some future ahead of us, and I almost did things that I didn't really want myself (she had swallowed a great amount of pills) so I just got home. I still have to calm down but I couldn't relax at the crisis centre either, and my husband says he will help me.' The woman put herself under his control and protection again (Van Stolk and Wouters 1983). A longing to submit themselves again to their husbands' control and to retrace their rebellious steps can be heard also in other interviews with these women. Nevertheless, sensitivity towards inequality has grown more intense, which indicates a change in the power ratio between men and women. With growing power equality, not only do the weaker have to think about the feelings of the stronger, but the latter also have to take into account the wishes, feelings and sensitivities of the former. Much of present-day marital conflict has to do with these shifts, with the fact that these changes are not identical among more and less empowered groups. Women's wishes for change often develop faster than men's willingness and capacity for adaptation. That is suggested by, among other things, differences in the speed of change, such as between women's entering the labour market and men's taking over household duties (which has hardly happened so far). This unequal tempo of change is responsible for much friction and women's work overload, as nowadays they cope with a job and in many cases still do the lion's share of household duties and childcare.

Shifts in the figuration ideal of harmonious inequality towards growing equality do not take place without conflict and fierce strife, both in relations between the sexes and in the men's and women's emotional economy: in their ideals concerning themselves and the other, and the mutual identification and emotional control which fit the figuration in which they live, the figuration of partner relations in a changing patriarchal culture.

In the working environment too, where most formal barriers for women have been eliminated, a number of mechanisms still operate – deliberately or not – to keep women in their former place. Ideals of women's emancipation and equal division of power notwithstanding, women still rarely occupy top positions. They are highly underrepresented in decision-making positions of important branches of the social order, such as trade and industry, education, politics, government and the medical world. This phenomenon, referred to as the 'glass ceiling', is not only caused by more or less subtle ways of exclusion of women by men. Women also withdraw or do not dare enter this arena. One reason is that it is hard to combine a job with family care, which is still mainly women's work. There are other reasons too. Women do not feel at ease in this arena, are not treated with trust by the already established men; sometimes they are invited there enthusiastically but then become critically and suspiciously watched, and are harshly reprimanded for every fault and every instance of violation of the existent codes (Fischer 1998, 2000; Brinkgreve 1999). Women often feel uncomfortable in male-dominated organizations, and are uncomfortable with the male manner of work, behaviour, and the prevailing concepts of professionalism that not only demand total availability but also a specific mode of emotional control. The top-management cultures demand total availability and involvement in business, and a particular type of emotional control, according to which emotions may not be man-ifested, especially those which suggest weakness, uncertainty and sen-sitivity. In contrast, emotions which suggest strength, ambition, rivalry, focus on power and control are highly appreciated. Showing doubt and uncertainty is often regarded as a sign of weakness, incompetence or lack of professional qualities. Men feel more comfortable than do women in a competitive environment, seeing competition as challenge, whereas women tend to perceive it as an obstacle, as something that stands in their way. Women find it more difficult than men do to move in circumstances which are stressful and competitive (Fischer 1998, 2000; Keizer 1997). The findings of studies of communication suggest that women are more sensitive about harmony in their relations, and that men are more worried about their status, and want to force respect from others in order to keep control (Tannen 1994).[8]

The central question here is who has the power to define the rules of the game: the standards of competence, the codes of behaviour and of emotional control. The persistent pattern of inequality is the provisional outcome of a battle in which women have gained some ground, but in the field of labour and the professions men still largely have the power to determine the rules of the game. In this context, men are still the established and women the outsiders.

Looking at the present time, and especially at the developments which have taken place in recent decades, we cannot but notice a diminishing inequality of power between the sexes. Women's and men's domains are less separated from each other than they were before. An important aspect of this process consists in a loosening of the division of labour between the sexes. Women have made their way into previously 'male areas', or at least those in which men long predominated: work outside the home, and the public sphere – such as politics, journalism, public debates, the world of out-of-home entertainment. In the reverse direction, less transgression of borders is noticeable. Although some men have indeed taken over part of caring for household and children, on average their share in these traditionally 'feminine' tasks has hardly increased.

These, however, are not the only tasks and activities where male and female performance and attitudes have begun to converge. Differences between the sexes as far as ways of behaviour and ambitions are con-cerned also seem to be blurred. Characteristics and attitudes which used to be regarded as definitely masculine, such as self-confidence, willpower, social ambitions and courage are also sought after by women. Traits which used to be considered appropriate for women, such as modesty, gentleness and patience are now experienced by women as impeding relics of education which hinder their lives and social advancement. The acquisition by men of characteristics for long considered feminine, such as gentleness, caring and patience, seems to be slower and less pronounced than the converse adoption of male attitudes and sensibilities by women. Belonging for centuries to the stronger party of the sex struggle, many men tend to experience it as degrading to take over qualities of the sex which for such a long time has been regarded as weaker and of lower rank.

Reflecting on the changing balance of power between the sexes, we can say that it does not only concern equality as an ultimate norm, especially not in the sense that women would have to appropriate the behaviour and habitus of men, without changes in the reverse direction affecting men. Investigating shifts in the balance of power, we need also to inquire into the evaluation of behaviour and qualities related to women, and behaviour related to men and masculinity. That boils down to the question of who has the power to define what is and what is not highly valued in society, and what is esteemed or underestimated socially.

To put Elias's perspective in the simplest terms possible: changes in the balance of power between the sexes cannot be understood without taking into account the broader development of society. For that reason, we have to take into consideration not only the stage of state formation, the development of the labour market, and the protection provided by law, but also the question of who enjoys the power to define what forms of behaviour and emotional expression are or are not valued, which aspirations are allowed to whom, and what level of emotional control is required from whom. The established can set the rules, but if erstwhile outsiders win power, they also make their voice heard, and are also going to participate in setting the rules of the social game, and force the established to reckon with that fact. This process is now in progress, and it is not taking place without tension and conflict. It leads to conflicts between and within individuals that are part of the processes through which the balance of power becomes less unequal.

NOTES

1. The line of thought in this section is broadly indebted to Goudsblom's essay.
2. In her theory of the evolutionary origins of patriarchy, Smuts (1995) mentions two comparable factors: organization (formation of coalitions and alliances) and monopolization of important power resources. Her hypothesis is that young adult women would move locations (upon marrying) and form no firm coalitions with other adult women, unlike men who did form alliances among themselves. Men's relations were of hierarchical order. Owing to the organization of those relations, men managed to monopolize economic resources as well. Since the origin of language, Smuts argues, men have also succeeded

in influencing language as well as thinking in such a way that patriarchal ideologies formed another source of their power over women.

3. This article was a later reconstruction by Elias of the opening section of what he had intended to be an entire book about changing relations between the sexes, but unfortunately it is the only part that is extant. The story goes that, in 1972, when Elias was spending a period at the University of Konstanz, the cleaners at the University of Leicester took the rest of the manuscript-in-making for waste paper and threw it in the dustbin. Elias's perspective is easy to reconstruct from that single piece, in the way he connects the level of state formation and manners.

4. Quite recently, modern armies have come to admit women soldiers.

5. In the Netherlands until 1957 it was legal to dismiss women employees after they married. In the same year legal incapacity of married women was repealed too. The clause that the man was the head of the marital union disappeared only in 1970.

6. Both economic independence and the development of their own voice are significant goals of the women's movement and form important themes in women's studies (Kapteyn 1977).

7. Aletta Jacobs was the first woman in the Netherlands to attend a comprehensive high school (Hogere Burgerschool or HBS) as well as university. She studied medicine in Groningen in 1871, and obtained a doctor's degree in medical science in 1879.

8. Psycho-linguist Deborah Tannen also presents such findings, and offers a succinct formula to describe this difference, saying that men have a tendency towards 'report talk' whereas women tend towards 'rapport talk'. Within the field of psychiatry this topic is elaborated by Jean Baker Miller, who also points to the importance women attach to relations which they enter. Baker classifies this as an 'organizing feature' of women's – but not men's – development. According to Miller, women are more orientated towards the relational, men towards division and dissociation (Miller and Stiver 1993). See also Carol Gilligan's influential book about the psychic and moral development of women, seen to be different to that of men (Gilligan 1982).

REFERENCES

Bertels, K. *et al.* 1978, *Vrouw, man, kind*. Lijnen van vroeger naar nu, Baarn: Ambo: pp. 44–78.

Brinkgreve, C. 1999, 'Old boys, new girls: De toegang van vrouwen tot elites', *Amsterdams Sociologisch Tijdschrift* 26 (2): 164–84.

Dobash, R.E. and Dobash, R. 1979, *Violence Against Wives: A Case Against Patriarchy*, New York: The Free Press.

Dresen-Coenders, L. 1978, 'Machtige grootmoeder, duivelse heks', in K. Bertels *et al.*, *Vrouw, man, kind*, Baarn: Lijnen van vroeger naar nu, pp. 44–78.

Elias, N. 1987, 'The changing balance of power between the sexes – a process-sociological study: the example of ancient Roman state', *Theory, Culture and Society* 4 (2–3): 287–316.

Elias, N. and Scotson, J. 1965, *The Established and the Outsiders*, London: Frank Cass, 2nd edn, London: Sage, 1994.

Fischer, A. 1998, *De top (m/v): de paradox van emoties*, Amsterdam: University of Amsterdam.

Fischer, A. *et al.* 2000, *Masculiniteit met een feminien gezicht*, Den Haag: Ministerie van Sociale Zaken en Werkgelegenheid.

Gilligan, C. 1982, *In a Different Voice*, Cambridge, MA: Harvard University Press.

Goffman, E. 1959, *The Presentation of Self in Everyday Life*, London: Allen Lane.

Goudsblom, J. 1997, *Het regime van de tijd*, Amsterdam: Meulenhof.

Kapteyn, P. 1977, 'Aletta Jacobs and female emancipation in the Netherlands', in P. Gleichmann, J. Goudsblom and H. Korte (eds.) *Human Figurations. Essays for/Aufsätze für Norbert Elias*, Amsterdam: Amsterdams Sociologisch Tijdschrift, pp. 284–92.

Keizer, M. 1997, *De dokter spreekt: Professionaliteit, gender en uitsluiting in medische specialismen*, Delft: Eburon.

Klapisch-Zuder, C. 1991, *Geschiedenis van de vrouw*, vol. II, Middeleeuven, Amsterdam: Agon.

Miller, J.B. and I.P. Stiver 1993, 'A relational approach to understanding women's lives and problems', *Psychiatric Annals* 23 (8): 424–31.

Ozment, S. 1986, *Magdalena and Balthasar: An Intimate Portrait of Life in Sixteenth-century Europe, Revealed in the Letters of a Nuremberg Husband and Wife*, New York: Simon and Schuster.

Ribberink, A. 1998. *Leidsvrouwen en zaakwaarneemsters: Een geschiedenis van de aktiegroep, Man Vrouw Maatschappij (MVM)*, Hilversum: Verloren.

Römkens, R. 1992, *Gewoon geweld? Omvang, aard, gevolgen en achtergronden van geweld tegen vrouwen in heteroseksuele relaties*, Amsterdam/Lisse: Swets & Zeitlinger.

Sevenhuijsen, S.L. 1992, 'Mothers as citizens: feminism, evolutionary theory and the reform of Dutch family law 1870–1910', in C. Smart (ed.), *Regulating Womanhood: Historical Essays on Marriage, Motherhood and Sexuality*, London: Routledge, pp. 166–86.

Smuts, B. 1995. 'The evolutionary origins of patriarchy', *Human Nature: An Interdisciplinary Biosocial Perspective* 6 (1): 1–32.

Van Stolk, B. and Wouters, C. 1983, *Vrouwen in tweestrijd: Tussen thuis en tehuis*, Deventer: Van Loghum Slaterus.

Tannen, D. 1994, *Woorden aan het werk (Talking from 9 to 5)*, Amsterdam: Prometheus.

Zweigenhaft, R. and Domhoff, G.W. 1998, *Diversity in the Power Elite. Have Women and Minorities Reached the Top?* New Haven, CT: Yale University Press.

Part III

The formation of individuals and states

9 Not so exceptional? State-formation processes in America

Stephen Mennell

Introduction

'America', said Alexis de Tocqueville in 1840, 'is . . . the one country in the world where the precepts of Descartes are least studied and most followed' (2000: 403). In their common assumptions Americans sought 'to escape . . . from the yoke of habits, from family maxims, from class opinions, and, up to a certain point, from national prejudices; to take tradition only as information, and . . . to seek the reason for things in themselves and in themselves alone'. In short, 'each American calls only on the individual effort of reason'. To say nevertheless that Americans had rarely troubled to define the rules of this philosophic method was a little unfair. This rational individualism, which has remained a force in American politics and culture to the present day, is a legacy of the Enlightenment spirit to which so many of the great intellectuals among the Founding Fathers contributed. To adapt Keynes's famous remark, Americans in Tocqueville's perception were the slaves of long-defunct *philosophes*. If Tocqueville had been looking for really unrecognized philosophical debts, he might have pointed to another strain of idealism: Hegelianism. For with the passage of time, the United States, and especially its Constitution, came to be represented as almost an emanation of the human spirit. A very important component of 'American exceptionalism' has been the sense that – unlike European states that emerged from war, greed, inequality and exploitation – the United States arose from an individual and collective striving for the greater good. On the contrary, however, like other states elsewhere, the United States arose out of a long-term process of state formation that involved contests – frequently violent contests – between many rival groups of human beings.

There is an enormous literature on American political development, but most of it is slanted rather towards nation building than state formation, towards the construction of a sense of shared national identity rather than internal pacification and the forging of an effective monopolization of the means of violence (see, for instance, Lipset 1963, and Greenfeld

157

1992: 397–484). Such has been the strength of American social scientists' focus on the collective subjectivity of 'nation building' that the very term 'state formation' is a rare usage for them. The ambiguity of the word 'state' in the US context undoubtedly contributes to the avoidance of the term 'state formation' – what are called 'states' in the United States might be called 'provinces' or *Länder* in other federal constitutions – but perhaps also to a neglect of the factual process to which the term refers. For instance, after the United States invaded Afghanistan in 2002 to overthrow the Taliban regime, American spokesmen said they were not interested in becoming involved in 'nation-building' (which, if it depends on the creation of good and wise individuals, would certainly take a long time), and in consequence resisted the deployment of either US or UN troops to maintain order beyond the capital city, thus nonchalantly handing back most of Afghanistan to regional warlords.

Of course, state formation and nation building by no means can be entirely separated. 'We-images' and especially 'we-feelings' are important, notably today when the United States has become the world's one superpower. Yet while there is no doubt that the formation of we-identities in the course of nation building is an important facet of state-formation processes, it is subsidiary to the central feature of the formation of a state in the sense in which Max Weber defined it: 'an organization which successfully upholds a claim to binding rule-making over a territory, by virtue of commanding a monopoly of the legitimate use of violence' (Weber 1978: I, 54). How such a monopoly is established is a Janus-faced process: on the one hand, it involves securing and extending the boundaries of a territory, to a considerable extent by means of the use of violence against external opponents; and, on the other, it involves the internal pacification of the territory. Elias's thesis is that internal pacification also, in the long term, comes to be embodied in a more pacific habitus: 'if in this or that region, the power of central authority grows, if over a larger or smaller area people are forced to live at peace with one another, the moulding of affects and the standards of emotion management are very gradually changed as well' (Elias 2000: 169; translation amended).

At first glance, state formation in North America may appear to have an entirely different starting point from the corresponding process in Western Europe. For one thing, by the time European settlement on a significant scale began in North America, the precursors of several of the states which constitute Europe today – England, France, Spain, Portugal, The Netherlands, Sweden, although not Germany or Italy – had already assumed something like their present territorial shape through processes that had begun centuries earlier in the Middle Ages. Internally, they already had relatively well developed state apparatuses, and, with necessary provisos about the prevalence of civil wars in seventeenth-century Europe, most of the settlers came from internally relatively pacified states. Yet, on closer inspection, there are interesting similarities beside the differences between North America and Western Europe. In particular, competition for territory – between rival groups of European settlers, between rival groups of indigenous people, and between Europeans and the indigenous population – was as essential a feature in North America as it had been and continued to be in Europe.

Elias's account of the formation of states in Western Europe

Elias's account of state formation takes its departure from Max Weber's definition of the state, but to the idea of a monopoly of violence, however, he added 'and taxation'. In the earliest stages of the formation of effective states, it is futile to try to draw a clear line between the 'economic' and the 'political'. Elias sought to show in much more detail than did Weber the long-term processes through which increasingly effective monopolies of violence and taxation have taken shape. The third section of *The Civilizing Process* (2000: 195–256) discusses the period of the early Middle Ages, after the fall of the Roman Empire in the west, when the centrifugal forces dominant in the process of feudalization resulted in the extreme fragmentation of western Europe into countless tiny territories each controlled by a local warlord. The principal reason why centrifugal forces dominated over centripetal tendencies – in an era of reduced population, decaying roads, declining long-distance trade and repeated invasions by marauding bands – was that the only means kings then had of paying subordinates to administer distant territories was to give them the land from which they could support themselves. The means of supporting themselves were identical with the means of making them rulers of the territory independent of the king to whom they nominally owed allegiance. Political autarky went hand in hand with economic autarky: they were mutually reinforcing.

Early in the second millennium AD, at least in the region that was to become France, the balance tilted once more in favour of centripetal, centralizing forces (Elias 2000: 257–362). It was not inevitable that there would be a single country corresponding to France in its present boundaries: it was not preordained nor in any sense planned that the kings whose principal seat was Paris would extend their territories until they reached the boundaries of the hexagon, and then stop. For much of the Middle Ages the Paris kings were locked in combat with other French-speaking kings whose principal city was London, but who often controlled more of what is now France than did the Paris kings. Even towards the end of the medieval period, there was a resurgence of centrifugal forces when members of the royal family, assigned regions as appanages to govern on behalf of the king, used them to reassert their autonomy.

Even if state formation in Europe did not unfold in linear fashion, and its outcome was in considerable measure affected by chance and accident, Elias was able to point to a number of part-processes running fairly consistently through it in the long term. State formation was a violent competitive process through which there emerged successively larger territorial units with more effective monopoly apparatuses. Initially, around AD 1000, there were relatively small disparities in strength between the rulers of the many small territories, who fought out an 'elimination contest' with each other, the victor in each round absorbing his defeated rival's land, so that a smaller number of steadily larger territories arose. In explaining this, Elias alluded to the westward expansion of America, quoting what was once said of an American pioneer: 'He didn't want all the land; he just wanted the land next to his' (2000: 312). The more or less continuous warfare between neighbouring magnates in the European Middle Ages is not to be explained primarily by the aggressive psychological characteristics of warlords. In an age when power was so directly correlated with the amount of land one controlled, it was impossible for a ruler of unusually pacific temperament to sit idly by as his neighbours slugged it out with each other, for the victorious neighbour would then control a larger territory and be able to defeat next the would-be passive observer. True, there is much evidence that most medieval warriors thoroughly enjoyed warfare, but they had to – they would not have survived in a social situation so structured had they not. Aggressiveness, remarked Elias, may more nearly be explained as the outcome of conflict than conflict as the outcome of aggressiveness – though, to be more accurate, it is a two-way relationship through time.

The state-formation process was two-sided. On the one hand, larger territories became internally pacified. On the other hand, the scale of warfare steadily increased through European history. In what became France, for instance, the local skirmishes in the early stages of the elimination contest gave way to a struggle between the Paris kings and the London kings prolonged over several centuries. The Valois' final victory brought them face to face with new rivals, and they immediately entered a prolonged contest with the Habsburgs and the Hohenzollerns, the process culminating in the Franco-Prussian War of 1870 and the two 'world wars' of the twentieth century.

Although the precise outcome differed from case to case (Elias 2000: 261–7), within each of the developing states of Western Europe certain common processes can be discerned. One of them Elias calls the *monopoly mechanism*. In the course of the elimination contest between many territorial magnates, a smaller number of central rulers emerged with more extensive lands and, by extension, with more of other power resources by which they were able gradually to make their monopoly of the means of violence and taxation within their territories more complete and effective. Alongside this operated the *royal mechanism*, the accretion of power to the social position of kings and princes through their ability to play off rival social interests against each other – typically, by the late Middle Ages, the relatively evenly balanced forces of the old warrior nobility and the rising commercial bourgeoisie. Kings often threw their weight on the side of the second most powerful group as a counterbalance to the most powerful. A necessary third component was the *transformation of private into public monopolies*. Administrative functions became too large and varied to be handled by a king and his immediate staff, so bureaucracies of an increasingly 'public' character developed.

If Elias pays most attention to the monopolization of violence within state formation, he sees it as only one important thread interweaving with others in a long-term overall process of social development which enmeshed individuals in increasingly complex webs of interdependence. It interweaves with the division of labour, the growth of towns and trade, the use of money and increasing population, in a spiral process. Internal pacification of territory facilitates trade, which facilitates the growth of towns and division of labour and generates taxes which support larger administrative and military organizations, which in turn facilitate the internal pacification of larger territories, and so on – a cumulative process experienced as an increasingly compelling, inescapable force by people caught up in it. Furthermore, according to Elias, the gradually higher standards of self-restraint engendered in people contribute in turn to the upward spiral – being necessary, for example, to the formation of gradually more effective and calculable administration. Unfortunately, space does not permit comparison of all these components of the overall process in Europe and America, so the focus will be on the growth of the territory of the United States and America's relations with its neighbours.

The North American elimination contest

The American elimination contest differed from that of medieval Europe in at least one very important way. The territorial struggle in North America was driven as much by rivalries between the various established states back in Europe as it was by local conflicts. In that respect it was somewhere intermediate along a continuum between the endogenously driven battles between numerous local warlords in early second-millennium Europe and the largely exogenous race for territory in Africa between European colonial powers in the nineteenth century. In the seventeenth century, England, France, Spain, Sweden and The Netherlands all established settlements in North America. The Swedes who settled in the Delaware River area in 1637 are often forgotten; after some years of conflict with the Dutch, they were eliminated as an independent player in the continent following their defeat in 1655. The Dutch lasted longer, from 1612 to 1664, but by the end of the seventeenth century, the English could claim to rule a consolidated strip of land along the entire eastern seaboard, between the vicinity of Maine and that of Georgia. The strip was not wide – rarely more than 200 miles. Nor was the territory internally wholly pacified, although government was gradually becoming more effective.

The consolidation of English rule along the eastern seaboard and the gradual extension of the frontier of trading and settlement westwards towards and beyond the Appalachians during the late seventeenth and eighteenth centuries led to battles with the French who were moving down from Canada in the interior. Fighting flared up in North America particularly during each of the successive European wars. The French and British colonists, with their respective Indian allies, launched steadily more ambitious raids on each other's settlements. The cycle of colonial violence came to a head in the fourth of the series, the Seven Years War (1756–63), known in America as the French and Indian War. It was at this time that Britain established its clear ascendancy over the French in India and in North America. Under the Treaty of Paris which concluded the Seven Years War in 1763 Canada was ceded to Britain along with all lands east of the Mississippi hitherto claimed by France. But the elimination of France as a major player had unforeseen consequences that made the triumph prove to be only short term.

Parallel with the elimination contest among European powers in North America, but thoroughly intertwined with it, was a similar contest among Indian peoples. In the 'French and Indian' wars, the French fought in alliance with Algonquian Indians, the British with the support of most of the Iroquois. The Iroquois, in particular, conducted themselves from an early stage as an independent power in their relations with the white settlers, allying themselves first with the Dutch and then, fairly consistently, with the British. But this formed part of their own striving for hegemony over other Indian peoples in a vast region to the west of the seaboard colonies. In particular, they effectively held the balance of power between the French and the British, opposing the expansion of French settlement southwards. At the end of the Seven Years War, the British were thus militarily indebted to their Indian allies, and that proved to be of some significance.

The standard histories of the American Revolution dwell especially on the issues and events connected with the slogan 'no taxation without representation'. At the end of the Seven Years War, Britain had acquired vast new territories and in seeking to control them faced a considerable problem of overstretch. Standing armies had to be paid for by raising revenue, and the attempts of the London government to tax the colonies led to steadily increasing resentment through the 1760s and early 1770s. Certainly 'no taxation without representation' was the kernel of the discourse through which the Revolution was justified by its leaders (and its supporters back in Britain), and there is no need to retell the story in any detail here.

In the background, however, is another consideration which although well known has been paid less attention. By royal proclamation in 1763, the British government reserved the Ohio Valley for the Indians – among whom their allies the Iroquois were the dominant power. They drew a line on the map between white and native Americans, without the means to police and enforce it.

In the years just preceding the war for independence, the frontier regions between British colonists and tribal Indians rocked in turmoil . . . Garrisons stationed in western forts were withdrawn to control eastern urban rebels, and squatters known as 'settlers' rushed to occupy lands for which they had only the most tenuous pretensions of right, when they had any at all. Deputy Superintendent George Croghan declared in 1769 that 'there were between four and five thousand, and all this spring and summer the roads have been lined with wagons moving to the Ohio'. (Jennings 2000: 216)

Theodore Roosevelt recognized the significance of this. In *The Winning of the West*, he described the American Revolution as 'fundamentally a struggle between England . . . and the Americans, triumphantly determined to acquire the right to conquer the continent', and pointed out that had they not won that right, 'we would certainly have been cooped up between the sea and the mountains' with the Alleghenies as the western frontier. Among modern historians, Francis Jennings in particular has argued that the American Revolution must be seen as a conflict over the control of conquests, and this underlines the parallels between the continuing elimination contest in North America and that which had unfolded much earlier in Europe. The colonists were also colonizers; while resisting the imperial ambitions of the British government, they were consciously seeking to create their own empires. This theme could scarcely be as prominent as 'no taxation without representation' in the rhetoric of the Revolution, but leaders such as Jefferson never made any secret of their vision of the immense possibilities offered by westward expansion. The opportunities for enrichment were irresistible:

> Though the crown made an effort to preserve 'crown lands' for the Indians, it was unable to prevent some of its own officials from the common rapacity . . . Governor Lord Dunmore launched war against the Shawnees in 1773 to open their territory to immigrants from Virginia who would have to buy from him. Mostly, however, crown officials acquired rights quietly that they hoped to cash in when times became quieter . . . The Revolutionaries, however, were in a hurry. (Jennings 2000: 216)

That tells a story startlingly reminiscent of the problem faced by aspirant central rulers in a feudal Europe with a pre-monetary economy.

Manifest destiny and latent dynamics

Whenever one looks at an historical process *a posteriori*, knowing what was the final outcome, it is difficult to perceive the uncertainties at each stage, the range of alternative outcomes that might have been. In retrospect, it may be hard to imagine how there could be any outcome other than a USA stretching from Atlantic to Pacific and between what are now the Canadian and Mexican borders. Certainly, by the 1840s it already appeared inevitable to a good many Americans. The term 'manifest destiny' originated just before the Mexican War which gave the continental United States more or less its present boundaries. Justifying expansion into Texas, Mexico and Oregon, the journalist John L. O'Sullivan wrote in 1845 that it was 'by right of manifest destiny' for the United States 'to overspread and to possess the whole of the continent which Providence has given us', both for 'the development of the great experiment in liberty and federative self-government entrusted to us' and for 'the free development of our yearly multiplying millions' (Boyer 2001: 470).

Yet destiny had not always been quite so manifest. Looking back to the period between the Declaration of Independence and the adoption of the Constitution, John Adams wrote in his diary, 'no-one thought of consolidating this vast continent under one national government' (Adams 1962: III, 352). So to what extent was the continental USA 'inevitable' or 'accidental', and how far was it the outcome of conscious plans or of unintended processes?

The overall territorial expansion of the USA was not as unplanned as that of France centuries earlier.[1] It is not just the probability of alternative outcomes that changes in the course of a process of social development, but also the foreseeability and plannability of such outcomes. This is – yet again – a function of changing power ratios between the groups of people whose interests and intentions are interweaving to produce the process. Without being blind to very important contrary movements, Elias sees one of the broad trends in the development of modern industrial societies as being towards 'functional democratization', by which he means that, on the whole, the power ratios within society – between, for instance, social classes, men and women, rulers and ruled – have become *relatively* less unequal. An important consequence of this dominant (if partial) trend is illustrated in Elias's series of 'game models' (1978: 71–103). Generally speaking, the more relatively evenly balanced are the power ratios between players, the more prevalent will be unforeseen outcomes that are not planned or intended by anyone. Elias illustrates the point at its simplest by reference to a basic two-person game like chess. Even when only two players are involved, a rather different situation emerges if, for whatever reason, their strengths in the game gradually become more equal. Two things diminish: the stronger player's ability to use his or her own moves to force the weaker to make particular moves, and his or her ability to determine the course of the game. The weaker player's chances of control over the stronger increase correspondingly. But, as the disparity between the players' strengths is reduced, the course of the game increasingly passes beyond the control of either. As Elias explains:

Both players will have correspondingly less chance to control the changing figuration of the game; and the less dependent will be the changing figuration of the game on the aims and plans for the course of the game which each player has formed by himself. The stronger, conversely, becomes the dependence of each of the two players' overall plans and of each of their moves on the changing figuration of the game – on the game process. The more the game comes to resemble a social process, the less it comes to resemble the implementation of an individual plan. In other words, to the extent that the inequality in the strengths of the two players diminishes, there will result from the interweaving of moves of two individual people a game process which neither of them has planned. (1978: 82)

A principle that is true in even a simple two-person game becomes still more evident in Elias's subsequent multiperson games, in which more players form more complex networks of interdependence with each other. The more players there are, the more likely it is that their moves will interweave to produce a game process than none of them has planned; and, furthermore, the likelihood is markedly increased the more relatively equal becomes the power balance between the players.

How does this relate to the question posed above? How far was the continental United States 'inevitable' or 'accidental', and how far was it the outcome of conscious plans or of unintended processes?

The most obvious part of the answer is that, whatever processes of functional democratization may have been in train *within* American society, the power ratios between the Unites States and its neighbours have steadily changed *in the opposite direction*. That is, the United States, like the proverbial pioneer, has over a prolonged period become more powerful in relation to the people who held 'the land next to its'. The result has been that, while the 'accidental' remained important in providing opportunities for expansion, the process overall came over time *more* to resemble the implementation of the stronger party's plans, and *less* a social process that no one had planned or intended.

The Louisiana Purchase of 1803 was the most dramatic and one of the most peaceful acquisitions of territory in US history. When President Jefferson bought all the remaining territory claimed by France in North America – about 800,000 square miles west of the Mississippi – he virtually doubled the national territory. His original intention had been to buy only New Orleans, which was vital to export trade from the then American western lands between the Appalachians and the Mississippi. Fortuitously, at that moment the Emperor Napoleon found himself overstretched in Europe and the Caribbean, and sold the whole vast territory for $15 million.

After the acquisition of such a vast additional territory, westward expansion need no longer be imagined to rest solely on individual pioneers nibbling at small parcels of land to establish squatters' rights; exercising the power of the federal government could gobble up huge mouthfuls of land. That was to become increasingly apparent. In 1803, territorial rights under international law had been gained through an entirely peaceful diplomatic transaction, by a country that was not then militarily very strong, but military power would come to play a more prominent part. This can first be seen in the complicated sequence of events leading to the incorporation of Florida into the Union. Force played its part, with incursions into Florida under President Madison in 1812 and President Monroe in 1818, pressure on the enfeebled Spaniards making possible the Adams–Onís Treaty of 1819, under which the USA finally became a transcontinental power. Florida was sold to the USA, and the boundary with remaining Spanish territories settled (temporarily, as it proved), running northward from the Gulf of Mexico along what is now the eastern boundary of the state of Texas, zigzagging to the forty-second parallel (now the northern boundary of California, Nevada and Utah), and then due west to the Pacific.

Spain in the early nineteenth century had long been declining in power; Britain decidedly was not. After the War of 1812, there was no resort to military force in Anglo-American relations. There were intermittent tensions over the boundary with Canada. As late as the end of the nineteenth century, leading Americans such as Theodore Roosevelt, Henry Cabot Lodge and James C. Blaine were still hankering after the annexation of Canada. Indeed it was a plank in the Republican platform in 1896, though it was dropped in the following election. But, in stages (1818, 1846, 1903), the boundary between the USA and Canada was agreed peacefully.

The role played by diplomacy in establishing the borders of the coterminous United States is not enough to establish any startling contrast with Elias's account of equivalent processes in medieval and early modern Europe. True, Elias placed most emphasis on wars between European neighbours, but he acknowledged the part that even then was played by diplomacy, with inter-dynastic marriages often cementing the settlements reached. But war and diplomacy are not separate things – as Clausewitz so famously observed 'war is the continuation of politics by other means', and the converse is also true. More precisely, war and diplomacy are functional equivalents in relations between states, and they are not mutually exclusive equivalents. The fate of many a princely daughter was settled as much by force of arms as by parleying between parents. The proportions of force and diplomacy depend largely on the power ratios between players in any particular situation. This principle can be seen clearly in the next important episode in the territorial growth of the United States, the annexation of Texas and a substantial part of Mexico.

Mexico had gained its independence from Spain in 1821, but it did not exercise much control over its sparsely populated province of Texas. By the early 1830s around 30,000 US immigrants had moved into the territory. In 1836 they had established effective independence from the Mexican government, and petitioned the United States to be admitted to the Union as a slave state (Mexico had abolished slavery in 1829). There was an outcry from abolitionists and, for a decade, the Texas Republic was tenuously independent. In 1845, under President Polk, Texas was finally annexed. The outcome of the Mexican War (1846–8), which saw the US army rout the Mexicans and occupy Mexico City, was that the American claim to all the land north of the Rio Grande was conceded. Under the 1848 Treaty that ended the war, the United States gained the lands that were to form the states of California, Nevada, Arizona, Utah, the western parts of Colorado and New Mexico, and the southwestern corner of Wyoming. Many Americans felt uneasy about the war at the time. Ulysses S. Grant, later Union commander in the Civil War and president, recorded his unease as a young officer during the Mexican War.

> Generally the officers of the army were indifferent whether the annexation [of Texas] was consummated or not. For myself, I was bitterly opposed to the measure, and to this day regard the war which resulted as one of the most unjust ever waged by a stronger against a weaker nation. It was an instance of a republic following the bad example of European monarchies, in not considering justice in their desire to acquire additional territory. (Grant 1885: 37)

'Poor Mexico! So far from God, and so close to the United States.'[2]

'Sovereignty' as a function of power ratios

It is curious that what came to be known as the Monroe Doctrine, a cornerstone of US foreign policy throughout the nineteenth and twentieth centuries, very nearly began life as a joint declaration by the United States and Britain. In 1823 both countries were concerned that the French, Spanish and the other European powers of the Holy Alliance were about to attempt to reassert Spain's rule over its Latin American colonies, nearly all of which had gained *de facto* independence. British Foreign Secretary George Canning proposed a joint declaration opposing all future colonization in Central and South America. Secretary of State John Quincy Adams strongly opposed a joint declaration, however – he said that it would make America 'come in as a cock-boat in the wake of the British man-of-war' (Remini 2002: 60) – and he had his way. Monroe's message to Congress in December 1823 stated that Europe and the Americas had different political systems, and that the United States would not interfere in European affairs. The United States furthermore recognized the existing European colonies and dependencies in the Western hemisphere, but asserted that the hemisphere was closed to future colonization, and that were any European power to seek to control or oppress any of the new nations of Latin America, the United States would take that as a hostile act against itself. At the time, though, the declaration attracted relatively little attention; it is easy to forget that the United States was not then a major military power, and the authors of the 'Doctrine' were aware that American intervention in Latin America would only have been possible with the support of the British navy. The Monroe Doctrine only gradually came into its own, at first nearer to home where America had a more credible power advantage. Only in 1895 was the Doctrine deployed against Britain, by President Cleveland's administration, with reference to a long-standing boundary dispute between British Guiana and Venezuela. By the turn of the century, America was building a substantial navy of its own, and in 1904 President Theodore Roosevelt added the so-called 'Roosevelt Corollary' to the Monroe Doctrine. Also known as the 'Big Stick Policy', this was an assertion of the USA's right to police the hemisphere. Given that the unruly and economically ill-managed states of Latin America were quite likely to provoke intervention by European creditor nations, the USA claimed an exclusive right to intervene in their affairs, and did so frequently throughout the twentieth century. Only when the power ratio between the USA and its hemispheric neighbours to the south had become very unequal could the Monroe Doctrine be taken to mean that the USA was 'practically sovereign' in the Western hemisphere, carrying with it the right to use force in the territories of lesser sovereignties.

The major gains in the territory legally claimed by the USA were embodied in treaties with the European powers and Mexico, reached with varying degrees of sabre-rattling and actual use of force. The same treaty-making power of the federal government was then employed in relations with the various Indian tribes who might have been under the impression that they themselves had some legal claim to the land. The Senate had to ratify the Indian treaties, which could be taken to imply that the tribes were independent and sovereign states just like the European powers. In fact, from the earliest decades after independence, the USA never viewed the tribes in that light (Remini 2002: 90–1). It did not need to. The power ratio between Indians and European settlers shifted steadily against the earlier inhabitants from shortly after the beginnings of European colonization, and violence characterized relations with the Indians – treaties or no treaties.

Beyond manifest destiny: the beginnings of an American empire

For more than a century, since Frederick Jackson Turner read his famous paper on 'The Significance of the Frontier in American History' (1986 [orig. 1893]: 1–38), historians and social scientists have debated the consequences of the so-called 'closing of the frontier' for the *internal* development of American society. Its consequences for the USA's *external* relations are even more speculative, but there was a striking coincidence of timing between the completion of the settlement of the West and the beginnings of an American external empire. In the 1890s, the USA began to compete with the European powers, not to settle its own North American borders but to acquire overseas dominions (Zimmerman 2002). The ambition to build a canal across the Panama isthmus, in order to facilitate trade and military deployments from the Atlantic to the Pacific, had implications beyond engineering the new state of Panama's secession from

Colombia. The USA had since the Civil War become a major world economic power. It looked to protect its trade routes from possible rivals, and built a navy third in size after those of Britain and Germany. The Hawaiian Islands, an independent Polynesian monarchy, lay athwart the great circle route from California and the canal to China and the Far East. American missionaries turned traders proved adept at insinuating themselves into the Hawaiian political structure, and they persuaded the USA to annex the islands. Almost simultaneously came the Spanish–American War of 1898 through which the USA acquired Cuba only temporarily, but kept Puerto Rico on grounds of its strategic location in relation to the eastern end of the canal. As a more or less accidental by-product of the war, the USA found itself a colonial power in the Philippines, where its rule began with the task of suppressing a rising by Filipino freedom fighters. As in the case of Hawaii, Guam, Midway and various other Pacific islands, the decision for annexation was driven by the competition with other world powers in which the USA was now ineluctably caught up. Specifically, it was feared that Japan might annex Hawaii and Germany the Philippines. These decisions were debated heatedly; many Americans felt uneasy at ruling any territory that did not become fully integrated into the USA, and whose inhabitants were not accorded the full democratic rights of American citizenship. That the advocates of annexation won is one small sign of the flaws in the 'emanation of the human spirit' interpretation of American political development, and of the strength of the model of a 'compelling process' Elias developed through his study of Western European history.

The sense of an inherent conflict between the democratic rhetoric of the era of the War of Independence on the one hand and the emergence of America as a world power on the other has endured. The USA's belated intervention in the First and Second World Wars, and the debate over the League of Nations, all reflect that. Even during the Cold War, there remained a constant need to present the conflict as a battle between a free and an unfree world.

Most western historians place the blame for the great falling out between the two wartime allies squarely on the shoulders of Josef Stalin, who not only snuffed out the democratic regimes of half a dozen countries in Central and Eastern Europe, which thanks to the Yalta agreement found themselves on the wrong side of the Iron Curtain, but who was also beyond dispute one of the great mass murderers of history. There is another, minority, viewpoint articulated by such critics as Noam Chomsky (1991) and Gore Vidal (2002: 166–85), who blame the onset of the Cold War on President Truman's reneging on the Yalta agreement by beginning the process of incorporating West Germany into the emergent Western alliance. But it scarcely matters who is right about the historical details.

In the historical big picture, the years immediately after VE Day were a classic illustration of how victory over one enemy brings the victor face to face with another powerful rival, and potentially (in accordance with the principle of the monopoly mechanism) into a bigger and better round of an elimination contest. Such processes have been familiar since antiquity: Thucydides (1972: 49ff.) began his account of the Peloponnesian War by recounting how a dispute over the small city of Epidamnus had brought Corcyra into conflict with Corinth, then Corinth with Athens, and so on until – after their joint victory over the Persians – there broke out the great war between Athens and Sparta. The standoff between the USA and the USSR, which endured for more than three decades, did not result in direct conflict between the two great powers for each other's territory; the hotter parts of the Cold War were to be found in a series of peripheral wars fought mainly by their proxies. In spite of the superficially grave threat of nuclear annihilation, mutually assured destruction (MAD) actually produced a period of global stability that was conducive to prosperity in the Western world (Bergh 1992).[3] It was the economic failure of the Soviet empire that brought about its collapse in 1989–90, and for once in the course of human history it left the victors as the overwhelmingly dominant power in the world; there no longer remained a further rival to be confronted – at least for the time being. In 2002 the USA, with about 5 per cent of the world's population, created and consumed about 30 per cent of Gross World Product; and it accounted for more than 40 per cent of all the world's expenditure on defence, its military expenditure being roughly equal to that of the next twenty highest defence-spending nations combined (Center for Defense Information 2003). This degree of predominance is without precedent in world history.

Conclusion: the Dubya Addendum

After the terrible events of 11 September 2001, President G. W. Bush announced what we may call the Dubya Addendum to the Roosevelt Corollary to the Monroe Doctrine, extending the USA's self-proclaimed right to intervene in other states beyond the western hemisphere to the rest of the world. In a speech at West Point on 1 June 2002, he stated that 'our security will require all Americans to be . . . ready for pre-emptive action when necessary to defend our liberty and defend our lives'. The 'Big Stick' was now to be used against any state anywhere. In effect, this amounts to an attempt to embark on the establishment of a world state exercising an effective claim to a monopoly of the means of violence, under the auspices of the USA rather than under the Charter of the United Nations. But Weber spoke of a monopoly of the *legitimate* use of the means of violence. While the internal pacification of the world is an attractive dream, the unilateral exercise of the monopoly by the USA is deeply problematic. The objections that Mark Twain and other anti-imperialists made to America's acquisition of its first colonies a century ago apply *pari passu* today. How are the 95 per cent of the world's population who are not US citizens to exercise any democratic constraint upon American policy? And if they do not, how long will an effective US monopoly survive?

NOTES

1. It is not helpful to think in terms of a polar dichotomy between history as following 'inevitable' laws and history as an unstructured sequence of more or less 'accidental' events (see Popper 1957; Mennell 1992, 1996; Dunning 1977). The question of whether a sequence of social development can ever be said to be 'inevitable' has tended to become entangled with the philosophers' metaphysical antithesis of 'determinism' and individual 'free will'. The muddle is then further compounded when 'free will' is linked to 'freedom' in the sense of political and social liberty, and 'determinism' to lack of liberty. This link is false. As Elias points out, 'it is usually forgotten that there are always simultaneously many mutually dependent individuals, whose interdependence to a greater or lesser extent limits each one's scope for action' (Elias 1978: 167). That simple sentence pithily cuts across centuries of metaphysical debate. More subtle and reality-orientated modes of thinking are necessary to come to grips with the issue of prediction and 'inevitability' in sequences of social development. Elias proposes that we think of such development as a continuum of changes, or figurational flow. Within the flow, we can identify a sequence of figurations, which we can label A, B, C, D; these are not static, discontinuous *stages* of development, but points inserted in a flow – various figurations of people, each figuration flowing from the previous one as the development takes its course from A to D. The kernel of Elias's argument is then as follows:

> Retrospective study will often clearly show not only that the figuration is a *necessary* precondition for D, and likewise B for C and A for B, but also why this is so. Yet, looking into the future, from whatever point in the figurational flow, we are usually able to establish only that the figuration at B is *one possible* transformation of A, and similarly C of B and D of C. In other words, in studying the flow of figurations there are two possible perspectives on the connection between one figuration chosen from the continuing flow and another, later figuration. From the viewpoint of the earlier figuration, the later is – in most if not all cases – only one of several possibilities for change. From the viewpoint of the later figuration, the earlier one is usually a necessary condition for the formation of the later. (1978: 160)

There is, then, an asymmetry in the two time-perspectives. The reason is that figurations vary greatly in their pliability, plasticity, potential for change (or, conversely, in their rigidity). Retrospective investigation will usually show that

the possible outcomes have to be thought of in terms of probabilities; moreover, as a particular figuration changes into another, and a scatter of possible outcomes narrows down to a single one, *another range of possible outcomes, once more with differing probabilities*, hoves into view in the next phase of development.
2. Mexican President Porfirio Díaz (1830–1915).
3. For an account of the friendly disagreement between Van Benthem van den Bergh and Norbert Elias (who in his later years was preoccupied with the danger of nuclear war), see Mennell (1990).

REFERENCES

Adams, John 1962, *Diary and Autobiography of John Adams*, ed. L. H. Butterfield, 4 vols., Cambridge, MA: Belknap Press of Harvard University Press.
Bergh, Godfried van Benthem van den 1992, *The Nuclear Revolution and the End of the Cold War: Forced Restraint*, London: Macmillan.
Boyer, Paul S., ed. 2001, *The Oxford Companion to United States History*, Oxford: Oxford University Press.
Center for Defense Information 2003, 'Last of the big time spenders: U.S. military budget still the world's largest, and growing' http://www.cdi.org/programme 29 March 2003.
Chomsky, Noam 1991, *Deterring Democracy*, Cambridge, MA: South End Press.
Dunning, Eric 1977, 'In defence of developmental sociology, a critique of Popper's *Poverty of Historicism* with special reference to the theory of Auguste Comte', *Amsterdams Sociologisch Tijdschrift* 4 (3): 327–49.
Elias, Norbert 1978, *What is Sociology?* New York: Columbia University Press. 2000 [originally 1939], *The Civilizing Process*, Rev. edn, Oxford: Blackwell.
Grant, Ulysses S. 1885, *Personal Memoirs of U.S. Grant*, New York: Smithmark.
Greenfeld, Liah 1992, *Nationalism: Five Roads to Modernity*, Cambridge, MA: Harvard University Press.
Jennings, Francis 2000, *The Creation of America: Through Revolution to Empire*, Cambridge: Cambridge University Press.
Lipset, Seymour Martin 1963, *The First New Nation: The United States in Comparative and Historical Perspective*, London: Heinemann.
Mennell, Stephen 1990, 'The globalization of human society as a very long-term social process: Elias's theory', *Theory, Culture and Society* 7 (3): 359–71.
1992, 'Momentum and history', in J. L. Melling and J. Barry (eds.), *Culture and History*, Exeter: University of Exeter Press, pp. 28–46.
1996, 'Introduction: bringing the very long term back in', in J. Goudsblom, E. L. Jones and S. J. Mennell, *The Course of Human History*, Armonk, NY: M. E. Sharpe, pp. 3–13.
Popper, Karl R. 1957, *The Poverty of Historicism*, London: Routledge.
Remini, Robert V. 2002, *John Quincy Adams*, New York: Henry Holt.
Roosevelt, Theodore 1889–99, *The Winning of the West*, 4 vols., Lincoln: University of Nebraska Press.
Thucydides 1972, *History of the Peloponnesian Wars*, Harmondsworth: Penguin.

Tocqueville, Alexis de 2000 [orig. 1835–40], *Democracy in America*, Chicago: University of Chicago Press.

Turner, Frederick Jackson 1986, *The Significance of the Frontier in American History*, Tucson, AZ: University of Arizona Press.

Weber, Max 1978, *Economy and Society*, 2 vols., Berkeley, CA: University of California Press.

Zimmerman, Warren 2002, *The First Great Triumph: How Five Great Americans Made their Country a World Power*, New York: Farrar, Straus & Giroux.

10 Armed peace: on the pacifying condition for the 'cooperative of states'

Paul Kapteyn

The issue: interdependency, compulsion and consensus in the establishment of peaceable and cooperative behaviour

No matter how complex human society may be, there is one distinctive trend that is simple to describe: more and more people are becoming dependent on one another in increasing numbers of ways. Although this is not a linear trend, it is clearly a dominant one, and it has been accelerating in recent years. One mundane example of this is the increasingly stressful phenomenon of road traffic. The emergent dynamics that arise from the interdependent decision-making of individual drivers are both palpable, but also abstruse, in the chaotic switching between traffic flows and jams. Participants ponder by the minute whether fellow drivers will give way, jump the queue and otherwise break or bend the rules and social conventions that regulate the 'game' of driving.

This chapter explores this issue of the emergent dynamics of intensifying patterns of interdependency in relation to the global pattern of cooperation between nation-states – the 'cooperative of states' – which has expanded and intensified in recent decades, and which now constitutes a higher level of social integration overarching the patchwork of national societies. The central question to be addressed is why hitherto autonomous states – which have been competing violently with each other since their inception – are now finding more and more means of peaceful cooperation. Phrased differently, what is the *pacifying condition* of this cooperative of states? The point of reference here will be the theory of state-formation articulated by Norbert Elias shortly before the Second World War in his magnum opus, *The Civilizing Process*. The conclusion will highlight an emerging worldwide *dual order* that may signal an end or paradigmatic transformation of the historical pattern. This dual order, at least in tendency, spurs nations towards a new form of supranational cooperation that is analysed under the rubric of a *three-stage progression to world cooperation*.

The historical pattern of the state process

If one asks why people cooperate, one 'obvious' answer presents itself. As people have more extensive and intensive dealings with one another, it is in the interest of all of them to coordinate their actions and – in order to guarantee the effectiveness of such cooperation – to create a higher authority strong enough to ensure that agreements are kept. In an orderly society, this is the rule. People enter into contracts and 'ask' the state to impose sanctions if these are breached. The greater the efficacy of this social contract the more the flywheel of mutual cooperation is propelled into motion. This in turn generates additional trust and confidence, which further enhances cooperation. Social harmony furthers economic expansion and civilization advances almost unnoticed. To use the analogy of road traffic again, the optimal, average speed is attained when all participants give equal consideration to one another, motivated by both mutual interest and propriety. It is expected that 'hot-rodders' will be fined by the higher authority, if not this time, then sooner or later.

The rule: violent pacification is the precursor to peaceful modes of cooperation and competition

In fact, as Norbert Elias showed, the history of state formation suggests a rather different process. Successful cooperation within states does not prove that states were set up with that purpose in mind. In other words, the *function* of state authority is not identical to the *condition of its emergence*. The establishment of state authority always entails a monopolization of the means of violence. It is from this strategic position that the state subsequently furthers peaceful cooperation through its panoply of legal sanctions. However, at the outset the process of state formation is the very antithesis of peaceful cooperation. States arose in the wake of violent competition between people, which, in turn, resulted from their condition of increasing interdependency. This basically means *war*. And in so far as war results in a victor, it is the subsequent extension of a coordinating authority that spurs people to both peaceful cooperation *and* peaceful competition. This is the rule that pervades the history of tribes, cities and states – a history repeatedly defined by the use of violence. Although *The Civilizing Process* refers only to state processes in Western Europe, the story itself began some 10,000 years ago, when the first tribes were settling in the deltas of great rivers in Mesopotamia, China, India and Pakistan (McNeill 1963). The evidence suggests a complex, spiralling relationship between processes of agrarianization and demographic growth, resulting in the gradual displacement and elimination of the hunter-gathering mode of subsistence. Agrarianization ushered in the curses and blessings of routinized work, at least for the vast majority of the population. It also facilitated the emergence of a division of labour and specialist social functions; these early agrarian societies saw the emergence of both priests, who began to assume control of the means of orientation, and warriors, who specialized in the means of violence. Warrior violence was necessary for both the defence and the extension of the basic condition of existence for military-agrarian society. This condition was its fertile soil. Over time, soils were degraded by intensive agriculture and land became a scarce resource coveted by both growing populations and neighbouring tribes. The latter were both lured and impelled by the manifest productivity of agriculture and the power accruing to communities with large populations.

This growing interdependence brought with it increasing competitive pressure. Violent tests of strength resulted in the elimination or absorption of neighbouring communities. Successful warlords, princes or monarchs emerging from such elimination contests thereby secured a double monopoly over the means of violence and of taxation in a territory that could carry on expanding, commensurate with the success of the ruler. Such nascent processes of state formation spread contagiously, eventually, over the course of many centuries, engendering a world-encompassing movement. This movement, as will be argued below, has now reached its ultimate limits, with the incorporation of all populations and communities within the regulatory ambit of nation-states.

In some ways, the struggle for state formation resembled successive rounds in a tournament, with many contestants occupying a myriad of small territories at the beginning, being reduced during the course of the game to a single winner controlling an integrated territory. The historical rise and fall of imperial states, however, bears witness to reversibility and instability in the state process. In the case of the agrarian empires, conquered territory was often simply too vast to hold together. Spontaneously or under external threat, imperial states have historically evinced a marked tendency to implode. But this 'disintegrative function' often simply cleared the way for the ensuing 'integrative function' – a further cycle of elimination contests. Sometimes such fluctuations followed each other in rapid succession, but sometimes the process took centuries. Where successive integrative and disintegrative phases were long and drawn out the condition of political unity or fragmentation was often naturalized, appearing to the subjects involved as an immutable, god-given characteristic of the state. Thus, for instance, whereas unity prevailed in ancient Egypt and other now-lost empires, as well as in China (the oldest state now existing), disunity was the rule in Europe. In the case of the latter, political fragmentation came firmly anchored in the form of stable nation-states, which are similarly perceived by Europeans to be a natural, 'apex form' of the state process.

Some of the conditions that account for such remarkable differences in the outcome of state processes are geographical. For instance, natural barriers such as watersheds, mountain ranges or deserts, often made a territory easier to defend once conquered, increasing the survival chances of the resulting political unit. This *low threshold for integration* character-ized China, Korea and Japan in Asia, England and (to a degree) France in Europe, and Turkey and Iran in the Middle East – all of which have existed as state entities from an early date, despite changing governmen-tal constellations and territorial dimensions. The opposite condition is evident in Central Europe, particularly in the case of Poland, which, lacking natural boundaries on either side, has seen its territorial bound-aries continually redrawn during the course of conflict with its larger neighbours. One of these neighbours, Germany, has itself been subject to a similar handicap. The lack of geophysical integrity presented an im-pediment to the national-state process which neither the Habsburgs, the Hohenzollerns nor the national-socialists proved capable of overcoming. Germany has recently been 're-united', but it did not achieve unification on the basis of its own strength. Just as with the division that preceded it, the unification was determined ultimately by the country's former rivals.

The consequences of such natural differences have been dramatic and far-reaching. Where state authority was weak, the process of internal pacification and cooperation stalled. In the opposite case, strength was self-reinforcing – the power of the victor's sword, after first wreaking death and destruction, subsequently went on to preserve and defend the peace, at least more or less. Ultimately it freed the subjects from what has been called 'the dilemma of collective action' – action that fails to materialize because all parties justifiably fear that others will not keep their agreements unless there is a third party to oversee them (Olson 1965, 1982; Swaan 1995). This notion from game theory again suggests the analogy of road traffic, where the experiential wisdom (and habitu-ated convention) of 'joining the queue alternately' nicely illustrates the cogency of the argument. By speeding up traffic, such cooperative con-ventions prove their value as collective assets – but assets that would never have been developed by the traffic participants themselves in the absence of an overt process of state regulation, as the authority of last resort. This rule has many variants, of course, and they are situated between two op-posite poles: at one end, the strongly centralized, formalized authority of a stable state; and at the other end, the informal authority of a dominant party, with vassals who, though not forcibly subjugated, have submitted to the authority more or less voluntarily for fear of subjugation. Such 'hegemonic' entities, to employ the usual term, contrast with centralized state entities. What they have in common, however, is the existence of one dominant party which constitutes a higher authority that is able to induce cooperation.

The exception: federalism or voluntary 'self-pacification'

A rare exception to the historical pattern of violent pacification might be called voluntary self-pacification: the voluntary leap to the formation of a higher coordinating authority. Though such an authority also holds sanctioning power, it is constituted not on the basis of force by a dominant party, but by a consensual decision taken by nominally equal parties on the basis of reciprocity. In common with its 'centralistic' counterpart, a form of violence also plays a decisive role in its emergence of this 'federal' arrangement. However, whereas in the centralistic variant the violence relates to the process of *internal* subjugation, the federal self-pacification, in the form of a higher authority, arises in response to a common *external* danger. Both such conditions culminate in a higher authority. But although the federal variant is more easily established, it is also weaker than the centralistic form. This weakness partly explains why federal forms are indeed exceptions from a historical point of view. Movements towards federal arrangements have been numerous, but they have generally either failed to materialize, or have been short lived, often being destabilized by the growing dominance of one of the constituent parties. This is what Elias was referring to when he wrote:

As long as no absolutely dominant power has emerged . . . units of the second rank seek to form a bloc against the one which, by uniting numerous regions, has come closest to the position of supremacy. The formation of one bloc provokes another; and however long this process may oscillate back and forth, the system as a whole tends to consolidate larger and larger regions about a centre. (Elias 1982: 123)

A good example of a federation that achieved success, but still collapsed more than two centuries later, was the Republic of the Seven United Netherlands, which arose in the sixteenth century as a very loose federation, in opposition to the centralistic ambitions of the Habsburg monarchy. Partly by virtue of the geographical protection afforded by its swampy terrain, the Dutch Republic managed to survive with this federal state structure intact for a considerable length of time, until France invaded and occupied the country shortly before 1800. France imposed a centralistic regime that the Dutch subsequently retained even after regaining their independence in 1814. It would seem that the forced centralization revealed 'a dilemma of collective action' from which The Netherlands became liberated under the French occupation. The irony is no accident. It is not unusual for an oppressor to demonstrate an administrative efficacy that the subjugated people had failed to accomplish on their own, but whose results they take advantage of after self-government is restored. Another example of a federation that later acquired more centralistic traits is the United States of America, which still likes to see itself as a voluntary cooperative entity set up in revolt against an oppressive motherland. That image is correct but incomplete; it ignores not only the fate of the Native Americans and African Americans, but also the Civil War, through which the North forced a more centralistic form of government onto the Southern states (see Mennell's chapter in this volume). Long-lived federations are rare exceptions to the centralistic pattern. But such exceptions are highly instructive. They demonstrate that the dilemma of collective action can also be resolved 'voluntarily', and that egalitarian relationships also have the potential to generate a hierarchical authority.

This outcome is supported by a different game theoretical notion – the *theory of reciprocity* which argues that interdependence generates cooperation, provided that three preconditions are satisfied (Axelrod 1990): firstly, that none of the parties involved is allowed to abandon the common 'field of interdependencies'; secondly, that their respective interests in the cooperative efforts must be approximately equal, *and* acknowledged as such by all parties; and thirdly, that punishments for disloyalty must fit the crime, no more and no less. Such a 'tit-for-tat policy', the reasoning goes, helps all parties to learn through experience, and teaches them to cooperate instead of competing.

Research and modelling experiments in the area of game theory have lent a degree of plausibility to the theory of reciprocity. When the three conditions are satisfied, cooperative strategies seem to predominate. However, closer inspection reveals limitations in the scope and applicability of Axelrod's model. In particular, the second condition, requiring a transparent and acknowledged equilibrium of interests is, in historical terms, very rare – except in situations in which a higher authority has already established itself. Axelrod's theory of reciprocity, however, denies the need for such a higher authority. He claims quite explicitly that the evolution of cooperation requires no third party and that his experiment proves this. But this ignores the fact that in Axelrod's game the leader of the experiment effectively performs the function of a higher authority by dictating fair, peaceful relations in advance. This 'blind spot' limits the demonstrative value of the experiments, and thereby undermines the validity of the theory.

Such criticisms do not render the theory useless, however. The approach definitely throws light on the problem of how a higher coordinating authority can come into being through voluntary means, on the basis of reciprocity, and in the face of external dangers. Even though this is an exception from a historical point of view, there is no reason why this should always be the case. This is perhaps what Elias was suggesting at the end of *The Civilizing Process* when he finally came to qualify the dominant role of violence leaving open the possibility that 'peaceful trials of strength' could also generate centralized organizations (Elias 1982: 123).

Recent developments

The rule: elimination and integration

How does this albeit schematic account of the state process relate to more contemporary developments? Whilst the historical record points to an almost invariable relationship between violent pacification and the establishment of internal peace this 'historical logic' seems of little help as a benchmark for present-day developments. What would the implications be otherwise? Played out to its logical conclusion, the principle of violent elimination contests would lead ultimately to a world war (really) to end all wars, and whose winner would then be in a position to impose a global peace. But in fact the coming of this Leviathan is a dream – or rather a nightmare – because such a trial of strength in today's world would have no winners. This is the widely held belief, at any rate, and this in itself makes a perpetuation of the historical logic rather improbable in the long run.

But this is not to say that the state process has come to an end, already. The logic of elimination still continues, albeit in a less extreme manner than just depicted. The Second World War might be considered a new starting point in this regard. Up to now it still remains the last extensive conflict in a long series. As we know, the war was decided by two relative outsiders – the USA in the West and the former USSR in the East. After the war, both of them held sufficient military power to act as higher coordinating authorities, each within its own sphere. Great differences existed between the two powers. Whereas coercion was the dominant force in the East, the perceived common threat from the USSR figured heavily in the West. This gave federalist features to the centralistic coordinating arrangement in the West, and most of the states involved also had a bourgeois character. States of this nature, as we shall see below, are more readily inclined towards cooperation. In this context, the USA became the enlightened 'hegemonist'. Its influence was immense and decisive, both within regional entities such as NATO and the OECD, and in broader arrangements such as the UN and its affiliated organizations. Although the UN had global pretensions, it actually embraced only the American sphere of influence, while a counter-configuration was established in the Russian counterpart. The competitive tension between East and West soon began to grow. This two-track regime of cooperation and competition during the Cold War lasted until around 1990, when the Communist Bloc collapsed and disintegrated making the USA the global winner. Its supremacy was reconfirmed in a series of military confrontations beginning in 1991 with the first Gulf War against Iraq. Though officially a United Nations operation, the war was actually an initiative of the USA, whose president spoke of a 'New World Order'. He was alluding to a global society consisting of the type of states described here as *bourgeois* – and thus characterized by *democratic rule of law, open market economies* and *respect for the autonomy of sovereign states* conditional upon the acceptance by these states of the existing order. Although this was a long-standing ideal, its achievement was impeded by international disunity and competition between the superpowers. From the perspective of the Americans, things would be different now. The great barriers between states had been lowered, and if the anticipated cooperation failed to materialize, the USA could always secure compliance through a combination of rewards and sanctions. The *Pax Americana* was dawning, with the USA as the highest authority on earth.

However, America's capacity to play the self-designated role of global policeman is not unlimited. Police officers are not always immediately on the scene and they cannot be everywhere. How far do the ambitions reach of the only superpower still existing in the world? Opinions are divided. Some believe that the New World Order coincides with US interests, while others think it overextends them. Correspondingly, the USA may be expected to pursue either more *proactive* or more *reactive* policies and, in whichever case, these may be expected to be more *multilaterally* or more *unilaterally* oriented. Both these perspectives, however, reflect the dominant position of the USA, which is founded on violence, but which at the same time establishes the preconditions for a worldwide peace as never known before.

The reverse rule: disintegration and the proliferation
of political territories

The historical pattern of the state process continues, but it may also operate in reverse, at least in some parts of the world. This observation refers first and foremost to the disintegration of the USSR, which ushered in the global domination of the USA. Such an erosion of a regional authority is a dramatic, intriguing affair. It confirms that the logic of the past is not a linear progression. Phases of expansion and contraction in the scale and intensity of state processes succeed one another, or may even coincide with and mutually reinforce each other.

Disintegration Disintegration conjures up images of vast empires imploding, after having expanded (according to the logic of elimination and integration) beyond the administrative and military capacity of the central state. The unity of such overstretched imperial states disintegrated with a violence equal to that with which they were created in the first place. This was generally the story in the military-agrarian empires of the past (Goudsblom 1996: 49–63) and so it went, more or less, in the case of the Soviet Union also. The empire had attained its largest dimensions following the Second World War and had proven ill-equipped to sustain this success. But additional factors were also at work. Invariably, a military-agrarian empire is authoritarian and grounded on the demonstrative use of force. Although the same was initially true of Russia, it is also true that its authoritarian traits had been easing in recent times. A dual transition had occurred: the shift from an agrarian to a more industrial mode of production, which in turn produced fewer instruments of production, had been followed more recently by the development of more consumer-oriented patterns of production. This economic process had become increasingly incompatible with the authoritarian, centralistic regime, which was therefore obliged to reduce the level of repression. In this respect there emerged a tension between the need for the economic growth necessary for social consensus, and the political repression required to keep the state together. As it turned out, the social and political liberalization of the Gorbachev era was not enough to sustain the economic growth, but too much for political cohesion. This is the classic problem in the transition from a military-agrarian to a bourgeois-industrial regime, and one which many other countries, most notably China, have also had to confront. And yet the Russian experience remains exceptional in that the transition process was relatively peaceful. Comparable 'revolutions' in places such as England and France, centuries before, were only resolved through the violence of war and internal strife. In Russia, uniquely, the authorities in power made little or no use of their instruments of force even in the face of an unequivocal threat to their position.

This relatively peaceable acquiescence is noteworthy and seems to be a departure from the historical pattern. How is it to be explained? The answer leads us from internal to external relations, and hence to the USA, which – had it indeed conformed to the role of the classical enemy – would have taken advantage of its arch-rival's internal troubles to deliver a knockout blow, resulting in world supremacy. But in fact the USA responded cautiously. It had already, in the period immediately preceding the disintegration of the USSR, been evolving from an arch-enemy into a potential friend. This rapprochement derived from the phenomenon of 'mutual nuclear deterrence', which had first been acknowledged officially in the ABM Treaty of 1972. The intensity of the nuclear stand-off had subsequently been mitigated in a series of joint consultations to reduce arms levels. This 'thaw' in the Cold War had been largely the initiative of the Russians, for whom the costs of military competition constituted a serious obstacle to economic modernization and the development of a more consumer-oriented economy. Partial disarmament was to offer a remedy. But in fact the outcome was different. Externally, the policy did proceed according to expectations, and arms levels diminished. But the policy had unforeseen internal consequences. It failed to relieve the domestic tensions as expected, and the 'soft-handed' approach brought social and political divisions to the fore. The ruling authority had apparently failed to fully appreciate the integrative function of the repressive regime, and since a return to repression might have jeopardized the external détente, the government kept its armies in the barracks on the domestic front too. Before long, all room for manoeuvre had vanished. In the summer of 1991, the rulers lost control of the situation, and following a failed coup attempt – aimed at restoring the grip of the central machinery – the USSR dissolved relatively peacefully into a multitude of sovereign states. The consequences of this disintegration were dramatic. After a short period of euphoria, the costs of imperial contraction and collapse began to become apparent: military and monetary decline; economic impoverishment of the many and enrichment of the few; an upsurge in serious crime; and a fall in average life expectancy. All these developments were in stark contrast to the period of sustained economic growth in the West. Contrary to our often naturalized image of the nation-state, the importance of the phases of expansion and contraction in the scale of state-regulatory processes, as well as the role played by higher authorities in such processes, becomes very obvious in this contrast between the ascendancy of *Pax Americana* and the collapse of the Soviet Union.

Integration   Ten years on, the worst seems to be over. The Russian Federation now seems to be achieving a greater degree of social integration. And, ironically, this is partly a response to the scale of American hegemony. This was demonstrated in the first Gulf War of 1991, which Russia unsuccessfully opposed. It was shown again in the military interventions in former Yugoslavia, where the USA again ignored Russian opposition. A third example was the expansion of NATO to include several former Soviet satellite states in the face of Russian disapproval. Such flexing of military muscle fits into the classical pattern of inter-state rivalry and 'trials of strength'. But it has not removed the ultimate sanction implied by mutual deterrence, especially in cases where the Russian sphere of influence is at stake. In such matters the USA shows deference to its former rival, as in keeping a neutral stance with regard to the war in the Caucasus, which the Russian central authority regards as the acid test of its restoration of power. Such deference also has more positive overtones. From the very outset, the USA has approached the new Russia as an ally. Invited with money and wise counsel to join the New World Order, Russia consented. It set course towards a democratic system of government with an open market economy. The road has proved long, and restoration of the central authority will be the decisive factor in its success. Much also depends on the USA and its continued willingness to make tactful use of its hegemony. This seems to be, more or less, the way that America defines its own role. Its ambition is not to rule the world, and understandably so. The country is not under threat in any classical sense of the word, and should any other reasons exist for such an ambition, the mutual nuclear deterrence effectively makes any such attempt unlikely. And furthermore, there *are* no such reasons. The USA is a democratic constitutional state with an open market economy, and Russia and the other rivals of yesteryear are in the process of becoming so. Such countries do not fight each other: they resolve disputes through negotiation, or by applying economic sanctions if need be. This is the rule, at least, for societies of this type where economic and humanitarian interests weigh heavier than violence-tinged sentiments of glory and honour. Democracies show two distinctive faces – strongly cooperative inwardly, but militantly competitive towards adversaries outside of the cooperative of states. Such an orientation has proven to have an exceptional survival value in the past, but the advantages of such militancy seem to diminish to the degree that the competing states develop more bourgeois attributes. Such developments strengthen the pacification of the world, and at the same time they reduce the need for the unilateral pacifying role of the dominant USA. Indeed, the drift of the USA towards unilateral supremacy has not yet proceeded as far as the logic of the past would predict. But it continues nevertheless, and it is now running up against the inherent limitations of imperial overstretch.

The exception: mutual nuclear deterrence

There remains a third possibility. But this more federal solution remains as yet hypothetical. There is no global federal authority established by mutual consent in the face of a common, external danger, nor does it look like one will be created in the foreseeable future. There is, however, a development in progress that does bear resemblance to the historically exceptional federal scenario. It has arisen in the face of a violent danger from *within* that is inherent in the integrative and cooperative functions. This shared danger has already been touched upon. It is the mutual nuclear deterrence between Russia and the USA that still serves the cause of peace today, even after the Russian disintegration.

In view of the broad reach and proven effectiveness of its pacifying impact, mutual deterrence is a new phenomenon in history (van Benthem Van den Bergh 1992; McNeil 1982; Kapteyn 1996). Yet the 'frozen clinch' already has a respectable record of service. It began some ten years after the Second World War, when the USSR had closed the nuclear gap with the USA, and the instruments of violence stockpiled by both societies had reached such levels that they seemed manifestly unusable. Unintentionally such stockpiles forced both parties into the stalemate of the 'Cold Peace'. At this point the historical pattern of the state process ceased to operate, having reached its own ultimate limits. The mutual threat did not result in an elimination contest and nor did it generate a 'winner' with a clear state-regulatory remit over an expanded territory. It produced rather a condition of 'mutual assured destruction'. It thereby set the stage for a two-track coordination regime in which this potentially apocalyptic, internal competition, functioning in place of a common external threat, fostered a form of *negative cooperation* that can be understood in terms of the theory of reciprocity discussed above. All the necessary ingredients were present. The relationships were equal, at least that was the assumption on both sides. They were also acknowledged as such by both parties, and deviant behaviour was subject to punishment. This resulted in a curious, paradoxical kind of coordination based on trustful distrust. This 'mutual hostage relationship' was accepted as the least of all evils, which might gradually develop into something more positive.

And that was exactly what happened, though much faster and in different ways than the experts of this Cold War had anticipated. After thirty years of distrust, arms levels were reduced in gigantic strides, while the deterrence was left intact by mutual understanding even after the disintegration of the USSR, at least on paper. This educational effect can also be understood through the theory of reciprocity: Russia constrains American dominance, whilst accepting the pacifying impact of that dominance, on the condition that Russia's own, now more limited, sphere of influence is respected. In this fashion, 'world peace' is 'doubly' secured, ostensibly at least, by the unipolar coordination of the USA and the bipolar coordination of the USA and Russia together. A third potential safeguard against violence – let it be said again – is that mature bourgeois states do not tend to show belligerence among themselves.

This situation does not completely ensure peace, if only because China has meanwhile developed into a fully fledged, nuclear power. Since the disintegration of the USSR, China has been pursuing its own course, thus necessitating the future creation of a tripolar coordination regime to maintain the pacifying effects of nuclear weapons. Although relations between these three powers have since grown more friendly, some of the tensions still run high, especially between the USA and China, which is the least integrated of all the world's large states into the New World Order, and is also the least dependent on the USA supremacy. That has been demonstrated by a whole series of incidents in which the USA has tested the limits of its power, encroaching on China's territory and meeting accusations of arrogance. What probably carries more weight, however, is the growing structural cooperation between the two countries, especially in the realm of trade, where they have reached a compromise that opened Chinese access to the World Trade Organization and other economic arrangements. If this trend continues, as seems likely, the odds of military cooperation will be reasonably high, and the double safeguard to world peace will be sustained.

Such a conclusion is much less certain when it comes to the proliferation of nuclear weapons among a growing number of smaller nations, that are now caught up in series of local arms races and that also present a threat to the larger states. Since any open conflict is liable to escalation, such local conflicts are a threat to world peace. Proliferation jeopardizes the bipolar or tripolar coordination, and a multipolar coordinating arrangement would be difficult to secure, if only for practical reasons. This problem is being addressed through treaties that prohibit the proliferation and testing of nuclear and other weapons of mass destruction. Although America would be the appropriate power to compel compliance, it in fact fails to keep to agreements itself and seeks to cancel them. In violation of earlier promises, it is now working on a military 'space shield' designed to make the country invulnerable to nuclear aggression from any direction – one consequence of which would be to nullify the reciprocity of nuclear deterrence (see *The Economist*, no. 18, 2001: 9). Should such a shield be realized, it would signal an end to the dual peace. The USA would at once be both dominant and invulnerable, and – the crux of the matter – it could be less relied upon to police the world. This explains the widespread opposition to US unilateralism in this regard. Other countries would remain vulnerable to US weaponry themselves, and would also become increasingly vulnerable to threats from one another. Russia, China and the European Union, the cooperative arrangement of European states, would all take steps to bolster their own military capabilities, possibly in some new alliance that would undermine the strength of the Atlantic-based NATO. Such new configurations would be long in coming, however, and in the meantime the world would be a more dangerous place.

All things considered, the further spread of nuclear weaponry and the potential invulnerability of the USA present an uninviting prospect. For that very reason, however, the chances are great that the USA will relinquish its ambition to construct 'the shield', or will at least postpone it indefinitely, or, if it does build it, that it will do its utmost to minimize the dangerous consequences. Whatever sentiments may prevail, autarky remains a fantasy, even for the USA. That is true not only economically and culturally, but also militarily.

If this appraisal is correct – and is acknowledged as such by the USA – then that country will continue its proactive stance with or without the shield. The greatest risk would then be the mini-danger that states of the second rank and their accomplices with modest weapons arsenals will try to circumvent the global regime.

How serious this 'mini-danger' already is was brought home by the terrorist attack on the USA in September 2001 – which, of course, was not carried out with nuclear weapons and was also not perpetrated by a foreign state, but by groups with political and religious motives. How would the United States react? The question had taken on new urgency in the light of the unprecedented, almost inconceivable, magnitude of the disaster. Would US policy become more proactive or more reactive, and would it be guided by multilateralism or unilateralism? At first it appeared that proactive multilateralism would predominate. But the mild euphoria of an activated cooperative of states dissipated rapidly when the USA ignored both NATO and the UN Security Council in its attack on Afghanistan, whose Taliban regime had supported the terrorist organization, and when, despite a brief impulse to the contrary, the USA deliberately allowed the related Israeli–Palestinian conflict to escalate by failing to intervene. The Bush government also resumed its earlier campaign to abrogate, frustrate or deny ratification of international agreements addressing a wide range of problems: e.g. the aforementioned ABM treaty; treaties against nuclear weapons testing and biological weapons production; global warming and carbon dioxide emissions (the Kyoto Protocol); the illicit trading in small arms; agreements establishing a permanent

International Court of Justice; and, to end with an issue of a different order, the provision of support to abortion clinics in the Third World.

Yet this unmistakable trend towards unilateral dominance on the part of the USA is likely to ease in the longer term in favour of a more cooperative reciprocity. After all, the terrorist attack itself has underlined the vulnerability of even the most powerful country in the world. It also demonstrated how problematic it is to overcome that vulnerability through strategies that violate the American way of life and political order, attacking the very assets it claims to defend. American vulnerability has increased sharply in recent decades, and the country seems gradually to be accepting and recognizing this reality. The same applies to the erstwhile enemies that are now participants in the cooperative of states. Russia and China expressed their condolences at the deaths of thousands of Americans and at the blow to national pride. They appealed for a strengthening of international cooperation. Notably absent here was the spiteful regime in Iraq, whose feelings of revenge had been gratified, but which might sensibly have feared a renewed conflict with the USA, fuelled by suspicions that Iraq was an accomplice in the attacks. And sure enough, tensions between the two countries mounted, with the USA levelling allegations of Iraqi complicity and non-compliance with disarmament obligations dating from the 1991 Gulf War. Initially US policy was tempered by multilateral concerns. What at first seemed a unilateral retaliatory act by a dominant party developed into a common concern of the cooperative of states, represented by the UN Security Council. However, when the Council proved ultimately to be divided about the urgency of the Iraq issue, the USA decided to proceed, together with the UK, to declare war and topple the Iraqi regime. Even though such a move had been anticipated, the assembly of states was shocked by this unilateral action. Most states denounced the decision, which they saw as not serving a policing function, but merely US interests. Although understandable, this international reaction ignored the simple fact that the world order is structured around the two principles of dominance and reciprocity. The USA is the dominant party, and it acts unilaterally on that basis until, sooner or later, self-interest dictates a shift towards multilateral reciprocity. It can be expected that this will also happen in relation to Iraq. Whatever impact the unilateral US actions may have, Iraq will return to the agenda of the cooperative of states sooner or later, thus strengthening the cooperative. In due course, something similar may also happen with the space shield. What began as a unilateral strategy may well evolve into a multilateral project. One thing is already clear. Whatever the exact balance may be at any given moment between a more reactive or proactive policy, or between a more unilateral or multilateral attitude, the world will remain dependent on US military supremacy and on the mutual deterrence between several world powers for a long time to come. Obviously this order of bourgeois states does not provide absolute security. Yet it still constitutes a pacifying condition previously unknown in human society.

Conclusion

The dual order: hegemony and reciprocity

The historical pattern of the state process has persisted into recent times, though less inexorably than anticipated by Elias in his book *The Civilizing Process*. Although a dominant party has indeed emerged on the global stage, its power is constrained by the reciprocity of violent deterrence. World peace now seems doubly ensured. This dual order of global peace is strengthened by the fact that the states involved are democracies with open market economies, or are moving in that direction. States of this type typically resolve their mutual disputes peaceably – a quality that forms a useful complement to the historical pattern of the state process as analysed by Elias. The dual order has already succeeded in preventing the 'last' world war. It is for this reason that no world government or global hub of administrative authority has emerged as the result of such a decisive elimination contest. In the context of nuclear weapons, the principle of elimination now seems to have lost its potency. The dual order navigates between two poles: the reciprocity of many states, especially the largest ones; and the dominance of one of them, the USA, which has the potential to act forcefully. This dominance is perceived positively to the extent that it engenders order, and negatively in so far as it compromises the autonomy of the other states. The same applies in reverse to the regime of reciprocity. The respect for autonomy engenders mutual confidence between states, but at the cost of the indecisiveness of so many officially equal parties. The present structure of the United Nations can be seen as an attempt to steer between these poles, reconciling the democratic reciprocity of the (failed) League of Nations, with the reality of *Pax Americana*. It is in this field of tension that the 'cooperative of states' sets its bearings, like a fleet of ships lacking an overseeing admiral, able to chart the course and enforce order. Here lurks the perpetual danger of 'every man for himself'. And yet the dual order still remains the least of many evils. It offers peace to the world, at least more or less. Although that peace may be imperfect, it is also unprecedented in history. It is unarguable that, perceptions aside, in pacified Western societies, more people live peaceably, in the absence of any realistic threat of war and without a pervasive certainty of violence in the context of daily life, than at any time in history. And this situation may be extended to incorporate more people and more countries. In time this may provide some sort of 'end to history', and a new beginning, opening up unparalleled opportunities for peaceful cooperation in military, economic and cultural realms.

Three stages of cooperation

Those opportunities are now being seized. Peaceful cooperation has spread across national frontiers, changing the classical sequence – today's cooperation does not presume a higher authority that is constituted in violent competition, but it creates that authority itself through what may be called the three stages of transnational cooperation. The *transfer of national autonomy* is the decisive factor. The first stage is *negative cooperation*. Parties refrain from doing something they previously did, and they do so with comparative ease, because their autonomy is reduced but not relinquished or transferred. Examples are the early disarmament agreements, and the lowering or removal of trade barriers in the context of the WTO, the EU or other regional organizations. The second stage is *positive cooperation*, whereby the participating parties actively seek to remedy the adverse consequences of negative cooperation. Positive cooperation generally demands more effort. National autonomy is shared in a collective entity, but is also protected by powers of veto, so that a dissenting vote may impede progress. Examples of positive cooperation are peacekeeping missions, and also common monetary policies to neutralize currency competition. The third stage of cooperation is the *formation of a higher authority*, whereby the cooperating states do away with the power of veto and transfer part of their autonomy to a new body, thus endowing that body with an authority of its own. This final step is the most difficult one. But it is increasingly being taken, primarily in order to resolve disputes between the participating parties. This stage of cooperation hence involves the international administration of justice through *ad hoc* or permanent international courts of justice, as well as dispute settlement through the WTO or the Court of Justice of the European Union. Each such institution is invested with a higher authority to which the participating states have voluntarily submitted.

Viewed in this way, the three stages of cooperation form an upward progression in which each lower stage generates tensions that can be resolved at a higher stage. Such a progression goes beyond the process of state formation identified by Elias in *The Civilizing Process*, and in which, as we have seen, cooperation is premised upon the existence of a higher authority, which itself is the outcome of a process of violent competition. This historical pattern seems now to have been transcended. Although this *three-stage progression to world cooperation* does presume the existence of the dual order as a condition for its continuation, it then proceeds further to generate its own higher authority.

REFERENCES

Axelrod, Robert 1990 [orig. 1984], *The Evolution of Cooperation*, London: Penguin.

Benthem van den Berg, G. van 1992, *The Nuclear Revolution and the End of the Cold War: Forced Restraint*, Basingstoke: Macmillan (in association with the Institute of Social Studies).

Elias, Norbert 1982 [orig. 1939], *The Civilizing Process, Vol. 2: State Formation and Civilization*, Oxford: Basil Blackwell.

Goudsblom, Johan 1996, 'The formations of military-agrarian regimes', in J. Goudsblom, Eric Jones and Stephen Mennell, *The Course of Human History*, Armonk, NY and London: M.E. Sharpe.

Kapteyn, Paul 1996, *The Stateless Market, The European Dilemma of Integration and Civilization*, London: Routledge.

McNeill, William 1963, *The Rise of the West: A History of the Human Community*, Chicago: University of Chicago Press.

1982, *The Pursuit of Power: Technology, Armed Forces and Society since 1000 AD*, Oxford: Blackwell.

Olson, Mancur 1965, *The Logic of Collective Action*, Cambridge, MA: Harvard University Press.

1982, *The Rise and Decline of Nations*, New Haven, CT and London: Yale University Press.

Swaan, A. de 1995, 'Rationale keuze als proces', *Amsterdam Sociologisch Tijdschrift* 22 (4): 593–609.

11 Changing regimes of manners and emotions: from disciplining to informalizing

Cas Wouters

Introduction

In this chapter, I outline changes in the regimes of manners and emotions in the West between the fifteenth and the twenty-first century. I will use the material and perspective developed by Norbert Elias in *The Civilizing Process*, and extend Elias's own investigation through to the end of the twentieth century. By studying manners books, Elias uncovered evidence of long-term changes in social codes as well as in people's psychic makeup. According to his theory, the dynamic momentum of these directional processes derives from 'the increasing division of functions under the pressure of competition' (2000: 433), tending to integrate increasing numbers of people in expanding and increasingly dense networks of interdependency. He showed these changes in power and dependency relationships to be connected with changes in sources of power and identity, in competition for status and a meaningful life, and also with changes in how the manners people of different class, sex or age showed a demand for respect or fear of the loss of. With Elias, I understand changes in the code of manners and feeling to illuminate changes in relationships *between* individuals and groups (social classes, sexes and generations – *sociogenesis*) as well as psychic processes *within* people, i.e. in how individuals manage their emotions and 'relate to themselves' (*psychogenesis*).

The history of Western manners and emotion management shows that the more extreme expressions of social and psychic distance between people of different social class, age and gender have declined and vanished. It shows a long-term trend of restricting expression of feelings of superiority and inferiority. However, whereas this trend continued into the twentieth century, in other respects the changes in regimes of manners and emotions showed marked discontinuities. Until the end of the nineteenth century there was a consistent trend towards the formalizing of manners and the disciplining of people. During this period the code of manners became increasingly strict and detailed, a development which corresponded to the spread of a type of personality with a rather stringent mode of self-regulation and a rather rigid conscience, functioning more or less automatically as a 'second nature'. In contrast to this long-term formalizing of manners and disciplining of people, the twentieth century has seen an extended process of informalization of manners along with a disciplined relaxation of people's conscience and self-regulation. Much that was strictly forbidden at the end of the nineteenth century came to be allowed in the course of the twentieth. Manners have become more lenient, more differentiated and varied for a wider and more differentiated public; an increasing variety of behavioural and emotional alternatives have come to be socially accepted and expected. There has been a collective 'emancipation of emotions', that is, a (re)entering of emotions into the centre of personality – consciousness. With increasing social integration and mutual identification the social and psychic distance between people has diminished and the expectation to be frank and at ease in expressing feelings has spread. From this perspective, the trend involves ongoing attempts to reconnect to deeper layers of the personality without losing control. This implies a rise in the demands on emotion management and on the self-steering capacities of people through reflection, presence of mind, consideration, role-taking and the ability to bear and control conflicts. The trend of social constraints towards self-restraints has continued.

Any code of manners functions as a regime, as a form of external social control demanding the exercise of self-control. Manners and sensibilities function as power resources in the competition for social status and meaning, they provide important criteria for social ranking. As a rule, the dominant code of manners serves to maintain the prevailing social dividing lines, particularly a social distance between the established classes and those trying to enter their circles. Manners are instruments of exclusion or rejection and of inclusion and group charisma: individuals and groups with the necessary qualifications are let in while the 'rude' – that is, all others lower down the social ladder – are kept out. The dual function of manners is evident in such comments as 'They are not nice people'; manners are a weapon of attack as well as a weapon of defence. Any code of manners contains a standard of sensitivity and composure, functioning to preserve the sense of purity, integrity and identity of the group.

Good manners usually trickled down the social ladder. The sensibilities and manners cherished by the established generally functioned as a model for people from other social groups aspiring to respectability and social ascent. Only at times of large-scale social mobility, when whole groups gained access to the centres of established power, did their manners to some extent trickle up with them. In contrast to individual social ascent, the ascent of an entire social group involves some mixing of the codes and ideals of the ascendant group with those of the previously superior groups. The history of manners thus reflects the social ascent of increasingly wider social groups. In general, specific national regimes of manners and emotions have developed from different national class structures, from their specific forms and levels of competition and cooperation.

Some changes in manners are symptomatic of changing power balances between states. As France became the most dominant power in Europe, French court manners increasingly took over the model function previously fulfilled by Italian court manners. In the nineteenth century, with the rising power of England, the manners of English 'good society' came to serve as a major example in many other countries. Likewise, after the Second World War, when the United States became a dominant superpower, American manners served more easily as a model. Before that war, the USA had already been rising as a model, in particular because of the relatively early development of a youth culture in that country, and, in close connection, of an appealing entertainment industry, summarized and symbolized as Hollywood.

The study of manners and emotion management

Interest in the history of manners is fairly new and has grown together with interest in the history of emotions, mentalities and everyday life, all of which only became serious topics of research after the 1960s. When it appeared in German in 1939, *The Civilizing Process* was the first systematic study of the history of manners and emotion management. Among the studies that prepared the way was the work of the Dutch historian Johan Huizinga, particularly *The Autumn of the Middle Ages*, originally published in 1919. This book had an unusual focus on manners, emotions, mentalities and everyday life in the fifteenth century; it presented a lively sketch of the wide range of behaviours, the intensities of joy and sorrow, and the public nature of life. However, this work was exceptional and remained marginal until, during the 1930s, the historians Lucien Febvre, Marc Bloch and others associated with the French *Annales* school, again took up an interest in mentalities, lifestyles and daily life.

As a serious object of study, the history of manners and emotion management has faced a major obstacle in the strong social pressures of status competition. No matter what social definition of 'good manners' may prevail, if these 'good manners' do not come 'naturally', that is, more or less automatically, the effect is ruined. Only manners springing from the inner sensitivity of 'second nature' may impress as 'natural'. Otherwise, the taints of status-aspiration and status-related anxiety attach to an individual, provoking embarrassment and repulsion. For this reason, status-competition and inherent status anxieties have exerted pressure to associate the entire topic of manners with lower classes and with 'lower instincts'. That is, as good manners themselves were taken for granted, the subject of manners was limited to spheres in which good ones were taken to be absent. Throughout the period from the 1920s to the 1960s, manners were discussed mainly in the context of the behavioural 'problems' of lower classes, of children having to learn such things as table manners, as well as of social climbers and *nouveaux riches* who were usually seen as being too loud and too conspicuous. Status fears have in this way functioned as a barrier to developing the level of reflexivity needed for serious interest in the subject. These fears have impeded the development of an historical perspective by making people less inclined to perceive their own manners as the outcome of social and psychic processes.

More recently, social integration, the social ascent of certain groups – the working classes, women, youth, homosexuals and blacks – spurred the development of the level of detachment and reflection needed for studies in the social history of manners and mentalities. In the 1960s and 1970s these groups were emancipated and further integrated within nation-states. Accompanied by an avalanche of protest against all relationships and manners perceived as authoritarian, they succeeded in having themselves treated with more respect. This implied a decline in the social and psychic distance between people and a widening of their circles of identification (Swaan 1995). Similarly, processes of decolonization saw whole populations emancipated and integrated, however poorly, within a global network of states. As differences in power and rank diminished, the motive to keep up a social and psychic distance lost vigour, resulting in greater interest in the daily lives of 'ordinary' people. With increased mobility, and more frequent contact between different kinds of people, has come the pressure to look at oneself and others with greater detachment, to ask questions about manners that previous generations took for granted: why is this forbidden and that permitted or prescribed? These processes have been the driving forces behind the growing interest in the study of manners, mentalities and emotion management.

The period of courts and courtesy

The manners books studied by Elias included prominent ones that were translated, imitated and reprinted again and again. These books were directed primarily at the secular upper classes, particularly people living in courtly circles around great lords. Early modern terms for good manners such as 'courtesy' derive from the word 'court'. With few exceptions, these books address adults and present adult standards. They deal openly with many questions that later became embarrassing and even repugnant, such as when and how to fart, burp or spit. These changes in feelings of shame and delicacy become vividly apparent in the chronological sequence of excerpts presented by Elias. The series on table manners, for example, shows that people at feudal courts ate with their fingers, using only their own general-purpose knife or dagger. The main restriction on using the knife was not to clean one's teeth with it. Everyone ate from the same dish, using a common spoon to transfer the food onto a slice of bread. Readers were advised to refrain from falling on the dish like pigs, from dipping already bitten or nibbled food items into the communal sauce, and from presenting a tasty morsel from their own to a companion's mouth. Diners were not to snort while eating, or blow their noses on the tablecloth (as this was used for wiping greasy fingers) or into their fingers.

This kind of advice was repeated throughout the Middle Ages. Then, from around the sixteenth century, the regimes of manners and emotions entered a period of continuous flux. Codes became more differentiated and more demanding. In the sixteenth century the fork was introduced as a proper item of cutlery, although only for lifting food from the common dish. Likewise, handkerchiefs and napkins begin to appear as albeit optional items of tableware; if you had one, you were to use it rather than your fingers. Only by the mid-eighteenth century had plates, knives, forks, spoons and napkins for each guest, and also handkerchiefs, become more or less indispensable utensils for the courtly class. In this and other aspects, the code of these upper classes was then beginning to resemble the more general usage of later centuries.

Erasmus wrote that it was impolite to speak to someone who was urinating or defaecating; he discussed these acts quite openly. In his conduct manual, *Il Galateo ovvero De' Costumi* (1558), Giovanni della Casa wrote that 'it is not a refined habit, when coming across something disgusting in the sheet, as sometimes happens, to turn at once to one's companion and point it out to him' (Elias 2000: 111). This warning is in line with other evidence from early manners books, which indicate that urinating and defaecating were not yet punctiliously restricted to their socially designated, proper places. Often enough, needs were satisfied when and where they happened to be felt. Over time, these bodily functions increasingly came to be invested with feelings of shame and repugnance, until eventually they were performed only in strict privacy and not spoken of without embarrassment. Likewise, certain parts of the body became increasingly 'private parts' or, as most European languages phrase it, 'shame parts' ('pudenda', deriving from the Latin word meaning to be ashamed).

The same trend is apparent in relation to behaviour in the bedroom. As the advice cited above indicates, it was quite normal to receive visitors in rooms with beds, just as it was very common to spend the night with many in one room. Sleeping was not yet set apart from the rest of social life. Usually people slept naked. Special nightclothes slowly came into use at about the same time as the fork and the handkerchief. Manners books specified how to behave when sharing a bed with a person of the same sex. For instance, a manners book from 1729, as quoted by Elias, warns that 'it is not proper to lie so near him that you disturb or even touch him; and it is still less decent to put your legs between those of the other'. From the 1774 edition of the same book, an advance in the thresholds of shame and repugnance can be deduced, for this pointed instruction was removed and the tone of advice became more indirect and more moral: 'you should maintain a strict and vigilant modesty'. The new edition also noted that to be forced to share a bed 'seldom happens' (Elias 2000: 137). Gradually, to share a bed with strangers, with people outside the family, became embarrassing. As with other bodily functions, sleeping slowly became more intimate and private, until it was performed only behind the scenes of social life.

In general, as Elias's examples showed, what was first allowed later became restricted or forbidden. Heightened sensitivity with regard to several activities, especially those related to the 'animalic' or 'first nature' of human beings, coincided with increasing segregation of these activities from the rest of social life; they became private. Again and again, what was once seen as good manners later became rude or, at the other extreme, so ingrained in behaviour as to be completely taken for granted. Social superiors made subordinates feel inferior if they did not meet their standard of manners. Increasingly, fear of social superiors and, more generally, the fear of transgression of social prohibitions took on the character of an inner fear, shame.

All new prescriptions and prohibitions were used as a means of social distinction until they lost their distinction potential. Gradually, ever-broader social strata were willing and anxious to adopt the models developed above them, compelling those above to develop new means of distinction. For instance, it became a breach of good manners to appear naked or incompletely dressed or to perform natural functions before those of higher or equal rank; doing so before inferiors could be taken as a sign of benevolence. Later, nakedness and excretion not conducted in private became general offences invested with shame and embarrassment. Gradually, the social commands controlling these actions came to operate with regard to everyone and were imprinted as such on children. Thus all references to social control, including shame, became embedded as assumptions and as such receded from consciousness. Adults came to experience social prohibitions as 'natural', emanating from their own inner selves rather than from the outer realm of 'good manners'. As these social constraints took on the form of more or less total and automatically functioning self-restraints, this standard behaviour had become 'second nature'. Accordingly, manners books no longer dealt with these matters or did so far less extensively. Social constraints pressed towards stronger and more automatic self-supervision, the subordination of short-term impulses to the commandment of a habitual longer-term perspective, and the cultivation of a more stable, constant and differentiated self-regulation. This is, as Elias called it, a civilizing process.

In his explanation, Elias emphasized the importance of processes of state formation, in which taxation and the use of physical violence and its instruments were progressively centralized and monopolized. Medieval societies lacked any central power strong enough to compel people to restrain their impulses to use violence. Over the course of the sixteenth century, families of the old warrior nobility and some families of bourgeois origin were transformed into a new upper class of courtiers; impulsive war-lords became tamed nobles with more muted affective drives. In this way, the territories of great lords were increasingly pacified, and at their courts, encouraged especially by the presence of ladies, more peaceful forms of conduct became obligatory. Such conduct was a basic part of the regime of courtly manners, and its development, including ways of speaking, dressing and holding and moving the body, went hand in hand with the rise of courtly regimes.

Within the pacified territories of strong lords, the permanent danger and fear of violent attack diminished. This relative physical safety facilitated the growth of towns, burgher groups, commerce, wealth, and, as a result, taxation. Taxes financed larger armies and administrative bodies, thus helping the central rulers of the court societies to expand their power and their territory at the expense of others. The dynamic of the competition for land and money went in the direction of expanding the webs of interdependence, bonding together the people of different territories. Political integration and economic integration intertwined and reinforced each other, culminating in the absolute monarchies of the later seventeenth and the eighteenth centuries.

The inhabitants of these states were increasingly constrained to settle conflicts in non-violent ways, thus pressuring each other to tame their impulses towards aggressiveness and cruelty. Moreover, families of bourgeois origin had risen in power, enough to compete with the nobility and forcefully to demand more respect. Their former social superiors were obliged to develop the habit of permanently restraining their more extreme expressions of superiority, particularly violent ones. Such displays were successfully branded as degrading. As they came to provoke shame and repulsion, impulses in that direction and the corresponding feelings of superiority (and inferiority) came to be more or less automatically repressed and rejected. Thus, in a widening circle of mutual respect and identification, the more extreme displays of superiority and inferiority were excluded from the prevailing regime of manners and emotions.

The taming of aggressiveness coincided with an increase in sensibility towards suffering, that is, in the scope of mutual identification. Growing sensitivity to violence, suffering and blood can be deduced also from changes in manners such as increasing restrictions on the use of the knife as an instrument and symbol of danger. For instance, it was frowned upon to eat fish or cut potatoes with a knife, or to bring the knife to one's mouth. In a related trend, the slaughtering of animals and carving of their meat were removed from the public scene into slaughterhouses. The carving of large cuts of meat was also increasingly removed from the dinner table to the kitchen.

From courtesy to etiquette

In the absolute monarchies all groups, estates or classes, despite their differences, became dependent upon each other, thus also increasing the dependence of each of the major interest groups on the central coordinating monopoly power. Administration and control over the state, its centralized and monopolized resources, first expanded and spread into the hands of growing numbers of individuals. Then, with the rise of bourgeois groups no longer dependent on privileges derived from the Crown, royal or 'private' state monopolies were gradually transformed into societal or 'public' ones. With the exception of The Netherlands, where monopoly administration had in 1581 already been taken over by merchant patricians, this shift from private to public occurred in the late eighteenth century, first in France and later in many other European countries. This process accelerated in the nineteenth century, with the rising power and status of wealthy middle classes and the declining importance of courts, formerly the aristocratic centres of power.

The transition from the eighteenth-century 'courtesy genre' of manners books to the nineteenth-century 'etiquette genre' reflects this change. The new genre presented a blend of aristocratic and bourgeois manners. The aristocratic tradition persisted, for example, in the continuing importance of being self-confident and at ease. Even the slightest suggestion of effort or forethought was itself bad manners. Whereas courtesy books typically advocated ideals of character, temperament, accomplishments, habits, morals and manners for aristocratic life, etiquette books focused more narrowly on the sociability of particular social situations – dinners, balls, receptions, presentations at court, calls, introductions and salutations. Etiquette books were directed at sociability in the centres of power and their 'good society', a term referring to the social groups that possessed the strength of a social establishment. Here, the dominant social definition of proper ways to establish and maintain relationships is constructed. Particularly in England, etiquette books specified how to maintain public and private boundaries, how to practise reserve and to avoid intruding on another's privacy (Curtin 1987). The manners of good society were decisive in making acquaintances and friends, and for gaining influence and recognition. They also functioned as a means of winning a desirable spouse. In comparison to court circles, the circles of good society were larger, and sociability in them was more 'private'. In many of those circles the private sphere was more sharply distinguished from the public and occupational spheres.

The life and career of the bourgeois classes both in business and the professions depended heavily on promise-keeping and on the rather punctual and minute regulation of social traffic and behaviour. Accordingly, nineteenth-century manners books placed great emphasis on acquiring the self-discipline necessary for living a 'rational life'; they emphasized time-keeping and ordering activities routinely in a fixed sequence and at a set pace. The entrepreneurial bourgeoisie needed to arrange contracts, for which a reputation of being financially solvent and morally solid was crucial. To a large extent this reputation was formed in the gossip channels of good society. As occupational and political businesses depend on trust building, that is, on making friends and acquaintances in the field, these people developed the custom of inviting each other to dinner and to the other sociable occasions that good society provided, such as parties organized in their private drawing rooms. Thus professional success and social success strongly overlapped.

The reputation of moral solidity referred to the self-discipline of orderliness, thrift and responsibility, qualities needed for a firm grip on the proceedings of business transactions. Thomas Haskell (1985) has pointed to the 'disciplinary force of the market' in connection to the norm of promise-keeping and the ascendancy of conscience. The expectation that everyone would live up to promises – as comprised in contracts made on 'the market' – became a mutually expected self-restraint, which became taken for granted to the extent that it came to function as part of conscience. This type of conscience formation presupposes state formation, 'for everything in the contract is not contractual', as Durkheim has put it, or more precisely: the order behind the contract, 'in current parlance, is designated by the name, state' (1964 [1893]: 211–19). In the terms of Elias – the monopolization of the use of violence by the state and ensuing pacification of larger territories provided a necessary condition for the expectation of living up to promises and contracts to become taken for granted and engrained in the personality as conscience.

Moral solidity also pertained to the social and sexual sphere; without demonstrable control over wives and family, working bourgeois men would fail to create a solid impression of reliability and ability to live up to the terms of their contracts. Therefore, bourgeois means of controlling potentially dangerous social and sexual competition depended to a substantial degree on the support of wives for their husbands. Her support and social charm could make a crucial difference, as is implied in the opinion that 'nothing makes a man look more ridiculous in the eyes of the world than a socially helpless wife' (Klickmann 1902: 25). At the same time, these pressures offered specific opportunities to women. Whereas men dominated the courtesy genre of manners books, in the etiquette genre women gained a prominent position, both as authors and as readers. As the social weight of the bourgeoisie increased, middle-class women enjoyed a widening sphere of opportunities. Although confined to the domain of their home and good society, in the nineteenth century upper- and middle-class women more or less came to run and organize the social sphere. The workings of good society in large part took place in women's private drawing rooms. To a considerable extent, women came to function as the gatekeepers of this social formation, as arbiters of social acceptance or rejection (Curtin 1987; Davidoff 1973).

The expansion of good society

Compared to courts, circles of good society were larger, more open and more competitive, and as they expanded the people in them developed increasingly detailed and formal manners for social circulation – a complicated system of introductions, invitations, leaving cards, calls, 'at homes' (specified times when guests were received), receptions, dinners and so on. Entrance into good society was impossible without an introduction, which usually required the previous permission of both parties. This regime of manners not only regulated sociability, it also functioned as a relatively refined system of inclusion and exclusion, as an instrument to screen newcomers into social circles, to ensure that the newly introduced would assimilate to the prevailing regime of manners, and to identify and exclude undesirables. Sometimes, this was made quite explicit, as in

Etiquette for Ladies of 1863: 'Etiquette is the form or law of society enacted and upheld by the more refined classes as a protection and a shield
against the intrusion of the vulgar and impertinent' (quoted in Curtin
1987: 130). A basic rule of manners among those acknowledged as belonging to the circle was to treat each other on the basis of equality. Quite
often this was expressed in what became known as the Golden Rule of
manners: do to others as you would have them do to you. Others were
treated with reserve and thus kept at a social distance. In short, members
treated everyone either as an equal or as a stranger; in this way more
extreme displays of superiority and inferiority were avoided.

As a rule, differentiations in social distance among those included in
good society ran parallel with differentiations in social status. Thus, even
within the ranks of good society the practice of reserve functioned to
keep people considered not equal enough at a social distance and thus
to prevent (other) displays of superiority and inferiority. Procedures of
precedence, salutation, body carriage, facial expression and so on, all
according to rank, age and gender, functioned to regulate and cover status
competition within the ranks of good society.

As large middle-class groups became socially strong enough to compete in the struggle for power and status, they also demanded to be
treated according to the Golden Rule. As good society expanded in
the nineteenth century, circles of identification widened and spread, becoming increasingly multilayered. As ever-wider groups ascended into
these ranks, status competition intensified, pressuring all towards greater
awareness and sharper observation of each other and of themselves. Sensitivities were heightened, particularly to expressions of status difference.
As standards of sensibility and delicacy rose, the manners of getting acquainted and keeping a distance became more important as well as more
detailed.

To keep a distance from strangers was of great concern. Especially in
cities, the prototypical stranger was someone who might have the manners
of the respectable but not the morals. Strangers personified bad company
that would endanger the self-control of the respectable, prompting loss of
composure in response to repulsive behaviour or, worse, the succumbing
to temptation. In the nineteenth century, authors of manners books came
to describe the fall of innocent young men as lessons in moral virtue and
vigilance. Their repeated warnings against strangers expressed a strong
moral appeal, revealing a fear of the slippery slope towards giving in to
immoral pleasures. These warnings were directed at young men in particular. Playing a single game of cards with strangers, for example, would
'always end in trouble, often in despair, and sometimes in suicide', an
early-nineteenth-century advice book warned. By its nature, any careless

indulgence in pleasure would lead to 'a lethal fall' (Tilburg 1998: 66/7; Newton 1994; Blumin 1989). This strong moral advice was intended to teach young men the responsibilities needed not only for a successful career but also, as marriages were no longer arranged by parents, for choosing a marriage partner. Advice betrayed the fear that such choices would be determined mainly by sexual attraction. Social censorship verged on psychic censorship – warnings expanded to the 'treacherous effects' of fantasy. This kind of high-pitched moral pressure stimulated the development of rather rigid ways of avoiding anything defined as dangerous or unacceptable via the formation of a rigorous conscience. The pressures of this conscience formation and of growing interdependencies stimulated the rise of conflict-avoiding and nature-loving persons, obsessed with self-discipline, punctuality, orderliness and the importance of living a rational life. For them, the view of emotions came to be associated predominantly with dangers and weaknesses. Thus the successive ascent of large middle-class groups and their increasing status and power relative to other groups were reflected in the regimes of manners and of self-regulation.

Processes of formalization and conscience formation: second nature

Developments from the Renaissance to the end of the nineteenth century can be described as a long-term process of formalizing and disciplining; more and more aspects of behaviour were subjected to increasingly strict and detailed regulations that were partly formalized as laws and partly as manners. In this process, expression or display and, at its zenith, even references to emotions, especially those that could provoke violence, were curbed and tabooed. This regime of manners also expanded to include restrictions on behaviour defined as arrogant and humiliating, as wild, violent, dirty, indecent or lecherous. As this kind of now unacceptable behaviour became sanctioned by increasingly vigorous practices of social shaming, emotions or impulses potentially leading to that behaviour came to be avoided and repressed via the counter-impulses of individual shame. Any admission of these 'dangerous' emotions and impulses was likely to provoke compelling feelings of shame and anxiety. Thus, via an expanding regime of manners, a widening range of behaviours and feelings disappeared from the social scene and the conscious minds of individuals. In the nineteenth century, among upper and middle-class people this resulted in the formation of a type of personality characterized by an 'inner compass' (Riesman 1950) of reflexes and rather fixed habits, increasingly compelling regimes of manners and self-regulation. Impulses and emotions came to be controlled increasingly via the more or less automatically functioning counter impulses of an authoritative conscience, with a strong penchant for order and regularity, cleanliness and neatness. Negligence in these matters indicated an inclination toward dissoluteness. Such inclinations were to be nipped in the bud, particularly in children. Without rigorous control, 'first nature' might run wild. This old conviction expresses a fear that is typical of rather authoritarian relationships and social controls as well as a relatively authoritative conscience. The long-term trend of formalization reached its peak in the Victorian era, from the mid nineteenth century to its last decade; the metaphor of the stiff upper lip indicated ritualistic manners and a kind of ritualistic self-control, heavily based on an authoritative conscience and functioning more or less automatically as a 'second nature'. Particularly in the last decades of the nineteenth century, the 'domestication of nature', including one's own (first) nature, increasingly came to trigger both the experience of an 'alienation from nature' and a new romanticized longing for nature (Frykman and Löfgren 1987).

The twentieth century: a long-term process of informalization

By the end of the nineteenth century social groups with 'new money' were socially rising, creating strong pressures on 'old-money' centres of power and good societies to open up. Whole groups and classes were still outspokenly deemed unacceptable as people to associate with, but as emancipation and integration processes accelerated, the old avoidance behaviour of keeping up a considerable social and psychic distance became increasingly difficult. People from different social classes had become interdependent to the point where they could no longer avoid immediate contact with each other. Especially in expanding cities, at work and on the streets, in public conveyances and entertainment facilities, people who once used to avoid each other were now forced to try either to maintain or recover social distance under conditions of rising proximity, or to accommodate and become accustomed to more social mixing: 'Sometimes farmhands, fishwives or other such people come to sit down next to you. Cringing in your seat with a gesture of alarm or looking down at them with an expression of contempt, such behaviour does not exhibit any upbringing at all' (Stratenus 1909: 10). At the same time, people were warned against the dangers of familiarity, of being too open and becoming too close. From another direction came attacks on traditional ways of keeping a distance as an expression of superiority. As some social mixing became less avoidable, more extreme ways of keeping a distance and showing superiority were banned. Manners became less hierarchical and less formal and rigid.

The same trend is apparent in manners regulating the relationship between the sexes. From the end of the nineteenth century onwards, women gradually escaped from the confines of the home and good society (or its functional equivalent among other social strata). Chaperonage declined, and upper- and middle-class women expanded their sources of power and identity by joining the suffragette movement, attending university, engaging in social work or playing sports. Women, especially young women, wanted to go out, raising the question of whether they should be allowed to pay for themselves. The respectability of meeting places and conditions of meeting became more flexible, as young people began to exert control over the dynamics of their own relationships, whether romantic or not.

In the 1920s many newly wealthy families were jostling for a place within the ranks of good society. The rise of whole social groups triggered a formidable push toward informalization, and rules for getting acquainted and keeping a distance declined. The expansion of business and industry, together with an expansion of means of transportation and communication, gave rise to a multitude of new types of relationships for which the old formality was too troublesome. New meeting places for the sexes such as dance halls, cinemas, and ice-skating rinks were debated for the freedom that they offered. As women entered the wider society by going to work in offices, libraries and other places, office manners became a topic. The whole trend implied rising demands on the social-navigational abilities of the individual, such as a greater capacity to negotiate the possibilities and limitations of relationships easily and without tension.

Until the 1960s some manners books still contained separate sections on behaviour toward social superiors and inferiors. Later these sections disappeared. Ideals for good manners became dissociated from superior and inferior social position or rank. The trend was to draw social dividing lines less on the basis of people's belonging to certain groups – class, race, age, sex or ethnicity – and more on the basis of individual behaviour. The avoidance behaviour once prescribed toward people not deemed socially acceptable was increasingly discouraged. No longer could certain groups be legitimately targeted; rather, certain behaviour and feelings – including humiliating displays of superiority and inferiority – were considered inappropriate and could be shunned as such. An example of this process is the change in the introduction to America's most famous etiquette book by Emily Post. In the editions published from 1922 to 1937, this introduction still referred to superior groups of people, 'Best Society', and their advanced 'cultivation': 'Cultivation is always the basic attribute of Best

Society, much as we hear in this country of an "Aristocracy of wealth"' (1922: 1). In 1937, these formulations had been removed, and instead Mrs Post refers to personal qualities and instinct, using the term 'nature's nobleman' to state that 'the code of a thoroughbred . . . is the code of instinctive decency, ethical integrity, self-respect and loyalty' (1937: 2; Wouters 1998). Avoidance behaviour, no longer set out as explicit rules, thus tended to become internalized, transforming tensions between people into tensions within them. Accordingly, traditional ways of keeping a distance and being reserved when confronted with those outside one's social circles were transformed into the 'right of privacy', a concept which lacked a specific class component. The perception was that each individual should have the right to be left alone, to maintain a personal or social space undisturbed by unwanted intrusions.

Restrictions on ways and places of meeting sharply diminished from the 1960s onward. Mary Bolton, in *The New Etiquette Book*, observed (as though with a sigh): 'Boy meets girl and girl meets boy in so many different ways that it would be quite impossible to enumerate them' (1961: 15). This change in the conditions of 'respectable' meeting is in keeping with a general shift in the balance between external and internal social controls. Respect and respectable behaviour became more dependent upon self-regulation, and self-controls increasingly became both the focus and the locus of external social controls.

In the 1960s and 1970s, with entire groups rising socially, practically all relationships became less hierarchical and formal. The emancipation and integration of large social groups within welfare states coincided with informalization; the regimes of manners and emotions rapidly lost rigidity and hierarchical aloofness. Many manners that formerly had been forbidden came to be allowed. With the exception of expressions of superiority and inferiority, all other areas of expression – sexuality, the written and spoken language, clothing, music, dancing and hairstyles – exhibited this same trend towards informality. On the one hand, the spectrum of accepted behavioural and emotional alternatives expanded (with the important exception of displays and feelings of superiority and inferiority). On the other hand, an acceptable and respectable usage of these alternatives implied a continued increase in the demands made on self-regulation. At the same time, the spurt of emancipation and integration implied that '[m]ore, not fewer, people are involved in the world of social good form' (Edwards and Beyfus 1969: ix, x).

In increasingly dense networks of interdependency, more subtle, informal ways of obliging and being obliged demanded greater flexibility and sensitivity to shades and nuances in manners of dealing with others and oneself. The rise of mutually expected self-restraints allowed for what might be called a controlled decontrolling. Emotions that previously had been repressed and denied, especially those concerning sex and violence, were again 'discovered' as part of a collective emotional makeup; in the emancipation of emotions many re-entered both consciousness and public discussion. From a set of rules manners turned into guidelines, differentiated according to the demands of the situation and relationship. This was accompanied by a strong decline in social as well as psychic censorship. Both the fear and awe of fantasy or dissident imagination diminished together with the fear and awe of the authorities of state and conscience. On the level of the personality, an authoritarian conscience made way for a conscience attuned to more equal and flexible relationships. As a psychic authority, conscience lost much of its more or less automatic ascendancy, a change that can be described in shorthand as a transition from conscience to consciousness.

Within families, commanding children and presenting them with established decisions came to be seen as dangerous. Acceptance of peremptory authority – do it because I said so – was seen as a symptom of blind submissiveness, estranging children from their own feelings. Parents invested more intensely in their children's affective lives, and family ties gained in confidentiality and intimacy. Pedagogical regimes stressed mutual respect and affection, and parents and teachers sought to direct children to obey their own conscience and reflections rather than simply the external constraints of adults.

In the 1980s the collective emancipation that had flourished in the 1960s and 1970s disappeared and a market ideology spread. This change reflected a shift in West European power structures; politicians and governments came to side less with unions and social movements, and more with commercial and managerial establishments. From the 1980s onwards the prevailing power structures allowed only for individual emancipation. Individuals aspiring to respectability and social ascent came to feel strongly dependent once again on the established elites and they adjusted their manners accordingly. Thus the sensibilities and manners prevailing in the centres of power and their good societies once again functioned more unequivocally as a model. This shift was reinforced in the 1990s. The events that followed the collapse of the Iron Curtain – breaking out into violence in some cases, such as in the former Yugoslavia – intensified feelings of fear, insecurity and powerlessness. The events of 11 September 2001 and the subsequent US 'War on Terrorism', expanding from Afghanistan to Iraq and the Middle East, added new impetus to this trend. In the USA, the impetus to identify more strongly with the established order has emerged from belief in the possibility of controlling global processes via this global 'War on Terrorism'. Most Europeans, for opposite reasons, or so it seems, also tended towards further identification with the established. For them, increased awareness of their nation-states' lack of control over global processes has stimulated both identification with the established order and concern about anything perceived as a threat to it – criminality and bad manners, in particular. Accordingly, the whole regime of manners became somewhat more compelling. To a large extent, informal behaviours that had become socially acceptable in the 1960s and 1970s remained so, through their endorsement by and integration into the standard, dominant code of manners.

Conclusion

In the twentieth century the long-term process of formalization gave way to a long-term process of informalization: manners became increasingly relaxed, subtle and varied. As more groups of people came to be represented in the various centres of power and their good societies that functioned as models for manners, the extreme differences between all social groups in terms of power, ranking, behaviour and management of emotion diminished. Increasing numbers of people belonging to these social groups directed themselves to uniform national codes of behaviour and feeling. Thus, as power inequalities lessened, the Golden Rule and the principle of mutual consent became expected standards of conduct among individuals and between groups.

The turn of the twentieth century, the Roaring Twenties, and the permissive decades of the 1960s and 1970s were periods in which whole groups collectively became involved in emancipation processes. Power differentials decreased sharply. They were also periods with strong spurts of informalization. As power and status competition intensified, and sensitivities over social inequality increased, demonstrations of an individual's distinctiveness became more indirect, subtle and hidden. References to hierarchical group differences, particularly to 'better' and 'inferior' kinds of people, became increasingly taboo; social superiors were less automatically taken to be better people. Yet it was not until the 1960s that the once automatic equation of superior in power and superior as a human being declined to the point of embarrassment.

As bonds of cooperation and competition blended, the people involved came to experience more ambivalence in their relationships. At the same time, many people felt increasingly compelled to identify with other people, a process expressed and reinforced by welfare state institutions. Widening circles of identification implied less rigid boundaries of nation, class, age, gender, religion and ethnicity, and provided a basis for a rising societal level of mutual trust. Expanding and intensified cooperation and competition have prompted people to observe and take the measure of themselves, and of each other, more carefully, and to show flexibility and a greater willingness to compromise. Social success did become more strongly dependent on a reflexive and flexible self-regulation, the ability to combine firmness and flexibility, directness and tactfulness. The overall emancipation and integration of 'lower' social groups in (Western) societies has allowed for the emancipation and integration of 'lower' impulses, and the opening up of emotions in the personality structure. Both emancipations demanded a more strongly ego-dominated process of self-regulation, because drives, impulses and emotions, even those which could provoke physical and sexual violence, tended to become more easily accessible, while their control became less strongly based upon an authoritative conscience, functioning more or less automatically as a 'second nature'. As people's unthinking – their more or less automatic – acceptance of authorities decreased, the respect and self-respect of all citizens have become less directly dependent upon external social controls and more directly upon their reflexive and calculating abilities, and therefore upon a particular pattern of self-control in which the 'unthinking acceptance' of the dictates of psychic authority or conscience also decreased. In this way, these social processes – i.e. the relationships and manners between social groups becoming less rigid and hierarchical – are connected to psychic processes: less hierarchical and more open and fluent relationships between the psychic functions of people's emotions and impulses, their regulation via the counter-emotions and counter-impulses of conscience, and their self-regulation via consciousness. As social and psychic dividing lines have opened up, social groups as well as psychic functions have become more integrated, that is to say, the communications and connections between both social groups and psychic functions have become more flowing and flexible. Lo and behold, the sociogenesis and psychogenesis of a 'third-nature personality'!

I have introduced the terms 'third nature' and 'third-nature personality' as sensitizing concepts to illuminate these changes (1998a, 1999). The term 'second nature' refers to a self-regulating conscience that to a great extent functions automatically. The term 'third nature' refers to the development of a more reflexive and flexible self-regulation. Ideally, for someone operating on the basis of third nature it becomes 'natural' to attune oneself to the pulls and pushes of both first and second nature as well as the dangers and chances, short term and long term, of any particular situation or relationship. As national, continental and global integration processes exert pressure toward increasingly differentiated regimes of manners, they also exert pressure toward increasingly reflexive and flexible regimes of self-regulation.

REFERENCES

Blumin, Stuart M. 1989, *The Emergence of the Middle Class: Social Experience in the American City, 1760–1900*, Cambridge: Cambridge University Press.

Bolton, Mary 1961, *The New Etiquette Book*, London: Foulsham.

Curtin, Michael 1987, *Propriety and Position: A Study of Victorian Manners*, New York: Garland.

Davidoff, Leonore 1973, *The Best Circles: Society Etiquette and the Season*, London: Croom Helm.

Durkheim, Émile 1964 [1893], *The Division of Labour in Society*, trans. G. Simpson, London: Glencoe.

Edwards, Anne and Drusilla Beyfus 1969 [orig. 1956] *Lady Behave: A Guide to Modern Manners*, London: Boswell & Co.

Elias, Norbert 2000 [1939], *The Civilizing Process: Sociogenetic and Psychogenetic Investigations*, trans. Dunning and Mennell, Oxford: Blackwell.

Frykman, Jonas, and Orvar Löfgren 1987, *Culture Builders: A Historical Anthropology of Middle-Class Life*, New Brunswick, NY and London: Rutgers University Press.

Haskell, Thomas 1985, 'Capitalism and the humanitarian sensibility', *American Historical Review* 90: 339–61, 547–66.

Klickmann, Flora 1902, *The Etiquette of Today*, London: Cartwright.

Newton, Sarah E. 1994, *Learning to Behave: A Guide to American Conduct Books Before 1900*, Westport, CT: Greenwood Press.

Post, Emily 1922, *Etiquette in Society, in Business, in Politics and at Home*, New York: Funk and Wagnalls (revd. edns: 1923; 1927; 1931; 1934; 1937; 1942; 1950; 1960).

Riesman, David with N. Glazer and R. Denney (1950), *The Lonely Crowd*, New Haven: Yale University Press.

Stratenus, Louise 1909, *Vormen. Handboek voor de samenleving in en buiten huis*, Gouda: Van Goor.

Swaan, Abram de, 1995, 'Widening circles of social identification: emotional concerns in sociogenetic perspective', *Theory, Culture & Society* 12: 25–39.

Tilburg, Marja van 1998, *Hoe hoorde het? Seksualiteit en partnerkeuze in de Nederlandse adviesliteratuur 1780–1890*, Amsterdam: Spinhuis.

Wouters, Cas 1999, 'Changing patterns of social controls and self-controls: on the rise of crime since the 1950s and the sociogenesis of a "third nature"', *British Journal of Criminology* 39: 416–32.

1998a, 'How Strange to Ourselves Are our Feelings of Superiority and Inferiority, *Theory, Culture & Society* 15: 131–50.

1998b, 'Etiquette books and emotion management in the twentieth century: American habitus in international comparison', in Peter N. Stearns and Jan Lewis (eds.), *An Emotional History of the United States*, New York: New York, University Press, pp. 283–304.

12   Elias and modern penal development

John Pratt

Introduction

Modern societies like to think of themselves as 'civilized'. When they make this claim, it becomes a way of self-evidently distinguishing themselves from non-Western, uncivilized societies, which are then seen, given the teleological qualities that have now come to be associated with this concept, as being at a more primitive, less-advanced stage of social development. But what are the distinguishing features of a society that professes to be civilized? We can draw from a number of social indicators to demonstrate such characteristics: levels of health care, literacy rates, those for infant mortalities – and, as well, the way in which a given society punishes its offenders. What sort of punishments, though, make one society seem civilized, another uncivilized?

For those of us in the modern world, this question can perhaps be best answered by reference to what it is that strikes us as 'uncivilized punishment'. This is likely to include excessive, brutalizing public punishments: floggings, stonings, amputations, bodies hanging from nooses – almost certainly, we think, 'civilized people don't want to see that sort of thing' (Smith 1996). Other identifiers of uncivilized punishment relate to squalid, corrupt and brutal prison conditions (in movie representations, they have come to be associated particularly with Thailand, Turkey and Viet Nam), which seem disgusting and degrading to our sensibilities. Others still involve shaming punishments of varying kinds, whereas in modern Western societies shaming punishments disappeared during the course of the nineteenth and twentieth centuries (Pratt 2002; Scheff this volume). However, it is probably easier to identify these characteristics of what seems to us to be 'uncivilized punishment' than to provide an outline of 'civilized punishment' since one of its particular characteristics, surely, is that we not only neither see nor hear of any such sights, but in addition we – the general public – have little at all to do with it, and very little knowledge of what it might involve. There are fairly clearly defined parameters to how much suffering should be imposed by punishment in the civilized world (and all the above examples go well beyond this), but at the same time, very little else is known about it. This is because of another of its identifying characteristics. Punishment in the civilized world has largely disappeared from public view and access because it has come to be presided over by government bureaucracies and their experts, whose task has been to administer it according to principles of rationality and humanitarianism. This, in fact, has become the regular theme in the annual reports that these bureaucracies produce, that take the form of an official discourse and 'true' account of their work.

And yet, in the last two decades or so, there have been significant indicators in societies such as the USA, United Kingdom, Canada, Australia and New Zealand (in other words, this is an Anglophone development: the rest of Western Europe looks rather different) that this longstanding framework, these longstanding expectations, are beginning to unravel; not disintegrate altogether – it is not as dramatic as that – but certainly unravel to varying degrees, thereby allowing the rekindling of penal forms long since thought to have vanished from the civilized world. These include the return of shaming and humiliating public punishments, such as chain gangs in the Deep South of the United States. In another manifestation of this unravelling, it is as if the consensus on what constituted an acceptable level of societal punishment has also begun to change, as imprisonment levels, particularly in the United States, escalate upwards to new heights. In other words, those cultural parameters that helped distinguish between punishment in the civilized world and its uncivilized counterpart are changing and are by no means as clear cut as they were, say, thirty years ago. How, then, do we explain such developments and what is their sociological significance?

Elias, sociology and punishment

To date, the sociology of punishment, although a burgeoning sub-strand of the discipline, has primarily reflected the work of Marx (issues of economic determination) or Foucault (issues of power/domination). What is clear from the above outline of modern penal development, however, is the way in which cultural values are one of its determinants, and in relation to which it would not seem possible to say very much within the parameters of either. More generally, for Marxist scholarship, in respect of which for the purposes of this essay the classic text remains Rusche and Kirchheimer (1939), the origins of modern imprisonment are connected initially to labour shortages during the eighteenth century, followed by its use, in the nineteenth, as an instrument to terrorise the emergent industrial working class into subjection. However, and aside from the book's historiographical shortcomings (see Garland 1990), what such an analysis cannot address is the way in which economic interests have been regularly tempered, and at times completely overridden, by other forces at work on penal development – religious, cultural, humanitarian, administrative etc. In these ways, neither the complexity of prison development in modern society nor the differential nature of prison development (for example, in the nineteenth century, the unique ferocity of the way in which less eligibility was applied to in British prisons only, see Pratt 2002) and rates of imprisonment between seemingly similar societies is given any significant regard.

For Foucault (1978), modern penal arrangements effectively begin with Jeremy Bentham's late-eighteenth-century blueprint for a model prison, the panopticon. However, the panopticon itself never actually became much more than a blueprint, and what is neglected are issues of prison location (usually at the outskirts of modern cities on elevated sites) and design (architects with competing ideas designed prisons built in the style of the extraordinary grandeur of early-nineteenth-century gothic and neo-classicism, but these were then replaced by the functional austerity that came to dominate prison building from the mid-nineteenth century, see later). In these respects, Elias's work, even if he himself has virtually nothing to say about punishment as such, has the potential to provide a very different but very significant contribution to this area. That is to say, the way in which it came to be assumed that modern Western societies should punish their offenders in ways that were in keeping with the values of the civilized world, can be seen as another example – in many respects, a particularly apposite one – of the 'civilizing process' (Elias 1939, 1984) at work. This was characterized by (i) the growth of the central state's monopolistic control on the use of violence and taxation (state process); (ii) the increasing scale and scope of interdependencies between citizens of modern societies as a result of the heterogeneous division of labour characteristic of them and the attendant shift from rural to urban life (sociogenesis) and (iii) the internalization of constraints in relation to displays of emotion which also led to a growing sensibility towards 'disturbing events' (psychogenesis). By implication, at least, modern penal development, I want to argue, can be subsumed under these three headings.

Yet, at the same time, it is not a simplistic reiterative fit that can be fashioned, but one that comes about only through critical reflection on and development of Elias's ideas, particularly in *The Civilizing Process*, but also in relation to *The Germans* (Elias 1996) and *The Established and Outsiders* (Elias and Scotson 1965).[1] *The Civilizing Process* itself effectively ends by the mid nineteenth century and as such does not really address the significance of features quite specific to social development in the civilized world thereafter. That is to say, firstly, central state monopolistic control and regulation of taxation, violence and (by inference) the power to punish, ultimately led to the creation of modern bureaucracies through which such powers would then be exercised and deployed over an increasing arena of public policy. The settlement of disputes and grievances, for example, thus came to be resolved by these bureaucratic organizations rather than by the efforts of ordinary people. One of the consequences of this, and one of the characteristics of punishment in the civilized world, was that an administrative veil would be drawn across these events, effectively shutting the public out from any significant involvement – nobody would know what was going on; in this way, the prison came to be one sub-realm of a specialist sector in the social structure of modern society with (almost exclusive) responsibility for punishment and penal development. Within this, the prison, as it were, took on a life – became a figuration – of its own, as the professional interdependencies within it excluded those from the non-prison world and created sets of reciprocal obligations, rules, codes and so on as to its management.

However, secondly, another qualification that needs to be made to Elias's work relates to the issue of sensitivities themselves. It is fairly obvious that sensitivities to suffering have never been uniformly applied. For much of the nineteenth and twentieth centuries, sympathy for the suffering of animals (certainly in Britain) has probably outstripped sympathy for the suffering of humans, most certainly in the cases of criminals who, bar a few exceptions,[2] would be seen as one of the extreme outsider groups in modern society (Elias and Scotson 1965; although the way in which the social distance between them and the penal establishment at least came to be reduced over this period, represents another of the contours of punishment in the civilized world. Pratt 2002). At the same time, this revulsion may have also contributed to the desire to have such distasteful citizens hidden away in institutions, again providing one of the channels for the way in which disturbing events came to be hidden behind the scenes in the civilized world.

Thirdly, in these respects, nobody would know what was going on behind the administrative veil that had been drawn across penal systems in the civilized world because, by and large, *nobody would want to know* what was going on. In such societies, the self-restraint characteristic of the habitus of the civilizing process would be likely to turn into moral indifference to the fate of others, particularly when combined with the individuating factors characteristic of them (the loss of community, remoteness of the extended family, anonymous employment in large organizations, to name just a few). Indeed, it was the fatal combination of bureaucratic and technocratic efficiency on the one hand and indifference on the other in Nazi Germany that led to the Holocaust, it has been claimed by Zygmund Bauman (1989). More specifically for our purposes here, the general public welcomed the way in which penal development went 'behind the scenes'. What then took place – the development of the secretive, closed-off prisons as the focal point of punishment – would be acceptable to a public that did not wish to become involved, and would only reluctantly become involved when it appeared through scandal, for example, that the parameters of 'the civilized' had been breached in some way. Importantly, then, the civilizing process provides no guarantee of civilized eventualities; instead, the effect could be just the opposite. As such, the civilizing process itself helped to make possible some of the greatest barbarities of the twentieth century, a point Elias made clear in his later work on the Holocaust (Elias 1996). And, in a different context, the assumptions in official discourse that have been made about punishment in the civilized world, for example, have regularly been contradicted by those who have experienced them – as prisoners' memoirs reveal. In these respects, the sociological task then becomes one of ascertaining how it was that official penal discourse came to be accepted as 'the truth' about prisons and punishment, and this at the expense of any counter-claims that were put forward by the prisoners themselves.

Fourthly, how do we account for the current fragmentation of the penal framework characteristic of punishment in the civilized world? In Eliasian terms, the breathing of life into penal forms long since thought to be extinct would seem to be indicative of a 'decivilizing interruption' to the civilizing process (see Mennell 1990; Dunning and Mennell 1998). In other words, there is no certainty that the civilizing process will continue on its processual terms; it can be interrupted at any time by war, massive social and economic change and so on. But the issue here, surely, revolves around the term 'interruption'. To what extent do decivilizing forces have the potential to completely overturn the course of the civilizing process to date? Given the way in which the bureaucratic structures of modernity have become so deeply embedded over the last 150 years or so, it would surely require an unparalleled catastrophe (such as nuclear war) to completely break down these foundations of modern society itself and effectively turn the clock of civilization backwards. On the other hand, significant, but non-catastrophic events, such as the social and economic changes of the last twenty years or so, or what Wacquant (this volume, p. 98) more forcefully refers to as 'the multifaceted retrenchment on all levels . . . of the . . . state and the correlative crumbling of the public sector institutions that make up the organizational infrastructure of any advanced urban society', and their effects at the level of the individual and at the level of the state, are likely to produce smaller-scale but still effective impacts. Prima facie, the reappearance of previously extinct penal forms may signify the presence of decivilizing forces; the issue then becomes one of assessing the extent to which these forces are able to make intrusions to the civilizing process, or to push it off its long-determined route and into new directions. In other words, decivilizing forces are likely to run in conjunction with the civilizing process barring utter catastrophe and, in varying degrees, cross its path at various points, rather than bringing it to a halt altogether. This is the point that Elias (1996) makes in *The Germans* (and which also distinguishes his analysis of the origins of the Holocaust from Bauman's (1989) account of bureaucratic rationalism). Here, it was the particular combination of the technological and bureaucratic proficiency of the civilizing process, *in conjunction with* the hatred of Jews brought about by decivilizing influences powerful enough to burst through traditions of restraint, reserve and forbearance that made it possible. It represented a fusion of both the civilizing process and decivilizing counter-trends.

Civilized punishment

Let me now try to sketch in the main contours of penal development in the anglophone world from the early nineteenth century to around the 1970s – the point where the framework that had been set in place begins to fragment. The combined effect of these developments was to produce ways of punishing, ownership of which would signal to the rest of the world that that particular society punished its offenders in ways that were 'civilized'. This involved the disappearance of punishments to the body, the removal from view of both prisons and prisoners, the sanitization of penal language and the amelioration of penal sanctions.

The decline and subsequent disappearance of punishments to the human body

At the beginning of the nineteenth century, the human body was still the main target of punishment, involving in an elaborate, ritual-like form, whippings, duellings, use of the pillory and stocks, ducking stools, public executions and so on. By the 1860s, all of these had vanished. Like other raucous, disorderly public events of this time (e.g. fairs and sporting contests), these 'spectacles of suffering' seemed increasingly distasteful to middle-class sensibilities during the first half of the nineteenth century, rather than evidence of the growing 'mutual identification' thesis advanced by Wouters (this volume); my own argument is that dislike of these spectacles and all that they entailed was significantly more important than sympathy for those on the gallows (see Pratt 2002). As John Stuart Mill (1836: 130–1) noted, 'one of the effects of civilization . . . is that the spectacle, and even the very idea of pain, is kept more and more out of the sight of those classes who enjoy in their fullness the benefits of civilization'. If we use the death penalty as the most prominent example of this mode of punishing, then we find that its use in England had been scaled back from being available for over 200 offences at the beginning of the nineteenth century to, for all intents and purposes after 1861, murder only.

By the same token, middle-class elites, led by prominent novelists and social commentators such as Charles Dickens and William Thackeray, also reform groups such as the Society for the Diffusion of Knowledge upon the Punishment of Death, were prominent in the campaign to have public executions abolished. This reached a successful culmination with the passing of the Capital Punishment within Prisons Act 1868, described by *The Times* (14 August 1862: 12) as being 'in keeping with the spirit of the age' – although such spectacles, right up to the end, had remained enormously popular with the general public. It is also apparent that even most middle-class sensitivities had been disturbed mainly by *the sight of death*, rather than the existence of the death penalty; now that it was to be used more sparingly and in private, it was as if a satisfactory equilibrium of suffering had been arrived at ('the storm which once seemed to be gathering has subsided and has been followed by a great calm. Abolition [of the death penalty] no longer has a place among the real questions of the day' (*The Times* 14 March 1878: 9)). Thereafter, from the late nineteenth century through to the 1930s, the central focus of debate about the death penalty was not related to its abolition but instead to its sanitisation (whether this be in terms of further screening its effects from the officials who had been designated to observe it, or in terms of reducing the suffering of the executed – when the electric chair was first used in New York state, for example, the attendant doctor testified that death had been 'completely painless' (Report of the New York Prisons Department 1891)).

It was only after the Second World War that there was a further shift in the configuration of the civilizing process that created the momentum for the death penalty (and any other residual punishments to the human body, such as the flogging of prisoners, that were still in existence) to be abolished altogether across these societies during the 1960s and early 1970s. In this period, the power and authority of the central state was considerably strengthened, amidst growing faith in the ability of its experts in the government bureaucracies to redress and solve social problems. With the emergence of the idea of a strong, authoritative state in the West, allied to the post-war association of the death penalty with the vanquished totalitarian states, it no longer seemed to occupy a legitimate place in the penal repertoire of the civilized world ('[the death penalty] has no proper place in the institutions of a free democracy . . . repressive punishments belong to the systems of totalitarian states and not democracies. It was no accident that the chief exponents of violence and severity in the treatment of criminals in other times were the Nazi and Fascist states' (Hansard [449] 1014–15: 14 April 1948)).

Ultimately, the death penalty was abolished in Britain for a trial period (although it has never been brought back) in 1965 after a free vote in the House of Commons. In the United States, the Supreme Court declared it to be a 'cruel and unusual punishment' in 1972, while observing that 'one role of the constitution is to help the nation become "more civilized"'. This did not then include the use of the death penalty or any other punishments to the human body at that juncture.

The disappearance of prisons and prisoners

Replacing the pre-nineteenth-century carnival of punishment, the prisons came to be the dominant sanction of penal systems in the civilized world during the course of the nineteenth century. But from then it becomes possible to trace in another line of development whereby this sanction began to be removed from public access, view and scrutiny. Initially, these new prisons tended to be built on high prominences (for reasons of health, apart from anything else), overlooking contemporary urban development. Their architecture was elaborate and extravagant, in the manner of Victorian gothic or neo-classical formalism. However, the opening of Pentonville model prison in London, in 1843, was very influential on prison building for the next half century and represented a significant change in architectural style; it was built according to a kind of 'functional austerity' (Garland 1990), with an almost complete abandonment of external decoration in its design. This was in the aftermath of widespread criticism that the 'palace prisons' in the two other contrasting architectural styles were much too luxurious for prisoners. They not only seemed to indicate that crime would be rewarded and honoured, but also placed the living standards of prisoners on a higher level than that of more worthy subjects in other institutions (e.g. workhouse residents), and even above free labourers. However, all that was left in Pentonville of former architectural extravagances was the arched entrance to it, as if this represented the dramatic point of departure from everyday life into the new and very different world of the modern prison (even if its interior technology at that point still led it to be regarded as one of the wonders of the age (see Ignatieff 1978)).

By the end of the nineteenth century, however, attitudes to prison building – and location – had changed again. On the part of the general public, their presence was now seen as tainting local neighbourhoods – they should be built elsewhere; on the part of the penal authorities, attempts were made to try and 'beautify' the prisons, or at least alleviate their depressing austerity, by the planting of flowers and shrubs, and the provision of landscaped gardens to tone down the implicit deprivation of 'the prison look', now itself thought to be distasteful, at least on the part of the penal authorities; and on the part of governments, to move prisons out to more remote secluded locations, so that the contemporary urban landscape might be redeveloped ('the site of Kirkdale Prison has been sold to the Corporation of Liverpool . . . it is understood that the corporation propose to devote some of the site to "open spaces"' (Report of the Prison Commissioners 1895: 11)). Then, during the twentieth century, prison design became still more moderated, to the point where, by the 1960s, prison buildings gave away no exterior signs as to their purpose (Sparks *et al.* 1996). Where nineteenth-century urban prisons still remained in use, they now projected an appearance that set them and the localities in which they were situated apart from the rest of the civilized world – as if the rest of the world, as it bypassed them, turned its head away in disgust and thereby made these offensive sights, and the urban blight they now advertised, invisible.

It should also be noted that over this same period public access to the prisons became steadily more restricted, while the public presence of prisoners, either on public works, or as they moved from prison to prison, was removed or camouflaged ('in recent years advantage has been taken of the improvement in motor transport to convey a large proportion of prisoners by road and so avoid the publicity involved when they travel by rail' (Report of the Prison Commissioners 1935: 10)).

Overall, the result of these developments regarding both prisons and prisoners was that, by the 1960s, a physical veil had been drawn across modern prison development, a physical veil to accompany the administrative veil that the bureaucratic control of the prison and its inmates drew across it.

The sanitization of penal language

During the first half of the nineteenth century there seems to have been little distinction between the way in which crime and criminals were spoken about – by government, elites and the general public. Essentially, it was as if prisoners were simply brutish creatures to be feared and hated. As the well-known penal reformer Mary Carpenter (1864: 1) put the matter, 'the very name of "convicts" excites in the mind an idea of moral corruption which would make one shrink from such beings with a natural repulsion, which would lead one to wish only that like lepers of old they should dwell apart in caves and desert places, warning off the incautious passenger with the cry "unclean, unclean"'. Nonetheless, as the distinction and distance began to grow between a general public that was peripheral to the penal system and the bureaucracies that presided over it, that were able to invoke the expertise of specialists to concentrate on the reformation of prisoners, so we begin to find the development of two separate penal languages. On the one hand, that of the general public continued to be expressed predominantly in terms of fear, loathing, distrust and contempt, a language that also periodically found expression amongst the lower echelons of the penal establishment, such as prison officers (see, for example, Cronin 1967).

However, on the other hand, the formal language in which penal policy was developed and expressed by government bureaucracies (what became the 'official discourse' of punishment) began to change tone. While for Sir Edmund Du Cane (1875: 302–3), Head of the Prison Commissioners, criminals had characteristics 'entirely those of the inferior races of mankind', the Report of the Gladstone Committee (1895: 16, my italics) noted in contrast that 'so much can be done by recognition of the plain fact that *the great majority of prisoners are ordinary men and women*, amenable, more or less, to all those influences which affect persons outside'. During the first part of the twentieth century, these bureaucratic sensibilities and ideas of what it was possible to achieve in reforming prisoners through the practice of scientific expertise continued to shed a more positive light on them. Du Cane's successor, Sir Evelyn Ruggles-Brise (1921: 87, my italics), pointed out that 'upon a certain age, every criminal may be regarded as potentially a good citizen . . . *it is the duty of the state at least to try and effect a cure*'. Now, as the belief in professional expertise began to grow, so the central state itself began to assume broader responsibilities towards all its citizens, including its criminals (even if the rest of its citizens were unlikely to share this belief).

In the post-war period, with the further enlargement of central state authority and investment in the scientific expertise of bureaucratic officials, there was a further shift in this formal language of punishment. Far from treating and speaking of them as outcasts, it was now as if the state itself was prepared to assume some measure of culpability for their wrongdoing. As Edwin Glover (1956: 267), the eminent British psychiatrist, put the matter, '[criminals] have certainly injured their fellows, but perhaps society has unwittingly injured them'. There was now a duty on the expanding welfare states of this time to provide expert assistance both in relation to the correction of their individual deficiencies and at the same time the amelioration of disadvantageous social conditions that might have contributed to the causes of their crimes; such a commitment had now become a test of the extent to which a given society could claim to be civilized (Jones 1965).

The amelioration of penal sanctions

There are two features to this theme. Firstly, the way in which prison moved from being at the centre of the penal system in the nineteenth century to an increasingly peripheral role during the course of the twentieth, to the point where, in much of the penal literature of the 1970s, it was increasingly spoken of in terms of being a 'last resort' penal option (Bottoms 1977). It had come to be seen as too harsh, too ineffective (according to the scientific criteria of the penal system's own experts) for an ever-widening group of criminals: progressively, from the mid nineteenth century onwards, juveniles, alcoholics, first offenders, mentally ill offenders, the homeless, and even by the 1970s, petty persistent offenders. As the alternative sanctions for such constituencies began to proliferate, so the institution of prison became more residual to modern penal development.

Then secondly, the way in which prison conditions themselves were steadily improved over this period. As such, we see a steady retreat taking place from the well-known prison conditions of the nineteenth century – stigmatic uniforms, shaved heads, restrictive diets and so on. For example, 'a new style of clothing is being devised which though of the simplest kind will give a better chance to self-respect' (Report of the Prison Commissioners 1922: 14). As such, the Report of the Prison Commissioners (1924–5: 19) noted that 'the hangdog look so characteristic of many prisoners in former days tends to disappear'. By the 1960s, in accordance with the reduced social distance between prisoners as an extreme outsider group and the prison authorities as an establishment group (although I do not think that there was much reduction of the distance between ex-prisoners and the general public when they came into contact with each other over this period), prison conditions, at least in these official accounts became progressively more 'normalized'. In relation to food, for example, the Report on the Work of the Prison Department (1967: 19) noted that 'diets have been more interesting and more varied. Some establishments are able to offer as many as four choices at the main meal. Arrangements for both the preparation and the service of food are being modernized;

the cafeteria system has been introduced at some establishments, and new rotary bread ovens are installed in all new establishments.'

Overall, these four contours represented landmark indicators of what we had come to expect punishment to be like in a society that was civilized. The extent to which the framework of punishing that they made possible was actually set down obviously varied and was dependent upon 'local centrifugal forces' (Elias 1996). There was no uniform pattern to it – but my point is that it did come to be the normative framework by which societies professing to be civilized in the way in which they punished their offenders would be judged. Thus, those that punished the least and the most humanely – the Scandinavian countries and Holland, for example – were, around 1970, seen as setting the penal example for the anglophone countries to follow. By contrast, a shameful stain might be cast on those countries that departed from these standards, as in the case of the Southern United States, with its history of chain gangs, vigilantism and lynchings (see Pratt 2003; Dunning, this volume).

And what presided over this framework was an axis of penal power which was concentrated in the central state and its bureaucratic organizations – where the general public, as outsiders to the penal system, had come to have only the most peripheral involvement and influence.

Decivilizing counter-trends

However, as was noted at the outset, there have been indications since the 1970s that this framework – the contingent outcome of a particular configuration of the civilizing process then in place – has begun to unravel. The decivilizing consequences of the profound social and economic changes that have taken place across these societies in this period make possible the re-emergence of penal forms from previous eras which in varying degrees – there is again no uniformity to this process – set back the course taken by punishment in the civilized world up to this time; or, more precisely I think, help to reroute it by merging in varying degrees the decivilizing counter-trends with the continuing effectivity of the civilizing process. We can see this in a reshaping of the four contours set out above – thus.

Punishments to the human body

This is an area where these influences have had least effect. The exception to this has been the United States, where the death penalty was reintroduced in 1976. In that country, the sanitization of the execution process – death by lethal injection has become the predominant mode of despatch – helps to make it a culturally tolerable sanction. However, throughout these other societies – and Western society in general, for that matter – the movement against the death penalty and other corporeal sanctions has become even more strongly entrenched. Membership of the European Union is now conditional, inter alia, on a particular state renouncing the death penalty. For all intents and purposes, in the civilized world, at least, it would seem that outside of the United States, punishment to the human body has been consigned to history.

Prisons and prisoners

There are some fairly clear counter-trends here. In terms of the physical presence of prisons, there is no doubt that some communities are more tolerant of their presence now – they bring jobs at a time when more traditional industries have closed down (Christie 1992). And like the other more visible penal signs today, such as the chain gangs, their presence can be seen as a sign of security when this is no longer given out by the more familiar sources for this in the social fabric.

Penal language

We have seen the emergence and predominance of a much more severe penal language since the 1970s – 'zero tolerance', 'life means life' and 'three strikes',[3] for example, replace discourse on treatment and reform – and it is a language that is increasingly spoken by governments (if not their bureaucratic officials) and the general public. At the same time, there is no longer any reticence amongst politicians on speaking of their large and growing prison populations – the possession of which is seen as an indicator of political strength rather than a source of shame.

Penal sanctions

Again, there have been significant reversals to the long-standing trend whereby the pain and severity of penal sanctions were reduced, both in terms of the way in which this has allowed the reintroduction of explicitly shaming, humiliating sanctions, and in terms of the way in which prison terms have become significantly longer, while conditions in prisons in some of these jurisdictions have been made considerably more severe.

Overall, as the central state has assumed a more retracted role in the governance of everyday life, with the authority of its own bureaucracies and scientific experts tarnished because of their association with unnecessary expense, inefficiency and remoteness from the general public, there has been a growing readiness on the part of the state to allow public sentiment to have a greater impact on penal development than had previously been the case. At the same time, the public themselves, increasingly anxious in an era of 'no guarantees' against insecurity of various kinds become increasingly intolerant of the seemingly intractable menace of crime. The lowering of their threshold of embarrassment and self-restraint means that instead of indifference to the punishment of criminals, they increasingly demand a right to have 'a say' in penal affairs. What this then makes possible is the emergence of a new axis of penal power, between the state and the general public, with bureaucratic expertise increasingly sidelined.

The greater the commitment to the neo-liberal polity of small, anti-public sector and bureaucratic government that has become the norm since the 1970s, the more this axis is likely to influence penal development. In that space vacated by the state and the scientific, bureaucratic rationalism that had previously guided such matters, local cultural traditions can be reactivated – whether this be in the form of restorative justice in New Zealand and parts of Canada; chain gangs as in the Deep South of the United States, as also with the concentrated use of the death penalty in that region. On other occasions, these volatile human sentiments that have been set loose may break out of the existing penal framework altogether and manifest themselves in vigilante activity, as happened across Britain in the summer of 2000 (see Pratt 2001, 2002).

In effect, what this points to are significant changes in the direction of penal development in the last two or three decades. The decivilizing influences at work have had sufficient force to reverse the path taken by punishment in the civilized world at some points. More generally, however, the framework characteristic of this still remains in place – but has been pushed by these decivilizing forces into directions and towards horizons previously unthinkable, previously incompatible with any claim to be civilized.

NOTES

1. There is no doubt that Elias's work and ideas came very late to the sociology of punishment and to criminology in general. In relation to the latter, the most significant use of his work is still that of Gurr (1981) on the history of violence. Indeed, there seem to be very few other applications of his work in criminology (although on the subject of violence, see Fletcher 1997). In relation to the former, his work first seems to have received extended consideration in

Spierenburg (1984), which relates the decline in use, and relaxation in severity, of the death penalty in pre-modern Europe to state-formation and the rise of middle-class sensibilities, a theme that author then continues in relation to the origins of eighteenth and early-nineteenth-century imprisonment in Europe (Spierenburg 1990). The potential of Elias's work for understanding the history of punishment was most clearly and expertly set out by Garland (1990). He was then given critical and mistaken consideration (in so far as the civilizing process was seen as a teleological construct) by Christie (1992). Braithwaite (1993) uses his precepts as normative assertions. Elias received some consideration in Gatrell (1994) on the nineteenth-century decline of public executions in England. Franke (1995) used his work – particularly his ideas on 'functional democratization' – to explain the post-war liberalization of Dutch prisons. In my own recent work (Pratt 2002), Elias becomes the central theorist in an explanation of the history of punishment in modern society.

2. Nonetheless, some criminals, by virtue of their particular circumstances, are still capable of being understood more as glamorous, romantic heroes – Ronnie Biggs, for example, the former Great Train Robber of the early 1960s, later escaping from a maximum security prison, eluding the police in Australia, and coming to surface in Rio de Janeiro, where he then spent almost the next thirty years (see Mackenzie 1975).

3. These are forms of language that emerged initially in the United States during this period, but have now reached the official penal language of these other countries. 'Zero tolerance' refers to the police practice of prosecuting *all* crime that they come across, however trivial, to give a particular message to criminals. Originating in New York city around 1990, it was attributed (almost certainly mistakenly) to the subsequent fall in crime in that region. 'Life means life' refers to the practice of keeping those sentenced to life imprisonment in jail for life without parole. 'Three strikes' refers to the sentencing practice which emerged in the early 1990s of sentencing those who already have two imprisonable convictions to life imprisonment in some cases, a minimum term of twenty-five years in others.

REFERENCES

Bauman, Z. 1989, *Modernity and the Holocaust*, Cambridge: Polity Press.
Bottoms, A.E. 1977, 'Reflections on the renaissance of dangerousness', *Howard Journal* 16: 70–96.
Braithwaite, J. 1993, 'Shame and modernity', *British Journal of Criminology* 33: 1–18.
Carpenter, M. 1864 (1969), *Our Convicts*, Montclair: Paterson Smith.
Christie, N. 1992, *Crime Control as Industry*, London: Martin Robertson.
Cronin, H. 1967, *The Screw Turns*, London: Longmans.
Du Cane, E. 1875, 'Address on the repression of crime', *Transactions of the National Association for the Promotion of Social Science*, London: Longmans Green, pp. 271–308.

Dunning, E. and Mennell, S. 1998, 'On the balance between "civilizing" and "decivilising" trends in the social development of Western Europe: Elias on Germany, Nazism and the Holocaust', *British Journal of Sociology* 49(3): 339–57.

Elias, N. 1939 (1984), *The Civilizing Process*, Oxford: Basil Blackwell.

1996, *The Germans*, Cambridge: Polity Press.

Elias, N. and Scotson, J. 1965, *The Established and the Outsiders*, London: Sage.

Fletcher, J. 1997, *Violence and Civilization*, Cambridge: Polity Press.

Foucault, M. 1978, *Discipline and Punish*, London: Allen Lane.

Franke, H. 1995, *The Emancipation of Prisoners*, Edinburgh: Edinburgh University Press.

Garland, D. 1990, *Punishment and Modern Society*, Oxford: Oxford University Press.

Gatrell, V. 1994, *The Hanging Tree*, Oxford: Oxford University Press.

Glover, E. 1956, *Probation and Re-education*, London: RKP.

Gurr, T. 1981, 'Historical trends in violent crime', in M. Tonry and N. Morris (eds.), *Crime and Justice*, vol. III, Chicago: University of Chicago Press, pp. 295–353.

Ignatieff, M. 1978, *A Just Measure of Pain*, London: Macmillan.

Jones, H. 1965, *Crime in a Changing Society*, London: Penguin.

Mackenzie, C. 1975, *Biggs: The World's Most Wanted Man*, New York: W. Morrow.

Mennell S. 1990, 'Decivilising processes: theoretical significance and some lines for research', *International Sociology* 5(2): 205–3.

Mill, J.S. 1836 (1977), 'Civilization', in J. Robson (ed.), *Collected Works*, vol. XVIII, Cambridge: Cambridge University Press, pp. 119–47.

Pratt, J. 2001, 'Beyond gulags western style: a reconsideration of Nils Christie's "Crime control as industry"', *Theoretical Criminology* 5: 283–314.

2002, *Punishment and Civilization*, London: Sage.

2003, 'The decline and renaissance of shame in modern penal systems', in B. Godfey *et al.* (eds.), *Comparative Histories of Crime*, London: Willan Publishing (in press).

Report of the Gladstone Committee, 1895, London, PP LVII.

Report of the New York Prison Department, 1891, Albany, NY: New York State Prison Department.

Report of the Prison Commissioners, 1895, London, PP LVI.

1922, London, PP (1922–3), cmd 1761.

1924–5, London, PP (1924–5), cmd 2307.

1935, London, PP (1936–7) XV cmd 5430.

Report on the Work of the Prison Department, 1967, London: PP (1967–8), cmd. 3774.

Ruggles-Brise, E. 1921, *The English Prison System*, London: Macmillan.

Rusche, G. and Kirchheimer 1939, *Punishment and Social Structure*, New York: Russell and Russell.

Scheff, T. 2003, 'Shame as the master emotion: Goffman, Elias and Freud', in S. Loyal and S. Quilley (eds.), *The Sociology of Norbert Elias*, Cambridge: Cambridge University Press, pp. 229–42.

Smith, G. 1996, 'Civilized people don't want to see that sort of thing: the decline of physical punishment in London 1760–1840', in C. Strange (ed.), *Qualities of Mercy*, Vancouver: UBC Press, pp. 21–51.

Sparks, R., Bottoms, A.E. and Hay, W. 1996, *Prisons and the Problem of Order*, Oxford: Clarendon.

Spierenburg, P. 1984, *The Spectacle of Suffering*, Cambridge: Cambridge University Press.

1990, *The Prison Experience*, New Brunswick: Rutgers University Press.

13   Elias, Freud and Goffman: shame as the master emotion

Thomas J. Scheff

Introduction

There is a surprising similarity between three of the giants of modern social science, Freud, Elias and Goffman. For each of them, their first published work took the extremely unusual step of proposing that shame and embarrassment were crucially important in human affairs. It would not be exaggerating to say that each implied that it was the master emotion, rather than love, anger, fear, anxiety, grief or guilt. Since shame, especially, was little discussed in Western societies at the time that these authors were writing, this focus was very much against the grain.

Surprising also are the immense differences in relation to the topics, methods, writing styles, perspectives and training of the authors. Freud was a medically trained Austrian psychiatrist, and Elias a historical sociologist, born and raised in Germany. Goffman was a Canadian, schooled in ethnography and sociological social psychology. Freud's first published work (Freud 1895) was a study of hysteria based upon his own cases, and one of his mentor, Breuer. The method that Freud applied involved a careful analysis of the words, manner and behaviour of these patients, all of whom were women. Freud's writing style, even in his first book, is clear, evocative and elegant, written in the manner of poetry or a novel, but based upon real, rather than fictional episodes.

Elias's first publication (Elias 1939) involved a history of European culture based on excerpts from etiquette and advice manuals over a period of some 600 years. His method involved a close analysis of excerpts from these manuals, but in the context of the surrounding culture, its time and place. Elias's prose lacks the charming style of Freud, as well as the playfulness of Goffman. In contrast, his writing is straightforward and clear.

Goffman's first book (Goffman 1959) began as an ethnographic study of the Shetland Islands. But the actual book is much broader and less easy to characterize. It is built on examples, often excerpts from books or newspapers. His writing style, although engaging, is extremely complex and involuted. His style appears to charm the casual reader, but a close reading reveals many ambiguities. This aspect of his writing style contrasts particularly with the straightforward prose of Elias. Unlike the first works of the other two authors, *Presentation of Self in Everyday Life* itself requires considerable analysis in order to understand its basic thesis.

Of the three studies, Elias's *TCP* comes closest to realizing Spinoza's method of part/whole analysis (Sachsteder 1991; Scheff 1997: ch. 1). Spinoza proposed that human conduct is so complex that the only hope for understanding it is to be able to relate what he called 'the least parts and the greatest wholes'. That is, to link the smallest parts, such as words used in actual discourse, to the largest wholes, general theories, social institutions, historical eras and civilizations. Much more than Freud or Goffman, in *TCP*, Elias was at least partially successful in applying Spinoza's method. Since Spinoza's time, increasing specialization has made linking parts and wholes increasingly rare. Virtually all modern studies specialize in the perspective of a single discipline or sub-discipline, and separate micro and macro levels. They have also opened a huge gap between those who focus on theory, method or descriptive data. For this reason, Elias's seems to me a singular achievement. Although *TCP* overemphasizes data and underemphasizes method, both data and method are completely in the service of a general theory. The quest for integration of disciplinary perspectives, level, and theory, method and data will hopefully become a model for future work in social science.

Freud on shame and repression

This review will begin with Freud's and Breuer's study of hysteria (1895), not only because it was the first published of the three, but also because of the influence it seems to have had on Elias. Although not acknowledged, Elias's first writing appears to be strongly indebted to Freud. In *Studies on Hysteria* (1895), Freud and Breuer stated early on (p. 40) that hysteria is caused by hidden affects, and named the emotion of shame (*scham*) as one of these affects. Near the end of the book, this idea is urged more strongly: '[The ideas that were being repressed] were all of a distressing nature, calculated to arouse the affects of shame, self-reproach and of psychical pain and the feeling of being harmed' (1895: 313). Note that all of the affects mentioned can be considered to be shame derivatives or, for one of the four, a general name for emotional pain. Self-reproach is a specific shame cognate, the feeling of being harmed (as in rejection) somewhat broader, and finally, the quite abstract phrase 'psychical pain', which, like 'hurt' or 'emotional arousal' can be applied to any emotion. In this passage and several others, shame is given a central role in the causation of psychopathology. The idea that it is shame that causes repression would give it the leading role in the causation of all mental illness, not just hysteria. Freud seems to have stumbled upon the idea that shame is the principal agent of repression, without ever being able to assimilate it. In one of his statements many years later, Freud declared that repression was the central motor of human development and emotional illness, but psychoanalysis knew very little about it. Apparently Freud had not actually understood, or perhaps had forgotten, his earlier discovery that shame was the agent of repression. With the publication of *The Interpretation of Dreams*, Freud (1905) permanently renounced his earlier formulation in favour of drive theory, especially the sexual drive. At this point, anxiety and guilt became the central emotions in psychoanalytic theory. Since 1905, shame has been ignored in orthodox formulations. Although individual psychoanalysts have made crucially important contributions to shame knowledge, these contributions helped make them marginal to mainstream psychoanalysis.

In his mature years, because he saw so little evidence of shame in himself and in his male colleagues, Freud was dismissive of shame as an adult emotion in modern societies. He considered guilt to be the moral emotion of adults, being acutely conscious of it in himself and his male circle. Seeing little shame in himself and his friends, he found it, in his earliest work (1895) in his patients, all women. Reflecting the ageism, sexism and racism of his time, Freud seemed to think that shame was the emotion of children, women and savages. However, in *Studies on Hysteria*, Freud proposed two ideas which seem to have strongly influenced Elias: first, the concept of repression, and secondly, the idea that shame and other emotions were the agents of repression.

Elias on civilization

Elias's analysis of the 'civilizing process' (1939) shows how shame went underground in modern societies, yet became increasingly important as a means of social control. He traced changes in the development of personality in the onset of modern urban/industrial civilization. Like Weber, Elias gave prominence to the development of rationality. Unlike Weber, however, he gives equal prominence to changes in the threshold of shame: 'No less characteristic of a civilizing process than "rationalization" is the peculiar molding of the drive economy that we call "shame" and "repugnance" or "embarrassment"' (1982: 292).

Using excerpts from advice manuals in five languages from the Middle Ages to the nineteenth century, Elias outlined a theory of modernity. By examining advice concerning etiquette, especially table manners, body functions, sexuality and anger, he suggested that a key aspect of modernity involves shame. Elias's central thesis is that decreasing shame thresholds at the time of the breakup of rural communities, and decreasing acknowledgement of shame, have had powerful consequences on levels of awareness and self-control. The following excerpt suggests the flavour of Elias's study. He first presents an excerpt from a nineteenth-century work, *The Education of Girls* (von Raumer 1857), that advises mothers on how to answer the sexual questions their daughters ask:

Children should be left for as long as is at all possible in the belief that an angel brings the mother her little children. This legend, customary in some regions, is far better than the story of the stork common elsewhere. Children, if they really grow up under their mother's eyes, will seldom ask forward questions on this point . . . not even if the mother is prevented by a childbirth from having them about her . . . If girls should later ask how little children really come into the world, they should be told that the good Lord gives the mother her child, who has a guardian angel in heaven who certainly played an invisible part in bringing us this great joy. 'You do not need to know nor could you understand how God gives children.' Girls must be satisfied with such answers in a hundred cases, and it is the mother's task to occupy her daughters' thoughts so incessantly with the good and beautiful that they are left no time to brood on such matters . . . A mother . . . ought only once to say seriously: 'It would not be good for you to know such a thing, and you should take care not to listen to anything said about it.' A truly well brought-up girl will from then on feel shame at hearing things of this kind spoken of. (1978: 180)

Elias first interprets the repression of sexuality in terms of unacknowledged shame:

In the civilizing process, sexuality too is increasingly removed behind the scenes of social life and enclosed in a particular enclave, the nuclear family. Likewise, the relations between the sexes are isolated, placed behind walls in consciousness. An aura of embarrassment, the expression of a sociogenetic fear, surrounds this sphere of life. Even among adults it is referred to officially only with caution and circumlocutions. And with children, particularly girls, such things are, as far as possible, not referred to at all. Von Raumer gives no reason why one ought not to speak of them with children. He could have said it is desirable to preserve the spiritual purity of girls for as long as possible. But even this reason is only another expression of how far the gradual submergence of these impulses in shame and embarrassment has advanced by this time. (1978: 180)

Elias raises a host of significant questions about this excerpt, concerning its motivation and its effects. His analysis goes to what I consider to be the central causal chain in modern civilization: denial of shame and of the threatened social bonds that both cause and reflect that denial. I concur with Elias's analysis of the causal process in repression, the arousal of shame and the denial of this arousal:

Considered rationally, the problem confronting him [von Raumer] seems un-
solved, and what he says appears contradictory. He does not explain how and
when the young girl should be made to understand what is happening and will
happen to her. The primary concern is the necessity of instilling 'modesty' (i.e.,
feelings of shame, fear, embarrassment, and guilt) or, more precisely, behaviour
conforming to the social standard. And one feels how infinitely difficult it is for
the educator himself to overcome the resistance of the shame and embarrassment
which surround this sphere for him. (1978: 181)

Elias's study suggests a way of understanding the social transmission of
the taboo on shame and the social bond. The adult, the author von
Raumer, in this case, is not only ashamed of sex, he is ashamed of
being ashamed, in accordance with Kaufman's (1989: 3–4) analysis of
taboo: shame about shame cascades leading to complete repression. The
nineteenth-century reader, in turn, probably reacted in a similar way; being ashamed, and being ashamed of being ashamed, and being ashamed
of causing further shame in the daughter. Von Raumer's advice was part
of a social system in which attempts at civilized delicacy resulted and continue to result in an endless chain reaction of unacknowledged shame.
The chain reaction is both within persons and between them, a 'triple
spiral' (Scheff 1990). Elias understood the significance of the denial of
shame: i.e. that shame goes underground, leading to behaviour that is
outside of awareness. As he comments: 'Neither rational motives nor
practical reasons primarily determine this attitude, but rather the shame
(*scham*) of adults themselves, which has become compulsive. It is the social prohibitions and resistances within themselves, their own superego
that makes them keep silent' (1978: 181). Like many other passages, this
one points not only to a taboo on shame, but at the actual mechanisms by
which it is transmitted and maintained. In particular, he shows a possible
route of transmission in the chain that connects author with reader, and
reader, presumably a mother, with a daughter. This chain is then linked
to the beliefs and practices of a specific society and historical era. Elias's
close reading of the passage from von Raumer's book, and his exploration
of its emotional and relational sources and effects illustrates what I mean
when I say that Elias analysed parts and wholes, in the manner suggested
by Spinoza.

As already indicated, Elias's sustained use of the concept of repression
is one indication of his debt to Freud, and the importance Elias put on
shame as an agent of social control in European history. There is also
a third indication of Freud's influence; Elias's idea that not only shame,
but also disgust was an important force in social control. In his study
of hysteria, and in *Three Essays on the Theory of Sexuality* (1905), Freud
names not only shame, but also disgust as the basis for repression. Elias

seemed to have picked up this idea from his reading of early Freud. In *TCP* (1939), shame is the emotion that is most frequently invoked. However, in that book, Elias often mentions embarrassment and disgust (translated in English as 'repugnance') along with shame. In the excerpts chosen by Elias as illustrations of his theory, disgust often plays a role at least as important as shame. It is particularly important in his discussions of mealtime manners and the etiquette of the body and its products. For example, there are many excerpts concerning spitting and picking one's nose. These excerpts are used, I believe, to actually evoke disgust in the reader. One fourteenth-century excerpt used by Elias warns the reader that if one is forced to blow one's nose in public, it should be wiped with a handkerchief, not on one's sleeve, and one should avoid looking at what comes out as if searching for treasure.

The idea that disgust can be an important force in social control is suggested in the work of the anthropologist Mary Douglas. In *Purity and Danger* (1966) she shows how the status quo in tribes and other groups is maintained by thoughts/feelings of clean and unclean. Surprisingly, although she does mention fear several times, she doesn't explicitly name disgust. But virtually all of her examples, coming as they do from the arenas of food, sex and the body, evoke disgust rather than fear. Under the heading of 'bodily excreta', Goffman lists four types: 'corporal excrete (or their stains) that contaminate by direct touch, odor, bodily heat (as on toilet seats), and markings left by the body in which excreta can be imagined, plate leavings are an example' (1971: 46–7). Goffman seems to have been particularly interested in the last category, since he goes on for another page about defilement fears connected with food (p. 48). (I am indebted to Amelia George for calling these passages to my attention.) Miller (1997) is also forthright; he names disgust, as well as shame, as the crucial emotions in social control.

Reception of Elias's book

From the point of view of attracting readers, the translator of *TCP* from German into English made what I consider to be a gross mistake. He translated the word that Elias used, *scham*, into the word shame. Although technically correct, it is an error in terms of emotional content. Perhaps if he had used the word embarrassment instead of shame, the reception of the book in the USA might have been less tepid. Although one of the great landmarks of social science research in England and Europe, the book is still little known in the USA. Why was *TCP* well received in England? Because of the long hiatus between the original publication in German in 1939 and its first translation into English in 1982, the scholars in England who became followers of Elias had read *TCP* only in German. Knowing German, they were able to accept Elias's emphasis on *scham*. Writing about the early reviews of *TCP* in Europe, Goudsblom (1977) noted that many of them were especially appreciative of the first part, the history of manners. Since French and Dutch each have a word that is the exact equivalent of 'scham', perhaps they were able to take his unusual emphasis on shame in their stride. If Elias had used the word *schande* (the German equivalent of the word shame in English), rather than *scham*, the book might have received a less enthusiastic reception in Europe, paralleling its reception in the USA. In terms of taboo, it should also be noted that many years passed before reviewers or users of *TCP* referred to the central role of shame in Elias's study of manners. Goudsblom didn't note it in his 1977 review, nor did any of the reviewers cited by Goudsblom.

The only researcher who made use of Elias's shame work was Sennett, who cited Elias in his own chapter on the way managers use shame to control workers (Sennett 1980). Sennett's earlier work, *The Hidden Injuries of Class* (1972), implied that shame was the hidden injury, but did not make it explicit. Perhaps Sennett was encouraged by Elias's book to be explicit about shame in a chapter of his 1980 book. However, neither reviewers nor anyone else took note of that chapter. Perhaps both Sennett and Elias noted the lack of response, since neither one ever wrote directly about shame again.[1] The taboo on shame is maintained through silence, first by the readers of the books, then by the authors themselves. This taboo extends even into psychoanalysis and social psychology, disciplines in which emotion is a central concern.

Goffman's looking-glass self

The Presentation of Self in Everyday Life (1959, henceforth *PSEL*) has sold over a million copies, probably more than any other book in sociology. Yet scholars are still unsure of its meaning. Some background will be necessary to uncover its message. In order to understand the central thread in *PSEL*, it will be necessary to locate it in the work of Mead and Cooley. Mead (1934) proposed that the self is a social phenomenon as much as a biological one. His fundamental insight into consciousness was that it arose out of role taking, of seeing things from the point of view of the other(s), as well as from one's own point of view. This idea is central to the social psychology of Mead, Cooley and Goffman.

Mead himself gave very little attention to shame or any other emotion. The problem that he attacked was the basis of reflective intelligence. He needed the idea of role taking to explain the origins of intelligence and objectivity. However, a contemporary of Mead's, Charles Cooley, in his version of role taking, noted that reading the mind of the other would usually generate emotions. For Cooley (1922), shame and pride both arose from seeing oneself from the point of view of the other. In his discussion of what he called the 'self-sentiments', pride and shame are mentioned as two of the emotions possible. But his concept of 'the looking glass self', which implies the social nature of the self, refers directly and exclusively to pride and shame. Cooley saw self-monitoring in three steps: 'A self-idea of this sort seems to have three principal elements: the imagination of our appearance to the other person; the imagination of his judgment of that appearance, and some sort of self-feeling, such as pride or mortification' (1922: 184). In this passage he restricts self-feelings to the two he thought to be the most significant, pride and shame (considering 'mortification' to be a shame variant). To make sure we understand this point, he mentions shame three more times in the passage that follows:

The comparison with a looking-glass hardly suggests the second element, the imagined judgment, which is quite essential. The thing that moves us to *pride or shame* is not the mere mechanical reflection of ourselves, but an imputed sentiment, the imagined effect of this reflection upon another's mind. This is evident from the fact that the character and weight of that other, in whose mind we see ourselves, makes all the difference with our feeling. We are *ashamed* to seem evasive in the presence of a straightforward man, cowardly in the presence of a brave one, gross in the eyes of a refined one and so on. We always imagine, and in imagining share, the judgments of the other mind. A man will boast to one person of an action   say some sharp transaction in trade   which he would be *ashamed* to own to another. (1922: 184–5, emphasis added)

The way in which Cooley linked intersubjective connectedness, on the one hand, with pride and shame, on the other, could have been the basis for a general social psychological theory of bond affect. Even though the looking glass self was appreciated and frequently cited in mainstream sociology and social psychology, the part involving pride and shame was simply ignored. Why?

Like most of the pioneers in the study of emotions, Cooley didn't attempt to define what he meant by pride or shame. He simply used these words as if their meaning were simple and singular. But in Western societies, the meaning of pride and shame is neither simple nor singular. The meaning of these words is complex, and laden with emotion. Unless prefaced by an adjective like genuine or justified, the word pride carries a strong connotation of arrogance and selfishness, the kind of pride that 'goeth before the fall'. The unadorned word pride, that is, is taken to be false pride or vanity.

As already indicated, the word shame alone also has negative connotations to the point that it is taboo. Perhaps because he was born in the nineteenth century, when these words may have been less weighted with feeling, Cooley could have been unaware of the problem. It appears that his readers didn't know what to make of his emphasis on pride and shame. In any case, his insights into the relationship between attunement and emotion were ignored until my review (Scheff 1990), a hiatus of 68 years.

Goffman also pursued the idea of emotions arising out of role taking, but more diffusely than Cooley. Rather than with shame alone, *PSEL* deals with what might be called the whole shame triad, embarrassment, shame and humiliation, with primary emphasis on embarrassment. More than Cooley, and much more than Mead, Goffman fleshed out the link between emotions and role taking by providing example after example (1959; 1963; 1963a; 1967). These examples allow the reader at least the illusion of understanding ideas that are only abstractions in Mead and Cooley. Goffman's use of examples to illustrate abstract ideas makes his work accessible to readers. The idea of impression management, crucial in most of Goffman's writing, made the avoidance of embarrassment a central motive of interpersonal behaviour. Goffman's 'Everyperson' is always desperately worried about his image in the eyes of others, trying to present himself with his best foot forward. Goffman's work vivifies Cooley's abstract idea of the way in which the looking glass generates emotion, giving the idea roots in the reader's imagination.

Goffman also made the key sociological point about embarrassment: it arises out of slights, real, anticipated or just imagined, *no matter how trivial* they might appear to the outside observer. Everyone is extremely sensitive to the exact nuance of deference they receive. This idea certainly cannot be derived from Cooley, whose few examples concern extreme situations of shame and humiliation. This is Goffman's key contribution to emotion knowledge. He liberated the shame triad from melodramatic circumstances, showing that it was also the stuff of everyday life. In Goffman's language: 'One assumes that embarrassment is a normal part of normal social life, the individual becoming uneasy not because he is personally maladjusted but rather because he is not . . . embarrassment is not an irrational impulse breaking through socially prescribed behaviour, but part of this orderly behaviour itself' (1967: 109, 111).

It was fortunate, perhaps, in terms of the size of his readership, that Goffman chose to focus on embarrassment, without connecting it to shame. It's not clear whether Goffman chose that strategy intentionally. One piece of the puzzle is suggested by his book *Stigma* (1963b). Since shame is the central topic of this work, it provided him with ample opportunity to explore the relationship between embarrassment and shame. But he did not, shame is mentioned only a few times, and in passing. In fairness to Goffman, although he emphasized embarrassment, in his early work he didn't avoid shame completely. In the 30 pages of chapter 6 (1959), he mentioned shame or being ashamed four times, guilt and humiliation once each, and embarrassment seven times. But this count underplays his consideration of everyday embarrassment, because there are many more images that imply it, rather than shame or humiliation. One example from the same chapter should be enough to make this point:

He may . . . add to the precariousness of his position by engaging in just those defensive manoeuvers that he would employ if he were really guilty. In this way it is possible for all of us *to become fleetingly for ourselves the worst person we can imagine that others might imagine us to be.* (1959: 236, italics added)

Like most of Goffman's images of emotion, this one, because it is so fleeting, invokes the idea of embarrassment rather than longer-term feelings such as shame or humiliation. This seems to me a limitation of Goffman's work on emotions, to which I will return below. But the basic idea, of seeing one's self negatively in the eyes of others, was perceived as the origin of embarrassment, shame or humiliation, by Darwin (1872), Cooley and Goffman himself. Although I haven't made an actual count, I propose that it is invoked constantly by Goffman, particularly in his most popular work. Although Goffman doesn't credit Cooley directly, the central theme of *Presentation of Self*, and much of Goffman's later writing, is an elaboration on Cooley's thesis – since we live in the minds of others, pride and shame (in its broad sense), are the master emotions of everyday life.

Discussion

This chapter, to this point, has been both a review and an analysis of the writings on shame, embarrassment and disgust by Freud, Elias and Goffman. I will now compare their advantages and limitations.

It was Freud who was the first Western writer to suggest the profound influence of shame, embarrassment and disgust in everyday life. In his first book (1895), Freud stated two concepts that he believed to be the causative agents in hysteria, repression of thoughts, memories and emotions, and how, in turn, shame and disgust are the causal agents of repression. The concept of repression was carried farther in Freud's later work to the point that it became the core idea. But the influence of the emotion part of theory was greatly diminished because Freud disowned it in all of his work that followed. Furthermore, even in the original study, the part played by shame and disgust was presented briefly and casually. A reader not particularly interested in emotions might miss it entirely. But it appears that there was at least one reader who did not miss it. Elias, it seems to me, was strongly influenced by both concepts. I will return to this idea in my discussion of Elias's work.

One further limitation of Freud's perspective is that it was almost entirely limited to individuals, ignoring relationships both at the interpersonal and societal levels. Freud subscribed to what is now being called 'the fundamental attribution error' (Ross and Nesbitt 1991). That is, he was so focused on the psychodynamics of individuals that he failed to incorporate situational, and especially social and institutional elements into his analysis.

The opposite limitation can be found in the *PSEL*, Goffman's first work. His focus was on social interaction, on what transpired between individuals, rather than within them He went so far as to suggest that the individual self was an illusion created by social arrangement. Like most sociologists, he was extremely suspicious and rejecting of individual psychodynamics.

Although not as many-levelled as Elias's approach in *TCP*, the *PSEL* had many strengths. One of them was the way in which Goffman used concrete examples copiously, to bring to life ideas that would otherwise be abstract and distant. As I have argued above, though Goffman didn't make it explicit, the *PSEL* may even have a central unifying theme, the theory of the looking-glass self and emotions. Although Cooley was not cited in this regard, much of the book, especially how it deals with emotions, can be seen as showing how we respond with shame or embarrassment when we consider how we are seen in the eyes of others. More than any other work, the *PSEL* vivifies Cooley's conjecture.

The frequent use of examples is also a strength of Elias's *TCP*. But unlike Goffman, whose examples seem to be completely random,[2] Elias's examples are excerpts from a larger study that is at least partly systematic. His examples come only from etiquette and advice manuals published in Europe from the thirteenth through the nineteenth centuries. Furthermore, the examples are all used for a single purpose, to illustrate and extend his general theory of the civilizing process, the way in which emotions are gradually co-opted in the service of social control.

Equally impressive is Elias's very detailed analysis of some of his excerpts. Although Goffman has a reputation for being a miniaturist, and is given credit for the microscopic analysis of his examples, in my opinion, Elias goes much more fully into his examples than Goffman does. Indeed, Goffman's examples nicely illustrate whatever point he is making, but they require very little analysis to do so. Although Elias's identification of shame in written texts is completely intuitive, my reading of the excerpts is almost always exactly as his.

Another strength of Elias is that all of his analysis of shame and disgust in *TCP* implies that these emotions played a central role in the development of our civilization. Although Elias often invokes embarrassment as well, since it is usually less intense and of shorter duration, it is much less crucial in his analysis. Goffman's emphasis on embarrassment, rather than shame, as already indicated, gives it a less important role in Goffman's social and personal scheme of things.

Although I am less qualified to evaluate the accuracy of the way Elias provides the larger social and institutional context for his excerpts, my impression from reading his critics is that they find no fatal flaws in his historical accounts.[3] Together, his detailed analyses of the excerpts, on the one hand, and his ability to place them in the larger cultural and historical context, give his work a breadth and range of vision missing in both Freud and Goffman. Elias's analysis of shame in specific instances, within the larger cultural context, provides the basic theme of the whole study.

I believe Elias's *TCP* is one of the very few sustained studies that follows Spinoza's suggestion for understanding complex human conduct by linking 'the least parts' to the 'greatest wholes'. To the extent that this is the case, *TCP* may provide a model for future research that would integrate perspectives from the different social sciences, sub-disciplines, micro and macro levels, and, perhaps most important, balanced use of theory, method and data.

NOTES

1. No longer true in 2003, since in his new book on respect, Sennett has a chapter on the shame of dependency. Perhaps my correspondence with him about untheorized shame in *The Hidden Injuries of Class* encouraged Sennett to be explicit about shame in the 2003 book.
2. When I was a graduate student, I once asked Goffman where he got his examples. Rather than answering directly, he told me about a comment by John Updike in his review of the book *The Batchelors*, by Muriel Spark. Impressed by the vast knowledge the ageing writer seemed to have of men in all kinds of class positions in London, Updike asked Spark how she came to know all these things. The response she gave him was 'A lifetime of combing lint.'
3. Miller (1997:170) offers this tribute: 'It is a trait of great works to be able to be proven wrong in particulars and still manage to offer a truth about the larger picture . . .' Miller makes the comment to discount the charges that Elias's description of medieval people as vulgar, uninhibited and childlike is a caricature.

REFERENCES

Cooley, Charles H. 1922, *Human Nature and the Social Order*, New York: Scribner's.

Darwin, Charles 1872, *The Expression of Emotion in Men and Animals*, London: John Murray.

Douglas, Mary 1966 (2002), *Purity and Danger*, London: Routledge.

Elias, Norbert [1939] 1978, 1982, 1983, *The Civilizing Process*: vols. 1–3, New York: Pantheon.

1994, *The Civilizing Process*, Oxford: Blackwell.

1996, *The Germans*, Cambridge: Polity.

Elias, N. and Scotson, J. 1965, *The Established and the Outsiders*, London: Frank Cass.

Freud, S. 1905, *Three Essays on the Theory of Sexuality*, vol. 7, pp. 135–244, standard edn, London: Hogarth.

Freud, S. and Breuer, J. 1895 (1966), *Studies on Hysteria*, New York: Avon.

Goffman, Erving 1959, *Presentation of Self in Everyday Life*, New York: Anchor.

1963a, *Behaviour in Public Places*, New York: Free Press.

1963b, *Stigma*, Englewood Cliffs, NJ: Prentice-Hall.

1967, *Interaction Ritual*, New York: Anchor.

1971, *Relations in Public*, New York: Basic Books.

Goudsblom, Johan 1977, 'Responses to Elias's work in England, Germany, the Netherlands, and France', in Peter Gleichmann (ed.), *Human Figurations*, Amsterdam: Sociologische Tijdschrift.

Kaufman, Gershon 1989, *The Psychology of Shame*, New York: Springer.

Mead, George, H. 1934, *Mind, Self, and Society*, Chicago IL: University of Chicago Press.

Metge, Joan 1986, 'In and out of touch: Whakamaa [bond affect]', in *Cross Cultural Perspective*, Wellington, NZ: Victoria University Press.

Miller, William, I. 1997, *The Anatomy of Disgust*, Cambridge, MA: Harvard University Press.

Ross, Lee, and Richard Nisbett 1991, *The Person and the Situation*, Philadelphia: Temple University Press.

Sachsteder, W. 1991, 'Least parts and greatest wholes: variations on a theme in Spinoza', *International Studies in Philosophy* 23 (1): 75–87.

Scheff, Thomas 1984, 'The taboo on coarse emotions', *Review of Personality and Social Psychology*, June.

1990, *Microsociology*, Chicago, IL: University of Chicago Press.

1994, *Bloody Revenge: Nationalism, War, and Emotion*, Boulder, CO: Westview. Re-issued by Universe (2000).

1997, *Emotions and the Social Bond: Part/Whole Analysis*, Cambridge: Cambridge University Press.

2000, 'Shame and the social bond', *Sociological Theory* 18: 84–98.

2002, 'Working-class emotions and relationships: secondary analysis of Sennett and Cobb, and Willis', in Bernard Phillips, Harold McKinnon and Thomas Scheff (eds.), *Toward a Sociological Imagination: Bridging Specialized Fields*, Lanham, MD: University Press of America, pp. 263–92.

2003, 'Shame in self and society', *Symbolic Interaction*, 26(2): 239–62.

Scheff, Thomas, and Retzinger, Suzanne 1991, *Violence and Emotions*, Lexington, MA: Lexington Books. Re-issued by Universe (2001).

Sennett, Richard 1980, *Authority*, New York: Alfred Knopf.

2003, *Respect and Inequality*, New York: Norton.

Sennett, R. and Cobb, J. 1972, *The Hidden Injuries of Class*, New York: Knopf.

Von Raumer, Wilhelm 1857, *The Education of Girls* (cited in Elias, 1978).

Part IV

Religion and civilizing processes: Weber and Elias compared

14 Weber and Elias on religion and violence: warrior charisma and the civilizing process

Bryan S. Turner

Introduction: charisma, routinization and the civilizing process

In a famous passage from the *Ynglingsaga*, we hear about the comrades of Odin who 'went without shields, and were mad as dogs or wolves, and bit on their shields, and were as strong as bears or bulls; men they slew, and neither fire nor steel would deal with them; and this is what is called the fury of the berserker' (Morris and Magnusson 1893:1, 16–17). This passage could usefully function as a preface to either *The Civilizing Process* or *Economy and Society*. We can interpret Norbert Elias's theory of the civilizing process as, amongst other things, a history of the decline of the warrior stratum in European feudalism and the rise of the court society. The emergence of a pacified court society and the technological development of weapons employing gunpowder eventually transformed the social functions and status of feudal warlords and their followers. These changes in civility also chart the formation of the nation-state and the centralization of institutional power. The transformation of the emotions is an important feature of this history. In the discussion 'On changes in aggressiveness', Elias (2000: 161–2) provides an important account of how violent passions in the early feudal period were slowly regulated as the civilized forms of court society evolved. In this chapter I develop an argument that there are important parallels between Max Weber's account of the routinization of charisma in military bureaucracies and Elias's analysis of the decline of militarized feudalism. The routinization of charismatic force in society brings about a predictable social environment in which risk and passion are routinely managed. However, I want to criticize Elias's historical sociology for its neglect of religion and the relationship of religion to military institutions and culture. In developing this interpretation of war and civilization, I shall coin the expression 'warrior charisma' in order to extend Weber's analysis of types of authority (Turner 2003).

Despite their shared interests in the historical sociology of power relations and state institutions, there are relatively few published commentaries by Elias on Weber's sociology. Weber was clearly important in the development of Elias's historical sociology. There is, for example, an extended discussion of Weber in *The Court Society*. Elias criticized Weber effectively for developing a unidimensional and ahistorical notion of rationality, and pointed out that patterns of rational behaviour would be specific to different social contexts. While Weber had in mind primarily 'bourgeois-capitalist' forms of rationality, Elias argued that the court had its own style of rational norms of action. Thus '[c]ourt rationality is generated by the compulsion of the elite social mesh; by it people and prestige are made calculable as instruments of power' (Elias 1983: 111). In *The Civilizing Process* (Elias 2000:469) Weber is criticized for his static view of 'the individual', and for his inability to reconcile the analytical tensions between 'the individual' and 'society'. Elias (2000: 472) treats Weber's failure to deal successfully with this artificial and static division as part of a general weakness of sociological theory, and argues that Weber and Parsons belong to 'the same provenance'. The same argument occurs in *The Society of Individuals* (Elias 1991: 164) where it is claimed that human society is not a loose collection of individuals or groups as 'depicted in some older sociological theories, including Max Weber's theory of action'. Elias's solution was to analyse the two concepts of individual and society as social processes 'in conjunction with empirical investigations' (Elias 2000: 473). In *The Court Society* (Elias 1983: 21) Weber is discussed with approval in relation to the problem of luxury in the court society, but his 'ideal type' method is rejected as historically inadequate, especially in Weber's treatment of patrimonialism.

My argument is broadly that Weber's 'rationalization process' in which legal-rational norms of conduct come to dominate social interaction is parallel to the civilizing process in which civil norms of self-restraint come to dominate social interaction. The routinizing process and the civilizing process have similar analytical functions and occupy the same space within the theoretical structure of Weber's macro-sociology and Elias's figurational sociology. In addition, much of Elias's criticism of Weber (and Parsons) is misplaced. Weber did not accept a static, ideal-typical analysis of the historical patterns of authority, but more importantly his sociology is not based on a rigid division between society and individual. The concept of the social actor in both Weber and Parsons was an analytical construct that emerged from their critical engagement with economic theory. By contrast, in his sociology of religion, Weber developed the sophisticated idea of 'personality' and 'life orders' in which a personality structure is not a given, but is cultivated through education and discipline. 'Personality' stands frequently in opposition to the 'life orders' of the economy and the state, and with the growth of capitalism personality is threatened by the regulatory impact of the practical rationality of this secular world (Hennis 1988). Different cultures have different regimes that produce these personalities. The violent personalities of medieval society are replaced by new life orders that emerge with new social technologies. In his studies of the Protestant sects, Weber examined the historical development of the ascetic personality in relation to the life orders of an emerging capitalist society. One can argue that the articles on European and American sectarianism were part of a larger project on the sociology of life conduct (*Lebensführung*) (Baehr 2001). It is not possible therefore to interpret Weber's sociology as yet another conventional dichotomy of the individual and society; the question for Weber was thoroughly anthropological and historical. Similar arguments might be developed in relation to Parsons who thought of personality as a type of institution and hence did not conceptualize society as simply a collection of individuals. Neither Weber nor Parsons adopted a behavioural epistemology of the individual, and both assumed that religion had historically played an important part in shaping the 'individual' as an historical construct (Bourricaud 1981).

Charisma, and especially warrior charisma, is important because it occupies a social and historical niche that appears to challenge the social practices that bring about civility and civilization. Charisma is opposed to the normalizing processes of tradition and incompatible with the rationalizing processes of the legal-rational bureaucracies in the modern state. Bureaucratization occurs in societies where the disruptive effects of charismatic claims have been contained and suppressed by the political power of the 'office' over 'the person', and by the centralizing of state power (Shils 1975). Civilizational processes in court society are parallel to the routinizing of charisma into the authority of office, and, while the habitus of the court and the office are very different, they are both incompatible with charismatic frenzy. The self-restraint of both settings is far removed from the warrior intoxication that is described in the *Ynglingsaga*. In particular, the rationalization of warrior charisma means the end of the intoxication of the berserk warrior and the growth of military discipline and training as techniques for producing a mass army. The training of the body in the feudal court and the monastery are early models of body techniques that were developed by educational and military institutions in the creation of professional training (Foucault 1977; Vigarello 1989).

The modern state emerges as an institution that secures a monopoly over legitimate violence, and hence it relies on specialised training and military discipline to produce professional men who are able to carry out their tasks in a spirit of neutrality and disinterest. The calling of the modern soldier does not include the sheer enjoyment of killing that was characteristic of the feudal warrior or the 'noble savage'. Although women in the modern army may not necessarily be combat troops, the fact that women are recruited into the military is an important indication that the emotional structure of the military, and modern warfare, are consistent with a professional rather than a charismatic culture. In this chapter I want to modify Weber's argument in two directions. In many 'primitive societies', warrior charisma is also a form of spiritual ecstasy in which the warrior is transformed out of an earthly and profane role into a sacred domain. I shall take the Cheyenne Plains tribes of North America as an illustration. Charisma, while commonly understood to be a spontaneous eruption into normal social relationships, is still governed by roles and expectations. In this sense, it is already partly 'cultivated' and hence partly 'civilized'. This issue is related to the problem in Weber's account in *Ancient Judaism* (Weber 1952) concerning the difference between true and false prophets. Can charisma be simulated and manufactured, or is it a blind force of the sacred? My second elaboration of Weber's sociology is that, while Weber's argument is correct that charisma is a rare form of authority in modern societies, charisma is increasingly manufactured and transformed into celebrity. In modern societies, charisma is democratized, and as a result of commercial routinization appears as popular celebrity. In the world of popular entertainment, any trivial and mundane activity of celebrities has charismatic worth, but the contents of the original notion have completely disappeared. The contrast with the intoxicated fury of the charismatic warrior could not be more profound and hence this discussion of warrior charisma provides a theoretical platform for examining the historical and social relationship between religion, discipline and (organized) violence.

Weber's development of the concepts of personality and life order can be understood as a sociological contribution to the study of character as a form of discipline. We can reasonably interpret Weber's notion of personality as an institutionalization of the individual, and thereby make some sensible comparisons with Michel Foucault's contribution to the 'technologies of the self' (Foucault 1997). The military training of the Cheyenne was designed to construct a technology of the self that was set within the sacred. Their mode of warfare can be defined as a form of spiritual violence, because warfare was bound up with religious norms of conduct and their military interaction was highly ritualized. War was a deadly serious game. Cheyenne warriors had a reputation for extreme forms of violence, but their mode of warfare was also highly controlled by ritual. The basic idea is to show how the training of the body as a technology of the self produced a capacity to define the person as (socially) dead prior to conflict. These spiritual technologies are therefore an important illustration of military technologies of self-creation.

There is no doubt that Elias produced one of the most influential theories of the transformation of violence in human societies in terms of the civilizing process. His argument is well known. In summary, it states that with the transformation of feudal society, the rise of bourgeois society and the development of the modern state, interpersonal violence was increasingly regulated by social norms that emphasized self-restraint and personal discipline. The theory can be regarded as a moral pedagogy of the body in which raw passions and emotions are self-regulated through disciplinary regimes. The theory shows how developments in social institutions (such as the court, the state and the bourgeois family) are important for and interact with the emotions and dispositions of individuals. Personal civility and civilizing institutions are bound together in a dynamic historical process. As a result, in contemporary societies, social restraint and social order require the development of self-attention in which through self-reflection (imagining what others think of us) we exercise self-surveillance and control (Barbalet 1998:86). In this sense, we can regard the theory as an historical psychoanalytic of violent emotions within the sociological paradigm of the modern state.

Given the important exposition of the contrast between culture and civilization in the introduction to Elias's major work, it is odd that he chose the title 'the civilizing process', because his argument is in fact about the cultivating process. Elias's historical study of the social processes that civilize behaviour through the development of a culture of restraint occurs within the context of an established European debate about the contrast between *Kultur* and *Zivilisation*. Through this discussion, Elias begins to establish the sociology of morals where different social classes are involved in a competitive struggle over the meaning and value of ethical conduct, and where different systems of training and discipline are seen to be appropriate to the cultural production of character. These differences were not only about the cultural conflict between social classes but also between nations and national character. The theory of *Zivilisation* was interpreted as part of an international struggle between Anglo-Saxon, specifically American industrial society and Germany. This perception of profound differences in national character was an important aspect of actual politics and social theory. Pessimism about intercultural conflict was evident in Weber's inaugural Freiburg lecture on social conflict as a Darwinistic struggle, in the pessimistic cultural analysis of the decline of the West by Oswald Spengler and in the literary works of Thomas

Mann (Herf 1984). Elias was sensitive to these historical struggles in the evolution of the notion of culture, and he argued that the dichotomy between (technological) civilization and (moral) cultivation was gradually transformed from a social distinction between classes to a national distinction as the German bourgeoisie rose in social power. Elias's sociology of morals is concerned therefore with the complex historical relationship between the production of character and the production of culture. This sociological concept of process is a major criticism of the traditional dichotomy of the individual and society that has dominated and frequently frustrated the development of sociological theory.

While this theory has been distinctively influential, it has also been subject to systematic criticism. In this chapter, I shall outline three obvious lacunae in Elias's theory. Firstly, the theory does not provide any adequate account of the role of religion in controlling human violence. One can develop this critical observation through a commentary on charisma and the sacred in human society, namely on the nature of sacred violence. Secondly, Elias had relatively little to say about the interaction between technology, particularly military hardware, and interpersonal norms. Against Elias's theory of the civilizing process, modern technology has made it possible, both in peace and war, for the state and modern military institutions to exercise control over instruments of mass destruction that were unimaginable in less civilised societies. Elias's analysis of the importance of constraints in terms of interpersonal violence is, however, consistent with the view that modern technology has obviously enhanced the capacity of the means of violence in civilized societies. This 'de-personalization' of violence is obviously consistent with Elias's civilization theory, and it is clearly compatible with Weber's discussion of rationalization. While the Holocaust raised basic questions about the civilization of Europe, the destruction of Jewish communities can however be interpreted as the rational application of the means of violence to an administrative objective (Bauman 1989). It was an aspect of 'the banality of evil' (Arendt 1994) that Nazi officers like Adolf Eichmann went about their bureaucratic tasks with clinical calmness. My point is that Elias has very little to say about technology as such. Thirdly, apart from Elias's interest in art in African society, possibly as a consequence of his teaching appointment in Ghana (1962–4), his theory was primarily concerned to explain aspects of social change in European society. My examination of the evolution of violence and warrior charisma among American Plains Indians, especially the Cheyenne, is intended to be an elaboration of the discussion of self-restraint in Elias's historical sociology. Elias made some important comparisons between contemporary societies and native American tribes in terms of the importance of self-restraint and time discipline in *Time: An Essay* (Elias 1992), and I shall draw upon this discussion in what follows.

Weber and Elias on religion and civilization

In the history of sociological theory it has been a commonplace to compare Elias favourably with the work of Talcott Parsons on the grounds that Parsons neglected historical processes, because his structural-functional analysis made static assumptions about the properties of social systems rather than historical transformations. The intention here is not to reassess Parsons's functionalism, but rather to explore an important difference between Elias and Parsons in order to develop a sociological account of charisma, the sacred and violence. While Elias had given special emphasis to military conflicts and social violence in his study of the civilizing process, he almost completely neglected the historical and comparative importance of religious cultures and institutions. *The Civilizing Process* is largely silent about the role of religious norms and institutions in European history in the regulation of social behaviour. By contrast, the centrality of the sociology of religion in Parsons's sociology was in part a consequence of his intellectual encounter with the legacy of Weber (Turner 1999). Parsons was steeped in Weber's sociological project, and recognized that the question of religion was the continuous thread in Weber's economic and political sociology. For example, Parsons translated *The Protestant Ethic and the Spirit of Capitalism* (Weber 1930), wrote an influential introduction to *The Sociology of Religion* (Parsons 1966) and edited *The Theory of Social and Economic Organization* (Parsons 1947). The absence of any sustained discussion of religious institutions in any part of Elias's *oeuvre* is remarkable, and provides a definite contrast with the sociological legacies of both Weber and Parsons. Parsons's criticisms of simple secularization theories and his recognition of the generic importance of religion to the building of institutions were major foundations of his sociology as a whole.

The absence of any sustained analytical interest in the regulative and restraining functions of religious norms in the historical process of civilizing military violence, the court and the bourgeois household is a significant problem in Elias's treatment of the institutional matrix of Western nation-states. Sociologists who are sympathetic to Elias's historical sociology have claimed that it was simply not possible for Elias to deal with all aspects of the civilizing process, and in any case his analysis was specifically concerned with secular institutions and processes (Russell 1996). This defence is not convincing, because, from a sociological and historical perspective, religion is fundamental to social regulation. Religion, to paraphrase Durkheim, includes the rites and rituals that bind people together into a moral community, and exercises constraint over their affective drives. Religion, to paraphrase Weber, disciplines the person, especially through ascetic practices, and creates life orders and personalities. Weber's sociology of religion can be read as a contribution to the idea that religion has been important in regulating the instinctual life in the interests of social order (Turner 1987). Freudian psychoanalysis, for example, was preoccupied with the tensions between instinctual gratification and religious asceticism, and the analysis of the relationship between psychic regulation and social requirements in *Civilization and its Discontents* (Freud 1930) was an important anticipation of the critical theory of Herbert Marcuse (1955) in such works as *Eros and Civilization*. The notion that religious norms play an important part in creating and establishing social order has been fundamental to social and political theory.

There are linguistic, philosophical and theological arguments that we separate and distinguish violence from the sacred, but further reflection shows that this separation is unwarranted and historically complex. The psychoanalytic analysis of ritual indicates the falsity of this cultural separation. In *Violence and the Sacred*, René Gerard (1988) showed how sacrifice was the root of religious ritual and the social contract. Sacrifice is a collective ritual that obscures the origins of religious practices in actual murder and physical violence. Sacrifice can be interpreted as a collective celebration that ritually undermined the prohibition or taboo on murder, especially of relatives and kinfolk. In general, collective rituals typically undermined and reversed the normal order of society to release charismatic powers that become available to the social group. Freud (1913) had almost unwittingly (re)discovered the true connections between sexual abstinence, sacrifice and the Oedipus Complex in *Totem and Taboo*. Primitive religious ritual is organized around the killing of a surrogate victim, and involves a fusion of opposites – violence and the sacred. The historical evolution of rituals typically obscures these primitive origins. The crucifixion of Christ was yet another sacrifice of the offspring in order to release the charismatic powers of the Father. From this psychoanalytic vantage-point, Elias's theory might also obscure this relationship, and allow us to argue that the evolution of the civilizing process involves the suppression of primitive violence behind the shield of civility. The periodic revivification of the social order requires a release of charismatic powers through what Durkheim called a collective effervescence. When these rituals are separated by any length of time, the intensity of their celebration 'sometimes attains to a sort of frenzy' (Durkheim 1961: 391–2). The study of these ritual practices led Durkheim to conclude that religion was the wellspring of social life, because 'nearly all the great social institutions have been born in religion' (Durkheim 1961: 466). These lasting institutional forms required a periodic restoration through moments of collective frenzy. It is appropriate to call this social frenzy a 'collective charisma'. In ancient cultures, warrior cults and military leaders were thus a common feature of religious organization (Wach 1944: 255).

In 'primitive society', there is no clear institutional differentiation between violence and the sacred, but with the rise of Christianity these spheres are distinguished in Christian theology which had a clear understanding of 'the world' and religion. Augustinian theology established a categorical separation of the secular world of violence and the Christian world of *agape*. The City of God was characterized by justice and forgiveness, whereas the secular world of the pagans was violent and cruel. But Augustine, partly as a result of his struggle with the Donatist sect, was compelled to compromise in recognizing the validity of the concept of the just war (Weithman 2001). This attempt to reconcile Christianity as a religion of salvation and imperial Rome produced a profound reaction against the materialism of secular society, namely Christian monasticism and mysticism. Augustine was critical of the alleged virtues of the pre-Christian Empire, arguing that the military advances of the Empire were not motivated by true virtues. He rejected Cicero's view of the glorious origins of Rome, and championed Christian virtue as the foundation of a civilized society based on love of neighbours. Augustine hated civil disturbance and war, and was compelled to accept the state as a necessary regulation of society.

Medieval political theory moved in a very different direction and was concerned to find some institutional reconciliation between Church and state, and, in particular, ecclesiastical teaching returned to a conception of the prince as a religious leader who ruled wisely and, where necessary, forcefully. The problem specifically was to develop a view of feudal kingship as, at least potentially, a religious institution. This theological trajectory was eventually established by Charlemagne (768–814), who was crowned the emperor of the Romans in 800 by Pope Leo III in St Peter's basilica. In the resulting Carolingian theory of rulership, theocracy was combined with some degree of popular consent. We can identify this amalgam in the writings of Charlemagne's teacher Alcuin, who claimed that the emperor had two swords, one to keep the Church internally free from heretical belief and the other to quell its external pagan enemies. In the tradition of the biblical King David, Charlemagne embraced the roles of ruler and priest.

With the creation of the Holy Roman Empire, an institutional fusion of religion and imperial power was achieved, but theologians still struggled to determine Christian norms of conduct that would regulate key areas of life, especially sex and the family, the economy and exchange, and war. In feudalism, religion provided an important institutional check on interpersonal violence by integrating the warrior into society. Christianity legitimized the social role of the knight as a necessary aspect of human society and redirected that military violence outwards during the Crusades. Religious norms clearly played an important part in the development of the chivalrous knight and were an important component of the social regulation of the violence of the man-at-arms in medieval society. In *The Canterbury Tales*, Chaucer's knight is the classic example of a warrior who has been civilized by the values and culture of Christendom (Chaucer 1969). For example, the knight who had recently returned from a military campaign undertook a pilgrimage to offer thanks to a saint for his safe return. The regulation of such warriors involved a complex and often contradictory mixture of secular, feudal values of hierarchy and duty, and Christian norms, such as respect for the honour of noble women.

Although Elias was clearly aware of such religious norms, ecclesiastical institutions did not play any significant part in his account of civilizing processes. However, this absence raises a more general issue about the relationship between spiritual and secular powers, and between charismatic force and military violence. In his account of power, Weber compared the role of the state that seeks a monopoly of military violence within a given territory and the Church that aims at a monopoly of spiritual or symbolic violence in human society. Therefore, the excommunication of heretics and sinners was a form of symbolic violence that excluded people from access to divine grace. The history of Western society can be interpreted as an unstable balance between these two systems of authority. As a liberal political theorist, Weber regarded the political system of caesaropapism, where religion and secular power are institutionally united, as the principal foundation of secular absolutism.

The symbolic capital of ecclesiastical institutions was closely connected to Weber's general theory of authority in which charisma remained a potent challenge to traditional forms of institutional regulation. Charisma is a theological concept that has been widely used in the social and religious sciences to describe the hierarchical organization of religious roles, social movements based on religious inspiration, and authority and leadership in society generally. In its religious context, charisma means a divinely conferred power. Charismatic power is tied to the sacred as an irresistible force in human societies, and people who possess charisma are thought to have extraordinary talents such as healing or prophecy. In shamanism, charismatic authority depends on a capacity to have visions and to perform healing (Eliade 1964). Weber's sociology of religion was particularly concerned to understand the tensions between folk religious leaders and formal religious authorities (Werbner and Basu 1998). As a result, charisma is conceptually part of an analytical framework that understands the dynamics of large-scale changes in religious institutions and the foundations of authority as outcomes of the violent impact of the sacred on the profane (Lindholm 1993).

In *Economy and Society* (Weber 1978: I: 241), charisma is 'applied to a certain quality of an individual personality by virtue of which he is considered extraordinary and treated as endowed with supernatural, superhuman, or at least specifically exceptional powers or qualities'. In the rise of religions, certain individuals have been recognized as having a capacity to experience ecstatic states that were perceived as the pre-condition for healing, telepathy and divination (Weber 1965: 2). Such charismatic power is either acquired by extraordinary means or inherited as a natural endowment. Often this religious capacity is conceived as an actual substance that may remain dormant in a person until it is aroused by ascetic practices or by trance. In everyday life, charismatic possession is a form of sacred intoxication that is not available (Eisenstadt 1968). Charisma is the foundation of claims to leadership over persons who become disciples or over groups that become as a result 'charismatic communities'. In 'primitive communities', these powers were 'thought of as resting on magical powers, whether of prophets, persons with a reputation for therapeutic or legal wisdom, leaders in the hunt, or heroes in war' (Weber 1978: I: 241).

Although Jesus Christ, Muhammed, Napoleon, Stefan George and the Chinese Emperor were all treated by Weber as charismatics, Weber was primarily concerned with religious charisma in the Old Testament prophets (Clements 1997). It is from his analysis of war prophecy in *Ancient Judaism* that I want to develop the idea of warrior charisma to designate the role of sacred force in military leadership. Such forms of charisma are very common in pre-modern society where the authority of military leaders was based on their charismatic capacities as illustrated by their power over enemies and their ability to avoid injury and death. Weber was particularly interested in the charismatic ecstasy of the Old Testament prophets who were called to defend the relationship between the Jewish people and their jealous God, Yahweh, in times of external threat and adversity. For example, Weber (1952: 98) drew attention to Saul who was 'seized by ecstasy and went around naked, spoke madly and for an entire day was in a faint'. He also compared Saul who was possessed with an 'explosive fury' to 'a warrior ecstatic like Mohammed'.

These forms of charismatic powers are by definition 'uncivilized' in the sense that this power is conferred on individuals as a result of the action of a divine force that cannot be easily controlled or cajoled. The early warlike charismatics were not in control of their actions and their intoxication was an indication of their extraordinary powers. Charisma is always spilling out of the institutions that are designed to house and domesticate it. Charisma thus is always imagined as breaking through and disrupting human relations, bringing confusion, conflict and violence in its train. This religious intensity has clear psychological consequences because 'religious life cannot attain a certain degree of intensity without implying a psychical exaltation not far removed from delirium. That is why . . . the men whose religious consciousness is exceptionally sensitive, very frequently give signs of an excessive nervousness that is even pathological' (Durkheim 1961: 258). Among the American Plains Indians, such warrior charisma was associated with transitions to manhood status where tribal rites of passage produced experiences of possession, trance and vision. Charisma erupts into human society, albeit in the context of rituals and institutions of liminal transition. While the training of the knight inculcates norms of bodily deportment, uprightness and chivalrous dispositions, shaking, convulsive and vibrating bodies mark the presence of charisma. Although warrior charisma is often manifest by the uncontrolled body, it is important to recognize that frenzied behaviour typically takes place in the context of ritual prescriptions and expectations. There are shared norms about the ritual context within which frenzy will occur, and also assumptions about which persons may enter such social roles.

Weber's sociology of charisma is useful in understanding the social strains that have faced traditional societies in their encounters with Western colonialism and postcolonialism. Charismatic leadership has also played a significant role in those new religious movements that have been a response to the social and economic disruptions associated with the decolonization of the Third World (Worsley 1970). For example, charismatic renewal has been a common theme of diverse religious movements in 'primal societies' (Wilson 1973; 1975). The collapse of aboriginal or tribal societies under colonial settlement resulted in the spread of charismatic movements against the supremacy of white-settler societies such as the Ghost Dance among the Cheyenne and Sioux tribes of the American Plains in the 1880s (Niezen 2000). A Paiute prophet called Wovoka had received a vision in which through ritual dance the dead would return to restore the pristine culture of native societies (Brown 1970: 433). This anti-white charismatic movement subsided after the murder of Sitting Bull and the destruction of his followers at Wounded Knee in December 1890. It is interesting that the beliefs associated with the Ghost Dance movement actually discouraged war, and ritual practices associated with it such as the war and scalp dances (Mooney 1996: 145). They also proscribed the mutilation of the body that was a traditional aspect of mourning.

Military techniques and charisma: the Cheyenne

Early historical records of the Cheyenne from the seventeenth century indicate that they were living west of the Mississippi River in Minnesota. The name 'Cheyenne' is an approximation of the name given to them by the Lakota or Dakota people and means a people whom the Lakota could not understand but were not enemies. Living on the edge of the Plains and equipped with primitive weapons, the Cheyenne were hunter-gatherers, being dependent on gathering wild rice and stalking buffalo. The archaeological evidence suggests that the Cheyenne constructed for-tified villages and lived in earth lodges in the eighteenth century on the Cheyenne River in North Dakota on the site known in the scientific liter-ature as Biesterfeldt (Wood and Liberty 1980). This village was attacked and burned by a Chippewa war party around 1790. By the end of the eighteenth century, Cheyenne groups were migrating south-westward on the great plains where they became nomadic tribes dependent on hunt-ing buffalo from horseback (Grinnell 1962). The history of the modern Cheyenne is bracketed by two tragedies, namely Wounded Knee 1 when the Seventh Cavalry massacred a large band and Wounded Knee 2 when members of AIM (American Indian Movement) came into bloody conflict with supporters of tribal leader Dick Wilson (Frazier 2000: 61).

Although the Plains Indian tribes shared a number of common war practices, the Cheyenne perfected and made explicit their underlying 'spiritual' and ritualistic characteristics. The Cheyenne, who became fa-mous among white settlers and military for the (alleged) practice of cut-ting off the arms of enemies as trophies, were renowned among native tribesmen for their concentrated use of ruthless violence against their enemies, and the spread of horses through the Plains region converted them into a formidable mobile military unit. Like other forms of ritu-alization of violence, Cheyenne warrior practices involved a remarkable discipline of the self to bring about the maximum effect of violence (real and symbolic) on an enemy. From a brief description of Cheyenne fight-ing protocols, we can learn something more generally interesting about the discipline of the body as a technology of the self to produce through specific institutions a spiritual violence.

Because people living in the militarized societies of the Plains had to face the prospect of an early and violent death, often accompanied by horrific torture, young children were trained to experience pain stoically.

The ideal warrior could undergo torture without any expression of pain, and would sing proudly about the military prowess of his own tribe as his captors tore flesh from his body. Plains warriors took great delight in humiliating their enemies through the grotesque torture of their prisoners, and as a result they too had to prepare themselves for an equally protracted and violent end. Elias (1992: 155–60) makes the important point that, in our nuclear age, modern military systems can destroy whole societies, but our social codes prohibit enjoyment of torture and regard interpersonal violence as uncivilized. In these 'pre-state societies', individuals enjoyed a wide margin of personal freedom because they were not subject to time constraints, but the price of such freedoms was a militarized environment in which they might anticipate a violent death.

These social codes trained men in the stoical acceptance of death. The fundamental point of Cheyenne military culture was that warriors already counted themselves among the dead prior to violent engagement, and hence they were spiritually oblivious to danger or death. They prepared for battle by saying farewell to their relatives, dressing as for a funeral and singing their death songs. They ritually consigned themselves to death, and they were as a result typically surprised to survive such encounters. Plains warfare was organized by a definite set of formal procedures. Warriors would line up to face their foes, and then issue taunts and other gestures calculated to humiliate the opposition. The men would dress in their best buckskin and ornaments, as if they were already prepared for death. Because Cheyenne warriors had already accepted death, their indifference to suffering and death was calculated to cause the maximum psychological terror. Taunts and insults preceded most engagements. Those warriors who had great medicine or warrior charisma would challenge the enemy to shoot them by riding in front of them.

Cheyenne tactics involved a ritualized sequence of attacks. There were firstly 'suicide boys' who were typically unarmed. They sought suicide because they had experienced some loss of face within their own community, or a woman had rejected them or they were grieving over a lost relative. These young men, with the encouragement of the warriors, threw themselves upon their enemy in an effort to tear them apart with their bare hands. The death of such boys was an indication that the Cheyenne had no concern for casualties. The next wave involved the 'dog rope men' who denied themselves the possibility of flight by fixing themselves to the ground with a sash tied to a stake. They fought from this ground position with long lances, clubs and bows and arrows. Singing their death songs, they invited the enemy to kill them. These men were often able to break up a mounted attack of the enemy. These preparations were followed by a genuine Cheyenne cavalry attack in which the soldiers concentrated their force on a single point in the enemy line. Once this attack was complete, the Cheyenne would remorselessly pursue those who attempted to escape the battlefield. These military engagements were normally concluded with victory songs expressing their joy and triumph over their enemies. These tactics, which expressed a spiritualized approach to symbolic self-destruction prior to battle, had the consequence of making the Cheyenne a dominant military force on the Plains (Moore 1999: 107–8). The Cheyenne were ferocious enemies who sought to destroy their enemies rather than engage them only in ritualized confrontation. Plains warfare in other tribal cultures often involved ritualized harassment of the enemy such as stealing horses or counting *coup* by striking an enemy with a stick as a form of humiliation.[1] Cheyenne warfare was more determined and systematic. It is claimed that they exterminated a tribe (the Owuqeo) as a form of tribal genocide (Moore 1999: 113).

The military victories of the Plains Indians over General Crook on the Rosebud River and George Custer at the Little Big Horn in 1876 were decisive. Cheyenne and Sioux warriors killed 254 members of Custer's troops and Custer's scalp became an important trophy. However, the retaliation of the United States troops was determined and ruthless, resulting in the dispersal of the Plains tribes and their final confinement to reservations by 1879. Reservation life had a devastating effect on people whose nomadic culture had been destroyed so rapidly and profoundly by the eradication of the buffalo herds, warfare and disease. In response, the Cheyenne joined the Ghost Dance movement of the 1880s, but Cheyenne involvement was terminated by the Wounded Knee massacre when approximately 300 men, women and children were killed by Hotchkiss machine guns. This sudden termination of their nomadic pattern of life was also the end of warrior charisma, because the sedentary life of the reservation undermined the hunter-gatherer economy and the sacred rituals that produced it. By a strange fate, the extraordinary warriors of this period of modern history – Sitting Bull, Crazy Horse, Red Cloud. Little Big Man and Dull Knife – became legends of the encounter between civilization and savagery (Klein 1997). As a result, the Cheyenne and Sioux were drawn rapidly into the emerging entertainment culture of modern society. Warriors who had terrified white settlers in the 1870s became figures in popular culture by the 1880s. They became celebrities rather than charismatic warriors.

Warrior charisma flourished briefly, but in a highly technological context, when Plains Indians served in large numbers in the United States forces in the two world wars and in Vietnam. In these modern wars, Native Americans were still able to draw upon their tribal military cultures. Many Plains Indians became war heroes in the US forces. In *The*

Cheyenne, Moore (1999: 108–13) recounts how Native American soldiers would count *coup* on surprised German soldiers during the Allied invasion of France, and Roy Nightwalker, a Cheyenne chief, collected scalps from German soldiers he had killed. These warriors of modern warfare were often welcomed back into the tribal communities with traditional ceremonies in which they received new names and tribal honours in respect of their bravery. Pima Ira Hayes, a Native American, was a member of the group of Marines who were photographed by the *Life* magazine reporter raising the American flag at Iwo Jima (Frazier 2000: 87). Native Americans also served in the Gulf War, but the occasions for warrior charisma are limited by the growing dependence on high technology and the reluctance of the American government to sustain war casualties in an era of intensive media coverage.

A central aspect of Foucault's social theory was the recognition that in the Western tradition acquiring knowledge, recognizing moral truths and developing the self required a government of the body. Put simply, body training is a critical method of training the self (Foucault 1997). These various practices amounted to techniques of the self. In particular, the warrior self is dependent on specific modes of body transformation through discipline. Don Levine (1991) has shown how the martial arts as a form of body training was linked to a specific educational regime. We might conclude from this research that the production of the self cannot be achieved without a corporeal pedagogy; in short, 'characterology' requires a specific form of embodiment to achieve its effects.

We can identify a range of practices in the culture of Plains Indians that were designed to produce a special warrior character. Religious training of the warrior body involved a number of preparations for adulthood. These included the Sweat Lodge, dance, fasting and Sun Dance. These rituals also gave rise to specific religious experiences that typically involved a vision, and as a result a change of name. The frenzied behaviour of charismatic warriors is a form of institutionalized violence. This behaviour requires a certain amount of training and preparation; it is organized into distinctive temporal sequences, for example, relating to initiation; the behaviour is comprehensible to indigenous observers; and it is channelled in particular directions. Rape and pillage against women were often ritually controlled (Eliade 1958: 83). It may not count as 'civilized behaviour' but it is certainly cultivated. Furthermore, as we have seen, the violence between individuals is often regulated. The Cheyenne warriors would count *coup* against their enemies in terms of the rules of war.

It is obvious that in this account of Cheyenne spiritual violence I have sought to show the possible connections between Foucault's notion of the 'technology of the self', Weber's 'personality' and 'life orders' and

Elias's 'civilizing process'. Elias's theory can be seen as an application of this insight to a long-term historical process in which civilizational norms have achieved a transformation of character through the education of embodied practices. However, the theory was not equipped to analyse how religious experiences were crucial to sustaining violent but spiritual personalities. In fact, he has no real theory of ritual at all. In Elias's work, the civilizing process is primarily a secular history of manners whereby crude, vulgar and rustic behaviour was converted into courtly dispositions. In particular, his approach was designed to explicate the normative regulation of the manners of the elite in European history. These processes contrast sharply with the meaning and intention of Cheyenne ritual which was constructed to sustain what we might call battle frenzy, where the warrior was induced to consider himself already dead. The civilizing process is designed to eliminate the forms of collective intoxication that produced warrior heroes in the Viking saga and Cheyenne folk memory. We might argue also that the civilizing process is related to the democratization of charisma that in its pristine form created a spiritual hierarchy of virtuoso religion. Whereas by definition charisma is in short supply, celebrity is subject to inflationary pressures, where everybody can be famous for 15 minutes. This conversion of charisma into celebrity also presupposes a democratization of personality, where spirit possession finds a substitute in narcotic addiction.

Conclusion

In this discussion of charisma and civility, I have drawn out some interesting and theoretically fruitful parallels between Elias and Weber in terms of their historical sociology of routinization and the civilizing process. However, while the analysis of religion was central to Weber's sociology as a whole, Elias was strangely silent about the macro-sociology of religious institutions in the formation of European society. Religion has played a major part in shaping the restraints on social behaviour that make social life orderly and predictable. If we interpret charisma as a form of risk, then religion is important in making social interactions predictable. The actual institutional relationships between military and religious institutions, as I have shown, are complex and contradictory. However, in its legitimation of the violence of knights, it is clear that religious institutions were important in the regulation of the scope and nature of violence. In this respect, my argument follows Weber closely in that warrior charisma was eventually routinized by the rise of military discipline. Although this lack of attention to religion is in my view a major and striking absence in Elias's otherwise comprehensive account of civility, it does not falsify his argument. There is no reason why the figurational paradigm could not include religious institutions in its account of civilizing processes.

NOTE

1. It was a common practice among Plains Indians to humiliate their enemies not by killing them but by striking them with sticks or other weapons. This practice of hitting or striking the enemy came to be described, from the initial observations of French explorers, as the practice of taking or counting *coup*. This practice further illustrates the fact that warfare resembled an elaborate game in which male aggression was channelled into ritualized combat (Hoxie, 1996: 667).

REFERENCES

Adorno, T. 1991, *The Culture Industry*, London and New York: Routledge.
Arendt, H. 1994, *Eichmann in Jerusalem. A Report on the Banality of Evil*, London: Penguin Books.
Baehr, P. 2002, 'Introduction' to Max Weber, *The Protestant Ethic and the "Spirit" of Capitalism and Other Writings*, New York: Penguin Books, pp. ix–xxxii.
Barbalet, J. 1998, *Emotion, Social Theory, and Social Structure. A Macrosociological Approach*, Cambridge: Cambridge University Press.
Bauman, Z. 1989, *Modernity and the Holocaust*, Cambridge: Polity Press.
Bourricaud, F. 1981, *The Sociology of Talcott Parsons*, Chicago and London: University of Chicago Press.
Brown, D. 1970, *Bury my Heart at Wounded Knee. An Indian History of the American West*, London: Book Club Associates.
Chaucer, G. 1969, *The Prologue and Three Tales*, Melbourne: Cheshire Publishers.
Clements, R.E. 1997, 'Max Weber, charisma and biblical prophecy', in Y. Gitay (ed.), *Prophecy and Prophets. The Diversity of Contemporary Issues in Scholarship*, Atlanta: Scholars Press, pp. 89–108.
Durkheim, E. 1961, *The Elementary Forms of the Religious Life*, New York: Collier.
Eisenstadt, S.N. 1968, *Max Weber on Charisma and Institution Building. Selected Papers*, Chicago: University of Chicago.
Eliade, M. 1958, *Rites and Symbols of Initiation. The Mysteries of Birth and Rebirth*, New York: Harper and Row.
 1964, *Shamanism. Archaic Techniques of Ecstasy*, Princeton: Princeton University Press.
Elias, N. 1983, *The Court Society*, Oxford: Basil Blackwell.
 1991, *The Society of Individuals*, Oxford: Basil Blackwell.
 1992, *Time: An Essay*, Oxford: Blackwell.
 2000, *The Civilizing Process. Sociogenetic and Psychogenetic Investigations*, Oxford: Blackwell.
Foucault, M. 1977, *Discipline and Punish. The Birth of the Prison*, London: Tavistock.

1997, 'Technologies of the self', in *Ethics: Subjectivity and Truth*, London: Allen Lane, pp. 225–51.

Frazier, I. 2000, *On the Rez*, New York: Farrar, Strauss and Giroux.

Freud, S. 1913, *Totem and Taboo, The Standard Edition of the Complete Psychological Works of Sigmund Freud*, vol. XIII, London: Hogarth Press.

1930, *Civilization and its Discontents, The Standard Edition of the Complete Psychological Works of Sigmund Freud*, vol. XIII, London: Hogarth Press.

Gerard, R. 1988, *Violence and the Sacred*, London: Athlone Press.

Grinnell, G.B. 1962, *The Cheyenne Indians*, New York: Cooper Square, 2 vols.

Heidegger, M. 1977, *The Question Concerning Technology and Other Essays*, New York: Harper.

Hennis, W. 1988, *Max Weber. An Essay on Reconstruction*, London: Allen & Unwin.

Herf, J. 1984, *Reactionary Modernism: Technology, Culture and Politics in Weimer and the Third Reich*, Cambridge: Cambridge University Press.

Hoxie, F. E. (ed.) 1996, *Encyclopedia of North American Indians*, Boston: Houghton, Mifflin.

Klein, K.L. 1997, *Frontiers of Historical Imagination. Narrating the European Conquest of Native America 1890–1990*, Berkeley: University of California Press.

Levine, D. 1991, 'Martial arts as a resource for liberal education: the case of Aikido', in M. Featherstone, M. Hepworth and B.S. Turner (eds.), *The Body. Social Process and Cultural Theory*, London: Sage: 209–24.

Lindholm, C. 1993, *Charisma*, Oxford: Blackwell.

Marcuse, H. 1955, *Eros and Civilization. A Philosophical Inquiry into Freud*, Boston: Beacon Press.

Mooney, J. 1996, *The Ghost Dance*, North Dighton: J.G. Press.

Moore, J.H. 1999, *The Cheyenne*, Oxford: Blackwell.

Morris, W. and Magnusson, E. 1893, *Heimskringla*, London: Sage Library.

Niezen, R. (ed.) 2000, *Spirit Wars. Native North American Religions in the Age of Nation Building*, Berkeley, CA: University of California Press.

Parsons, T. 1966, 'Introduction' to Max Weber, *The Sociology of Religion*, London: Methuen.

Ringer, F. 1969, *The Decline of the German Mandarins. The German Academic Community 1890–1933*, Cambridge, MA: Harvard University Press.

Russell, S. 1996, *Jewish Identity and Civilizing Processes*, Basingstoke: Macmillan.

Shils, E. 1975, *Center and Periphery. Essays in Macrosociology*, Chicago: University of Chicago Press.

Tocqueville, A. de 1968, *Democracy in America*, Glasgow: Collins.

Turner, B.S. 1987, 'The rationalization of the body: reflections on modernity and discipline', in S. Whimster and S. Lash (eds.), *Max Weber, Rationality and Modernity*, London: Allen & Unwin, pp. 222–41.

Turner, B.S. (ed.) 1999, *The Talcott Parsons Reader*, Oxford: Blackwell.

Turner, S. 2003, 'Charisma reconsidered', *Journal of Classical Sociology* 3(1): 5–26.

Vigarello, G. 1989, 'The upward training of the body from the age of chivalry to courtly civility', in M. Feher (ed.), *Fragments for a History of the Human Body*, New York: Zone, pp. 149–99.

Wach, J. 1944, *Sociology of Religion*, Chicago and London: University of Chicago.

Weber, M. 1930, *The Protestant Ethic and the Spirit of Capitalism*, London: Allen & Unwin.

1947, *The Theory of Social and Economic Organization*, New York, Oxford University Press.

1952, *Ancient Judaism*, Glencoe: Free Press.

1966, *The Sociology of Religion*, London: Methuen.

1968, *Economy and Society, An Outline of Interpretive Sociology*, Berkeley: University of California Press, 2 volumes.

Weithman, P. 2001, 'Augustine's political philosophy', in E. Stump and N. Kretzmann (eds.), *The Cambridge Companion to Augustine*, Cambridge: Cambridge University Press, pp. 234–52.

Werbner, P. and Basu, H. (eds.) 1998, *Embodying Charisma. Modernity, Locality and the Performance of Emotion in Sufi Cults*, London and New York: Routledge.

Wilson, B. 1973, *Magic and the Millennium: A Sociological Study of Religious Movements of Protest Among Tribal and Third-World Peoples*, London: Heinemann Educational Books.

Wilson, B.R. 1975, *The Noble Savages. The Primitive Origins of Charisma and its Contemporary Survival*, Berkeley: University of California Press.

Wood, W.R. and Liberty, M. 1980, *Anthropology on the Great Plains*, Lincoln: University of Nebraska Press.

Worsley, P. 1970, *The Trumpet Shall Sound*, London: Paladin.

15 Christian religion and the European civilizing process: the views of Norbert Elias and Max Weber compared in the context of the Augustinian and Lucretian traditions

Johan Goudsblom

Introduction

Religion does not play a prominent role in Norbert Elias's by now classical study *The Civilizing Process*.[1] This raises a question. Did Elias, as a critic once asserted, 'overlook religion'? Or, more precisely, did he underestimate the influence of Christianity in the civilizing process in Western Europe?[2]

Undoubtedly the absence of a systematic discussion of the role of religion in *The Civilizing Process* reflects a deliberate decision. One likely reason for this decision was Elias's relation to the work of Max Weber. It has been said that underlying a great deal of Max Weber's work is a running discussion with 'the ghost of Karl Marx'. A similar observation can be made about Elias; many of his writings can be read as a continuing discussion with Max Weber, sometimes explicit, more often tacit, even when Weber is not mentioned by name. Thus Elias took issue with Weber's conception of sociology as starting from 'subjective action'; with his treatment of the notion of charisma; and with his emphasis on capitalism, Protestantism and (by implication) the bourgeois and the ecclesiastical lines in the European civilizing process.[3]

In this chapter I shall focus on the latter issue, and I shall extend the argument beyond Weber. For beyond Weber looms an old and strong tradition in European thought that is still very much alive – the Augustinian view of the history of civilization, according to which religion, and the Christian religion, in particular, has been the prime moving force in the civilizing process in Europe. I shall give a brief sketch of this dominant tradition, and contrast it with its 'recessive' counterpart, which I shall call the Lucretian tradition. Elias's approach was in line with the latter school of thought.

Norbert Elias on the European civilizing process

The Civilizing Process is a very rich book; I shall not try to summarize it here. As Elias said in the opening sentence of the Preface to the first German edition, written in 1936, he was concerned first of all with modes of behaviour that appeared as 'civilized' to the members of modern Western societies in the early twentieth century. To many people those modes of behaviour seemed self-evident; but on closer examination they were highly problematic. The task Elias set himself was to gain a better understanding, based upon empirical inquiry and theoretical reflection, of how these modes of behaviour had developed in a process of socio-psychological change extending over many generations.

In *The Civilizing Process* Elias presented documentary evidence for changes in conduct and feeling among 'the secular upper classes' of European society since the late Middle Ages. He began with excerpts from manners books, containing instructions about what was regarded as proper conduct. Successive editions of those manners books showed remarkable changes, leading Elias to the conclusion that in the course of time the ruling strata in Western Europe cultivated standards of conduct that became more refined and increasingly demanded a continuously vigilant self-control. Similar standards, requiring a similarly constant self-restraint, spread to other social circles as well. Different social classes certainly continued to have their own distinct customs, but in general the ways in which they controlled their emotions tended to converge. All in all, Elias concluded that 'from the late Middle Ages and the early Renaissance on, there was a particularly strong shift in individual self-control – above all, in self-control acting independently of external agents as a self-activating automatism' (Elias 2000: 478).

There is a striking resemblance between the transformation sketched here by Elias and the transformation in mentality described by Max Weber in his famous essay *The Protestant Ethic and the Spirit of Capitalism*.

Max Weber on the Protestant ethic and the spirit of capitalism

Max Weber's study *The Protestant Ethic and the Spirit of Capitalism*, first published in German in 1905–6, has long been the most famous and prestigious work in sociology on an aspect of the European civilizing process. Although Weber did not use the term 'civilizing process', he dealt with a theme that was highly similar to the one that Norbert Elias treated in his *magnum opus*. Just like Elias, Weber observed in his essay on Protestantism and capitalism a profound historical change in mentality or habitus – a shift towards more regular and all-round self-restraint – and he tried to find an explanation for this change. In this section I shall summarize Weber's essay critically, in a way that will facilitate a comparison with the work of Elias.

In the Introduction, written in 1920, to the three volumes of *Collected Essays in the Sociology of Religion*, Weber began by stating that Western civilization was marked by an exceptionally high level of rationality in science, law, music, architecture, art, organization of the state and in 'the most fateful force in our modern life, capitalism' (1920: 17).[4]

Capitalism, he continued, is not to be equated with the pursuit of gain; that may be a universal human inclination. What distinguishes capitalism is 'the restraint, or at least a rational tempering, of this irrational impulse' (p. 17). A capitalist enterprise rests, for its success, on regularly recurring, calculable profits, on 'the utilization of opportunities for exchange, that is on (formally) peaceful chances of profit' (p. 17). Adventurers and speculators who seize a one-time chance have existed everywhere. However, the acquisition of booty by force is very different from rational capitalism.

In order to trace the origins of 'sober bourgeois capitalism' Weber decided to focus on those forces that traditionally were 'the most important formative influences on conduct' – the ethical ideas of duty bolstered by religious beliefs about the good life on earth and about rewards and punishments in the hereafter. He immediately added two caveats to this programme. Firstly, he noted that by focusing on ideas he would treat '*only one side of the causal chain*' (p. 27). Second, he stressed that '*the relative value of the cultures which are compared here will not receive a single word*' (p. 29). I italicize these caveats because I shall return to them. Their function seems to have been mainly rhetorical; the actual text contains many passages which flatly ignore these caveats.

Thus, even in the first substantive chapter, Weber was already arguing that there is a stronger tendency towards economic rationality among Protestants than among Catholics, and that the principal explanation of this difference 'must be sought in the permanent intrinsic character of their religious beliefs' (p. 40). Little or no heed is given here to the warning that we are dealing with only 'one side of the causal chain'. Similarly, the intention not to use value judgements seems forgotten when Weber speaks of the 'unexampled tyranny of Puritanism' (p. 37), and says that it 'was infinitely burdensome' (p. 36) and 'would be for us the most absolutely unbearable form of ecclesiastical control of the individual which could possibly exist' (p. 37).

Unlike Elias in *The Civilizing Process*, Weber did not give a chronological series of quotations showing a sequence of changes. He began his analysis of the spirit of capitalism with a lengthy quotation from Benjamin

Franklin's *Advice to a Young Tradesman* (1748) and *Necessary Hints to Those That Would Be Rich* (1736). Weber interpreted this text as exemplifying an ethic of duty – a 'value-rational' creed which was, according to Weber, more than purely utilitarian.

There was of course, as Weber acknowledged, a practical tinge to Franklin's recommendations: be industrious and frugal; show yourself to be trustworthy; remember that time is money and money, if well invested, breeds more money. All these virtues are useful because they assure a good reputation and improve one's credit. But, Weber added, Franklin's moral attitudes also contained something 'entirely transcendental and absolutely irrational' (p. 53).

In his commentary on Franklin, Weber lost sight of his own caveat that he was treating only one side of the causal chain. He noted with great emphasis that the spirit of industriousness and frugality could not be explained simply as an adaptation (a strategy of survival, we might say) to capitalist conditions. Such an explanation in what Weber called 'materialistic' terms would be putting the cart before the horse, for capitalism could not have developed without the spirit of capitalism. That spirit required an explanation; 'the causal relation is *certainly the reverse* of that suggested by the materialistic standpoint' (p. 56; italics added).

In almost personifying terms, making economic history sound like an ancient tragedy, Weber stated that 'the spirit of capitalism . . . had to fight its way to supremacy against a whole world of hostile forces' (p. 56). Its most important 'opponent' he considered to be 'that type of attitude and reaction to new situations which we may designate as traditionalism' (pp. 58–9). Thus, in his rejection of historical materialism, Weber adopted a kind of heroic idealism. He went very far in this:

> The question of the motive forces in the expansion of modern capitalism is not in the first instance a question of the origin of the capital sums which were available for capitalistic uses, but, above all, of the development of the spirit of capitalism. Where it appears and is able to work itself out, it produces its own capital and monetary supplies as the means to its ends, *but the reverse is not true.* (pp. 68–9; italics added)

This assertion is a long way from Weber's first caveat, about the one side of the causal chain. Nor is the second caveat, against value judgements, clearly observed in the passages that follow, describing the personality of the capitalist entrepreneur in terms of ethical qualities such as 'an unusually strong character', 'temperate self-control', 'clarity of vision', 'strength to overcome innumerable obstacles' – a set of 'very definite and highly developed ethical qualities' (p. 69).

In his further analysis of the origins of these character traits Weber did not turn to the social constraints and chances which prompted people to cultivate this particular mentality. He mentioned those social constraints only a few times, in passing. His main concern was to find 'the origins of precisely the irrational element which lies in this, as in every conception of a calling' (p. 78). He therefore narrowed his inquiry down to a search for theological ideas and practices which showed a similar insistence upon the duty towards one's calling in life.

This approach led him to an erudite and eloquent discussion of, first, 'the religious foundations of worldly asceticism', and then, as the final step, of 'asceticism and the spirit of capitalism'.

Weber sketched a chilling portrait of the ideal-typical Calvinist Puritan, who staunchly believed in the doctrine of predestination – a doctrine marked by 'magnificent consistency' as well as 'extreme inhumanity': 'In what was for the man of the Reformation the most important thing in life, his eternal salvation, he was forced to follow his path alone to meet a destiny which had been decreed for him from eternity' (p. 104). No magic, no sacrament was allowed him in this lonely journey.

At this point Weber's argument took a decisive turn. He translated the logic of predestination into a theory of personal motivation, more or less converting theology into psychology. In this view, the Calvinist sought relief from his religious agony in attitude of self-confidence, comforting himself with the impression that he actually belonged to the elect. To prove himself worthy of the state of grace he forced himself to live a life of 'systematic self-control' (p. 115).

The Calvinists did not have to invent all the rules of asceticism, for those had already been cultivated in medieval monasteries. Western monasticism 'had developed a systematic method of rational conduct with the purpose of overcoming the *status naturae*, to free man from the power of irrational impulses and his dependence on the world and on nature. It attempted to subject man to the supremacy of a purposeful will, to bring his actions under constant self-control with a careful consideration of their ethical consequences' (pp. 118–19). This form of 'quiet self-control', strengthening the motives of constancy against the volatile emotions, was taken over by the Puritans with the aim of destroying 'spontaneous, impulsive enjoyment' (p. 119). The 'gloomy doctrine of Calvinism' brought a regime of 'constant self-control' (p. 126). The resulting 'rationalization of conduct within the world, but for the sake of the world beyond, *was the consequence* of the concept of calling of ascetic Protestantism' (p. 154, italics added).

The next step led on to the road to Benjamin Franklin and to Weber's own time. After the seventeenth century, 'the intensity of the search for the

Kingdom of God commenced gradually to pass over into sober economic virtue; the religious roots died out slowly, giving way to otherworldliness' (p. 176). The great religious epoch of the seventeenth century bequeathed to later generations 'an amazingly good . . . conscience in the acquisition of money, so long as it took place legally' (p. 176).

The descent is clear: 'One of the fundamental elements of the spirit of modern capitalism . . . was born . . . from the spirit of Christian asceticism' (p. 180). 'Ascetism undertook to remodel the world' (p. 181). 'The idea of duty in one's calling prowls about in our lives like the ghost of dead religious beliefs' (p. 181). 'The Puritan wanted to work in a calling; we are forced to do so' (p. 181). According to an early Puritan, the care for external goods should only lie 'on the shoulders of the saint like a light cloak, which can be thrown aside at any moment'. Weber quoted those words, with the ominous addition: 'But fate decreed that the cloak should become an iron cage' (p. 181).

This semi-final passage, filled with captivating metaphors, is followed by a repetition of Weber's two initial disclaimers, now in a reverse order. First, 'but this brings us to the world of judgments of value and faith, with which this purely historical discussion need not be burdened' (p. 182). And second, 'it is, of course, not my aim to substitute for a one-sided materialistic an equally one-sided spiritualistic causal interpretation of culture and history' (p. 183). These disclaimers cannot take away the overall rhetorical tenor of the essay, which suggests a straight genealogy: capitalism is a product of the spirit of capitalism, which in turn was a product of ascetic Calvinism, which found its inspiration in medieval monasticism.

The Augustinian tradition

Weber's attitude toward the Calvinist creed in his study of Protestantism and capitalism was far from sympathetic. Yet, despite his critical stance, he attached great importance to the social and cultural impact of Calvinism. In singling out religion as a powerful force in the civilizing process, Weber followed a time-honoured intellectual tradition in which the Church father, St Augustine, was a towering figure.

Augustine (354–430) belonged to a generation of highly successful bishops during a formative period of the Roman Catholic Church who, in mutual collaboration and competition, did much to strengthen the organization of the Church and to canonize its doctrine. As a well-educated convert, Augustine was able to combine Roman learning with Christian teaching. His writings were soon taken up in the mainstream of European theology and philosophy. His books *Confessions* and, still more, *The City of God* left a strong mark on the development of ideas about morality and society. In his *Confessions* Augustine related how his conversion to Christianity brought him personally on the path to salvation and made him a better man; *The City of God* described the blessings of Christianity for humanity at large.

The City of God was written after the sack of Rome by the Visigoths in 410. Conservative Romans tended to attribute this humiliating event to the emasculating influence of Christianity, which had undermined the ancient Roman virtues of courage and patriotism. To counter that prevailing view, Augustine came forward with a very different interpretation. He pointed out that Roman history consisted of a brute succession of wars and civil wars, all waged with horrible cruelty. Seen against that background, did not the behaviour of the soldiers from the North after their conquest of Rome compare very favourably with the frightful atrocities committed again and again by the Romans themselves? Roman citizens who regarded their recent invaders as barbarians failed to see the high ethical standards espoused by these men thanks to the fact that they were Christians:

All the devastation, the butchery, the plundering, the conflagrations, and all the anguish which accompanied the recent disaster at Rome were in accordance with the general practice of warfare. But there was something which established a new custom, something which changed the whole aspect of the scene; the savagery of the barbarians took on such an aspect of gentleness that the largest basilicas were selected and set aside to be filled with people to be spared by the enemy. No one was to be violently used there, no one snatched away. Many were to be brought there for liberation by merciful foes; none were to be taken from there into captivity even by cruel enemies. This is to be attributed to the name of Christ and the influence of Christianity. Anyone who fails to see this is blind; anyone who sees it and fails to give praise for it is thankless; anyone who tries to stop another from giving praise is a madman. (Augustine I, ch. 7)

A large part of *The City of God* consists of a complete revision of the history of Greece and Rome. All the well-known episodes pass in review, but they appear in a new context, together with the history of Israel as recorded in the books of the Jewish–Christian tradition. Just as the *Confessions* described Augustine's own life in terms of a moralizing developmental psychology, *The City of God* summarized the history of all known humanity in a theological synthesis. Every event was given a place in this synthesis; even facts which at first glance would seem to contradict Augustine's teleological view were shrewdly given a significance that made them fit in with the divine plan underlying human history.

The City of God is an impressive book. Because of its erudition and its lucid and ingenious argument, it lent itself very well to becoming an authoritative text in the expanding world of Christendom, helping to shape a new image of the development of civilization as guided by the hand of God. If later generations thought of themselves as more literate and more refined in manners and morals than their ancestors, they could humbly declare that they owed this advance primarily to their religion, to Christianity as embodied in the church and its representatives, the clergy.

Indeed, in the early Middle Ages, religious institutions, especially monasteries, were centres of literacy. Here ancient texts were rediscovered, re-read and reinterpreted, including the writings of such 'pagan' philosophers as Seneca and Cicero. Just as elements of Roman law helped to restructure legal and political organization, classical ideas about morality and personal well-being offered guidance towards individual self-restraint.

Because of the dominant position of the Church and clerical institutions, the texts were read, at first, mainly in a monastic setting. This lent them an aura of religiosity; they became 'sacralized'. Their secular origins were largely ignored and forgotten, and the models of temperance and moderation derived from these texts tended to be preached as representing exclusively Christian virtues.[5]

The merging of ancient 'pagan' and Christian ideas continued throughout the Middle Ages. Thus the ideal of temperance, advocated by the Stoics and other Roman schools of philosophy, was cultivated and formalized into the ascetic regime of newly founded monastic orders such as the Benedictines. A pagan legacy was transmitted in a religious guise. Parish priests and monks became self-appointed 'civilizing agents'.

Adopting Weber's imagery, we could say that the ancient spirit of asceticism was revived in the Christian monasteries, from where it then spread back into more mundane circles. As the medievalist C. Stephen Jaeger (1985) shows, clergymen played an important role among the high dignitaries at the medieval princely courts. Many of them were of noble descent themselves.

The lasting influence of the clergy rested largely on their virtual monopoly of literacy. As the literary class, they proclaimed themselves to be the First Estate. They made their own field of expertise, theology, into the first faculty at the new institutions for higher learning, the universities. They thus exerted a strong influence not only on practical conduct, but also on the intellectual justification of the rules of ethics and etiquette.

Their influence went very far, to the extent that, in the modern age, non-religious critics such as Friedrich Nietzsche and Menno ter Braak were able to detect residual Christian beliefs in systems of thought that professed to be thoroughly secular, and to recognize the Christian ideal of equality before God in the popular political ideologies of their own days. Similarly, the idea of divine providence could be shown to resonate with the notion of an 'invisible hand' ruling economic action, central to the ideology of liberalism, as well as with the Marxist tenet of 'the laws of history'.

Such residues can also be detected in Weber's essay on Protestantism and capitalism. Just like Elias in *The Civilizing Process*, Weber was concerned with the unintended consequences of long-term social processes. He did not, however, try to bring to light the dynamics generated by social interdependencies; he contented himself with speaking of a 'spirit' that apparently went its own way and determined the course of human affairs. Weber's implicit suggestion that terms like 'spirit' and 'fate' refer to decisive actors on the historical stage testifies to the tenacity of the Augustinian tradition; while determined not to let his own religious ideas interfere with his sociological analysis, Weber still adhered to a quasi-theological philosophy of history.

The Lucretian tradition

Medieval Christianity could easily absorb the practical moral teachings of such authors as Cicero. The innovators of monastic discipline found in classical philosophy a source of inspiration for their rules. One strand in the intellectual tradition of ancient Greece and Rome, however, contained elements that medieval theologians found unpalatable. This was Epicurean philosophy, represented in its most elaborate and elegant form by the Latin poet Lucretius (96?–55 BC), one of the most radically 'secular' authors in the late republic.

The Roman Republic and the early Roman Empire were political entities in a military–agrarian society which, remarkably, lacked a strong priestly class. There was nothing in the republican and early imperial social structure comparable with the organization of ecclesiastical administrators that emerged in the later empire at the time of Augustine. In the absence of a strong establishment of priests, a wave of secularization in thought could manifest itself in the earlier era, which was swamped again from the late fourth century AD onwards by a process of 'sacralization' under the influence of the triumphant Christian Church (cf. Elias 1991: 136).

Lucretius, in his didactic poem *De rerum natura* ('On the Nature of Things'), presented a coherent account of the development of the world and of humankind that in many ways strikingly anticipated the modern theory of evolution. He avowedly wrote the poem as an antidote to religion – the belief in supernatural beings and in a life after death, with terrifying phantoms of eternal punishment. According to Lucretius, people were susceptible to religious beliefs because they were uninformed about the principles underlying the cosmos and life on earth. In their ignorance they attributed all the many events they did not understand to the will of gods before whom they then trembled with obsessive fear. A reasonable survey of the real nature of the universe should dispel that fear; it would help people to appreciate their own limited powers and to reconcile themselves with the fact that, for each and every individual, death is inevitable and final. It should teach us 'that the universe was certainly not created for us by divine power' (Lucretius V: 232). But it can also show that humans have been able to improve the conditions of their lives:

So we find that not only such arts as seafaring and agriculture, city walls and laws, weapons, roads and clothing, but also without exception the amenities and refinements of life, songs, pictures, and statues, artfully carved and polished, all were taught gradually by usage and the active mind's experience as men groped their way forward step by step. So each particular development is brought gradually to the fore by the advance of time, and reason lifts it into the light of day. Men saw one notion after another take shape within their minds until by their arts they scaled the topmost peak. (Lucretius V: 1448–57)

Because the Epicureans were unwilling to take part in the mandatory religious cults, they were accused of atheism – a charge that was later also made against the first Christians who likewise rejected the prevailing 'superstitions' and refused to worship the officially venerated 'idols'. Apart from this shared (and, needless to say, for the Christians unjust) indictment, the Epicureans and the Christians had little in common; its hostility towards religion made Epicurean philosophy anathema to the Christians.

Consequently, the reputation of Lucretius was badly tainted and almost erased by the censorship of the triumphant early Church. The only data that were allowed to come down to us are the words noted in the chronicle of Augustine's contemporary, the Church Father, St Jerome, according to whom 'the poet Titus Lucretius Carus . . . lost his mind through drinking an aphrodisiac, and committed suicide at the age of forty-four, after having written in his lucid intervals some books which Cicero later corrected'.[6] This brief 'life of a heathen', the very opposite of a hagiography, is about all the information available about Lucretius. Its negative overtones keep recurring in modern encyclopaedias in which he continues to be characterized with such expressions as 'a tortured spirit'.

Still, Lucretius was disparaged but never completely forgotten. A battered manuscript of his poem was rediscovered in 1414 by Poggio

Bracciolini, and from then on humanist writers began referring again to the Lucretian view of the human condition and history – first with circumspection and later in open agreement. Eighteenth-century 'free-thinkers' such as Edward Gibbon and Voltaire wrote works of history in which religion was treated in purely secular terms – not as something that had come to people through divine revelation from some external, suprahuman source, but as an institution with specific social functions. This became an almost self-evident point of departure for the British historian Henry Thomas Buckle (1821–62) who, in his widely read *History of Civilization in England*, declared the view that religion was a prime mover of human affairs to be obsolete and 'altogether erroneous'. Instead of seeing religion as a 'cause' of civilization, we should see it as an 'effect' (Buckle 1865: 235).

To the best of my knowledge, neither Max Weber nor Norbert Elias ever referred to Buckle. Weber would probably have dismissed Buckle's position as materialistic. It would certainly have been more congenial to Elias – but with some significant qualifications. Elias did not share the unmitigated faith in progress that Buckle, like Lucretius, professed. And he avoided framing the relations between religion and the civilizing process in a simple model of 'cause' and 'effect'.

The two traditions reconsidered

The risk of any distinction is, of course, that it may block the view of resemblances and interconnections. After the revival of the Lucretian tradition in the fifteenth century, there were many exchanges between the Augustinian and the Lucretian traditions, leading to a blurring of the distinction. Max Weber, too, leaned towards the Lucretian tradition in most of his writings – and its influence is visible even in *The Protestant Ethic and the Spirit of Capitalism*, his most Augustinian publication.

Still, the long-lasting dominance of the Augustinian tradition in European thought about the civilizing process is indisputable. It has promoted, first of all, a persistent tendency to conceive of the civilizing process in terms of providence and teleology – as if that process has always been guided by a divine or otherwise transcendental plan. Secondly, it has given pride of place to the church or, more broadly, to religion as the driving force in the entire process. Thirdly, as a strong side-effect, all theories of sociocultural development – including those in which the ideas of providence and teleology are explicitly rejected (as in Elias's book *The Civilizing Process*) – tend to be interpreted by many readers as if they too were still predicated on Augustinian assumptions.

The idea that religion is an ancient element of human culture is compatible with the Augustinian as well as the Lucretian tradition. The two views diverge, however, where the Lucretian tradition considers religion as a means of orientation that has lost its validity; just as magic has been superseded by technology, religion has been superseded by science. While Elias by and large accepted the Lucretian thesis, Max Weber avoided an outspoken statement on this issue; but he did come very close to the Lucretian view when he wrote about the inevitable advance of rationalization and the concomitant 'disenchantment of the world'. Yet he always resisted embracing what he considered to be an evolutionary perspective of society and culture. Therefore, in order to account for the long-term processes of rationalization and secularization he eventually had recourse to dark phrases suggesting that those processes were 'decreed' by 'fate' (p. 181).

In some passages Weber also followed a tendency, common among adherents of almost any religion, to present religious doctrines and rituals as timeless and unchanging. Thus, when speaking of the Puritans, he referred to 'the permanent intrinsic character of their religious beliefs' (p. 40). At the same time, Weber knew all too well that religion is never a constant factor, in spite of the inclination among the believers themselves to 'eternalize' their creeds.

In fact, of course, both religious and secular ideas have changed over time; and, remarkably, in the course of change they have tended in the long run to converge. From the early Middle Ages on, the civilizing process in Europe has affected all the major social 'estates' – the clergy, the nobility, the bourgeoisie and the 'fourth estate' of farmers and workers – and the institutions in which their members were primarily engaged. Religion, the realm *par excellence* of the clergy, was not exempt from the forces of change that transformed society at large. For this reason Elias stated, in often-quoted words that are distantly reminiscent of Buckle:

Religion, the belief in the punishing or rewarding omnipotence of God, never has in itself a 'civilizing' or affect-subduing effect. On the contrary, religion is always exactly as 'civilized' as the society or class which upholds it. (Elias 2000: 169)

Elias carefully avoided the word 'cause', used by both Buckle and Weber. He also insisted that it would be futile to look for a 'zero point' in the European civilizing process – the process never started from scratch. In later work on the sociology of knowledge, Elias suggested as a mental experiment that his readers try to imagine a 'knowledge-less group' (Elias, 1987: 230). Clearly our imagination would fail here; no such human group could ever have existed. Nor can we conceive of a group that would be 'civilization-less' or completely 'uncivilized' – its members lacking any form of socially acquired self-restraint.[7]

An analogy with the theory of biological evolution may be illuminating at this point. There is no life on earth in units smaller than one cell; 'semi-cellular' life cannot exist. From this it follows, as Stephen J. Gould (1996) argued, that once unicellular life had come into being it could not evolve into smaller units; any development in that direction was blocked by a wall of impossibility – if life was able to evolve at all, it could only do so by forming larger units, with higher levels of organization. Gould used this argument to demonstrate that the theory of evolution need not involve any appeal to teleology. The same line of reasoning can also be applied to the civilizing process. Like the evolution of life, the civilizing process, too, could conceivably have gone in a whole gamut of directions; but one major direction was closed off. What Gould described as an imaginary wall may also be seen as a point (or a line) of no return: for any group to go beyond it in a 'negative' direction would amount to self-annihilation. On the other hand, we can conceive of a wide range of 'positive' directions in which the civilizing process can move at any given stage; that range includes possible 'regressions' in the sense of a loosening of self-restraints. But then, again, there is a limit to such regressions.

No human group can function without a minimum of self-restraint on the part of its members. That self-restraint has to be learned, learned from others. Civilizing processes are therefore universal; they occur in all human groups. But they take different forms at different stages of social development.

As I have argued before, at a certain stage of agrarian development, societies *with* priests had greater chances of survival than societies *without* priests (Goudsblom 1996: 42). Priests provided orientation and discipline which helped farming communities to cope with a whole range of problems raised by an agrarian existence – problems related to work and production, but also to the storage, distribution and consumption of food. I did not state in so many words, however, that priests stimulated an advance in the civilizing process. I only noted that they insisted on greater (socially induced) self-restraint.

I am now prepared to argue, in more general terms, that human groups stand a better chance of survival in the long run with an advance in the civilizing process than do groups that lag behind in this sense. This is a huge generalization; the clause 'in the long run' is indispensable if it is to be upheld. The formulation does not rule out temporary tendencies (or 'lapses') in the opposite direction. In many historical instances, groups with less regard for highly civilized strictures turned out to have an advantage over groups with greater respect for such strictures. In the very long run, however, the constraints of competition and collaboration put a premium on socially induced self-restraint.[8]

It is an empirical generalization, and not just a theoretical assumption, that in the very long run, the entire web of human relations has changed, and is continuing to change, in the direction of more far-reaching social interdependence and greater complexity. The 'master process' is the external expansion of the anthroposphere, which is inseparably accompanied by its internal transformation (see Goudsblom 2002). As a part of that transformation, human sensitivities have been changing, including their sensitivity for religious ideas and practices.

Conclusion

The Augustinian and the Lucretian traditions view the civilizing process from opposite angles. This leads to different impressions, with different emphases. If the Augustinian tradition overestimates the importance of religion in the civilizing process, the Lucretian tradition contains an anti-clerical sting that may bring about underestimation. There can be no doubt that what we now classify as religious forces have at times exerted a strong pressure towards socially induced self-restraint. That pressure should be seen, however, in the context of wider social and ecological pressures. Whatever influence religion had was always subject to histori-ical circumstances. Religion was never the sole civilizing factor. And in many instances it gave impetus to decivilizing spurts such as crusades, persecutions, civil war and as it has come to be called in our own days, 'ethnic cleansing'.

The concept of a civilizing process applies to 'societies of individuals' – that is, to individuals linked with other individuals in social figurations (Elias 1991; see also De Swaan 2001). In all figurations the potential for civilizing as well as decivilizing tendencies is continuously present. In Western Europe in the period studied by Elias, decisive civilizing shifts were initiated by various powerful groups: courtiers, priests, lawyers, busi-ness people and politicians; even the military played a part (see McNeill 1982: 125–39).

As the webs of human interdependence have expanded and differenti-ated, social figurations have generally become more dependent on forms of self-restraint that are attuned to these complex interdependencies. It is conceivable that – as the Augustinian tradition suggests – institutions focused on religion will further this socially driven civilizing process;

but – as the Lucretian tradition suggests – it is hard to imagine how the process could continue if people were to rely only on their religions.

NOTES

1. This article has a long history. It was first presented as a paper at seminars organized by Bryan Wilson at All Souls College, Oxford, by Dilwyn Knox at the Institute of Romance Studies of the University of London, and by SISWO (the Foundation for Inter-Academic Research in the Social Sciences) in Amsterdam. Earlier versions were published in Dutch in the *Amsterdams Sociologisch Tijdschrift*, 21 (4) 1995: 90–101, in my book *Het regime van de tijd* (Amsterdam: Meulenhoff 1997), pp. 144–55, and more recently the *Irish Journal of Sociology* 12 (1): 2003. I wish to thank Eric Dunning, Stephen Mennell and Nico Wilterdink for helpful comments on a draft of this version.
2. The first critic who found that Elias paid insufficient attention to religion in *The Civilizing Process* was Franz Borkenau. The assertion that Elias had overlooked religion was made by the Dutch sociologist I. Gadourek; see Goudsblom (1977).
3. See Elias (1978) ('subjective action'), Goudsblom and Mennell (1998) (charisma), Elias 2000 (Protestantism and the bourgeois line in the European civilizing process).
4. All quotations from Weber's essay in this section refer to Weber (1958).
5. Many examples are given by Bast (1995), Jaeger (1985), and Knox (1991, 1995).
6. Hieronymus (1994: 149).
7. On the connections between Elias's theory of the civilizing process and the sociology of knowledge, see Mennell (1989: 159–99).
8. As one example (which in itself offers no proof) I may mention the Third Reich, which, although intended to last a thousand years, failed to survive for more than twelve years.

REFERENCES

Augustine 1972 *The City of God*, translated Henry Bettenson. London: Penguin Books.
Bast, Robert J. 1995 'Honour your fathers: reform movements, catechisms, and the "civilizing process" in late medieval and early modern Germany', *Amsterdams Sociologisch Tijdschrift* 21: 116–25.
Buckle, Henry Thomas 1868 [1857], *History of Civilization in England*. 5 volumes, Leipzig: F.A. Brockhaus.
Elias, Norbert 1978 *What Is Sociology?* New York: Columbia University Press.
 1987 'The retreat of sociologists into the present', *Theory, Culture & Society* 4 (2–3): 223–47.
 1991a *The Society of Individuals*. Oxford: Basil Blackwell.
 1991b *The Symbol Theory*. London: Sage.
 2000 *The Civilizing Process: Sociogenetic and Psychogenetic Investigations*, rev. edn, Oxford: Blackwell.

Goudsblom, Johan 1977 'Responses to Norbert Elias's work in England, Germany, the Netherlands and France', in Peter R. Gleichmann, Johan Goudsblom and Hermann Korte (eds.), *Human Figurations: Essays for/Aufsätze für Norbert Elias*, Amsterdam: Stichting Amsterdams Sociologisch Tijdschrift: 37–98.

1996 'Ecological regimes and the rise of organized religion', in Johan Goudsblom, Eric Jones and Stephen Mennell, *The Course of Human History. Economic Growth, Social Process, and Civilization*, Armonk, NY: M.E Sharpe, pp. 49–62.

2002 'Introductory overview: the expanding anthroposphere', in Bert de Vries and Johan Goudsblom, *Mappae Mundi: Humans and their Habitats in a Long-Term Socio-Ecological Perspective*, Amsterdam: Amsterdam University Press, pp. 21–46.

Goudsblom, Johan, and Stephen Mennell (eds.) 1998 *The Norbert Elias Reader: A Biographical Selection*, Oxford: Blackwell.

Gould, Stephen Jay 1996 *Full House: The Spread of Human Excellence from Plato to Darwin*, New York: Harmony Books.

Hieronymus 1994 *Die Chronik des Hieronymus*. Berlin: Akademia Verlag.

Jaeger, C. Stephen 1985 *The Origins of Courtliness: Civilizing Trends and the Formation of Courtly Ideals 939–1210*, Philadelphia: University of Pennsylvania Press.

Knox, Dilwyn 1991 '*Disciplina*. The monastic and clerical origins of European civility', in John Monfasani and Ronald G. Musto (eds.), *Renaissance Society and Culture: Essays in Honor of Eugene F. Rice, Jr.*, New York: Italica Press: 107–35.

1995 'Erasmus' *De Civilitate* and the religious origins of civility in Protestant Europe', *Archiv für Reformationsgeschichte* 86: 7–55.

Lucretius 1951, *On the Nature of the Universe*, trans. Ronald Latham. London: Penguin Books.

McNeill, William H. 1982 *The Pursuit of Power: Technology, Armed Force and Society since AD 1000*. Chicago: University of Chicago Press.

Mennell, Stephen 1989 *Norbert Elias: Civilization and the Human Self-Image*, Oxford: Basil Blackwell.

Swaan, Abram de 2001 *Human Societies: An Introduction*. Cambridge: Polity.

Weber, Max 1958 *The Protestant Ethic and the Spirit of Capitalism*, New York: Charles Scribner's Sons.

Index

Index

double hermeneutic 20
functional democratization 14, 37
individualization 36
informalization 37
Kris on 28, 29–30
Mannheim on 28–9
mutual identification 36, 37
psychic functions 36, 37
reflection 31
reflexivity 36
secondary involvement 33–5, 44
sociological vocation 33–5, 37–8
Third Nature psychic structure 36, 37
value-freedom 25–6, 27, 30, 31, 32, 37
'whole people' 27
Iraq 182, 185, 189
  see also Gulf War
Israeli–Palestinian conflict 188

Jacobs, Aletta 153
Jaeger, C. Stephen 272
Jefferson, Thomas 164, 166
Jencks, Christopher 107
Jennings, Francis 163, 164
Johnson, H. M. 1

Kahl, J. A. 78
Kant, I. 62, 66, 67
Katz, Michael 106
Kaufman, Gershon 233
Kaufman, S. 43
Keynes, J. M. 157
Kilminster, Richard 18, 34
Kirchheimer 213
Klickman 202
knowledge
  conception of 59–60
  Durkheim and Elias 60–1
  object-adequacy 61
  self-knowledge 27
  theory of 5, 15, 20
  see also sociology of knowledge
Kotlowitz, Alex 100, 105
Kris, Ernst 28, 29–30
Kuhn, T. S. 59
Kuzmics, H. 18

language 6, 44, 50
Layder, Derek 18
Leach, E. R. 78
Levine, D. 260
Levine, Lawrence W. 109
life orders 246
Lockwood, D. 76, 77
Lodge, Henry Cabot 167

Löfgren, Orvar 205
looking-glass self 235–8, 239
Lucretian tradition 273–6

Madison, James 166
Magnet, Myron 107
Magnussin, E. 245
Mann, Thomas 249
manners, and emotions
  absolute monarchies 200
  bedrooms 198
  bodily functions 197
  bourgeoisie 200, 201–2
  children 208
  civilizing process 199–200
  conscience formation 201, 204, 208, 210
  courts and courtesy 196, 200
  distance 203, 205, 207
  dress 198
  emancipation of emotions 194, 208, 210
  equality 203
  etiquette 200–2, 203, 206
  family 208
  fifteenth century 195
  formalization 193, 204
  Golden Rule 203
  good society 201, 202–4
  informalization 193, 194, 205–10
  interdependency 193, 205, 207
  market ideology 208
  marriage 202, 204
  meeting 202, 206, 207
  morals 203
  national regimes 195
  parts of the body 197
  personal behaviour 206
  privacy 197, 207
  psychogenesis 193
  reputation 201–2
  second nature 194, 196, 198, 204, 210
  self-discipline 201, 204, 207
  sensitivity to violence 200
  and social aspiration 194, 196
  social integration 196, 205, 207, 209
  social status 194, 198, 199, 203, 205, 207, 209
  sociogenesis 193
  strangers 203
  study of 195–6
  table manners 197
  third nature 210
  women 202, 206
  see also shame
Mannheim, Karl 3, 4, 17, 28–9

UNIVERSITY LIBRARY
LOMA LINDA, CALIFORNIA